The Rhetorical Approach to 1 Thessalonians

The Rhetorical Approach to 1 Thessalonians

In Light of Ancient Funeral Oration

Ezra JaeKyung Cho

☙PICKWICK *Publications* • Eugene, Oregon

THE RHETORICAL APPROACH TO 1 THESSALONIANS
In Light of Ancient Funeral Oration

Copyright © 2020 Ezra JaeKyung Cho. All rights reserved. Except for brief quotations in critical publications or reviews, no part of this book may be reproduced in any manner without prior written permission from the publisher. Write: Permissions, Wipf and Stock Publishers, 199 W. 8th Ave., Suite 3, Eugene, OR 97401.

Pickwick Publications
An Imprint of Wipf and Stock Publishers
199 W. 8th Ave., Suite 3
Eugene, OR 97401

www.wipfandstock.com

PAPERBACK ISBN: 978-1-7252-5888-4
HARDCOVER ISBN: 978-1-7252-5889-1
EBOOK ISBN: 978-1-7252-5890-7

Cataloguing-in-Publication data:

Names: Cho, Ezra JaeKyung, author.

Title: The rhetorical approach to 1 Thessalonians : in light of ancient funeral oration / by Ezra JaeKyung Cho.

Description: Eugene, OR: Pickwick Publications, 2020 | Includes bibliographical references and index.

Identifiers: ISBN 978-1-7252-5888-4 (paperback) | ISBN 978-1-7252-5889-1 (hardcover) | ISBN 978-1-7252-5890-7 (ebook)

Subjects: LCSH: Bible. Thessalonians, 1st—Criticism, interpretation, etc. | Bible. Thessalonians, 1st—Socio-rhetorical criticism. | Funeral orations—History and criticism

Classification: BS2725.55 C56 2020 (print) | BS2725.55 (ebook)

Manufactured in the U.S.A.   10/08/20

To
Mary, Joanna, Ezra,
and Esther

Contents

List of Tables | xi
Preface | xiii
Introduction | xv

CHAPTER 1: **The History of Interpretation and Methodology** | 1
    Overview of the History of Interpretation | 1
    Proponents of Rhetorical Approach and Methodology | 8
        The Methodology of Rhetorical Criticism | 11
        The Rhetorical Invention of Argument and the Reconstruction of the Rhetorical Situation | 14

CHAPTER 2: **The Philosophy and Theology of Death and Dying in Funeral Orations and 1 Thessalonians** | 25
    Pagan Theology and Philosophy of Death (Epicureans and Stoics) | 25
    Philosophers' Consolatory Letters and Funeral Orations | 28
    Epitaphs in Greek and Latin | 32
    The Philosophy and Theology of Death in 1 Thessalonians | 33

CHAPTER 3: **Funeral Oratory in Speeches** | 36
    The Rhetorical Genre of 1 Thessalonians as Epideictic Rhetoric | 36
    Features that Identify Epideictic Discourse | 38
    The Four Types of Pure Epideictic Speech | 45
    Proto-typical, Exemplary Funeral Orations for Later Writers: The Athens Funeral Oration (5th—4th B.C.) | 52
        Isocrates | 52
        Thucydides | 55
        Pseudo-Lysias | 58
        Plato | 59

viii CONTENTS

    Demosthenes | 62
    Gorgias | 63
    Hyperides | 64
  Summary and Conclusion on Athenian Funeral Orations | 65

CHAPTER 4: **The Roman Oratory and the Jewish Oratory** | 70
  The Roman Funeral Oration (2nd B.C.—4th A.D.) | 70
    Tacitus | 73
    Appian | 75
    Dio Cassius | 77
    Plutarch | 79
    Cicero | 85
    Pliny the Younger | 88
    Seneca | 89
    Galen | 91
    Julian | 92
    Libanius | 94
    Dio Chrysostom | 95
    Lucian | 97
    Symmachus | 98
    Lucretius Vespillo | 99
  Summary and Conclusion on Roman Funeral Orations | 101
  Jewish Funeral Orations: 4 Maccabees | 106
  Summary and Conclusion on the Roman Funeral Oration and the Jewish Funeral Oration | 110

CHAPTER 5: **Funeral Orations in Rhetorical Handbooks** | 111
  Overview of Funeral Orations in Rhetorical Handbooks | 111
  The Handbooks on Funeral Orations | 112
    Aristotle | 112
    Cicero | 115
    Quintilian | 117
    Menander of Laodicea | 119
    Pseudo-Dionysius | 123
    Polybius | 127
    Dionysius of Halicarnassus | 128

CHAPTER 6: **Comparing 1 Thessalonians 1–3 and Funeral Oratory** | 130
 Discernible Disposition | 131
 The *Exordium* (1:2–3) | 132
 The *Narratio* (*Encomium*, 1:4—3:10) | 135
  The Identity and Exigency of the Long *Narratio* | 135
  First Section of *Narratio* (1:4–10) | 140
  Second Section of *Narratio* (2:1–12) | 146
   A Survey of Study in 2:1–12 | 146
   The Elements of Funeral Oration in 2:1–12 | 154
    The Repetitive and Lengthy Amplification in Content and Structure
    The Repetitive Contrast/Comparison in Character and Deeds in 2:1–12
    The Suffering and Persecution Context in 2:1–12
    Textual Criticism of 1 Thess 2:7 as "Gentle"
  Third Section of *Narratio* (2:13–16) | 174
  Final Section of *Narratio* (2:17—3:10) | 177
 Summary of *Narratio* in 1:4–3:10 (Elements of Funeral Oration) | 179
 Transitus with the Prayer Patterns (3:11–13) | 182

CHAPTER 7: **Comparing 1 Thessalonians 4–5 and Funeral Oratory** | 184
 Handbook of Funeral Oration (Consolation/Exhortation) | 186
 First Exhortation (4:1–8) | 187
 Second Exhortation (4:9–12) | 189
 Third Exhortation/Consolation (The Hope for the Parousia, 4:13–18) | 191
  Imperial Funerary Motifs in 1 Thessalonians 4:13–18 | 197
   Roman Imperial Funeral Procession | 198
   Extant Works of Roman Imperial Funeral Procession | 200
   Triumphal Image of Jesus' Parousia | 202
    Three Ways of Referring to Jesus' Triumphal Parousia
    The Funerary Language (4:17) and the Triumphal Language
    The Collective and Funerary Language of "We"
    The Funerary Language of Immortality and Consolation (4:17b–18)

Reverse of Order in the Funeral Procession with Triumphal Procession
Fourth Exhortation to the Living (5:1–15) | 222
　The Exhortation, Closely Connected with Consolation (5:1–11) | 224
　The Exhortation to the Living (5:1–11) | 231
　The Power of Images | 233
　Continuing Exhortation to the Community (5:12–15) | 236
Peroratio (5:16–22) and Wish Prayer/Closing (23–28) | 238
Conclusion of Consolation/Exhortation in 4:1—5:28 (Elements of Funeral Oration) | 239

CHAPTER 8: **Conclusion** | 242

Bibliography | 249
Index of Ancient Documents | 261

Tables

Tria Genera Causarum | 40
1:5–10 compared to 2:13–16 | 152
2:5–8 compared to 2:9–12 | 155
Paul's triple-repetitive metaphor in the *narratio* (2:1–18) | 157
Names of God and Jesus in 3:11–13 and 4:1—5:11 | 186
Clauses and commands in 3:10–12 | 189
Paramythia in Roman funeral orations and consolatory literature | 194
Paramythia in Athens funeral orations | 195
Funeral procession and funeral oration comparison | 201
The verb ἁρπαζω in the funeral context | 209
4:16–18 compared to 5:9–11 | 210
Cohesion and identity in 5:3–9 | 228
Paul's exhortation to the living in 4:16–18 and 5:9–11 | 230

Preface

My first foray into Rhetorical Criticism occurred in 2007 at Asbury Theological Seminary as their first Korean student with a Doctorate of Philosophy in Biblical Studies. I remember being captivated by Dr. Ben Witherington III's Socio-Rhetorical approach to the Pauline epistles. I first encountered 1 Thessalonians through an epistolary approach in 2005 through the ThM program at Calvin Seminary. Hearing Dr. Witherington's methodology inspired me to delve further into 1 Thessalonians with a more rhetorical approach. This book attempts to show the merits of the rhetorical approach for biblical interpretation in 1 Thessalonians over other methodologies and to prove how Paul used the rhetorical strategies in his messages. My contention in this book is that in writing 1 Thessalonians, Paul employs elements of epideictic funerary oratory to persuade his audience, and that elements of epideictic funerary oratory illuminate his language and arguments.

The book's uniqueness lies in the way it brings together the history of interpretation of 1 Thessalonians, the philosophy and theology of death in 1 Thessalonians, the prevalent phenomenon of funeral oration in ancient society, and Paul's unique employment of rhetorical strategy, that is, the epideictic rhetoric of funeral oration. This oration would match the rhetorical situation for addressing the prevalent issue of the death of believers in their church community.

Historically, there have been several key advocates of the thematic and doctrinal approach, the epistolary approach, and the mirror-reading approach. However, they had critical problems for correctly interpreting 1 Thessalonians according to the author's intentions. In this book, I propose a solution for a clearer interpretation of 1 Thessalonians that takes into account the particular elements of the funeral oration. Like today, people of ancient times were deeply concerned with death and kept it on their minds. There is much ancient material describing death as being "snatched away," as well as the consolation to the death of loved ones. In 1 Thessalonians,

Paul offers several consolatory rationales for why the community should not allow grief to overtake them.

For this argument, this book explore the materials of the Athens Funeral Oration (5th—4th B.C.), the Roman Funeral Oration (2nd B.C.—4th A.D.), and Jewish Funeral Oration. Furthermore, this book carefully examine some parallels among Aristotle, Cicero, and Quintilian concerning their funeral orations. This analysis provides a background showing how funeral orations reflect the theory of epideictic rhetoric found in the handbook of rhetoric.

Finally, this book compares 1 Thessalonians 1–5 with the funeral oratories in terms of their rhetorical strategies, rhetorical elements, and rhetorical situation the Thessalonian church faced. This book contributes to showing the exact meaning of 1 Thessalonians according to Paul's original intention, revealing many parallels between 1 Thessalonians and the ancient funeral oratories.

For several years I had the opportunity to teach a course on the New Testament and rhetorical approaches to Scripture at various seminaries. Through preparing for lessons, I felt the need to develop this program for a more correct interpretation of Scripture. I believe that this book would contribute to this need for future generations to build upon.

I am greatly thankful for the many people who have supported me to make this book possible. Most of all, to God be the glory forever! My ultimate gratitude ought to be given to my Lord, the basis of existence and thought, the source of heavenly wisdom, and the precious promise of triumphal hope.

> *Therefore, my beloved, be steadfast, immovable, always excelling in the work of the Lord, because you know that in the Lord your labor is not in vain.* (1 Corinthians 15:58)

Introduction

My contention in this book is that Paul employs elements of epideictic funerary oratory to persuade his audience in writing 1 Thessalonians—although the letter itself is not a funeral oration—and thus an examination of elements of epideictic funerary oratory illuminate the language and arguments of Paul in this letter.

In chapter one, I will briefly review the history of interpretation for 1 Thess. Through examining key advocates of the thematic and doctrinal approach, the epistolary approach, and the mirror-reading approach, I will argue that each of them has some critical problems. F. C. Baur and the Tübingen school argued that the church of 1 Thess was under the control of Judaizers, but there is no evidence of the central issues of Judaism. Walter Schmithals sees the apostle fighting off Gnostic intruders from his newly founded congregation, but there is no evidence of dualism or a docetic view of Christ. The epistolary approach has also been overly formalistic and the comparative basis of that activity has been too narrowly focused on the nonliterary papyrus letters of the past. I will propose the best solution for a clear interpretation of 1 Thess is to take into account the particular elements of the funeral oration, which is one of the main types of epideictic speech. Subsequently, I will endeavor to substantiate this in a number of ways through the following chapters.

In chapter two, I will explore the philosophy and theology of death in funeral orations and in 1 Thess. This exploration will contribute to the thesis in light of the circumstances of the ancient time. Ancient peoples were deeply concerned with death and often had it on their minds. In the ancient materials there are many descriptions of death as "snatching away" and consolation to the death of loved ones. In 1 Thess, Paul offers several consolatory commonplaces for why the community should not allow grief to overtake them. In this chapter I will examine and compare the philosophy and theology of death in funeral orations and in 1 Thess.

In chapters three and four, I will categorize the rhetorical genre of 1 Thess in order to consolidate my assertion. Through the process of invention, the rhetorician sets the purpose and the strategies to persuade the audiences. For my assertion that Paul employs elements of epideictic funerary oratory for persuading his audience in writing in 1 Thess, I will examine the actual funeral orations in ancient times. Due to the limitation of extant material, I will only examine key orations: (1) The Athens Funeral Oration (5th–4th B.C.); (2) The Roman Funeral Oration (2nd B.C.—4th A.D.); (3) Jewish Funeral Oration. Through this process, I will summarize them all and focus on a few most pertinent for 1 Thess.

In chapter five, I will carefully examine some parallels among Aristotle, Cicero, and Quintilian concerning funeral oration. After this, I will try to determine if what those three rhetoricians said was actually done in the epideictic rhetoric of funeral orations. I will also examine the rhetorical handbook of epideictic rhetoric from Menander Rhetor. This process of study will provide the background showing how funeral orations reflect the theory of epideictic rhetoric found in the handbooks of rhetoric.

In chapter six, I will compare 1 Thess 1–3 with funeral oratory. In this chapter I will try to determine the parallels and similarities between 1 Thess 1–3 and the *exordium* and *narratio* of funeral orations. The extant funeral orations fall chiefly under three heads: references to ancestry and encomium (family, birth, nature, nurture, education, accomplishments); lamentation; and consolation. In this chapter I will indeed endeavor to find the elements of encomium to the Thessalonian church, the martyred believers, and Paul himself (1 Thes 1–3), which conform to the exordium and narratio of funeral oration. Through this, it is possible to assert that Paul builds a paraclectic model in chapters 1–3 to achieve rapport with an audience and to prepare a good relationship for the following eschatological exhortations in chapters 4–5.

In chapter seven, I will compare 1 Thess 4–5 with funeral oratory. In this chapter I will continue to examine some elements of epideictic funerary oratory which illuminate the language and arguments of Paul in the discourse in 1 Thess 4–5 (exhortation and consolation). Paul's eschatological exhortations (4:13—5:11) and other exhortations to the Thessalonian church members (5:12–22) may conform to the pattern of consolation and instruction of funeral orations.

In chapter eight, I will summarize my assertions and also draw the argument of the book to a conclusion.

CHAPTER 1

The History of Interpretation and Methodology

Overview of the History of Interpretation

IN 1 THESSALONIANS, PAUL deals with the problems of persecution and the deaths of church members (1:6b; 2:2b, 14–15; 3:1–5; 4:13–18), problems of his own ethos (2:1–12), problems of holiness in an eschatological time (1:5, 6; 2:10; 3:13; 4:1–8; 5:5, 12–22, 23), problems of parousia (1:3b, 10a; 2:19; 3:13; 4:13–18; 5:1–11, 23), and problems of the ἄτακτοι (the disorderly, 4:11–12; 5:14). The research that has been done on the structure and theme of the letter of 1 Thess has fallen into two general categories: analyses of the logical, or thematic development, and analyses of the epistolary pattern.[1]

Some scholars attempted to establish models of what the Thessalonian church was like to shed light on the language and argument of 1 Thess. In the nineteenth century, F. C. Baur and the Tübingen school argued that the Thessalonian church was under the control of Judaizers, Jewish Christians who required Gentile Christians to obey the religious demands of Judaism before they could be fully Christian.[2] This view is clearly wrong based on the fact that Paul nowhere addresses in this letter any of the central issues of Judaism, such as the law, circumcision, Sabbath, dietary regulations, or cultic days.

While the Baur and Tübingen schools consistently interpreted Paul as combating Judaizing, Walter Schmithals continually saw the apostle fighting off Gnostic intruders in his newly founded congregations. Schmithals claims Paul, in 1 and 2 Thess, is addressing the problem of Gnosticism. For instance, Paul's concern for holiness is linked to the problem of Gnostic libertinism, and the concern about Christ's return is connected to the Gnostic rejection of future eschatology, to the conviction that the "day of

---

1. Jewett, *Thessalonian Correspondence*, 68.
2. Baur, *Paul the Apostle of Jesus Christ*, 85–97.

the Lord has already come," and the idea that believers have already experienced a spiritual resurrection.[3] Schmithals concludes, "in Corinth, so also in Thessalonica the charges come from Jewish or Jewish Christian Gnostics."[4] Schmithals drew this conclusion from his analysis of 1:5—2:12. Despite Schmithals' assertions, several distinctive elements of Gnosticism are not found in the Thessalonian letters: e.g., dualism of flesh and spirit, the speculative use of Gen 1–3,[5] and the docetic view of Christ. Furthermore, if the church was indeed being threatened by Gnostic teachers, Paul would likely be much clearer in his denunciation of their false teachings. On the contrary, Paul seems to be generally pleased with the condition of the Thessalonian church (1:2–10; 2:13–14).

Some scholars, notably Jewett and Lütgert, have claimed an enthusiastic model of the Thessalonian church. Jewett, developing further the view of Lütgert,[6] has argued that certain members of the Thessalonian church radicalized some of Paul's teaching, which resulted in problems of libertinism and idleness. This argument is based on the idea that the parousia had already arrived and was the basis of the spirit's manifestations.[7] Thus, this group viewed both the coming of Christ and the resurrection as past events, and the benefits of the resurrection had become a reality in the present.[8] Jewett and Lütgert hold that the identity of this group was idlers who resisted the structures of everyday life, including work ethics, sexual ethics, and the authority of congregational leadership. Wanamaker, however, correctly critiques Jewett and Lütgert in saying there is no sign of the connection between the problems associated with eschatology and the possession of the Spirit in this letter. Further, when compared to 1 Cor, 1 Thess has no evidence of spiritual enthusiasm.[9]

3. Schmithals, *Paul and the Gnostics*, 136–55.
4. Schmithals, *Paul and the Gnostics*, 155.
5. Jewett, *Thessalonian Correspondence*, 149.
6. Lütgert, "Die Volkommenen," 547–654.
7. Jewett, *Thessalonian Correspondence*, 143.
8. Lütgert, "Die Volkommenen," 632–38.
9. Wanamaker, *Epistles to the Thessalonians*, 55. He also claims that 1 Thess 5:19–22, the only injunction regarding spiritual gifts in this letter, cannot support the weight of the hypothesis because it could have been construed by spiritual enthusiasts to favor their basic activity. Further, E. Best criticizes both Schmithals and Jewett by saying the basic fault in their position is methodological. In other words, they assume there are opponents (one set of opponents) to be described and then they set out to discover them in every nook and cranny of the letter. Best asserts, however, instead of looking for one definite group Paul was attacking in Thessalonica, we must present a number of ideas from the Hellenistic atmosphere which were foreign to Christianity's Jewish cradle and which Paul had to refute (*First and Second Epistles to the Thessalonians*, 22).

After recognizing some of the weaknesses of the "enthusiastic model," Jewett employed a social-scientific, or sociological approach, to understanding the situation of the Thessalonian church and suggested a "millenarian model."[10] The term "millenarian" is used by sociologists to indicate "religious movements that expect the total transformation of this world to occur in connection with a cataclysm in the near future."[11] Some characteristics typical of millenarian movements include the following: (1) a belief in a messianic figure who is gone now but will return to usher in a new age; (2) a tendency of members to drop out of economic and civil obligations; (3) a strong criticism of the current political and civil order; and (4) involvement in activities that challenge existing rules or standards.[12] Jewett argues that the major concerns Paul addresses in the Thessalonian church match the characteristics of a typical millenarian movement and, thus, concludes a "millenarian radicalism" existed in Thessalonica. Jewett's contribution to the study of 1 Thess is his attempt to include sociological factors in the reconstruction of the Thessalonian church. Nevertheless, the connections between the problems in the Thessalonian church and the characteristics of a "typical millenarian" movement cannot be conclusively established.

There are other views concerning Thessalonica that attempt to see a relatively average congregation whose problems stemmed from two general sources. First, there were external pressures from those who harassed and ridiculed these recent converts for their faith and who charged Paul with selfish, impure motives. Second, internal confusion arose from (1) their new experience with the spirit and the power that He gives and (2) the relatively brief exposure they had to the teachings of Paul due to his rapid departure. Marshall states, "This may not be as exciting a hypothesis as those which find an organized and hitherto unsuspected group of opponents of Paul in Thessalonica, but it has the distinct advantage of doing better justice to the evidence."[13]

Another main methodology is the epistolary approach. In emphasizing the epistolary approach in the Pauline letters, Robert Funk states that "the first order of business in the interpretation of Paul's letters is to

---

10. Jewett, *Thessalonian Correspondence*, 161–78.
11. Jewett, *Thessalonian Correspondence*, 161.
12. Talmon, "Millenarian Movements," 159–200; Talmon, "Millenarism," 349–62.
13. Marshall, *1 and 2 Thessalonians*, 20. With minor variations, some scholars offered similar positions: Best, *First and Second Epistles to the Thessalonians*, 13–22; J. Moffatt, *Introduction to the Literature of the New Testament*, 69–73; Findlay, *Epistles of Paul the Apostle to the Thessalonians*, 35–39; Milligan, *St. Paul's Epistles to the Thessalonians*, 31–35; Schmidt, *Der erste Thessalonicherbrief*, 96–100; Bruce, *1 and 2 Thessalonians*, xxxv–xxxix; Kaye, "Eschatology and Ethics," 47–57.

learn to read the letter as a letter. This means, above all, to learn to read its structure."[14] In other words, the reader needs to look carefully not only at the content of a letter, but also its form or structure. The form or structure of a letter sometimes suggests important clues and gives information that helps one better understand, or interpret, what the person is really intending to say in the letter. In addition, Calvin Roetzel emphasizes the letter-writing conventions in interpreting the Pauline letters by saying a reader must understand Paul's "letter-writing conventions" to understand his creative use of those conventions.[15]

A letter structure, or epistolary approach, involves two kinds of analysis: (1) Comparative/Form critical analysis compares epistolary conventions in one Pauline letter with those found in the rest of the Pauline corpus in order to determine any unique formal features;[16] (2) Literary analysis understands the form and function of stereotyped formulae, which are relatively fixed or established epistolary conventions in Paul's letters, many of which have been borrowed and often adapted by the apostle from the letters of his day.[17]

Standard letter form is composed of "a tripartite structure" of prescript (or opening formula), body, and postscript (or closing formula).[18] Some scholars, such as White, Sanders, Doty, and Funk, do not consider such features as thanksgiving, prayer of supplication, and paraenesis as the body of the letter.[19] In other words, they include all of these elements in the thanksgiving section, which they emphasize in the structure of the Pauline letters. Paul Schubert highlights the importance of the thanksgiving section in foreshadowing the central themes to be developed in the body of the letter saying, "Each thanksgiving not only announces clearly the subject matter of the letter, but also foreshadows unmistakably its stylistic qualities, the

---

14. Funk, "Form and Function of the Pauline Letter," 8.

15. Roetzel, *Letters of Paul*, 30. Ann Jervis similarly asserts, "It is my conviction that by a comparative investigation of certain formal features of the letters of Paul, the function of any particular Pauline letter can be distinguished" (Jervis, *Purpose of Romans*, 35).

16. This kind of comparative analysis is especially significant in the epistolary framework of Paul's letters (the Opening, Thanksgiving, and Closing).

17. This kind of literary analysis is especially helpful in the body section of Paul's letters.

18. Jeal, *Integrating Theology and Ethics in Ephesians*, 17; Aune, *New Testament in its Literary Environment*, 174–80.

19. White, *Light from Ancient Letters*, 198–203; Sanders, "Transition from Opening Epistolary Thanksgiving to Body," 348–62; Doty, *Letters in Primitive Christianity*, 27–47; Funk, *Language Hermeneutic and the Word of God*, 270; Jeal, *Integrating Theology and Ethics in Ephesians*, 17–18.

degrees of intimacy and other important characteristics."[20] His weakness, however, is to focus on the initial parts and patterns of the thanksgiving section, not taking into account the function and structure. Actually, from the perspective of the rhetorical approach, this part reflects upon the narrative of the past in the case of 1 Thess (1:2–10).

The difficulty with studies of epistolary form, however, is that the elements of epistolary form are difficult to relate to one another. In other words, this approach has been overly formalistic, and the comparative basis of that activity has been too narrowly focused on the nonliterary papyri in the past.[21] The epistolary approach is basically unable to deal with the issues of intention and meaning, and can only address the fragments of epistolary elements without addressing the text as a whole.[22]

Of course, it is possible to find some overlapping elements between the epistolary approach and a rhetorical approach. For example, John White applies epistolary analysis to the opening and closing convention of Paul's letters and to the introductory and concluding conventions (disclosure formulae and transitional formulae) of the body-middle (the main content section) of his letters. He then asserts the relevance of analyzing the body-middle of Paul's letters in terms of rhetorical style and rhetorical argumentation. His approach, however, displays the fact that epistolary analysis has significant limitations and must be supplemented with rhetorical analysis of the body-middle if we want to know Paul's letter-writing practices and communication goals.[23] In the case of 1 Thess, apart from the opening and closing greetings, the thanksgiving, the reference to the wish prayer, and the greeting with a holy kiss and benediction, there is little evidence of the use of regular epistolary

---

20. Schubert, *Form and Function of the Pauline Thanksgivings*, 77. Peter O'Brien similarly emphasizes the existence of thanksgiving in the Pauline letters: "We note in these periods an epistolary function, i.e., to introduce and indicate the main theme(s) of the letters . . . Paul's introductory thanksgivings have a varied function: epistolary didactic and paraenetic, and they provide evidence of his pastoral and/or apostolic concern for the addressees. In some cases one purpose may predominate while others recede into the background. But whatever the thrust of any passage, it is clear that Paul's introductory thanksgivings were not meaningless devices. Instead they were integral parts of their letters, setting the tone and themes of what was to follow" (*Introductory Thanksgivings*, 263).

21. White, "Apostolic Mission and Apostolic Message," 158–59; Wanamaker, "Epistolary vs. Rhetorical Analysis," 284.

22. Wanamaker, "Epistolary vs. Rhetorical Analysis," 284.

23. White, "Apostolic Mission and Apostolic Message," 148–49. White also conceded this limitation of the epistolary analysis.

conventions. Even when epistolary forms are employed, they are modified and adapted thoroughly to serve Paul's pastoral purposes.[24]

Jan Lambrecht attempts to subsume 1 Thess 1–3 under a thanksgiving period or a triple period (thanksgiving: 1:2–10; 2:13–16; 3:9–10) on the basis of epistolary analysis.[25] In the ancient letters, however, two verses are about the normal length of a wish prayer and thanksgiving, and, in 1:2–3, Paul already gives a wish prayer and thanksgiving to God. From the perspective of rhetorical analysis, this section (1:4—3:10) corresponds to the long *narratio* in chronological order, presenting his past pastoral ministry.[26]

It is worth noting that there is some convincing evidence to support a rhetorical approach for Paul's letters from a social context. First of all, in the ancient world, dissemination was achieved through formal oral proclamation of the texts by appointed readers.[27] Achtemeier correctly claims that although a wide variety of written materials and literature existed, "the oral environment was so pervasive that no writing occurred that was not vocalized."[28] To support this assertion, William Harris, who studied the literacy and illiteracy of the Greek and the Roman worlds, concludes that "at least 15 percent of the adult male population reached the level of semi-literacy or some higher level . . . 5 percent or more of the total adult population (including women and slaves) was literate . . ." in this period.[29] In this social context, it is natural for the communication and the conveying of information to be delivered to the audience through the voice of the speaker or through a speech. For example, Paul's request, "I solemnly command you by the Lord that this letter be read to all of them" (1 Thess 5:27), is a testament to the aural and oral orientation of the authorial audience of 1 Thess. Similarly, in Acts 8:30, the story of the Ethiopian reading out loud from Isaiah and Philip hearing and approaching, indirectly displays the oral culture and public reading in ancient times. Written materials,

---

24. Witherington, *1 and 2 Thessalonians*, 21.

25. Lambrecht, "Thanksgivings in 1 Thessalonians 1–3," 200–202. He uniquely warns against "far-fetched and strained, *genre hunting*" with J. White's "the disclosure formula of 2:1–12," R. Funk's "an apostolic parousia of 2:17–3:13", and F. Schnider and W. Stenger's "a double epistolary recommendation of 2:1–12 and 2:17–3:8" (195–200).

26. Witherington, *1 and 2 Thessalonians*, 20.

27. Toorn, *Scribal Culture*, 12.

28. Achtemeier, "Omne Verbum Sonat," 12–17.

29. Harris, *Ancient Literacy*, 323–30. Actually, he continues to assert that the combined literacy level in the period before 100 BC is unlikely to have much exceeded 10 percent, and the level of women's literacy is likely to have been well under 5 percent. Small farmers and the poor will generally have been illiterate.

including letters, became surrogates for oral speech and communication,[30] and the rhetorical conventions of public speech and discourse could be carried over into such letters.

Another piece of evidence for the rhetorical nature of Paul's letters is that New Testament letters, including Paul's, tend to be longer than other ancient letters. Achtemeier claims the average length of a letter of Cicero is 295 words and that of Seneca is 955, but the average length of a Pauline letter is 2,500 words.[31] Paul's lengthy letters indirectly reflect the fact that though Paul uses the normal form of an ancient letter, he employs the rhetorical conventions in his letters to persuade his audience, a Christian community. Paul likely adapted rhetorical conventions to meet the rhetorical situation of his Chrisian community through the surrogate of oral communication. As long as there was no mass production of written texts, the spoken word remained the main channel of communication.[32]

Secondly, additional evidence of support for the rhetorical approach of Paul's letters may be his rhetorical education. Kennedy, approaching the New Testament in terms of Greek rhetorical ideas, says "rhetoric was a systematic academic discipline universally taught throughout the Roman empire."[33] Particularly, the historical fact that "the greatest rhetorician of the second century of the Christian era was Hermogenes, who was born in Tarsus, the home of Saint Paul, and who taught in the cities of the Ionian coast, where Christian churches had an early development," could indirectly mirror the dominant atmosphere of the rhetorical education of Paul.[34] In this sense, Paul may be familiar with the rhetorical skills and oral culture of his churches and strategically employ the rhetorical conventions in his letters for persuasion.

The rhetorical tendency and categories analyze argumentative texts based on the assumption that works of early Christian authors were written using the compositional standards, categories, and assumptions of Greco-Roman rhetoric, which are earlier and more influential than the epistolary conventions.[35] This makes better sense from a historical perspective.

30. Witherington, *Conflict and Community in Corinth*, 56.

31. Achtemeier, "Omne Verbum Sonat," 22. Cicero's letters range from 22 to 2,530 words; Seneca's from 149 to 4,134; Paul's from 355 to 7,101.

32. Toorn, *Scribal Culture*, 13.

33. Kennedy, *New Testament Interpretation*, 8–9.

34. Kennedy, *New Testament Interpretation*, 9. Concerning Paul's education and familiarity with Hellenistic rhetoric, there is probable evidence in light of social and historical background (Acts 22:3): Hengel and Deines, *Pre-Christian Paul*, 54–61; Murphy-O'Connor, *Paul*, 46–51.

35. Betz, *Galatians*.

Jeal points out the shortcomings of the epistolary analysis of the Pauline epistles:

> The value of a functional approach to the epistolary format . . . is that it emphasizes the message that an author is attempting to communicate through the medium of the whole letter, rather than employing what may at times be an *a priori* subtraction of features such as thanksgiving, prayer of supplication and paraenesis in an attempt to find the message by isolating it . . . Decisions about how letter components fit into a document, then, should not be made solely on formal grounds, but should take into account the pragmatic function of the text of an epistle . . . That is, the fundamental concern is not how the author views the written material, but how the author views the audience and how the author wishes the audience to be affected by the message of the letter.[36]

A fundamental advantage of the rhetorical approach is that it focuses on both the text being treated and the rhetorical situation, which gave rise to its composition, "rather than some supposed earlier sources, forms or editions of the text."[37] Functionally, the rhetorical approach is able to relate the smaller units of meaning to the text in terms of a whole effort in order to persuade the audience. Historically, it includes the historical dimension or rhetorical situation, which shows the rhetorical exigency for the author to meet the demand of the audience in the lecture.

Proponents of Rhetorical Approach and Methodology

The assertions of the methodologies about 1 Thess discussed above derived from their negligence of the clear rhetorical signals and epideictic nature of this material. *My thesis is that Paul employs elements of epideictic funerary oratory to persuade his audience in 1 Thessalonians, although the letter itself is not a funeral oration.* Elements of epideictic funerary oratory illuminate the language and arguments of Paul in the epistle which I will prove by showing a more systematic analysis of how funeral orations shed light on the whole of 1 Thessalonians in the exordium (1:2–3), the narratio (1:4—3:10), and the probatio/exhortatio (4:1—5:15). The following discussion attempts to examine 1 Thessalonians as a speech, that is, to consider 1 Thessalonians as a spoken discourse whose purpose is to affect and to persuade its audiences. The discussion will focus on why and how

---

36. Jeal, *Integrating Theology and Ethics in Ephesians*, 21–22.
37. Jeal, *Integrating Theology and Ethics in Ephesians*, 33.

1 Thessalonians fits into what may be called the category or genre of "epideictic" and "funerary oratory," and how a rhetorical approach shows both the nature of 1 Thessalonians and the function and structure of the whole epistle.

An Approach through Historical-Rhetorical Criticism

Juel correctly asserts the need to investigate the rhetorical aspects of texts:

> Every rhetorical act discloses three characters, according to Aristotle: the character of the speaker (*ethos*), of the speech (*logos*), and of the audience (*pathos*) . . . The three are related and, as Aristotle argues, in rhetorical terms. That means simply that *literature, as all human communication, is rhetorical: It seeks to move an audience, to change minds or feelings.* We should expect that with something as intentional as a gospel narrative or letter, the rhetorical features should be identifiable . . . In reading a piece of literature, we become aware of an author pulling the strings behind the scenes; we are aware of the story; and we are—intentionally or not—an audience of some sort.[38]

A phrase of rhetorical criticism was introduced into biblical study by J. Muilenburg to refer to the method of analyzing argumentative texts on the assumption that "the works of early Christian authors were written using the compositional and argumentative standards, categories, and assumptions of Greco-Roman rhetoric."[39] After critiquing the limitations of form criticism, Muilenburg defined his new proposed methodology in the following words:

> What I am interested in . . . is in understanding the nature of Hebrew literary composition, in exhibiting the structural patterns that are employed for the fashioning of a literary unit . . . and in discerning the many and various devices by which the predications are formulated and ordered into a unified whole. Such an enterprise I should describe as rhetoric and the methodology as rhetorical criticism.[40]

There are two different tendencies in rhetorical criticism used to approach the texts: diachronic rhetorical criticism[41] and synchronic rhetori-

---

38. Juel, *Master of Surprise*, 123.
39. Aune, *Westminster Dictionary*, 416.
40. Muilenburg, "Form Criticism and Beyond," 8.
41. Aune, *Westminster Dictionary*, 417. This method regards rhetorical criticism as an aspect of historical criticism. In other words, it attempts to understand the rhetorical

cal criticism.[42] There are three primary differences between Greco-Roman rhetoric and Modern rhetoric (New Rhetoric). First, there is the difference of perspectives in interpreting. Greco-Roman rhetoric approaches the text from the point of view of the author. Kennedy claims rhetorical criticism is a more historical method in which texts are studied from the perspective of the author or editor's intent, the unified results, and how the text would be perceived by the audience of near contemporaries. To him, the writers of the New Testament had a message to convey and sought to persuade an audience to believe it. Thus, they are rhetorical, and their methods should be studied by the discipline of ancient rhetoric.[43] On the other hand, modern rhetoric approaches the texts from the perspective of the interpreters and modern readers. Vernon Robbins has adopted a wide definition of rhetoric that allows him to discover formal patterns. To him, a complete interpretation includes the interrelation among the author, the text, and the reader. The reason is that language is produced out of social interaction among people—there is not simply a speaker or writer; the speaking and writing presuppose the presence of a hearer or reader; texts were produced by authors and they are meaningless without readers. Robbins especially emphasizes reader-response analysis.[44]

Second, between Greco-Roman rhetoric and Modern rhetoric (New rhetoric) there is a difference in the way they examine the texts. Greco-Roman rhetoric considers the text as "the speech" from the perspective of the author. Therefore, the components of Greco-Roman rhetoric focus on logic and the methods of persuasion. Modern rhetoric, however, considers the text as "a symbolic language and a social product." It considers the text as "a thick tapestry," which means the text is a matrix, or an interwoven network of meanings and meaning effects.[45]

---

features of the texts within the context and categories of Greco-Roman rhetoric (Betz, *Galatians*, xv; Mitchell, *Paul and the Rhetoric of Reconciliation*, 6–17; Anderson, *Ancient Rhetorical Theory*, 35–107.

42. Aune, *Westminster Dictionary*, 417. This tendency reinterprets Greco-Roman rhetorical tradition as a subset of literary criticism. In other words, it emphasizes modes of human communication. It may be called the more comprehensive "new rhetoric." (Perelman and Olbrechts-Tyteca, *New Rhetoric*; Wuellner, "Where Is Rhetorical Criticism Taking Us?," 448–63; Amador, *Academic Constraints*).

43. Kennedy, *New Testament Interpretation*, 3–5.

44. Robbins, *Tapestry of Early Christian Discourse*, 18–43. He insists that the author, the text, and the reader presuppose historical, social, cultural, and ideological relations among people and the texts they write and read.

45. Robbins, *Tapestry of Early Christian Discourse*, 18–43. According to this concept, modern rhetoric consists of the following key elements: (1) Inner texture (getting inside a text): Authors create texts in their world; readers create a world of the text in

Third, there is a gap concerning historical judgment. Although Modern rhetoric has some insight, its critical weakness is the problem of anachronism. When the authors wrote the letters, they did not take into account these kinds of modern complicated concepts and forms of communication. As Mitchell stresses, modern rhetoric has the danger of revising and reappropriating the texts to a modern philosophical context. This could lead the practitioners to a lack of concern for proper historical judgment, that is, anachronism. In this sense, she correctly points out, "Rhetorical Criticism is one of the panoply of tools which bear the name 'historical-critical method.' . . . the rhetoric will be studied in the light of the Greco-Roman rhetorical tradition which was operative and pervasive at the time of the letter's composition. Thus the resources . . . are the ancient Greco-Roman handbooks, speeches and letters themselves, not the modern 'New Rhetoric.'"[46] I will employ Greco-Roman rhetoric in the following study.

The Methodology of Rhetorical Criticism

Rhetorical criticism, by definition, is based on the works of the classical rhetoricians of antiquity, such as Aristotle's *Art of Rhetoric*, Cicero's *de Inventione* and the *Rhetorica ad Herennium*,[47] and Quintilian's *Institutio Oratoria*. While the *Rhetorica ad Alexandrum* is the sole surviving rhetorical treatise before Aristotle,[48] Aristotle is actually the first rhetorician who wrote a still extant treatise about rhetoric. Aristotle defined rhetoric as "the faculty of discovering the possible means of persuasion" (*Rhetorica* 1.2.1). Quintilian, after surveying many definitions about rhetoric (*Institutio oratoria* 2.15), though most of them emphasized "power and manner of persuasion by speaking," defined rhetoric as "the art of speaking well and the orator knows how to speak well," (*Institutio oratoria* 2.17.37)[49]

---

their own world. (2) Intertexture (entering the interactive world of a text): Every text is a rewriting of other texts, an "intertextual activity." (3) Social and cultural texture (living with a text in the world). (4) Ideological texture (sharing interests in commentary and text). (5) Sacred texture.

46. Mitchell, *Paul and the Rhetoric of Reconciliation*, 6; Mitchell, *Heavenly Trumpet*, xxi.

47. These two works of Cicero are the earliest and systematic rhetorical treatises containing Hellenistic rhetorical theory. Quintilian respects and relies on Cicero's works.

48. Anderson, *Ancient Rhetorical Theory and Paul*, 38. For a survey of the ancient sources and history in detail see Kennedy, *Classical Rhetoric*, 41–107.

49. Witherington, *New Testament Rhetoric*, 10–11.

while emphasizing the quality of the orator with: "he must be a good man" (*Institutio oratoria* 12.1–4).

Concerning the rhetorical analysis of the texts and the practice of rhetorical criticism, Kennedy shows five stages in sequence, though each stage could be considered as part of a circular process.[50] First, he begins with a determination of the rhetorical unit. A rhetorical unit must consist of "a beginning, a middle, and an end."[51] Second, after determining the rhetorical unit, one must define "the rhetorical situation" of the unit, which is similar to the *Sitz im Leben* of form criticism. It can also be called "rhetorical exigency." Understanding the rhetorical situation (an exigency) is crucial because it indicates "the author's intention and motives, on the purpose for writing, the genre of the text, and the goal that the text is intended to achieve through its appeal and persuasiveness."[52] Thus, before analyzing the structure and the arrangement of the texts, it is crucial to know the rhetorical need and the rhetorical exigency in writing the letter. In other words, the first step for the rhetorical approach is to answer the questions, "What is happening here?" and "What is the issue here?" Bitzer defined rhetorical situation as the specific historical context of discourse, which consists of persons, events, objects, and relations showing an actual or potential exigence in response to which a speaker formulates an oral or written discourse.[53] Therefore, in the *narratio* it seems possible to assume the rhetorical situation because *narratio* usually is defined as "an exposition of events that have occurred or are supposed to have occurred" (*de Inventione* 1.19.27).[54]

Third, in the next stage for determining the rhetorical strategy, the theory of the three "species of rhetoric" is useful. There are three major species,

---

50. Kennedy, *New Testament Interpretation*, 33–38.
51. Kennedy, *New Testament Interpretation*, 33.
52. Jeal, *Integrating Theology and Ethics in Ephesians*, 34.
53. Bitzer, "Rhetorical Situation," 1–14.
54. Watson claims that "the exigence . . . is often clearly detected in the introduction (*exordium*) or beginning of the body (*probatio*) of a rhetorical work" (*Invention, Arrangement, and Style*, 9.) In the case of 1 Thessalonians, however, it seems the long *narratio* (1:4—3:10) touches on the rhetorical exigence.

or genres, of rhetoric:[55] judicial,[56] deliberative,[57] and epideictic.[58] Judicial rhetoric is the rhetoric of the court of law, concerned with accusation and defense, to persuade judges about "whether or not certain events of the past had occurred and whether the accused was therefore guilty or innocent."[59] Deliberative rhetoric is particularly used in the assembly setting, "whose purpose is protreptic (persuasion) or apotreptic (dissuasion) of an audience" for future decisions of action and direction.[60] Epideictic rhetoric is the speech provided to a ceremonial gathering in praise and blame of a person (contemporary, historical, or mythological), community, activity, or a thing that is to be celebrated.[61] Following Aristotle, Lausberg claims the basis for the major classification of rhetorical species is given to the relationship intended by the speaker between the topic and the listener. In other words, there are two intended relationships (1) the listener as a decision-maker (κριτης)—Judicial and Deliberative Rhetoric; (2) the listener as a passive, entertained spectator (θεωρος)—Epideictic Rhetoric.[62]

Fourth, as a next step, the rhetorical critic needs to consider the arrangement of material with invention. In speech, rhetoric consists of five parts: invention, arrangement, style, memory, and delivery.[63] Invention is

55. Watson, *Invention, Arrangement, and Style*, 9–10. He shows the ancient rhetorical source in detail. Aristotle, *Rhet.* 1.3.1358b.3; 1359a.9; Cicero, *Inv.* 1.5.7; 2.4.12–59.178; *Top.* 24.91; *De Or.* 1.31.141; 2.81.333–85.349; *Her.* 1.2.2; Quintilian, *Inst.* 2.21.23; 3.3.14–15. Lausberg, *Handbook of Literary Rhetoric*, 30–38; Kennedy, *Art of Rhetoric in the Roman World*, 7–23.

56. Aristotle, *Rhet.* 1.10–15; *Rhet. Alex.* 4, 36; Cicero, *Inv.* 2.4.14–51.154; *Top.* 24.92–26.96; Quintilian, *Inst.* 3.9; Lausberg, *Handbook of Literary Rhetoric*, 32; Aune, *Westminster Dictionary*, 418–20; Johanson, *To All the Brethren*, 39–42.

57. Aristotle, *Rhet.* 1.4–8; *Rhet. Alex.* 1–2, 29–34; Cicero, *De or.* 2.81.333–83.340; *Inv.* 2.51.155–58.176; *Her.* 3.2–5; Quintilian, *Inst.* 3.8; Lausberg, *Handbook of Literary Rhetoric*, 32–33; Mitchell, *Paul and the Rhetoric of Reconciliation*, 20–32; Kennedy, *Art of Rhetoric in the Roman World*, 18–21.

58. Epideictic (Aristotle, *Rhet.* 1.3.1358b.3; 1359a.9; *Rhet. Alex.* 1.1421b.7–8; Cicero, *Or. Brut.* 11.37; Quintilian, *Inst.* 3.4.12), demonstrativus (Cicero, *Inv.* 1.5.7; *Her.* 1.2.2; Quintilian, *Inst.* 3.4.14), laudativus (Quintilian, *Inst.* 2.21.23; 3.3.14; 3.4.12), laudatio (Cicero, *De or.* 2.84.341; *Top.* 24.91), encomiastic (Quint. 3.4.12), panegyricus (Quintilian, *Inst.* 3.4.13). See also Aristotle, *Rhet.* 1.9; *Rhet. Alex.* 3, 35; Cicero, *Inv.* 2.59.178; *De or.* 2.11.45–46; 2.84–85; *Or.* 11.37; *Her.* 3.6–8; Quintilian, *Inst.* 3.4.3; 3.7. Aune, *Westminster Dictionary*, 418–20.

59. Cicero, *De or.* 2.10; *Inv.* 1.5.7; *Her.* 1.2; Quintilian, *Inst.* 2.21.23; 3.3.14–15; Aune, *Westminster Dictionary*, 419.

60. Aristotle, *Rhet.* 1.3.1358b.4; 2.18.1392a.5; Quintilian, *Inst.* 3.4.7; 3.8.6; Aune, *Westminster Dictionary*, 419.

61. Lausberg, *Handbook of Literary Rhetoric*, 33.

62. Lausberg, *Handbook of Literary Rhetoric*, 30–31.

63. Kennedy, *New Testament Interpretation*, 13.

the discovery of ideas, that is, the discovery of "hidden possibilities for developing ideas."[64] The main concern of the invention is the development of proof to best support the case, as well as the determination of the species of rhetoric and stasis.[65] Long correctly points out with respect to invention and the rhetorical situation, "Determining the rhetorical situation is a preliminary consideration when doing rhetorical work . . . the rhetorical situation initially determines the genre of the writing."[66] In other words, the process of invention—of the determination of the rhetorical situation, and of the species of rhetoric—is not separated, but closely connected.

The step of arrangement (disposition/*dispositio*) is concerned with "what subdivisions it falls into,"[67] and the function of these sections to some overall purpose "to meet the demands of the exigency."[68] As a final step, one must see whether the analysis is consistent and whether its results satisfy the rhetorical situation. In the following rhetorical analysis of 1 Thess, Kennedy's methodology discussed above will be employed with some adaptation.

The Rhetorical Invention of Argument and the Reconstruction of the Rhetorical Situation

On the basis of Bitzer's assertion with respect to the rhetorical situation, Hester correctly points out the importance of the rhetorical situation for creating invention; "The situation is dynamic . . . In other words, the situation is the source of invention and rhetoric is always situational."[69] Emphasizing speech as rhetorical only when it corresponds to a rhetorical situation, Bitzer claims:

---

64. Lausberg, *Handbook of Literary Rhetoric*, 119.

65. Watson, *Invention, Arrangement, and Style*, 14; Aune, *Westminster Dictionary*, 234. The two types of proofs used in invention in the New Testament are the inartificial (quotations of Scripture, miracles, and witnesses) and the artificial (*ethos, pathos*, and *logos*).

66. Long, *Ancient Rhetoric and Paul's Apology*, 12.

67. Kennedy, *New Testament Interpretation*, 37; Aune, *Westminster Dictionary*, 62–64. Further, *dispositio* can be used for the analysis of the train of thought for an entire argumentative text and for identifying the various rhetorical devices and figures of speech. In the ancient rhetoric, there are two types of arrangement (*dispositio*): (1) Aristotle's four-part arrangements: *exordium, narratio, argumentatio*, and *peroratio*. (2) Cicero's six-part arrangements: *exordium* ("introduction"), *narratio* ("narrative"), *divisio* or *partitio* ("division" or "case"), *confirmatio* ("proof"), *confutatio* or *reprehensio* ("refutation"), and *peroratio* or *conclusio* ("conclusion").

68. Long, *Ancient Rhetoric and Paul's Apology*, 12.

69. Hester, "Invention of 1 Thessalonians, 260."

Rhetorical situation may be defined as a complex of persons, events, objects, and relations presenting an actual or potential exigence which can be completely or partially removed if discourse, introduced into the situation, can so constrain human decision or action as to bring about the significant modification of exigence. Prior to the creation and presentation of discourse, there are three constituents of any rhetorical situation: the first is exigence; the second and third are elements of the complex, namely the audience to be constrained in decision and action and the constraints which influence the rhetor and can be brought to bear upon the audience.[70]

In other words, before any rhetorical situation, the rhetor must contend with three things: exigence, the audience that decides, and constraints that influence action. Bitzer asserts that in a rhetorical situation, an imperfection marked by an urgency is serious and can only be solved by the intervention of discourse; the audience under some rhetorical exigency may change their decision or become the mediators of change; and the external/internal elements in historical context work together upon the rhetor and the audience. Thus, as discussed above, the rhetorical situation dominates a rhetorical invention, and the processes of invention and the rhetorical situation are closely connected and circular. Therefore, in order to reconstruct the rhetorical situation, it is crucial to know the urgent need and what event is happening behind the passages. Concerning the motives and the rhetorical exigency of Paul's writing of 1 Thess, B. C. Johanson convincingly offers that "1 Thessalonians appears to be Paul's response to the report that Timothy brought back from this visit (3:6–7). It is thus reasonable to see the concerns and themes of the letter as reflecting Paul's prior knowledge of the community's strengths and weaknesses . . . as updated by Timothy's report."[71] Traditionally, it may be suggested on the basis of a scholarly survey of 1 Thess that there are four main concerns and purposes for Paul's writing of this letter. First is the concern about Paul's honor and integrity. Many passages in 1 Thess, particularly 2:1–12, may show Paul's honor and integrity were challenged by some opponents who suspected Paul's motives for preaching (1:5 " . . . but also in power and in the Holy Spirit and with full conviction; just as you know what kind of persons . . . ": 2:1–12; 2:17—3:10; 5:12–13 " . . . to respect those who labor among you.").[72] Wayne Meeks

---

70. Bitzer, "Rhetorical Situation," 6.
71. Johanson, *To All the Brethren*, 51.
72. Marshall, *1 and 2 Thessalonians*, 61: "He must have felt that he was being accused or stood in danger of being accused of behaving like a second-rate philosopher, and he defended himself by claiming that . . . "

also comments that "An ancient audience would doubtless hear an allusion to Paul's concern about his honor; failure of the Thessalonian Christians to endure would bring shame on Paul. Paul makes no explicit mention of honor, but he does speak of the addresses as his ἐλπὶς ἢ χαρὰ ἢ στέφανος καυχήσεως (hope and joy and proud diadem; 2:19) and as ἡ δόξα ἡμῶν καὶ ἡ χαρά. (our glory and joy; 2:20)."[73] Further, the community of the Thessalonian Christians consisted of the fairly recent converts who had suffered (1:6; 2:14), and Paul abruptly left the Thessalonian Christians even though they were like infants in the faith (2:17–18; Acts 17:5–10).[74] Acts 17:1–10 suggests the circumstances and situation of the Thessalonian church. For three Sabbath days, Paul argued with them and, "That very night the believers sent Paul and Silas off to Beroea . . . "[75] Because of Paul's abrupt exit, the Thessalonian Christians doubted Paul's honor and integrity. In 2:17–20, Paul asserts, " . . . for a short time, we were made orphans by being separated from you . . . certainly I, Paul, wanted to come again and again—but Satan blocked our way." Thus, it may be presumed he urgently needs to reestablish his honor and integrity with the Thessalonian believers.

The second concern for the writing is about persecution and the Thessalonian believers' weakness in faith. There are many signs from 1 Thess that suggest the infant converts were experiencing some kind of persecution and a real threat (1:6b " . . . in spite of persecution you received the word with joy"; 2:2b, 14 "for you suffered the same things"; 3:3–4 "so that no one would be shaken by these persecutions . . . we were to suffer persecution"). Given his short stay and abrupt departure, Paul was greatly concerned with encouraging them to overcome the persecution from their

---

73. Meeks, "Circle of Reference in Pauline Morality," 308.

74. Vielhauer, *Geschichte der urchristlichen Literatur*, 88–89; Johanson, *To All the Brethren*, 50.

75. Concerning the use of the account in Acts 17:1–10, some scholars (H. Conzelmann and E. Haenchen) attempt to make a sharp distinction between primary sources (Paul's letters) and secondary sources (Acts) in the reconstruction of Paul's life. They assume Luke was so theologically motivated when writing Acts that its historical events cannot be trusted. I agree, however, with F. F. Bruce who asserts that "The account of Paul's movements which can be gathered from 1 Thessalonians agrees so well with the fuller record of Acts 16:6–18:5 that that record, though it is substantially later than 1 Thessalonians, may confidently be accepted as providing a historical framework within which the reference in 1 Thessalonians can be read with greater understanding" ("St. Paul in Macedonia," 339; Howard Marshall also takes the same position as Bruce (*Luke*). Additionally, ancient historians usually viewed their task as rhetorically framing existing, convincing information. Ancient historiography such as Acts, contrary to ancient biographies, was a rhetorical exercise to some extent, and it was undertaken to persuade on the basis of historical sources (Luke 1:1–4) (Witherington, *New Testament History*, 24–28).

own compatriots (2:14, τῶν ἰδίων συμφυλετῶν) or Jews (Acts 17:1-10). For this reason, Paul sent Timothy in order to "strengthen and encourage you for the sake of your faith . . . I sent to find out about your faith . . . that our labor had been in vain" (3:2-5).[76]

Third, Paul writes to address problems about holiness and the proper conduct of the Thessalonian believers. In 1 Thess, Paul emphasizes holiness in their lives when compared with other letters (2:10; 3:13 ". . . your hearts in holiness"; 4:1-8 ". . . For this is the will of God, your sanctification . . . For God did not call us to impurity but in holiness"; 5:5-7, 23 "for you are all children of light . . . not of the night or of darkness . . . sanctify you entirely; and may your spirit and soul and body be kept sound and blameless . . . "). Through all of these words about holiness and proper conduct, Paul may warn against a libertinistic movement in Thessalonica.[77]

Fourth, Paul is concerned about the Parousia (Second Coming of Christ). Judging from the length of Paul's debate and the number of references to Christ's return, one of the major concerns of Paul in 1 Thess is to correct and clarify the confusing matters of Jesus' Second Coming (1:3b, 10; 2:19 "For what is our hope or joy or crown of boasting before our Lord Jesus at his coming?"; 3:13; 4:13-18 ". . . God will bring with him those who have died . . . "; 5:1-11 ". . . For you yourselves know . . . that the day of the Lord will come like a thief . . . ").

Recently, Jewett suggested "millenarian radicalism in Thessalonica," particularly the ἄτακτοι, as the source of exigency and the controlling motif underlying the exigency of the rhetorical situation.[78]

> This radical form of millenarism was embodied by the ἄτακτοι, who resisted on principle the structure of everyday life . . . They refused to prepare for a future παρουσια of Christ because in principle they were experiencing and embodying it already in their ecstatic activities . . . It is clear that the ἄτακτοι were a distinct group within the congregation and that they alone had ceased working . . . By the time of writing 2 Thessalonians, their resistance against the admonitions of the congregational leaders and the counsel of Paul's letter led to the command that they should be ostracized (2 Thess 3:6).[79]

---

76. Marxsen, *Der erste Brief die Thessalonicher*, 54.
77. Lütgert, "Die Volkommenen," 619ff.
78. Jewett, *Thessalonian Correspondence*, 172-78.
79. Jewett, *Thessalonian Correspondence*, 176-77. The word ἀτάκτως derives from the verb τασσω, "to give instructions as to what must be done," "to order" (BDAG 991).

Colin Nicholl denies the eschatological background and explains the reason of the unwillingness to work as the fact that converted manual laborers, after cut off from their *collegia*, came to church to meet their needs and exploit wealthy Christians' generous charity, motivated by greed and laziness.[80] However, just as the problem of idleness (1 Thess 4:11–12; 5:14) is linked to the topic of Christ's return (4:13—5:11), the ἄτακτοι reflects the eschatological background.[81] Further, in church history, there have been many cases of the errant ethical phenomenon of not working because of a misunderstanding of eschatology. In this sense, Jewett's assertion may be the convincing evidence for the rhetorical situation of the Thessalonian church.[82] In 2 Thess 3:6–15, the problem of "millenarian radicalism in Thessalonica," particularly the ἄτακτοι, may have led to serious results in the Thessalonian church; in 1 Thess there is no convincing evidence of this problem yet.

M. Goulder also suggests the exigency of the Thessalonian church with four points: (1) Giving up work for the Kingdom because of their realized eschatology; (2) Death and the kingdom because of their expectation of immortality; (3) Celibacy and the kingdom because of the realized eschatology; and (4) Criticisms of Paul.[83] Goulder's problem, however, is that he excessively employs the realized eschatology in grasping the exigency of the Thessalonian church through parallels with 1 Corinthians. Regarding Jesus' Parousia, there is a clear difference between 1 Corinthians (Paul's correction of the misunderstanding of their realized eschatology) and 1 Thess (Paul's

---

80. Nicholl, *From Hope to Despair in Thessalonica*, 158–66. He also asserts that the most significant difficulty to reading this as an eschatological problem is the silence of eschatology in 2 Thess 3:6–15 and no suggestion that the eschatological problems in 2 Thess 2:1ff. had direct ethical consequences.

81. The majority of commentators treat this problem with an eschatological background. Best, *First and Second Epistles to the Thessalonians*, 334; Bruce, *1 and 2 Thessalonians*, 209; Gaventa, *First and Second Thessalonians*, 129; Beale, *1–2 Thessalonians*, 249–51; Menken, *2 Thessalonians*, 129; Morris, *First and Second Epistles to the Thessalonians*, 251; Whiteley, *Thessalonians*, 108; Hoekema, *Bible and the Future*, 153; Ridderbos, *Paul*, 511.

82. The example of this is the Dami Mission Church in Korea, whose members were expecting the immediate return of Jesus, particularly in 1992. They left homes and families, sold all their properties, and were engrossed in praying. Most members of Dami Mission Church were disgusted with normal life of faith and chased this misunderstood eschatology. They changed the prophesied time of Jesus' coming many times, and the remnants of it have transformed into a different form of a religious group that waits for Jesus' coming at some fixed time. David Koresh of the Branch Davidians is also a similar case in history (Holmes, *1 and 2 Thessalonians*, 242). These kinds of indirect but historical evidences could surely demonstrate the effects of a misunderstood eschatology.

83. Goulder, "Silas in Thessalonica," 87–106.

proclamation of the triumph and the encouragement of Jesus' Parousia) in regards to the exigency of each church.

A recent debate has emerged over whether or not 2:1–12 is an apology defending Paul himself from opponents who criticize Paul. J. Weima, from the perspective of epistolary approach and mirror reading, denied the widespread claims that this passage functions as a paraenesis in which Paul represents himself as a role model for the Thessalonian believers to imitate. He suggests some evidence to support his claim that the thanksgiving section (1:2–10), the apostolic parousia (2:17—3:10), and the antithetical statements of and the repeated appeals and reminding words to the witness language of 2:1–12, indicate that the primary function of 2:1–12 is defensive or apologetic, denying the rhetorical approach.[84] He, however, does not consider the element of rhetorical approach, particularly *narratio*. *Narratio* is generally employed to win or confirm belief from the audience, and *narratio* in 1 Thess functions as unique element of funeral oration in identifying Paul himself with the Thessalonian community.

Against Weima's assertion, Malherbe explored 1 Thess 2:1–12 from a Cynic background. He found striking similarities between 1 Thess 2:1–12 and the characteristics of the Cynic philosopher described by Dio Chrysostom. On the basis of parallels, Malherbe claimed Paul was not defending himself against criticism made by real opponents, because Dio was not responding to particular charges leveled against him personally.[85] Many scholars take the same position as Malherbe, such as Lyons, Jewett, Wanamaker, A. Smith, E. Richard, Johannes Schoon-Janssen, Koester, Hock, D. W. Palmer, Stowers, D. E. Aune, F. W. Hughes, J. Hill, deSilva, Gaventa, Merk, and Donfried. In addition, Lyons, who examines the autobiographical statements of Paul in Gal and 1 Thess, denies a widely held assumption that Paul writes autobiographically only infrequently, reluctantly, and almost always apologetically. He concludes that the autobiographical reference of 2:1–12 (1:2—2:16) is Paul's rhetorical and argumentative goal to present and to establish his ethos as an embodiment of his gospel and his converts' ethos as an imitation of his, not functioning to defend his authority. Lyons supports his assertion through Paul's use of rhetorical antithetical construction in order to avoid the offensiveness of boasting and refutes the interpretive technique of "mirror reading."[86]

84. Weima, "Apology for the Apologetic Function of 1 Thessalonians 2:1–12," 73–99; Weima, "What Does Aristotle Have to Do with Paul?," 458–68; Weima, "Function of 1 Thessalonians 2:1–12," 114–31.

85. Malherbe, "'Gentle as a Nurse,'" 203–17; Malherbe, *Paul and the Thessalonians*, 1–4, 48; Malherbe, *Paul and the Popular Philosophers*, 35–48.

86. Lyons, "Function of Autobiographical Remarks," 34–44, 86–92, 99–106, 312–27,

This rhetorical approach sheds light on Paul's autobiographical reference, showing it to be paraenesis, not apology. However, it lacks elements of an epideictic funerary oratory, which illuminates the language and arguments of Paul in the discourse of 1 Thess wholly, which is beyond autobiographical paraenesis.

From the perspective of the rhetorical approach, Hughes rightly compares 1 Thessalonians to several traditions within Greco-Roman rhetoric and suggests the parallels between what Aristotle, Cicero, and Quintilian said about the narratio and 1 Thess 2:1—3:10. Furthermore, he rightly classifies 1 Thess into the *genus* of epideictic rhetoric and finds clues of this through showing exhortation at the end of speech. He points out and draws the parallels between 1 Thess and funeral speeches/consolatory speech according to Menander Rhetor.[87] His approach suggests just the possibility of funeral oration in 1 Thess, but does not fully show the elements, structure, and rhetorical situation of funeral oration. He neglects the function of narratio, of consolation, and exhortation in 1 Thess, which are the main elements in funeral oration, as well as in the rhetorical situation.

Bruce Johanson approaches 1 Thess with communication models attributed to text-linguistics, letter-conventional analysis, and rhetorical analysis to reconstruct the meaning of 1 Thess. He rightly concludes that Paul employs many rhetorical-persuasive strategies in 1 Thess as a whole to identify with "the deaths of fellow believers and the addressees' reactions of grief, perplexity and anxiety in the context of their expectation of direct assumption at the imminent parousia."[88] In other words, among the central panels (2:1–12; 3:1–8; 4:13—5:11) the first and second sections (2:1–12; 3:1–8) function as an exordial-like part to solve the issues emerging from rhetorical exigency in 4:13—5:11. Johanson rightly grasps Paul's rhetorical intentions in 1 Thessalonians wholly, but he overlooks some rhetorical elements, genre, and situation. Firstly, he misinterprets 2:1–12 as "an anticipative apologetic function." Secondly, though he suggests consolation elements in 1 Thess, like Kennedy, he wrongly classifies 1 Thess as of the deliberative genre, emphasizing the future-oriented focus and the response-changing function of dissuasion from grief to hope.[89] He loses the main function of epideictic rhetoric, because he misses funeral oration's elements and purpose.

374–82.

87. Hughes, "Rhetoric of 1 Thessalonians," 94–116; Hughes, "Social Situations Implied by Rhetoric," 250–51.

88. Johanson, *To All the Brethren*, 163.

89. Johanson, *To All the Brethren*, 49–144, 118–19, 163–67.

While Johanson combines consolation and correction without reproof and emphasizes the "dissuasive concern," which leads to his choice of the deliberative genre, Wilhelm Wuellner approaches 1 Thess with the rhetorical convention of the *paradoxon enkomion* (e.g., irony, paradox, oxymoron), which is a widely known sub-genre of the epideictic genre. He considers 1 Thess 1:6 as the centrality of the *oxymoron* and focuses on the special type of exordium, namely the *insinuatio* type. For him, throughout the rest of 1 Thess, on the basis of the *insinuatio* in 1:6, Paul amplifies an affirmation about the commitment and deepens the audience's understanding of God's community as "a church in God."[90] Though he is correct to classify 1 Thess as epideictic, he fails to prove his assertion. Firstly, the *paradoxon enkomion* in Greco-Roman epideictic rhetoric does not fit the characteristic of 1 Thess. Secondly, his assertion that Paul employs the approach known as *insinuatio* is not convincing, because 1:6 is just a clear description of Thessalonian believers in due chronological order according to the rhetorical rule of encomium.

Concerning the specific genre of 1 Thess, A. Malherbe proposes it to be the paraenetic letter because of its pastoral care. Recently, however, Juan Chapa, Stowers, and Abraham Smith have suggested a consolation letter pattern for 1 Thess. Chapa finds the parallels of consolatory topics between the letter of consolation in the Greco-Roman world and 1 Thess, and attempts to identify the pattern of 1 Thess. He suggests seven overlapping topics such as sympathy (2:2), commonplaces of suffering and human immortality (3:3–4), the noble way of facing sorrowful circumstances (1:6–10), consolation by *exempla* (2:14–15), and paraclectic exhortation (2:2–3; 3:2, 7; 4:1, 10, 18; 5:11, 14). However, he considers 1 Thess as "a consoling letter" rather than a letter of consolation with the characteristics of the prophets of the Old Testament and of the Jewish tradition (2 Macc).[91] On the other hand, Smith clearly defines 1 Thess as a letter of consolation and asserts that Paul exploited and inserted the rhetorical pattern to comfort the Thessalonian believers. Chapa sets the three large units (1:6—2:16; 2:17—3:13; 4:1—5:22) into the consolatory arguments following Stowers' definition of the letter of consolation.[92] Both Chapa and Smith contribute a new genre proposal

---

90. Wuellner, "Argumentative Structure," 117–36.

91. Chapa, "Is First Thessalonians a Letter of Consolation?" 150–60; Chapa, "Consolatory Patterns?," 220–28.

92. Smith, *Comfort One Another*, 42–92; Stowers, *Letter-Writing in Greco-Roman Antiquity*, 144. Stowers lists three fundamental elements for the letter of consolation: (1) The writer may have a wide range of positive relationships with the recipient. (2) The recipient has experienced some major misfortune that is apt to produce grief. (3) The writer expresses his grief and provides reasons why the recipient should bear up

to interpret and to reconstruct 1 Thess s. However, 1 Thess is beyond just a letter of consolation or a consoling letter. First of all, a letter of consolation is a personal letter rather than public letter. In contrast, 1 Thess is the public letter to the whole congregation of Thessalonica. Furthermore, consolatory letters actually follow the patterns of consolatory rhetorical speeches. The Latin consolatory letters are deeply influenced by funeral oration and serve as surrogates for oral forms. In other words, while consolatory letters use the form of letter, they actually contain the elements of epideictic speeches and follow rhetorical conventions.

First Thessalonians is more closely related to the funeral oration of epideictic rhetoric than to a consolatory letter. Throughout 1 Thess Paul's eschatological references are dispersed at 1:10; 2:12, 16, 19; 3:13; and 4:13—5:11. Duane Watson asserts the combination of apocalyptic discourse and imminent expectation pervades the entire letter, especially chapters 4–5.[93] Karl Donfried correctly points out the Thessalonians' suffering, to the point of martyrdom, and also claims the theme of the parousia dominates the entire letter. The analysis of the letter's social background by E. A. Judge and Holland Hendrix of the Thessalonian also supports Donfried's assertion.[94] Thus, 1 Thess may not be a paraenetic letter but a paraclectic one, mainly drawing on the funeral oration tradition of epideictic rhetoric. Nicole Loraux asserts the existence of the literary *genre* of funeral oration,[95] and it is possible to find some connections and clues of funeral language and purpose between 1 Thess and the ancient funeral oration of epideictic rhetoric, such as the phrase "we who are still alive" (1 Thess 4:15; *Menexenus* 235a5–6, 235d3–7). Furthermore, Loraux correctly asserts that funeral oration is public oration, not private oration, and as a didactic speech, the funeral oration does not so much console as it explains and exalts.[96] Demosthenes turns it into a celebration of valorous deeds; Thucydides describes the speech as an epainos; and Plato sees the epitaphioi as praise both of Athens and of the Athenians. Thus, with the characteristics of the *epitaphioi*, *enkomion*, *paraenesis*, and *paramythia*, the orators have a double aim: to instruct the young and to console the adults.[97]

---

under the grief.

93. Watson, "Paul's Appropriation of Apocalyptic Discourse," 61–80.

94. Donfried, "Cults of Thessalonica and the Thessalonian Correspondence," 336–56; Judge, "Decrees of Caesar at Thessalonica," 1–7; Hendrix, "Thessalonicans Honor Romans," 319–38.

95. Loraux, *Invention of Athens*, 1–14.

96. Loraux, *Invention of Athens*, 48.

97. Ziolkowski, *Thucydides*, 1–48.

Given the Thessalonian church's rhetorical exigencies, and the form and function of funeral orations in antiquity, it is probable that Paul employs the purpose and the topics of funeral orations in order to solve the present Thessalonian church's problems. Encountering the growing persecutions, sufferings, and even death of members (or martyrdom), the Thessalonian believers were perplexed and Paul needed some rhetorical strategy to answer their problems.[98] Through the employment of the funeral oration, Paul praises the dead and plants the hope of Jesus' Parousia and of eternal life, consoling and exhorting the Thessalonians to imitate their lives in the eschatological era (1 Thess 4–5). Succinctly and simply put, Paul employs elements of epideictic funerary oratory to persuade the audience by writing 1 Thess, though it is not a funeral oration.

Hester uniquely approaches 1 Thess to grasp the rhetorical exigency of the Thessalonian church through the structure and topics of a funeral oration. Given the audience's situation and the form and function of funeral orations in history, Hester proposes that Paul used the topics of a funeral oration, stating that "it was suggested by the death of one or more church members . . . The divisions and topics of the funeral oration allowed Paul to answer these and other questions and issues."[99] Hester's contribution is that he is different from the traditional perspectives in recognizing the rhetorical exigency. Further, he finds similarities in form and function between 1 Thess and a funeral oration and shows the possibility of Paul's employing and adapting of a funeral oration in antiquity to solve the Thessalonian church's problems. Hester's assertions are helpful in finding the rhetorical exigency and in interpreting 1 Thessalonians. From a similar position, W. Wuellner specifically identifies 1 Thess to be reflecting a context of suffering with joy and waiting for the Lord.[100]

Hester, however, neglects the eschatological tones of 1 Thess in grasping the rhetorical exigency, just as Luckensmeyer asserts that eschatology is the hermeneutical key to interpreting Paul's paraenesis in 1 Thess.[101] Further, Hester does not note the reason for death in 1 Thess, namely, a martyrdom of believers. He also does not deal with the structural problem of the long narratio and the purpose of a funeral oration from the perspective of rhetoric in history. In other words, Hester must have some more examples in the historical-social milieu. In order to grasp the purpose and structure of Paul's writing, it is necessary to take literary-genre problems into consideration

---

98. Hester, "Invention of 1 Thessalonians," 270.
99. Hester, "Invention of 1 Thessalonians," 270.
100. Wuellner, "Argumentative Structure of 1 Thessalonians," 117–36.
101. Luckensmeyer, *Eschatology of First Thessalonians*, 1–46.

within the discipline of ancient rhetorical criticism. In our next chapter, we will begin to explore funeral oratory going beyond what Hester and Hughes were able to demonstrate with a view to better understanding Paul's rhetoric in 1 Thess.

CHAPTER 2

The Philosophy and Theology of Death and Dying in Funeral Orations and 1 Thessalonians

ANCIENT PEOPLES WERE DEEPLY concerned with death. In the ancient materials, there are many expressions of sorrow over death as a form of "snatching away" and the consolation for the death of loved ones. Hopkins shows the atmosphere of the Romans who were under the pressure of death and sudden death.[1] In these frequent and unpredictable incidences of death, the Romans had ways in which people accommodated death, reacted to death, and coped with death. These ways are reflected in their philosophy of death utilizing semi-philosophical letters of consolation and funeral orations, and many epitaphs. In 1 Thess, Paul offers several consolatory commonplaces for why the community should not allow grief to overtake them through the use of funeral oratory topoi. Paul suggests that the Parousia overcomes mortal separation. In this chapter, I will examine: (1) The Philosophy of the Epicureans and Stoics, which affects the theology of death; (2) The Philosophy and Theology of Semi-philosophical Consolatory Letters and Funeral Orations; and (3) Epitaphs in Greek and Latin. Finally, I will compare the philosophy and theology of death in funeral orations and 1 Thess.

Pagan Theology and Philosophy of Death (Epicureans and Stoics)

Ancient people were vulnerable to sudden death and were dependent upon religion and philosophy for consolation regarding death. The philosophy of the Greeks had a great effect on their thought world. In the same context, both Cicero (*Tusculan Disputations*, 3:34) and Plutarch (*Consolatio*

---

1. Hopkins, *Death and Renewal*, 207.

as Apollonium, 102B) similarly point out the function of the philosopher to be a consoler, like a physician.[2] It is well-known that in Paul's age the Epicureans and Stoics were the chief rivals for the community of educated people (cf. Acts 17:18).[3] Naturally, both philosophical schools had a great influence in ethics and the thought world in the Hellenistic Age, particularly in the philosophy and theology of death and the afterlife.

In regards to death and the afterlife, the Epicureans (Lucretius: 94–55 B.C.; Lucian of Samosata: A.D. 120–180) opposed Plato claiming that death, the rest from torment, dispels the ills that afflict humankind and that beyond it there is neither joy nor sorrow.[4] The goal of the Epicureans was to achieve peace of mind and tranquility (*ataraxia*) in this world. When the physical body dies, the soul also disintegrates. When a person is dead, his whole self dies. Therefore, there is nothing to fear in death and there is no future punishment.[5] The most distinguishing maxim that reflects the unbelief in the afterlife is shown in the epitaph: "I was not; I was; I am not; I do not care" (Non fui, fui, non sum, non curo).[6] Therefore, the Epicureans denied the bodily resurrection of the dead, and in 1 Cor 15:30–34, Paul asserts the certainty of the bodily resurrection after death and makes fun of the Epicureans' maxim, "If the dead are not raised, 'Let us eat and drink, for tomorrow we die.'"[7] Paul's quotation of the Epicureans' maxim mirrors indirectly the prevalent thought of the pagan society in his age, including the Thessalonian Gentile people. Furthermore, Paul's exhortation in 1 Thess 4:13 "so that you may not grieve as others do who have no hope," may also reflect the thoughts of the Epicureans as "others who have no hope" because it is said hope is "for the living, but the ones who die are without hope" (Theocritus, *Idyll* 4.42).

If the Epicureans denied traditional religion and philosophy of immortality after death, the Stoics (Cicero: 106–43 B.C.; Seneca: A.D. 1–65; Epictetus:

---

2. Dio Chrysostom also describes the philosopher as a physician when someone is under suffering and death by saying, "if it is his misfortune to lose any of his relatives, either his wife, or a child, or a brother, he asks the philosopher to come and speak words of comfort, as if he thought it were only then necessary to consider how one may endure . . . be able to face the future" (*Twenty-seventh Discourse*, 7–9).

3. Ferguson, *Backgrounds of Early Christianity*, 333, 355.

4. Cumont, *After Life in Roman Paganism*, 8.

5. Ferguson, *Backgrounds of Early Christianity*, 351; Warren, *Facing Death*, 6–23. Its motto is "death is nothing to us; for what is dispersed does not perceive, and what does not perceive is nothing to us."

6. Cumont, *After Life in Roman Paganism*, 9–10. On a Roman tomb there are similar words inscribed: "We are and we were nothing. See, reader, how swiftly we mortals go back from nothingness to nothingness."

7. It is possible that this is taken directly from Isaiah, not the Epicureans.

A.D. 55–135; Plutarch: A.D. 45–120) believed in a divine fire, determinism from providence (pantheism), restricted immortality of the soul among the souls of the sages, and perfection in this world through virtue. The true belief of the Stoics can be summarized in that "souls, when they leave the corpse, subsist in the atmosphere and especially in its highest part."[8] When the Stoics are compared to Christianity, in some senses there are several similarities among belief in spirit, Logos, self-control, and immortatlity of soul. There are, however, some fundamental differences in contents and philosophy. The Stoics did not have a fully personal God but only an immanent god who, because of pantheism, has no sense of beginning, purpose, or end of the universe, and no personal immortality, just intellectual and restricted immortality.[9] The limitation of the Stoics regarding death and afterlife was clearly exposed through contemporary works as follows:

> But the idea of conscious survival after death was itself no longer looked upon as sure . . . we are struck by the small number of the epitaphs which express the hope of immortality . . . On by far the larger number of the tombs the survival of the soul was neither affirmed nor denied . . . Or else the authors of funeral inscriptions . . . used careful phrases which showed their mental hesitation: "If the Manes still perceive anything . . . If any feeling subsist after death . . . If there be reward for the righteous beneath the ground." Such doubtful propositions are most frequent . . . The future life was generally regarded as a consoling metaphysical conception, a mere hypothesis . . . a religious hope but not an article of faith. The lofty conclusion which ends Agricola's eulogy will be remembered. "If," says Tacitus, "there be an abode of the spirits of virtuous men, if, as sages have taught, great souls be not extinguished with the body, rest in peace."[10]

In the next section, I will explore the philosophy and theology of death which are reflected in the semi-philosophical consolatory letters and funeral orations.

---

8. Cumont, *After Life in Roman Paganism*, 15. The following epitaph shows the belief of the Stoics: "The holy spirit which thou didst bear has escaped from thy body. That body remains here and is like the earth; the spirit pursues the revolving heavens; the spirit moves all; the spirit is nought else than God."

9. Ferguson, *Backgrounds of Early Christianity*, 346–47.

10. Cumont, *After Life in Roman Paganism*, 18.

Philosophers' Consolatory Letters and Funeral Orations

In Roman conditions of high mortality, illness and death struck people in their prime without warning, as they also contended with the death of soldiers in a civil war. Because of the obvious arbitrariness of death and its pervasiveness, Romans, educated and uneducated, were engrossed in treating the matters of immortality of the soul and the afterlife.[11] Romans honored the dead and worried about their fate and location after death. Under the circumstances of frequent death the prospect of their own imminent death, consolatory letters and funeral orations naturally developed in Roman society. In consolatory letters and funeral orations, there are naturally emphasized reassuring words about the fate and the location of the dead.[12] These funeral orations' topoi are also found in 1 Thess, particularly in 4:13–18.

Representative authors of consolatory letters are Cicero, Seneca, Pliny the Younger, and Plutarch, most of whom were heavily influenced by Stoicism.[13] In keeping with Stoicism, Cicero (*Cicero's Letter to Titius*; *Tusculan Disputations*; *Somnium Scipionis as a Consolatio*) offers solace for one in distress and gives consolation to assuage the sorrow of death. Pliny the Younger (*To Calestrius Tiro*; *To Caninius Rufus*; *To Novius Maximus*) discusses the short and fleeting nature of human life and death as the escape from perpetual illness. However, he shows his limitations of solace in nihilism, "Nothing can heal his wound but acceptance of the inevitable, lapse of time, and a surfeit of grief."[14] Seneca (*The Consolatory Letters of Seneca to Lucilius*; *The Consolatio ad Marciam*; *On Despising Death*; *On Grief for Lost Friends*; *On Consolation to the Bereaved*) similarly offers solace to the dead. Seneca depends on the philosophy of Stoicism, but his hope for immortality of the soul is not certain, just as Fern correctly points out, Seneca shows "the hope of immortality; but his hope is expressed in a vague, uncertain manner."[15]

---

11. Hopkins, *Death and Renewal*, 230.

12. Witherington, *1 and 2 Thessalonians*, 23; Bauckham, *Fate of the Dead*, 19–32. Bauckham claims in Greco-Roman cultures there were many myths and traditions of descents to Hades, which may derive from both the myth of the cycle of nature as a descent to and return from the underworld and the shamanism of Greek religious traditions. These prominent traditions of descents to Hades show their deep concern about the afterlife and hope of a blessed immortality of the dead.

13. Hope, *Roman Death*, 132.

14. Hope, *Roman Death*, 136.

15. Fern, "Latin Consolatio as a Literary Type," 43. Seneca, in his prayer (*On Grief for Lost Friends*, 16) prays "perhaps, if only the tale told by wise men is true and there is a bourne (place) to welcome us, then he whom we think we have lost has only been sent on ahead."

Among consolatory philosophical letters, Plutarch (*Consolatio Ad Uxorem*; *Consolatio Ad Apollonium*), while following classical Stoicism for consolation topoi, moves nearest to the grief and consolation temperament of the N.T. Between Plutarch and Paul there are some parallels in content and in words, such as when Plutarch designates the grief of bereavement as λυπῆ and as πανθος and when he seeks consolation in his religious belief from the immortatlity of the soul (*Consolatio Ad Uxorem*, 611D–612B).[16] Plutarch's frequent consolatory reference of λυπῆ (grief, sorrow, and pain; 608B, 608D–F, 609E–610A, 610B, 611C) is reminiscent of 1 Thess 4:13–18 of consolation, particularly Paul's exhortation to the living of the Thessalonians, "so that you may not grieve (ἵνα μὴ λυπῆσθε)" since the dead will rise and be with the Lord together through Jesus' Parousia. Paul uses λυπῆ to express his deep sorrow toward actual death or spiritual pain near to death. In Phil 2:27, Paul expresses his grief (λύπην ἐπὶ λύπην σχῶ) as he would have if Epaphroditus died, just as in 1 Thess 4:13 he uses λυπῆ in the context of death. In Rom 9:2 and 2 Cor 2:1–5, Paul uses λυπῆ to indicate his deep pain and sorrow that is near to death in his spirit. In John 16:6, 20–22, in the context of his death and martyrdom, Jesus also employs λυπῆ to describe what his disciples would feel and experience in their hearts at his death.

Furthermore, Plutarch shows strong confidence in the immortality of soul, compared to other philosophers, "the soul (ψυχη), which is imperishable (ἄφθαρτὸν), is affected like a captive bird . . . before it is set free by higher powers . . . with flexibility and resilience unimpaired" (611D-E). In a similar context to 1 Thess 4:13–18, Jesus' Parousia in 1 Cor 15:50–54, Paul claims the immortality and imperishability of the resurrected body and spirit against death, "σαλπίσει. . .οἱ νεκροὶ ἐγερθήσονται ἄφθαρτοι. . .τὸ φθαρτὸν τοῦτο ἐνδύσασθαι ἀφθαρσίαν καὶ τὸ θνητὸν τοῦτο ἐνδύσασθαι ἀθανασίαν. ὅταν δὲ τὸ φθαρτὸν τοῦτο ἐνδύσηται ἀφθαρσίαν καὶ τὸ θνητὸν τοῦτο ἐνδύσηται ἀθανασίαν." In other words, whereas Plutarch traces his belief in the immortality of the soul to the Dionysiac mysteries and Platonic philosophy,[17] Paul's thought about spirit is Jewish. Like Pharisees of Paul's category, a positive bodily afterlife was envisioned. This stands in contrast to the Sadducees who maintained the O.T. theology of Sheol, where one simply died and was gathered to one's ancestors, the spirit of the dead, and no resurrection was envisioned. Therefore, in some senses, the Greco-Roman theology of the soul and the afterlife comported more with the O.T. theology of Sheol, than the later apocalyptic theology of resurrection first seen in Daniel 12. Paul thinks of the human spirit and personality surviving death,

---

16. Martin and Phillips, "Consolatio Ad Uxorem," 413.
17. Martin and Phillips, "Consolatio Ad Uxorem," 438.

but does not agree that the "body is the prison house of the soul and the soul is inherently immortal." To the contrary, Paul believes immortality is a gift from God experienced in the flesh at the resurrection by saying, "this mortal body must put on immortality" (1 Cor 15:53b). Paul believes the immaterial spirit of a believer survives death, but it is different from the Greek notion of the inherently immortal soul. It would be more reasonable to talk about the survival of death by the human spirit, remembering Jesus' final words, "Father, into your hands I commend my spirit" (Luke 23:46a). Plutarch (*Consolatio Ad Apollonium*, 121F) shows his confidence in the fact that the soul is "with the gods and is feasting with the gods." Therefore, these facts above indicate though Paul reflects the consolatory letters and funeral orations in topoi and in content in 1 Thess 4:13–18, his thoughts about death and spirit are different from the Greek notion of the inherently immortal soul. Paul's thoughts about immortality of spirit are related to pneumatikos (spiritual) body after Jesus' Parousia.

Since earlier Greek literature on consolation and funeral orations considerably influenced Cicero, Seneca, and Plutarch, Greek-Latin funeral orations are also related to and reflect similar philosophies and theologies of death with the consolatory letters. Pseudo-Lysias (*Funeral Oration*) contains some philosophy about death in consolation saying death is common to all. In the same way, Isocrates (*Evagoras*), Plato (*Menexenus*), and Demosthenes (*Funeral Speech*) claim the human being is mortal by birth, but by memory immortal; death is immune from the disease of body; and death is the noblest climax of all for mortal men. These philosophies about death in funeral orations are in some ways parallel to Stoicism. It is noteworthy that the epitaph for the Athenian war dead at Poteidia in 432 B.C. states that "the ether received their *psychai*, but earth, their bodies" and thus the war dead were considered and praised not only for civic immortality but also for celestial immortality.[18] Particularly, among the orators of funeral orations, Hyperides (*Oration*, 43) clearly shows the destiny/location of the war dead (the afterlife of the war dead), that is, the immortality of honor and the immortality of their souls in heaven.

Regarding the immortality in heaven of the dead in war, Christinae Sourvinou-Inwood explores fifth century Athenian public epitaphs and funeral orations for the war dead and shows evidence for the drastic change from the negative perception of death to the positive evaluation of death in war. She claims that, for the ideology in the city of Athens, death in battle is a glorious event that elevates the war dead collectivity to a higher status. Naturally, the funeral orations (the *epitaphioi*) and public epitaphs contain and confer on

---

18. Davies, *Death, Burial and Rebirth*, 179–80.

them three different types of immortality: civic immortality through glory, heroization, and celestial immortality.[19] Particularly, Thucydides excluded grief and lament for the war dead in favor of praise from the official rhetoric. Furthermore, the souls of the dead in war obtained special praise and glorification of existence in heaven with immortality.

This trend and philosophy of Greek funeral orations and epitaphs in the fifth century exerted an important effect upon the Roman funeral orations and epitaphs. Dio Cassius (*Roman History*) describes the destiny of the dead Emperor Augustus; "you finally made him a demigod, and declared him immortal . . . we should glorify his spirit, as that of god, for ever" (41.9a). When his dead body was consumed, an eagle released from the body flew aloft, which signified the flight of the Emperor's spirit to heaven (42.3–4). These also reflect the philosophy of the Stoicism about death, that is, immortality of the soul. Tacitus (*Agricola*), in peroration and prayer, expresses his hope for the immortality of the soul in heaven, but with some uncertainty; "if there be any habitation for the spirits of the just; if, as wise men will have it, the soul that is great perish not with the body, may you rest in peace" (46). This hope of Tacitus regarding the destiny of the dead soul, which also shows Stoic philosophy, is similar to Cicero (*On Despising Death*, 118), "let us regard it rather as a haven and a place of refugee prepared for us," and Seneca (*On Grief for Lost Friends*, 16), "perhaps, if only the tale told by wise men is true and there is a bourne to welcome us." In this sense, Fern correctly points out that the Romans had "the hope of immortality; but this hope is expressed in a vague, uncertain manner."[20] Therefore, their sense of immortality and the conception of the Elysian fields were always vague, often purely negative. In other words, their faith and expression of the afterlife were rather literary and conventional.[21]

In summary, consolatory letters and funeral orations commonly show the Stoics' philosophy of death. Both contain beliefs that human bodies are mortal; death is not pain or evil but is the release from the burden and prison of body; the soul of the dead is immortal, and the soul can achieve celestial immortality. Though believing and hoping for the immortality of the soul and existence with the gods in heaven, their hopes and prayers were not certain but vague and conventional. Paul's thought about the immortality of spirit is different from the Greek notion of the inherently immortal soul.

---

19. Sourvinou-Inwood, *'Reading' Greek Death*, 191–95; Loraux, *Invention of Athens*, 116–17.

20. Fern, "Latin Consolatio as a Literary Type," 43.

21. Dill, *Roman Society from Nero to Marcus Aurelius*, 257.

Epitaphs in Greek and Latin

Besides the consolatory letters and funeral orations, tombstone epitaphs also provide convincing evidence of the philosophy about the afterlife, which actually penetrated into people's lives. In the Roman period, pagan beliefs ranged from the completely nihilistic denial of the afterlife (Epicurean) to a concept of the individual soul's survival (Stoicism).[22] With a vague sense of the soul's ghostly existence and an uncertain hope of reunion with his dead daughter, a father showed his grief and hope: "My consolation will be that soon I shall see you . . . my shadow is joined with yours" (*CIL* 2.3771). But many epitaphs express a nihilistic philosophy concerning death: "We are nothing . . . We mortals return from nothing to nothing (*CIL* 6.26003)." Such sentiments were so predominant that there were also some jingles, half-prose, or initials *n f f n s n c* (*non fui, fui, memini, non sum, non curo*) using the same philosophy.[23] Thus, denial of immortality and the finality of death are prevalent on many epitaphs: "Death is the final depth to which all things sink . . . There is nothing left—for nothing awakens the dead—except to afflict the souls of those who pass. Nothing else remains" (*EG* 459, 7–8; *IG* 9, 2, 640, 8–9). Another ritual of the funeral process, reflecting a belief in immortality, was the funerary banquet with the dead. During the banquet, the dead were thought of as being present, and this hope was inscribed: "come in good health to the funeral feast and enjoy themselves along with everybody else" (*CIL* 6.26554).[24] The expression of closeness between the dead and the living was clearly shown by the fact that several surviving tombs have pipes in them so that food and drink for libation could be provided to the dead.[25] The departed spirit was believed to linger in a dim existence in the grave, and the dwellers in the tomb still remained members of the family.[26] This funeral banquet and ritual communion were related to faith in immortality and faith in the spirits of the dead nearer the celestial divinities, the banquet of the gods.[27] This belief, however, is also vague and uncertain as well as conventional just as claimed previously.

---

22. Hopkins, *Death and Renewal*, 227.

23. Lattimore, *Themes in Greek and Latin Epitaphs*, 84.

24. Hopkins, *Death and Renewal*, 233.

25. Toynbee, *Death and Burial in the Roman World*, 32, 52, 62; Cumont, *After Life in Roman Paganism*, 199–206; Hopkins, *Death and Renewal*, 234.

26. Dill, *Roman Society from Nero to Marcus Aurelius*, 486–87.

27. Cumont, *After Life in Roman Paganism*, 204.

The Philosophy and Theology of Death in 1 Thessalonians

As the absence of O.T. quotations in 1 Thess indirectly reflects the circumstances of the Thessalonian church, the members of the Thessalonian church consisted of mainly Gentile converts who were familiar with the pagan environment. Of course, the pagan social environment surrounding death and the afterlife in some ways shows the hope and faith in the immortality of the dead in philosophy and in epitaphs, as discussed above. These hopes and beliefs were, however, uncertain and vague, having only a conventional expression; rather the main trends and environment were deep sorrow and despair with a sense of the finality of death. The symbolic attitude of the pagan world toward death and the afterlife is succinctly summarized by Theocritus: "hopes are for the living, but the ones who die are without hope" (*Idyll* 4.42). Thus, Paul, as a strategic rhetor to meet the spiritual need and rhetorical situation of the audience, made a strong constrast between the pagan thought world and Christian beliefs about death. The thoughts and attitudes, which characterized the way of the ancient people about death and the afterlife, are about hopelessness. A letter of consolation (P.Oxy. 115) shows a symbolic contrast with Paul's letter of 1 Thess in light of hopelessness and hopefulness. This letter was written by Irene, who had recently lost her husband and son, to comfort the grieving couple, Taonnophirs and Philo, whose son died also. It reads, "I sorrowed and wept over your departed one . . . but nevertheless, one is able to do nothing against such things (death). So, comfort each other (yourselves)." This letter clearly indicates the fact that there are human beings who are both helpless against death and hopeless about the afterlife.

Another symbolic example of the pagan's hopelessness about death is well expressed in Julian's letter to Himerius (*Epistle to Himerius* 69), who grieved his wife's death. Julian comforts Himerius as his wife was prematurely "snatched away like a torch" and gives a true story of consolation which Democritus spoke to Darius, king of all of Asia. When Darius was in great grief for the death of his wife, Democritus could not, by any argument, succeed in consoling him so he promised Darius that he would bring the departed wife back to life if Darius could afford to supply him what he asked with everything necessary for the purpose. The story goes that, "if he [Darius] would inscribe on his wife's tomb the names of three persons who had never mourned for anyone, she would straightway come to life again" (69, B–C). Darius was in a dilemma and could not find any man who had not had to bear great sorrow. This consolation symbolically shows that all people are under the grief of death and no one can escape the hopelessness of death. Rather, the inescapable hopelessness of all people before death is consolation to the pagan world. In this pagan environment, Paul may see epitaphs on the tombs and experience the fatalistic and hopeless attitude of the Thessalonians about death. Paul attempts to implant new faith and hope about death, which the Thessalonians encounter because of the martyrdom of church members. Though employing the same expression to "comfort each other" used in the pagan consolatory letter in 1 Thess 4:18; 5:11, Paul's attitude toward death and the afterlife forms a striking contrast to the pagan attitude. In other words, Paul may intentionally and strategically stand as a stark contrast to the pagan attitude of definite hopelessness through an absolute future hope. Paul defines pagan people as "others . . . who have no hope" (4:13b). In 1 Thess, Paul, in every partial conclusion, draws a clear boundary between pagan people and the Thessalonian believers (1:9–10; 4:5b, 12a, 13; 5:6a, 23). Furthermore, the future hope for Jesus' Parousia functions as the foundation of that boundary. In 1:9–10, Paul refers to the Thessalonian believers as those who "turned to God from idols, to serve a living and true God, and to wait for his Son from heaven." In 4:4–5b, because of this hope, the believers keep themselves in holiness and honor, "not with lustful passion, like the Gentiles who do not know God." In 4:12–13, Paul divides both pagan people and the believers using the problem of future hope for Parousia. Finally, in 5:6a, 23, Paul exhorts the attitude of those who have this future hope in their lives. Thus, the themes of future hope about death, the afterlife, and God's people are interwoven through 1 Thess like threads. For Paul, death is not the end of life but the beginning of the resurrection of hope in the future. Death is not something to grieve with despair and sorrow because through resurrection (4:14, 16) they will be renewed with a spiritual and everlasting existence (1 Cor 15:51–54a). Death is not forever bereavement but the hope of reunion, the dead and the living, through new creation with Christ forever (4:17; 5:10). Death is not the defeat under Satan's power but the triumphal victory over death through Jesus' Parousia (1 Cor 15:54b–55; 1 Thess 4:16). Therefore, death is not an object to fear or to comfort each other without any hope, but to comfort each other with future hope. As an eschatological community of Christ, though being new, they encountered the martyrdom of church members, the Thessalonian church should comfort each other with the hope of the resurrection and Jesus' Parousia. Paul, through utilizing the purpose of funeral oration for enhancing the group identity and topoi,[28] repeatedly encourages them in consolation (4:18) and in exhortation (5:11).

28. In 1 Thessalonians, some topoi of funeral oration are the destiny of the dead, resurrection with certainty, being with God forever like a reunion of the Christian community, and the funeral banquet of pagans, triumphal images over death through

In conclusion, the pagan philosophy of death, particularly Epicurean and Stoic views, shows a limitation of hope after death. Though believing and hoping for the immortality of the soul after death, hopes and prayers were uncertain, vague, and conventional. While employing the rhetorical *topoi* of the ancient funeral oration, Paul made a strong contrast against pagan thought, which represents the hopelessness about the afterlife. Paul's theology of death is the hope of reunion of the living with the dead. It is the new creation in Christ, the triumphant Messiah, through his Parousia. Paul's thoughts on the immortality of spirit is different from the Greek inherent immortal of the soul, but is rather the immortal spirit of the pneumatikos body after Jesus' Parousia.

Christ, and judgment over the world.

CHAPTER 3

Funeral Oratory in Speeches

The Rhetorical Genre of 1 Thessalonians as Epideictic Rhetoric

GENERALLY, THE MAIN BRANCHES of ancient rhetoric consist of forensic/dicanic/judicial, deliberative/demegoric/political, and epideictic/encomiastic/demonstrative. It is, however, already known that the three classical genres are not enough to encompass every type of ancient oration. Reflecting Aristotle's view of rhetorical genres, Jamieson and Campbell define rhetorical genres as "dynamic fusions of substantive, stylistic, and situational elements and as constellations that are strategic responses to the demands of the situation and the purposes of the rhetor."[1] Quintilian correctly points out the flexibility and overlap of rhetorical genres:

> I cannot even agree with those who hold that *laudatory* subjects are concerned with the question of what is honourable, *deliberative* with the question of what is expedient, and *forensic* with the question of what is just: the division thus made is easy and neat rather than true: for all three kinds rely on the mutual assistance of the other. For we deal with just and expediency in *panegyric* and with honour in *deliberations*, while you will rarely find a *forensic* case, in part of which at any rate something of those questions just mentioned is not to be found.[2]

For example, Gorgias's *Encomium of Helen* (the end of the fifth century), rather than being an epideictic speech in praise of Helen, is actually a defense of her actions. Thus, Gorgias may employ "the medium of a defensive/

---

1. Jamieson and Campbell, "Rhetorical Hybrids," 147. Aristotle claims that a genre is defined by the kind of audience that makes a certain sort of decision on a distinctive issue, developed through recurring lines of argument, characterized by a typical style, and employing certain strategies that are particularly apt for these circumstances (*Rhetoric*, 3–10).

2. Quintilian, *Inst.* 3.4.16.

encomiastic speech to promote his epistemological views."[3] However, the general and traditional categories of ancient rhetoric will help in understanding the nature, purpose, structure, and function of 1 Thess.[4]

M. Mitchell asserts that genre designation in a New Testament text must precede compositional analysis so the arrangement can be investigated to see if it is appropriate to that species. One should not deduce a genre designation by individual details, but the designation must correspond with a holistic reading of the text. In other words, individual passages must be seen in their relation and function to the rhetorical whole.[5] It is not easy to deduce a genre designation such as epideictic, deliberative, or forensic, just as was discussed above. Aune claims that with few exceptions, early Christian letters were either written with a basically deliberative purpose or included major deliberative elements.[6] Actually, in 1 Thess there are some elements of deliberative rhetoric, such as Paul's use of imitation, as well as moral and religious exhortation (1 Thess 4–5). Mitchell asserts, of the three rhetorical species, the deliberative most appropriately employs proof by example, while the use of example *per se* does not prove the text is deliberative. Thus, she concludes that the more important factor for determining the rhetorical species is the function that those examples play in the whole argument.[7]

For example, in 1 Cor Paul's primary task is to reconcile members of a faction-ridden congregation. For this goal, Paul uses various kinds of persuasion, particularly with his own examples (4:1, 9, 16; 7:7–8; 9:1–27; 11:1–2; 13:1–13; 15:9–10, 30–32). Thus, 1 Cor is deliberative rhetoric, but there is a semi-forensic cast to ch. 9, which Mitchell considers deliberative.[8] There is also an epideictic character to ch. 13 and an encomium, both of which digress from the main trajectory of the argument.[9] Therefore, though 1 Cor has some elements of forensic and epideictic rhetoric, the whole and main genre of the rhetoric is deliberative.

In the same way, Paul's example in 1 Thess 2:1–12 of panegyric digression is sandwiched between Paul's laudations of the Thess (1:9, 10; 2:13; 3:6–9), and functions as Paul's identification with the believers of Thessalonica as well as achieving rapport with the audience and preparing a good

---

3. Long, *Ancient Rhetoric and Paul's Apology*, 24–25.
4. Jeal, *Integrating Theology and Ethics in Ephesians*, 41.
5. Mitchell, *Paul and the Rhetoric of Reconciliation*, 11–13.
6. Aune, *New Testament in Its Literary Environment*, 199.
7. Mitchell, *Paul and the Rhetoric of Reconciliation*, 39–42.
8. Mitchell, *Paul and the Rhetoric of Reconciliation*, 243–45.
9. Witherington, *Conflict and Community in Corinth*, 46.

relationship for the following eschatological exhortation in ch. 4–5. Concerning the rhetorical effect of "identification," Kenneth Burke claims that "You persuade a man only insofar as you talk his language by speech, gesture, tonality, order, image, attitude, idea, *identifying* (Burke's emphasis) your ways with his."[10] While 1 Thess has the elements of deliberative rhetoric (exemplary model), its function is Paul's identification with the audience.

Actually, 1 Thess has many elements of epideictic rhetoric including the following: amplification and embellishment with hyperbole (1:8; 5:16–22) instead of proof and argument, the ongoing stress on anamnesis (remembrance), an epideictic contrast between praiseworthy and blameworthy behavior (between Jews and the Thessalonians), and the prayer (3:11–13) and exhortation at the end of 1 Thess. These characteristics are also found in the funeral orations. Further, in 1 Thess there are no direct quotations of the OT because in epideictic rhetoric, it is not necessary to have proofs—either artificial (those based on the creativity of the speaker) or inartificial (those based on shared customs, laws, and traditions, such as Scripture quotes). Thus, the primary and main genre of rhetoric in 1 Thess is epideictic, though there is some use for deliberative rhetoric.

Features that Identify Epideictic Discourse

All epideictic (*epideiktikon*) oratory is generally distinguished by one of three things: (1) it is simply the oratory of the universal phenomenon of praise and blame under such banners as "panegyric," "eulogy," or "encomium;" (2) epideictic rhetoric is a general term embracing all non-deliberative, non-forensic oratory ("occasional oratory"); (3) epideictic rhetoric is considered synonymous with such epithets as "The Oratory of Display," "Demonstrative Oratory," or even "Ceremonial Oratory."[11] Epideictic is the form of oratory closest in style and function to poetry; both epic and drama are also delivered before spectators rather than before judges of fact or policy.[12] Cicero comments on the characteristic stylistic features of epideictic:

> the name *epideictic* because they were produced as showpieces ... for the pleasure they will give, a class comprising eulogies, descriptions, histories, and exhortations like the *Panegyric* of Isocrates, and similar orations by many of the Sophists ... and all other speeches unconnected with battles of public life ... This style increases one's vocabulary ... the ornamentation is done

10. Burke, *Rhetoric of Motives*, 55.
11. Chase, "Classical Conception of Epideictic," 293.
12. Kennedy, *Art of Persuasion in Greece*, 153.

of set purpose, with no attempt at concealment, but openly and avowedly, so that words correspond to words as if measured off in equal phrases, frequently things inconsistent are placed side by side, and things contrasted are paired; clauses are made to end in the same way and with similar sound. (Cicero, *Orator* 37)

In other words, what would be expected from epideictic rhetoric is "more use of metaphor, use of more elaborate, euphonious, elegant, or attractive words, and arrangements of words to sound better."[13] Following Cicero, Quintilian similarly describes the aim of epideictic rhetoric:

To begin with the primary classification of oratory, the same form of ornament will not suit demonstrative, deliberative and forensic speeches. For the oratory of display aims solely at delighting the audience, and therefore develops all the resources of eloquence and deploys all its ornament, since it seeks not to steal its way into the mind nor to wrest the victory from its opponent, but aims solely at honor and glory. Consequently the orator, like the hawker who displays his wares, will set forth before his audience for their inspection, no, almost for their handling, all his most attractive reflections, all the brilliance that language and the charm that figures can supply, together with all the magnificence of metaphor and the elaborate art of composition that is at his disposal. (*Inst.* 8.3.11–12)

In the same sense, Kennedy defines a more prominent role for epideictic in that "Epideictic is perhaps best regarded as including any discourse, oral or written, that does not aim at a specific action or decision but seeks to enhance knowledge, understanding, or belief, often through praise or blame, whether of persons, things, or values."[14] Therefore, some of its main functions are religious preaching and "cultural or group cohesion."[15]

D. A. G. Hinks categorized ancient speeches into three types of rhetoric (*Tria Genera Causarum*) in light of the functions: rhetorical situation, purpose, and time aspect.[16] See table "*Tria Genera Causarum*", which summarizes and compares three types of rhetoric in terms of function, time, argument, and purpose.

In terms of rhetorical exigency, when compared to forensic rhetoric in which the judicial setting is important, there is no conflicting issue and no setting of debate, accusation, defense, or diatribe in epideictic. Rather,

---

13. Witherington, *1 and 2 Thessalonians*, 23.
14. Kennedy, "Genres of Rhetoric," 45.
15. Kennedy, "Genres of Rhetoric," 45.
16. Hinks, "Tria Genera Causarum," 170–76.

epideictic employs a tendency to embellish. There is too little concern as to "whether it be legitimate or not," and even truth may be disregarded in the interests of eloquence.[17] For example, in Isocrates's *Busiris*, which was written as a eulogy of a famous mythical king of Egypt, Isocrates recommends regarding a eulogy that "those who wish to praise a person must attribute to him a larger number of good qualities than he really possesses, and accusers must do the contrary" (*Busiris*, 4). Aristides (Sp. II, 505) comments that the encomiastic part, among other things, employs *insinuatio* (παραλειψις) and ευφημια. In the former, only the praise is put forward, and ευφημια is a euphemistic way of stating facts that are, in reality, unfavorable to the one praised (1 Thess 2:2–12).

Tria Genera Causarum

	Judicial rhetoric	Deliberative rhetoric	Epideictic rhetoric
main matter	right or wrong	advantage or disadvantage	honor or dishonor
function	accuse or defend	hortatory or admonitory recommend or dissuade	praise or blame
time aspect	Past	Future	present (sometimes past or future)
type of argument	Enthymeme	Examples	Amplification
Setting	oration in court	oration before assembly	oration before a audience
Purpose	the just	the useful	the noble

In light of the rhetorical function, the epideictic rhetoric usually is more closely connected with deliberative rhetoric than with legal oratory. The *Panegyricus* of Isocrates, for example, is deliberative but employs encomiastic material.[18] Isocrates's own ideal is expressed in *Panegyricus*: "I have singled out as the highest kind of oratory that which deals with the greatest affairs and, while best displaying the ability of those who speak, brings most profit to those who hear; and this oration is of that character" (*Panegyricus*, 4). Thus, Isocrates claims a mixture of deliberative and epideictic rhetoric as ideal. In technical terms, "it is an oration on some theme of general interest, elevated in style and of real importance, preferably a speech of advice, to

---

17. Burgess, "Epideictic Literature", 94.
18. Burgess, "Epideictic Literature," 95.

be treated in epideictic style."[19] In the same sense, Jamieson and Campbell, asserting rhetoric hybrids (fusions of generic elements), recently argue that a functional hybrid will occur "when deliberative appeals are subordinate to the eulogy, when they can be viewed as a memorial to the life of the deceased, when they are compatible with positions advocated by the eulogist, whose motives must not appear self-serving, and when advocacy will not divide the audience or community."[20]

In light of function and type of argument, just as Kennedy defines epideictic as "an important feature of cultural or group cohesion,"[21] epideictic is distinguished from deliberative and forensic oration by the absence of any αγων, any question that is an immediate issue. Thus, there is "no vote or verdict to be given, no issue to be definitely decided one way or another; the function of the orator is not to prove a point but to make a lively presentation to his hearers."[22] For example, the purpose of a funeral oration, which is an epideictic speech, is not to prove but to celebrate the virtues of the dead; nor is the audience there to learn whether he was good or not. The speaker's main attention is to impress the audience. Instead of methods of argument for forensic rhetoric such as artificial proofs, inartificial proofs, and enthymeme, "The proper function of panegyric is to amplify and embellish its themes" (Quintilian, *Inst.* 3.7.6).

Isocrates shows the reason why the encomium should not be made an apology. In *Helen*, Isocrates rebukes Gorgias's apologetical tone in *The Encomium on Helen*[23] and shows the conventional pattern for an encomium:

19. Burgess, "Epideictic Literature," 101–2.

20. Jamieson and Campbell, "Rhetorical Hybrids," 149. Isocrates's *Panegyricus*, belonging to the deliberative species, is constructed of encomiastic material. Demosthenes's *On the Crown*, belonging to the judicial species, consists of self-praise and an attack on Aeschines.

21. Kennedy, "Genres of Rhetoric," 45.

22. Hinks, "Tria Genera Causarum," 172–73. Isocrates defends the artistic character of epideictic speech as follows: "Yet there are some who carp at discourses which are beyond the powers of ordinary men and have been elaborated with extreme care, and who have gone so far astray that they judge the most ambitious oratory by the standard of the pleas made in the petty actions of the courts; as if both kinds should be alike and should not be distinguished, the one by plainness of style, the other by display" (*Panegyricus*, 11).

23. Gorgias of Sicily actually takes a tone defending rhetoric in that "It is the duty of the same individual both to proclaim justice wholly, and to declaim against injustice holily, to confute the detractors of Helen . . . Now, it has been shown that, if Helen was won over by persuasion, she is deserving of commiseration, and not condemnation. The fourth accusation I shall now proceed to answer with a fourth refutation . . . with no difficulty will she be acquitted of the crime attributed to her . . . How, then, is it fair to blame Helen who, whether by love captivated, or by word persuaded, or by violence

> This is the reason why, of those who have wished to discuss a subject with eloquence, I praise especially him who chose to write of Helen, because he has recalled to memory so remarkable a woman, one who in birth, and in beauty, and in renown far surpassed all others. Nevertheless, even he committed a slight inadvertence—for although he asserts that he has written an encomium of Helen, it turns out that he has actually spoken a defense of her conduct! But the composition in defense does not draw upon the same topics as the encomium, nor indeed does it deal with actions of the same kind, but quite the contrary; for a plea in defense is appropriate only when the defendant is charged with a crime, whereas we praise those who excel in some good quality. (*Helen*, 14–15)

In *Progymnasmata*, Aelius Theon, Hermogenes, Aphthonius the Sophist, Nicolaus the Sophist, and Sopatros, all deal with encomion and ecphrasis as characteristic of epideictic rhetoric. Aelius Theon defines encomion as "language revealing the greatness of virtuous actions and other good qualities belonging to a particular person," and "The term is now specifically applied to praise of living persons, whereas praise of the dead is called an *epitaphios*, and praise of the gods a hymn."[24] Further, he asserts that in encomion, "One should either not mention things which are against the man—for these become a reminder of his mistakes—or disguise and hide them as much as possible, lest without knowing it we create an apology instead of an encomion."[25] Nicolaus the Sophist recommends that in encomion, one should employ comparisons (*synkrisis*) everywhere, avoiding excessive flatness and aiming at an account of virtues so the discourse may be alive. Regarding the question about whether encomion admits antithesis (opposition, criticism, disputable material), he comments that "if antithesis results from some particular material which we are not able to conceal because the hearer seeks to know about it, we shall demolish these things in the treatment and add stronger rebuttals," so we might remove any harm done by the antithesis.[26] In other words, encomion does not admit the consideration of objections to what consists of virtue. It may, however, allow possible objections to be raised about the virtue or vice of some action, with room for rebuttal of those objections.[27]

---

dominated, or by divine necessity subjugated, did what she did, and is completely absolved from blame?" (Gorgias, *Hel.*).

24. Theon, Sp. II, 109–10, in Kennedy, *Progymnasmata*, 50.
25. Theon, Sp. II, 112, in Kennedy, *Progymnasmata*, 52.
26. Nicolaus, Sp. III, 53, in Kennedy, *Progymnasmata*, 158.
27. Kennedy, *Progymnasmata*, 158.

Among the elements of *Progymnasmata*, the most important one likely to be characterized by epideictic qualities is the ecphrasis (*descriptio*, description).[28] Hermogenes (Sp. II, 16ff.), Aelius Theon (Sp. II, 118ff.), Aphthonius (Sp. II, 46ff.), Nicolaus (Sp. III, 491ff.), and John of Sardis all define the ecphrasis as descriptive language, bringing what is portrayed vividly and clearly before the eyes (of the hearers).[29] Particularly, Hermogenes claims that the virtues of an ecphrasis are, most of all, "clarity (*sapheneia*) and vividness (*enargeia*); for the expression should almost create seeing through the hearing."[30] Further, it is conceded by all that ekphrasis is involved to some extent in all other forms of *Progymnasmata*, especially in the synkrisis and encomion.[31] There are ekphrases of "persons and actions and times and places and seasons and many other things."[32] Nicolaus claims that whenever one composes ekphrases, it is necessary to add an impression because "explanations contribute to vividness," and "ekphrasis will practice us for the narrative part . . . but what is elaborated in ekphrasis incorporates clarity and brings before the eyes those things with which the words are concerned, and all but makes spectators."[33] John of Sardis comments that in composing an ekphrasis one should use "a relaxed style without periods and enthymemes," and adorn it with different figures. Further, emphasizing the characteristic of vividness in ekphrasis, he supports the function of imagination saying, "for the language inscribes what is described in the eyes of the spectators and paints the truth in the imagination."[34]

It is natural that ecphrasis is appropriate for the elaborate style of narrative and is part of the *narratio*. A *narratio* is meant to state those facts that have generated the discourse, and they make clear, to a certain extent, "the rhetorical situation or exigency that prompted the discourse."[35] Just as Hermogenes and Theon claim, "In describing actions we shall treat them by starting from what went before and continuing with what happened in them and what followed," Quintilian asserts a narration in epideictic rhetoric is normally to be done in chronological order: "Praise awarded to character is always just . . . it has sometimes proved the more effective course to trace

---

28. Burgess, "Epideictic Literature," 201.

29. Kennedy, *Progymnasmata*, 45, 86, 117, 167, 218; Anderson, *Glossary of Greek Rhetorical Terms*, 40.

30. Kennedy, *Progymnasmata*, 86.

31. Burgess, "Epideictic Literature," 200.

32. Kennedy, *Progymnasmata*, 45, 86, 117, 167, 218.

33. Kennedy, *Progymnasmata*, 167.

34. Kennedy, *Progymnasmata*, 219.

35. Witherington, *1 and 2 Thessalonians*, 25.

a person's life and deeds in due chronological order" (*Inst.* 3.7.15). In *Rhetorica ad Herennium* (1.8.12), the author states that, in epideictic rhetoric, the *narratio* functions to reaffirm and remind the audience of what they already know to be true about themselves. There should be a distinct account of facts, persons, times, and places related in a positive way (Quintilian, *Inst.* 4.2.36), and there is a stress on conveying the mental attitudes and motives of the one who is speaking or writing (Aristotle, *Rhet.* 3.16.10; Quintilian, *Inst.* 4.2.52).[36] Cicero also claims this form of *narratio* in epideictic rhetoric "should possess great vivacity, resulting from fluctuations of fortune, contrast of characters, severity, gentleness, hope, fear, suspicion, desire . . . pity, sudden change of fortune, unexpected disaster, sudden pleasure, a happy ending to the story" (*De Inventione* 1.27).[37]

At this juncture, it is necessary that one of the sub-characteristics in ekphrasis is vividness (*enargeia*). Εναργεια is the art of vivid expression, often described in terms of setting matters before the eyes of the audience and including all manner of detail.[38] Quintilian defines *enargeia* as a virtue of the *narratio* (διηγησις), saying that "the *statement of facts* should not merely be magnificent, but attractive in style . . . There are others who add palpability (Sunt qui adiiciant his evidentiam), which the Greeks call εναργεια . . . Palpability . . . is no doubt a great virtue, when a truth requires not merely to be told, but to some extent obtruded . . . " (*Inst.* 4.2.63; Cic. *Top.* 97) Jane Heath asserts εναργεια, which could be used "when they (mimetic arts) represented what was actually not there in a way that made it seem so vivid, so clear, so animated or immediate that it appeared to be practically perceptible to the sense."[39] Dionysius of Halicarnassus explains εναργεια as follows:

> Lysias's style has abundant εναργεια. This is a certain power of conveying the things being spoken of to the senses, and it comes from his grasp of circumstantial details. No one who applies his mind to Lysias's words will be awkward, so difficult to please or so slow-witted as not to suppose that he is seeing the things being presented actually happening and that he is face-to-face in the company of the people the orator introduces as if they were present.

36. Witherington, *1 and 2 Thessalonians*, 25.

37. In the same pattern, Nicolaus says that in panegyrical subjects, the elements of ecphrasis are capable of producing pleasure in theater-audiences. John of Sardis suggests that in composing an ecphrasis one should adorn it with different figures.

38. Anderson, *Glossary of Greek Rhetorical Terms*, 43. Εναργεια is foundational to the more specific devices of portrayal (*descriptio*), ecphrasis and phantasy.

39. Heath, "Absent Presences of Paul and Christ," 4–5.

Through the εναργεια, the audience's own imaginative memory is evoked by prompts in the orator's speech, that they could experience what he describes via experiences and expectations contained within them.[40] Both *Rhet. Her.* 4.69 and Cic. *De Orat.* 3.202 state that "vividness" (εναργεια) is useful in the amplification (αυξησις), and *Rhet. Her.* 4.45 notes that metaphors may also be used *rei ante oculos ponendae causa* (for the sake of creating a vivid mental picture).[41]

The Four Types of Pure Epideictic Speech

Gorgias, 5th century B.C. "founder of artistic prose," may be said to have begun epideictic literature as a distinctive division of oratory.[42] Both Aristotle (*Rhet.* III, 17) and Quintilian (*Inst.* 3.7.6) assert the importance of amplification and embellishment in epideictic rhetoric. Aristotle says of the chief τοποι of epideictic rhetoric, "This aim is happiness and its component parts . . . If, then, such is the nature of happiness, its component parts must necessarily be: noble birth, numerous friends, good friends, wealth, good children, numerous children, a good old age; further, bodily excellences, such as health, beauty, strength, stature, fitness for athletic contests, a good reputation, honour, good luck, virtue" (*Rhet.* I, 5. 4).

Historically, the development of epideictic rhetoric shows several strands. First, by late 5th century B.C., great festivals attracted orators and poets, and Gorgias's *Olympic Speech* was the model speech. Second, the Athenian custom of praising the war-dead in prose oration appeared as epideictic genre. Third, the sophists and philosophers were concerned with the question of the nature and purpose of praise and blame.[43]

It may be possible to classify epideictic discourse into four types of pure epideictic speech according to their own characteristics: funeral oration (επιταφιος), festal gathering/party orations (πάνηγυρικος), paradoxical encomium (πάραδοξα εγκώμια), and encomium of person. G. Kennedy

---

40. Heath, "Absent Presences of Paul and Christ," 10.

41. Anderson, *Glossary of Greek Rhetorical Terms*, 44.`

42. Burgess, "Epideictic Literature," 102. The rhetorical devices attributed to Gorgias are as follows: (1) amplification (*cf.* Quintilian, VIII, 3.53); (2) brevity; (3) an answering of jest with earnest and earnest with jest; (4) teaching by example rather than by precept; (5) a style characterized by flowing expression and bold metaphor; (6) some figures of language: antithesis, paronomasia, repetition of sound and alliteration, repetition of words, likeness of sound in final syllables of successive words or clauses, and arrangement of words in nearly equal periods.

43. Russell and Wilson, *Menander Rhetor*, xiii.

classifies the epideictic discourse into three broad types of rhetoric: funeral orations, festival orations, and sophistic oratory.[44]

In the 3rd century A.D., Menander defines epideictic rhetoric and categorizes epideictic speech into 23 types in detail. His classification of the epideictic speech are as follows: (1) praise of a country; (2) praise of a city; (3) praise of harbours; (4) praise of bays; (5) praise of a citadel; (6) praise of a city under the head of origin; (7) praise of cities for accomplishments; (8) the imperial oration (βασιλικος λογος): The imperial oration is an encomium of the emperor; (9) the speech of arrival; (10) the talk (λαλια);[45] (11) the propemptic talk; (12) the wedding speech; (13) the bedroom speech; (14) the birthday speech; (15) the consolatory speech (παραμυθητικος λογος);[46] (16) the address; (17) the funeral speech; (18) the crown speech; (19) the ambassador's speech; (20) the speech of invitation; (21) the leavetaking; (22) the monody; (23) the sminthiac oration.[47]

Encomium of Person (Βασιλικος λογος)

Βασιλικος λογος is a presentation that extravagantly praises good qualities of a person. Usually, the encomium shows the three characteristic features. First, it presents the glorification of the individual. For this purpose, "facts may be selected at will, grouped in any order, exaggerated, idealized, understated, if detrimental points must be touched upon."[48] Second, the connection between encomium and biography is intimate. A portrayal of character is the main aim in each, so events may be treated in summary fashion. Third, the encomium is not to be made an apology.[49]

The primary topoi of encomium are suggested in thorough form by Aphthonius:

---

44. Kennedy, *Art of Persuasion in Greece*, 152–203.

45. Burgess asserts there are two kinds: one is deliberative form and the other more purely epideictic. It may be used to praise kings or states, or to advise and exhort, or to announce some fact, pleasant or grievous. Thus, this speech is a union of deliberative and epideictic genres ("Epideictic Literature," 111; Jeal, *Integrating Theology and Ethics in Ephesians*, 51).

46. Menander says the speaker of a consolatory speech himself also laments the fallen and raises the misfortune to great significance, amplifying the emotion as best he can in his speech by means of the topics (origin, nature, nurture, education, accomplishments, actions). (Russell and Wilson, *Menander Rhetor*, 161).

47. Russell and Wilson, *Menander Rhetor*, 29–225; Burgess, "Epideictic Literature," 110–12.

48. Burgess, "Epideictic Literature," 116.

49. Burgess, "Epideictic Literature," 117–18.

(i) προοιμιον (a prooemion)

(ii) γενος (the person's origin)—nation, homeland, ancestors, and parents

(iii) ανατροφη (upbringing)—habits, acquired skill, and principles of conduct

(iv) πραξεις (deeds)—(1) mind: courage and prudence; (2) body: beauty, swiftness, strength; (3) fortune: power, wealth, and friends

(v) συγκρισις (comparison)—attributing superiority to what is being celebrated by contrast

(vi) επιλογος (an epilogue)—fitting a prayer[50]

Festal Gathering/Party Orations (πάνηγυρικὸς)

In *Art of rhetoric* (1.2 ff.), Dionysius says that a panegyric, the technical name for a festival speech, consists normally of praise of the god associated with the festival, praise of the city in which the festival is held, praise of the contest itself and of the crown awarded, and, finally, praise of the king or officials in charge.[51]

Paradoxical Encomium (πάραδοξα εγκώμια)

Menander did not deal with paradoxical themes. However, a widely known and popular sub-genre of the epideictic genre, known as the *paradoxon enkomion*, was prevalent in Hellenistic antiquity.[52] The paradoxical encomium is a display of ingenuity, that is a pun of words, and the other main motive is the desire to startle; to win admiration and applause by a mere exhibition of smartness.[53]

Further "in the general rhetorical treatment of the encomium there is prominent mention of some features which lie along the line of the πάραδοξα εγκώμια."[54] Aristotle, *Rhet.* III, 11, 6, approving the employment of the paradoxical style in encomium, says as follows:

---

50. Kennedy, *Progymnasmata*, 108.
51. Kennedy, *Art of Persuasion in Greece*, 167.
52. Wuellner, "Argumentative Structure of 1 Thessalonians," 126.
53. Burgess, "Epideictic Literature," 157–58.
54. Burgess, "Epideictic Literature," 158.

Most smart sayings are derived from metaphor, and also from misleading the hearer beforehand. For it becomes more evident to him that he has learnt something, when the conclusion turns out contrary to his expectation, and the mind seems to say, "How true it is! But I missed it." . . . And what Theodorus calls "novel expressions" arise when what follows is paradoxical, and, as he puts it, not in accordance with our previous expectation.

Funeral Oration (επιταφιὸς) History and Contents of Funeral Oration

The Greek funeral speech developed from the formal laudation or commemoration of those who had fallen in battle for their country as public ceremonial occasions when the fallen are collectively praised for their bravery.[55] The earliest extant speech is from Pericles (431 B.C.) reported by Thucydides in his history of the Peloponnesian wars. Hester explains a rather elaborate ceremonial ritual was observed during which the bones of those fallen in battle were put into a common repository, paraded through the streets of Athens with lamentation provided by the women, and then put into a sepulcher in a burial ground in the most beautiful suburb of Athens. The funeral oration was given by a person who had been selected by the city council, and at its close, the people were dismissed to go to their homes and consider the ramification of the whole ritual.[56] Martin McGuire considers Isocrates's (427–329 B.C.) *Evagoras* as one of the most effective and original funeral orations. Isocrates apparently was the first to compose a funeral oration about a historical individual. His speech on Evagoras of Cyprus, addressed to the latter's son Nicocles, and the *Epitaph* or funeral speech of the Attic orator Hypereides on his friend Leosthenes, in their form and content had considerable influence on the development of the funeral speech as a literary genre.[57]

In the period following Alexander the Great, the funeral oration was regarded chiefly as a branch of epideictic oratory, and a special schema with a whole series of topoi, or commonplaces, was elaborated for this as well as for

---

55. McGuire, "Christian Funeral Oration," viii; Hester, "Invention of 1 Thessalonians," 266; Russell and Wilson, *Menander Rhetor*, 171; Kennedy, *Art of Persuasion in Greece*, 154; Burgess, "Epideictic Literature," 146; Loraux, *Invention of Athens*, 1–14; Ziolkowski, *Thucydides*, 13.

56. Hester, "Invention of 1 Thessalonians," 266.

57. McGuire, "Christian Funeral Oration," viii.

other branches of the epideictic genre.[58] G. Kennedy correctly points out that the traditional history of classical funeral orations has an underlying continuity in rhetorical situation, structure, and rhetorical features as follows:

> Pericles (Thucydides 2.35) speaks as though the custom were long established. According to Thucydides (2.34) public funeral orations were delivered regularly throughout the Peloponnesian war. The most interesting rhetorical feature of such speeches is the highly formulaic quality . . . Not only general organization but the topics to be mentioned became traditional in the way that gradually happened in other forms of oratory and poetry. The religious nature of the occasion no doubt helped to effect this; it was a kind of rite . . . The traditional funeral oration led the way toward a traditionalism in all of literature.[59]

The development of the Greek treatise on consolation and the Latin *consolatio* are closely related with and have influence upon the Greek and Latin funeral orations respectively. Democritus of Abedera (460–370 B.C.), Plato (427–347 B.C.), Xenophon (430–354 B.C.), Antisthenes (450–366 B.C.), and Diogenes of Sinope (400–325 B.C.), the founders of Cynic philosophy, Aristotle (382–322 B.C.), Xenocrates of Chalcidon, Plato's successor as head of the Academy (339–322 B.C.), and Theophrastus (372–288 B.C.), Aristotle's successor in the Peripatetic School, all dealt with the theme of death and the problem and means of consolation.[60] Further, because the Greco-Roman philosopher was considered to be a moral physician (Cicero, *Tusculan Disputations*, 3.34; Seneca, *Ira*, 2.10.7; Dio Chrysostom, *Oration* 8.8; 27.8–9) able to diagnose and give prescriptive cures to the soul's distressful diseases, he was readily summoned to scenes of tragedy to speak words of comfort.[61] Regarding the origin and purpose of funeral oration of Athens, N. Loraux correctly concludes:

> My own inclination is rather to assign the funeral oration its original place between the two poles of the lament and the eulogy, which, in the aristocratic society, expressed the relationship between the living and the dead . . . even if the funeral oration derives from the lyric *threnos*, there is much more in this refusal to lament, since it involves the relationship between a community and its dead and, through these dead, with its present and its past . . . the Athenian ceremonial allowed ritual

---

58. McGuire, "Christian Funeral Oration," viii.
59. Kennedy, *Art of Persuasion in Greece*, 154.
60. McGuire, "Christian Funeral Oration," x.
61. Smith, *Comfort One Another*, 48.

laments while restricting them to a minimum; but, by means of the funeral oration, the city recalled that those who had died in battle deserved something better than laments ... So from now on we shall study the funeral oration as an *epainos* (praise); it is certainly as such that the Athenians understood it. Demosthenes turns it into a celebration of valorous deeds; Thucydides, in his excursus on the funeral, describes the speech as an epainos; and Plato sees the epitaphioi as praise both of Athens and of the Athenians. By defining the speech as a eulogy I do not mean to minimize the element of exhortation and consolation in the funeral oration, but on the contrary, to show the profound interdependence, within the epitaphioi, of enkomion, *parainesis*, and *paraymthia*. Indeed, in praising the dead, the orators have a double aim: to instruct the young and to console the adults.[62]

Earlier Greek literature on consolation and funeral oration considerably influenced Cicero (105–43 B.C.), Seneca (5 B.C.–A.D. 65), and Plutarch (A.D. 46–120).[63] The consolation, as a literary genre, was introduced into Latin literature by Cicero. His first work, *On Consolation* (*De consolation*), was written to console himself on the death of his daughter Tullia, and themes of death and consolation are found in Books I and III of his *Tusculan Disputations*. Seneca's most influential contributions to the genre of consolation are the *Ad Marciam de consolation*, *Ad Helviam matrem de consolation*, and *Ad Polybium de consolatione*.[64]

Closely connected with Latin consolation, and much earlier in date, was the native Roman *laudatio funebris*. It was an ancient Roman custom for a kinsman or friend to give a funeral speech at the death of a member of a prominent Roman family. Such funeral orations had a strong influence on the Greek writers Polybius (*Hist.* 6.53–54), Dionysius of Halicarnassus (*Rom. Antiq.* 5.17.2–6), and Plutarch (*Publicolar* 9.7).[65]

O. C. Crawford describes the traditional Roman *laudatio funebris* as an interruption in the funeral procession from the home of the deceased to the place of burial or incineration. The cortège turned into the Forum (Dionysius Halicarnassensis, *Antiq. Rom.* V, 17, 2; xi, 39, 5; Plutarch, *Lucul.* Xliii; Polybius vi, 53, 1) and came to a halt before the rostra, from which place the speech was

62. Loraux, *Invention of Athens*, 43–49.
63. McGuire, "Christian Funeral Oration," x–xi.
64. McGuire, "Christian Funeral Oration," xi. Seneca, *Epist.* CII, 15, places the funeral oration in that division of oratory called *laudatio* as follows: (1) *laudationes iudiciales*, (2) *laudationes in senatu*, (3) *laudationes pro contiones*: a) *militum*, b) *civium*, c) *funebri*.
65. McGuire, "Christian Funeral Oration," xii.

delivered."[66] In Roman culture, funeral orations were divided into two types, that is, public and private funerals. The custom of delivering a funeral oration, either at public or private funerals, seems to have originated with the Romans in early times.[67] Plutarch, *Pub.* ix, 7, 102 (B. Perrin, LCL), describing the first *laudatio funebris* by Valerius Publicola, says:

> The people were also pleased with the honors which Valerius bestowed upon his colleague at the funeral ceremonies. He even delivered a funeral oration in his honor, which was so admired by the Romans and won such favor that from that time on, when their great and good men died, encomiums were pronounced upon them by the most distinguished citizens. And this funeral oration of his is said to have been earlier than any among the Greeks.

It is important to note the big differences between the Athenian funeral orations and the Roman *laudatio funebris*. In Athens, funeral orations were reserved for public funerals of those who fell in battle because Athens felt that "no one except soldiers should be conspicuous in death." The Romans gave the honor to all distinguished citizens—those who were commanders of campaigns or magistrates; "not only to men who died in their boots, but also to those who had died in their beds, 'thinking that praises were due good men for a completely virtuous life as well as for those who had found a natural death'" (Dionysius, *Rom. Antiq.* V. 17. 6).[68]

Cicero defines the rule of *laudatio funebris* as "brevity of testimony, simple and unadorned" (*De Orat.* II, 84, 341),[69] and Quintilian describes the delivery as being "melancholy and subdued" (tristes atque summissae, *Instit.* XI, 3, 153). Regarding the purpose of the *laudatio funebris*, Crawford asserts that "the purpose of the *laudatio funebris* was to mark the place of the defunct in the long train of descendants from a common ancestor, and to set in relief his lofty actions and honors as his contribution to the family glory."[70]

---

66. Crawford, "Laudatio Funebris," 18–19. He adds that when the funeral procession had arrived in the forum, the bier was placed, and the corpse, clothed in splendid raiment, was propped into a sitting or standing posture facing the people, in order to make it conspicuous. The orator and those who were wearing the ancestral masks mounted the rostra and took their places in ivory chairs facing the assembled people.

67. Crawford, "Laudatio Funebris," 20.

68. Crawford, "Laudatio Funebris," 21.

69. Cicero here highlights Rome's pattern of *laudatio funebris* (testimonii brevitatem habent nudam atque inornatam), comparing it with Athens's pattern.

70. Crawford, "Laudatio Funebris," 24.

52   THE RHETORICAL APPROACH TO 1 THESSALONIANS

Proto-typical, exemplary Funeral Orations for later writers—examples of orations related to 1 Thessalonians: The Athens Funeral Oration (5th–4th B.C.)

Menander categorizes encomia or eulogies into two main classes: the imperial oration (*the basilikos logos*) for the living and the funeral speech (the *epitaphios*) for the dead.[71] The typical funeral oration had four divisions: (1) exordium; (2) encomium (laudation proper, combined with lament and developed under the following *topoi* or commonplaces: family, birth, natural endowment, upbringing, education, life and occupation, with emphasis on moral qualities, achievements, fortune, and comparison with others, especially the great and famous)[72]; (3) consolation of the living or Paramythia (parents, siblings, wives and children of the fallen); (4) epilogue with final exhortation and prayer.[73]

Isocrates (*Evagoras*) [La Rue Van Hook, LCL]

Like the *Encomium of Helen* and the *Busiris*, *Evagoras* shows characteristics of epideictic rhetoric. Isocrates's *Evagoras*, however, is a sincere panegyric of the murdered king whom he personally knew and adored. Thus, the delineation of the character of the hero, Evagoras, is much exaggerated, and this embellishment was an essential characteristic of the rhetorical funeral oration.

(Exordium, 1–11) Isocrates, honoring the tomb of Evagoras, the father of Nicocles, exalts his excellence and his glorious death by comparing "his principles in life and his perilous deeds to all other men," (*Evagoras*, 9.2) and his preference of "a glorious death to life . . . a memory of themselves that shall never die" (9.3). He also confesses his inability to praise Evagoras (9.8–11).

(Encomium/Epainos, 9.12–69) Isocrates respects the birth and ancestry of Evagoras; "he proved himself not inferior to the noblest and greatest example of excellence . . . the noblest of the demigods . . . Achilles . . . Ajax . . . Teucer . . . So distinguished from the beginning was the heritage transmitted to Evagoras by his ancestors" (9.12–14,17–19). According to the

---

71. Russell and Wilson, *Menander Rhetor*, 77–95, 171–79.

72. Dionysius of Halicarnassus says (VI, 2) the *topoi* of the funeral oration are the same as those of the encomium. Burgess also admits the funeral oration employs the contents of the encomium ("Epideictic Literature," 120–21).

73. McGuire, "Christian Funeral Oration," ix; Hester, "Invention of 1 Thessalonians," 267–68.

primary topoi of encomium, Isocrates continually praises Evagoras's body (9.22), mind (9.24), guiding principles (9.28), valour, and the greatness of his deeds by using comparisons (9.33–34). Finally, Isocrates proclaims Evagoras' character and virtue with historical facts and comparison (9.51–64), saying nothing of the portents, oracles, and visions; "In truth, how could one reveal the courage, the wisdom, or the virtues generally of Evagoras more clearly than by pointing to such deeds and perilous enterprises? For he will be shown to have surpassed in his exploits, not only those of other wars, but even those of the war of the heroes" (9.65).

(Consolation, 9.70–79) With the concluding words of encomium, Isocrates praises Evagoras's superiority and immortality; "if any men of the past have by their merit become immortal, Evagoras also has earned this preferment . . . but Evagoras continued from the beginning to be not only the most admired, but also the most envied for his blessings . . . and though a mortal by birth, he left behind a memory of himself that is immortal. . .nor afflicted with the infirmities attendant upon that time of life" (9.70–72). Further, Isocrates confesses his inability to eulogize his encomium (9.73) and shows his purpose of writing this discourse. "For you, for your children, and for all the other descendants of Evagoras, it would be by far the best incentive," (9.76) for the continuity between Evagoras and the present generation.

(Epilogue, 9.80–81) Isocrates finally urges and admonishes Nicocles and the other descendants of Evagoras to imitate the examples both at present and in the future "to incite you to strive eagerly after those things which even now you do in fact desire; and you it behooves not to be negligent, but as at present so in the future to pay heed to yourself and to discipline your mind that you may be worthy of your father and of all your ancestors" (9.80–81).

Isocrates (*Panegyricus*) [George Norlin, LCL]

Just as Burgess points out, considerable similarities exist between Isocrates's *Panegyricus* and the *Epitaphios*,[74] though not in funeral oration by itself; the *Panegyricus* as epideictic discourse contains some topoi of the funeral oration. Through employing topoi of exordium, encomium of the ancestors, and encomium of exhortation, Isocrates claims Athens must regain her lost supremacy (over the barbarians) and prove by her past history not only her right but also her ability to unite the Greeks in a common cause.[75]

(Exordium, 1–14, 186) Following the usual elements of exordium such as the inadequacy of the human tongue to match the immortal deeds

---

74. Burgess, "Epideictic Literature," 149.
75. Isocrates, *Volume I*, 117–18.

of the dead and the lack of time for preparation, Isocrates comments about the general beginning: "sometimes alleging that their preparation has been on the spur of the moment . . . it is difficult to find words to match the greatness of their theme" (13). Uniquely, Isocrates, in the exhortation/peroration section, again expresses his inability to adequately express the deeds of the dead, "how great must we think will be the name and the fame . . . if they die in battle . . . For if those who made war against an Alexander and took a single city were accounted worthy of such praise, what encomiums should we expect these men to win who have conquered the whole of Asia?" (186) (1 Thess 2:19–20; 3:9)

(Encomium/Epainos, 15–159) Isocrates begins the encomium by praising Athens and the ancestors' deeds. He praises the greatness of Athens in various ways (origin, upbringing, deeds, and comparison) such as land— "our city is the oldest and the greatest in the world . . . for we alone of all the Hellenes have the right to call our city at once nurse and fatherland and mother" (23–25; 1 Thess 2:7, 11); the outstanding benefits and blessings (29, 38); and the education of philosophy and the teachers in the rest of the world (47–50). Furthermore, Isocrates exalts the excellence of the ancestors' deeds in the war, such as standing by the weaker even against their interests (53, altruism), returning bodies to their kindred for burial against Thebes (52, 58), displaying valor and courage surpassing the numbers at Marathon (72, 82–84, 91), dying honorably for their country (77, 84, 95, 186), quickly winning trophies of victory (87), battling for freedom in the interests of all of Greece (95–98), and having a spirit of harmony, not of masters (104). Just as Isocrates says, "upon which the very ablest speakers among our citizens have many times addressed you at the public funerals," (74) all these elements of praise above show the topoi of the funeral orations.

(Exhortation and Conclusion, 160–189) Isocrates does not finish with consolation and lamentation like other funeral orations; instead, he ends this discourse with an exhortation and a conclusion. He exhorts that "we must be quick and not waste time . . . it is much more glorious to fight against the King for his empire than to contend against each other for the hegemony. . .For all these reasons, we must make it our paramount duty to transfer the war with all speed . . . " (163–166, 172–173). Finally, he concludes that "this war is the only war which is better than peace; it will be more like a sacred mission than a military expedition" (182). With peroration and encomium (186–189), Isocrates challenges and encourages an expedition led by the Athenians and the Lacedaemonians and again exhorts, "Therefore you must come to my aid . . . those among you who are men of action must exhort one another to try to reconcile our city with Lacedaemon" (187–188).

Thus, though omitting the consolation and lamentation, this discourse also contains the topoi and structure of funeral orations.

Thucydides (*History of the Peloponnesian War*) [C. F. Smith, LCL]

Regarding Thucydides' funeral oration, Usener and L. Radermacher correctly point out that Thucydides combined the genres of epideictic encomium with deliberative exhortation:

> Thucydides combined two rhetorical genres . . . For a funeral oration naturally belongs to the encomiastic genre, but the deliberative genre is blended in. He is not only praising the dead but also summoning the living to war . . . Of the three main parts of funeral speeches—praise (epainos), lament (threnos), and consolation (paramythia)—he omits the threnos. For lamentation would not contribute to advice (symbouleutic) or exhortation (protrope), as Thucydides himself says: "Therefore I do not lament the parents who are present more than I exhort you." He must do this since he is delivering the speech at the beginning of the war and if he had lamented the men who had died first he would have discouraged those who intended to fight. This is the practical reason for the two-fold genre . . . For blending is the art of creating rhetorical figures. The main part of the encomium is (genos), for by narrating the deeds of the ancestors speakers can exhort their audience to war. Thus the praise of the ancestry leads to the exhortation (symboule). Furthermore, the main part of encomia is the comparison (parabole) of these to be praised with their famous predecessors . . . But in deliberative speeches the speaker shows that the war is easy by juxtaposing the circumstances at home with those of the enemy. By the use of juxtaposition, therefore, he connects both the encomium and the exhortation.[76]

In this sense, funeral orations have the combined figures of epideictic oration and deliberative oration, in light of their function and form.

(Exordium, II, XXXIV-XXXV) Pericles, son of Xanthippus, was chosen to speak for the first victims of the war. Just as a commonplace of the exordium he says, "the general inadequacy of any human tongue to do justice to the immortal deeds of those whose death is thus publicly

---

76. Usener and Radermacher, *Opuscula,* 2:xxiii–xxiv, "On Figurative Expressions" (*peri eschematismonon* 9).

honored."[77] He shows his inability but obeys the law, which established this public celebration in honor of the hero in battle, saying, "I also, rendering obedience to the law, must endeavour to the best of my ability to satisfy the wishes and beliefs of each of you" (3).[78]

(Encomium/Epainos, II, XXXVI-XLII) Thucydides begins the encomium with a short praise of the ancestors, "it is right . . . to give them this place of honor in recalling what they did," (36.1) but then changes the emphasis from the ancestors to the contemporary warriors,[79] "and not only are they worthy of our praise, but our fathers still more; for they, adding to the inheritance which they received, acquired the empire we now posses and bequeathed it, not without toil, to us who are alive to-day" (36.2). He finally praises Pericles's and his own generation by saying, "And we ourselves here assembled, who are now for the most part still in the prime of life, have further strengthened the empire in most respects" (36.3). It is noteworthy that Pericles, when compared with givers of other funeral orations, lessens the praise of the ancestors and emphasizes praise of the present generation. Thus, in his funeral oration, he increases the effectiveness of his praise by presenting them with "we" language, so that he might include his audience in his glorification of Athens.[80] Thucydides develops his speech according to the statement of the main *topoi* in encomium, "But I shall first set forth by what sort of training we have come to our present position . . . with what political institutions . . . of what manner of life our empire became great, and afterwards proceed to the praise of these men" (36.4). First, he praises Athens as a model of democracy in areas such as equality, freedom, and law, not being the imitators of other people (37.1–3). Second, he praises the great land and soil (38) and stresses their superiority in the systems of training and education (39.1). "Depending on a courage which springs more from manner of life than compulsion of law . . . our city is worthy of admiration in these respects" (39.4). Then, he praises the character of "lovers of beauty, of wisdom" and "nobility of spirit . . . with confidence in the spirit of liberality which actuates us" (40.1–5). In conclusion, Thucydides praises the city of Athens, saying, "In a word, I say that our city as a whole is the school of Hellas . . . Athens alone among her contemporaries is superior . . . Such is

---

77. Burgess, "Epideictic Literature," 150.

78. For Ziolkowski, the traditional features of the funeral exordium (*prooemium*) are an approving attitude towards the tradition (*nomos*), a precautionary statement of the difficulty of praising the dead adequately (*logos*), and some specific statements of praise (*epainos*), commonly revealing the extraordinary *arete* of the dead and thereby justifying the speech (*Thucydides*, 72).

79. Ziolkowski, *Thucydides*, 76.

80. Ziolkowski, *Thucydides*, 187.

the city for which these men nobly fought and died, deeming it their duty not to let her be taken from them" (41.1–5). Finally, he praises the deeds and courage of the dead in battle; "regarding such a hazard as the most glorious of all, they chose to be avenged upon the enemy . . . thinking it better to defend themselves and suffer death rather than to yield . . . at the crowning moment not of fear but of glory, they passed away" (42.1–4).

Poulakos considers "the glorification of Athens's earliest origins and her subsequent development" as prominent *topoi* of public burial speeches, saying, "The discourse in praise of Athens's origins is governed by the principle of repetition and establishes a continuity between ancient and present inhabitants, a continuity sustained by glorifications of the recent dead as men who had lived up to the ideals of their ancestors."[81] For example, Thucydides proclaims the dead "after a manner that befits our city" (43.1). Thus, the lengthy exaltations of ancient ideals in Athens are "narrative presentations that seek not to recover the past but to constitute the present in terms of past valuations."[82] In the same way, Hayden White correctly points out that narrative accounts display the past "not as an end in itself, but as a way of providing perspectives on the present that contribute to the solutions of problems peculiar to the present."[83] Thus, it may be that Paul's lengthy *narratio* (1 Thess 1:4–3:10) functions to provide perspective and attempt unity in the Thessalonian church.

(Consolation of the living and exhortation/Paramythia, II, XLIII-XLV) Burgess classifies the consolation into seven common topics on the basis of Lysias's consolation as follows: (1) death is common to all; (2) it is fortunate to die honorably; (3) such gain the glory of a public funeral and the honor of games; (4) they are to be envied; (5) their bodies are mortal, but their fame, immortal; (6) there is no occasion for mourning; (7) there is a future life and one's ancestors ought to be imitated.[84] In other words, in the Paramythia, the speaker attempts to console his audience and to give exhortation for future conduct. Thucydides arranges his consolation and exhortation for the whole assembly, "And so these men then bore themselves after a manner . . . but you who survive should resolve . . . their glory survives in everlasting remembrance . . . For the whole world is the sepulcher of famous men . . . Do you, therefore, now make these men your examples" (43), to the parents of the dead, "Wherefore, I do not commiserate the parents of these men . . .

---

81. Poulakos, "Historiographies of the Tradition of Rhetoric," 178.
82. Poulakos, "Historiographies of the Tradition of Rhetoric," 179
83. White, *Tropics of Discourse*, 41.
84. Burgess, "Epideictic Literature," 156.

but will rather try to comfort them . . . and be comforted by the fair fame of these your sons" (44), and to their children, brothers, and wives (45).

(Epilogue, II, XLVI) The epilogue includes the concluding statements of the Paramythia and the dismissal; "thus offering both to the dead and to their survivors a crown of substantial worth as their prize in such contests. For where the prize offered for virtue are greatest, there are fond the best citizen." (46.1-2)

Pseudo-Lysias (*Funeral Oration*) [W. R. M. Lamb, LCL]

(Exordium, 1-2) According to the *topoi* of epideictic funeral orations, Lysias says that he lacks time for preparation and the ability to match their deeds in speech in order to gain sympathy from the audience; "for their valor/courage has provided matter in such abundance." He stresses his need to "glorify the valorous deeds of these men" (2).

(Encomium/Epainos, 3-70) The encomium has two chief themes: noble birth and deeds as mentioned above. According to Aristotle's definition (*Rhet.* II, 1390b, 15), "noble birth is a heritage of honor from one's ancestors." The narrative account of the idealized record of Athens's achievements in history became the most important part of the funeral orations.[85] With such a lengthy mythical (4-16) and historical (21-70) narrative, Lysias develops the encomium chronologically according to three broad divisions: ancestors (3-19), descendants (20-66), and the dead (67-70).[86] He recounts first the ancient ordeals of the ancestors by remembering and glorifying them and finding lessons for the living (3). He uses the story of the Amazons (4-6), the story of the Seven against Thebes who were slain (7-10), and the Children of Heracles (11-16), which all include the topic of valor of the ancestors. Lysias makes autochthonous origin the identifying badge of the Athenians; "They had not been collected . . . they were born of the soil," (17) and praises them for establishing democracy and freedom (18-19).

Just as Poulaskos correctly points out, the continuity between ancient origins and present times is maintained by noble birth, as a bridge between the ancestors and the descendants. Lysias says that "being of noble stock and having minds as noble . . . but ever memorable and mighty are the trophies that their descendants have everywhere left behind them owing to their valor" (20). In the rest of the encomium, Lysias, employing the historical order, deals with the story of the Persian wars with Darius (21-26),[87] the

---

85. Burgess, "Epideictic Literature," 150.
86. Ziolkowski, *Thucydides*, 80-81.
87. Lysias mainly emphasizes the Athenians' valor, "but holding that a glorious

battle of Salamis with Xerxes (27–47), other Greeks (48–53), the Athenian empire (54–57), and the defeat and the restoration of Athens in 403 B.C. (58–66). In the same context, Lysias maintains the continuity between the ancestors and the present warriors by praising the valor of the dead; "But these men are enviable . . . in manhood they preserved that ancient fame intact and displayed their own prowess." (69)

(Lamentation/Threnos, 71–76) Lysias says it is natural for the living to lament and bewail the dead (71) and to hold their parents and children in the same high regard (75).

(Consolation of the living and exhortation/Paramythia, 77–80) In the funeral speech, the statement that the dead would have an immortal reputation is one of the most appealing consolations in antiquity because one of the aims of the State funeral ceremony was to perpetuate the memory and honor of those who had died for the state.[88] Thus, Lysias begins Paramythia by contrasting lamentation. "But I do not know what need there is to lament so sadly" (77), rather "it is fitting to consider those most happy who have closed their lives in risking them for the greatest and noblest ends . . . those who have fallen in war are worthy of receiving the same honors as the immortals"(79–80).

(Epilogue, 81) In concluding Paramythia, Lysias repeats an immortal memory arising from their valor.

Plato (*Menexenus*) [R. G. Bury, LCL]

(Exordium, 236d–237b) When compared to other funeral orations, Plato alone omits the commonly used general inadequacy of any human tongue to do justice to the immortal deeds of the dead. This matches the satirical tone of the opening dialogue between Socrates and Menexenus (235). As is the nomos (custom), Plato says the honor of the dead should be commemorated both in respect of deeds and of words and particularly by means of funeral speech through which the dead are remembered and honored. Further, Plato shows the right order in funeral oration, saying, "[it] will adequately eulogize the dead and give kindly exhortation to the living, appealing to their children and their brethren to copy the virtues of these heroes, and to their fathers and mothers and any still surviving ancestors offering consolation" (236d–e). Following the order of the encomium, he suggests

---

death leaves behind it a deathless account of deeds well done" (*Lysias*, 23) "for death, in their opinion, was a thing for them to share with all men, but prowess with a few" (24–26).

88. Ziolkowski, *Thucydides*, 142–43.

the order of eulogy as their nobility of birth, their nurture and training, and the character of their exploits (237a-b).

(Encomium/Epainos, 237b-246b) In the section of origin (γενος) Plato praises the autochthony of the ancestors and the nurture of his mother-country (237b-c) and continually praises the land's human nourishment. Regarding a civic polity and upbringing (ανατροφη), he emphasizes the continuity of "democracy and an aristocracy" between ancient forefathers and their descendants of the present age, including the dead (238c-d). Thus, Plato stresses legal equality by one mother, consequently leading to the unity and identification between the ancestors and the present descendents, including the dead.[89]

In the section of πραξεις (deeds), before setting forth the long story of ancestors' deeds historically and chronologically, Plato proclaims the continuity and identification between all generations: "Wherefore the forefathers of these men and of us and these men themselves, having been reared up thus in complete freedom . . . achieved before all men many noble deeds both individual and national, deeming it their duty to fight in the cause of freedom alike with Greeks on behalf of Greeks and with barbarians on behalf of the whole of Greece" (239a-b). Particularly, when saying "already their valor has been adequately celebrated in song by poets," Plato describes, in chronological order, the stories of Eumolpus, the Amazons, other earlier invaders, the Seven against Thebes, and the Heracleidae (239a-c). Further, he embellishes the story of Athenian history from the Persian wars down to the Peace of Antalcidas in 387 B.C. (239d-246b). His points of praises are: (1) their valor (241a), (2) fighting at sea without fear (241e), (3) the salvation of Greece (241c). Because of "their valor we pronounce their eulogy now, as our successors will in the time to come" (241d), and "for these reasons it behooves us to have them in remembrance and to praise them always" (243d).

Just as Ziolkowski says, Plato makes no distinction in describing the stories of wars between the deeds of the present dead and the deeds of their ancestors.[90] Through the long description of Athens's wars against barbarians, Plato sets the groundwork for unity (identification) between ancestors and the present generation, including the dead, in order to "exhort these men's children, just as in time of war, not to fall out of rank with their fathers nor to give way to cowardice and beat a retreat" (246b).

89. Poulakos, "Historiographies of the Tradition of Rhetoric," 178.

90. Ziolkowski, *Thucydides*, 82. Plato also concludes the stories of Athens's wars, saying, "And now we have related many of the noble deeds done by the men who are lying here, and by all the others who have died in defence of their city" (Ziolkowski, "Thucydides," 246a).

(Consolation of the living and exhortation/Paramythia, 246d–249c) Since the Paramythia is intended to alleviate the grief of the living, it is usual for the orator to employ praises of the dead again, particularly about the glory of dying in battle for their country.[91] Plato glorifies their death, "As for our own fortunes, they have already reached that climax which is the noblest of all for mortal men" (248b-c). He also urges the living not to lament because of their fortune "and not join in their lamentations . . . Rather should we mollify and assuage their sorrow by reminding them that in the greatest matters the gods have already hearkened unto their prayers" (247d). Both fathers and mothers should be "well assured that it is not by mourning and lamenting us that they gratify us most" (248b). As for children, "first and last and always, in every way to show all zeal that you may exceed, if possible (πρωτὸν καὶ ὑστατὸν καὶ διὰ παντὸς πασαν πάντως προθυμιαν πειρᾶσθε ἔχειν. . .ὑπερβαλεισθε. . .)" (247a)[92] and "I myself, on their behalf, entreat the children to imitate their fathers" (248e). Thus, in Paramythia, Plato particularly recommends two main behaviors. First, he appeals to the children to zealously imitate their fathers in their valor to die for their country. Second, he commands his hearers not to lament more because of their fortune, but rather assuage their sorrow. The defining characteristic of the Paramythia is the limitation of grief. Like Thucydides, Plato employs more direct imperatives with crh (must/it is necessary/it ought) for the more forceful effects: "you must practice it in union with valor" (246e); "you must be consoled and . . . must not weep" (247c); "we should exhort the city" (248d); "you must bear your misfortune" (249c).[93] Finally, Plato pushes the protection of the city toward the children and the parents of the dead; "endeavoring to render them as little conscious as possible of their orphaned conditions" (249a).

(Epilogue, 249c) Plato ends his discourse with some repeated words.

---

91. Ziolkowski, *Thucydides*, 140.

92. These hypobolic repetitive expressions in funeral oration, particularly in closing, are also found in exhortation/peroration of 1 Thess 5:16–18:

16 Πάντοτε χαίρετε,

17 ἀδιαλείπτως προσεύχεσθε,

18 ἐν παντὶ εὐχαριστεῖτε·

93. Ziolkowski, *Thucydides*, 159.

Demosthenes (*Funeral Speech*)
[N. W. and N. J. DeWitt, LCL]

(Exordium, 1–3) Traditionally, Demosthenes follows the conventions of funeral orations: (a) norm and the law—"the duty of delivering over them (those who repose in this tomb) the customary speech" (1–2); (b) logos of the inadequacy of human tongue—"to speak as these dead deserve was one of those things that cannot be done" (1); (c) praise of the dead—"nobly born and strictly brought up and to have lived with lofty ideals" (3).

(Encomium/Epainos, 4–31) Demosthenes, after showing in detail the epainos of the dead (4–26), summarizes the topoi of the epainos; "The considerations that actuated these men one and all to choose to die nobly have now been enumerated,—birth, education, habituation to high standards of conduct, and the underlying principles of our form of government in general" (27).

Thus, Demosthenes firstly comments on the autochthony of the ancestors (4), and then on the mother-land (5). Next, he describes the ancestors' deeds and the wars against the Amazons and Eumolpus, the story of the Heracleidae and of the Seven against Thebes (8), and the Persian wars (10). Now, he focuses on the praise of the dead, particularly on their superior qualities; "willingness to do their duty . . . they were not sparing even of their lives" (15–18). Finally, Demosthenes concludes with the value of the dead during the Persian Wars; "what has become manifest to all living men alike is this—that in effect, the freedom of the whole Greek world could be preserved only with the lives of these men . . . the valor of these men was the very life of Greece" (23). Through this praise, Demosthenes attempts to connect the development of Athens into a Greek superpower to the valor of the dead and finally to subsequent generations.[94]

(Consolation of the living and exhortation/Paramythia, 32–37) Traditionally Demosthenes follows the conventions of Paramythia: (a) the glory of death—"of the glory and honour the source is found in the choice of those who willed to die nobly" (37); (b) the immortality of reputation/honour—"they leave behind them an ageless fame . . . it is a proud privilege to behold them possessors of deathless honours and a memorial of their valour" (32, 36); (c) release from sorrows—"immune from disease of body and beyond the reach of anguish of spirit" (32); (d) encouragement and imitation to the dead—"It is painful for children to be orphaned of a father . . . But it is a beautiful thing to be the heir of a father's fame" (35–37).

---

94. Poulakos, "Historiographies of the Tradition of Rhetoric," 179.

(Epilogue, 37) Demosthenes ends his speech by stating his real intention and commands his audience to disperse to their homes.

Gorgias (Fragment from a Funeral Oration) [James Hynd and Douglass Parker]

Regarding which section Gorgias's "Fragment" belongs to, Kennedy claims that it deals with praise of the dead with Gorgias's characteristic balanced, rhyming style.[95] This is evidenced by its lack of topoi and other commonalities of the epilogue (norm, logos, and praise) and the topoi of the consolation (immortality of fame, limitation of grief, and exhortation to imitation), and epilogue (concluding sentence of Paramythia and dismissal). It conforms to the pattern of the epainos of the deeds and attitude of the dead.

First, Gorgias confirms the merits and good deeds of the dead through questions; "For what did these men miss that makes a man? What did they manifest that makes amiss?" Next, he focuses on deeds and the attitude (arete) of a heavenly mettle that the dead demonstrated:

(a) they were loyal to a law they held as most divine and binding most all men: to maintain in the moment's need what most was needed and befriend those who floundered undeservingly;

(b) they were disposed to decorum and intellectual right: raging against the outrager, composed to meet the composed, fearless before the fearless, dreadful among the dreadful;

(c) they were victorious over enemies—"As witness to all this they raised a monument to mark their enemies' defeat;"

(d) they possessed no inborn flair for battle, were devout in probity to deities, pious in their attentiveness to parents, unimpeachable in parity to their people, and irreproachable in faithfulness to friends.

Finally, Gorgias praises their immortality of valour and reputation; "Therefore desire for them though they have died with them has not died; deathless/immortal (ἀθανατὸς), rather, despite these forms not deathless, still it lives, for these who have lost their lives."

---

95. Kennedy, *Art of Persuasion in Greece*, 156.

Hyperides (*Oration*) [J. O. Burtt, LCL]

The funeral speech of Hyperides, delivered in 322 B.C. over the Athenian dead in the Lamian war, is unusual to give to one man. But here Hyperides gives a speech for the prominent Leosthenes while still observing certain rigid conventions. Among other funeral orations there is no other example of a passage in which the leader is described in Hades as welcomed by the heroes of old.[96]

(Exordium, 1–5) According to the usual practice of exordium, Hyperides expresses his inability, "lest my speech may prove unworthy of their exploits" (1). In order to get the good-will of the audience, he exalts them as "no random audience... but the persons... (who) have witnessed the actions of these men" (2; 1 Thess 2:5, 10; witness-language in the funeral speeches). He omits praise of the virtues of Athens, great though they are (4–5).

(Encomium/Epainos, 6–40) Hyperides mainly focuses on praising the general Leosthenes and his soldiers instead of the ancestors and the city of Athens (6). While touching upon the Athenians' pure lineage and their education (6–9), Hyperides attempts to highlight their courage in battle for their country and the rest of Greece. First he praises the virtues and deeds of the general, Leosthenes, in the battle: his leadership, his devotion to his country in the cause of freedom, his victory in the war, his superiority over heroes, and his death (10–14, 35). After this, Hyperides praises the courage and valor of his comrades who were prepared to risk their lives for the freedom of the Greeks (15–19). Then, he shows the superiority of their endurance under extreme severities of weather and hard privations "almost beyond description... what speech could be of greater profit" (20–23, 33, *Panegyrisuc* 186, 1 Thess 2:19–20; 3:9). Finally, he adds the eulogy of the dead with emphasis on their undying glory, the prowess and blessings of these men, and their example (24–34). Uniquely and with imagination, Hyperides shows the welcome Leosthenes will receive from the heroes of old (35–40). This expression shows similarities to Seneca's *On Grief for Lost Friends* (16, "perhaps, if only the tale told by wise men is true and there is a bourne to welcome us") and Tacitus's *Agricola* (46, "If there be any habitation for the spirits of the just; if, as wise men will have it...") Just as Fern comments, the expression and prayer are "the hope of immortality; but this hope is expressed in a vague, uncertain manner."[97]

(Consolation and Exhortation, 41–43) With a little lamentation (41a), Hyperides consoles the living in that "we must take heart, and restrict our

---

96. Hyperides, in Burtt, *Minor Attic Orators* 2.532–34.
97. Fern, "Latin Consolatio as a Literary Type," 34.

grief as best we may," (41b) because their conduct claims the highest praise and they became immortal children (42) and have been released from sickness and from grief (43). Thus the listeners should envy their death and strive to take as an example these men's lives (31).

Summary and Conclusion on Athenian Funeral Orations

Rhetorical Situation (Rhetorical Exigency)

The importance of recognizing the rhetorical situation (exigency) is crucial because it has an important effect on the author's intention and motives, on the purpose for writing, the genre of the text, and the goal of rhetorical discourse.[98] In the occasion of the Greek funeral speech, the rhetorical exigency develops from the circumstances of war. The Greek funeral orations derive from the commemoration of those who had fallen in battle for their country as public ceremonial occasions.

Thus, all Greek funeral orations have the similar rhetorical situation of war, such as Hyperides (the funeral oration for the Athenians killed in the Lamian War, 322 B.C.), Demosthenes (the Persian Wars), Pseudo-Lysias (the Corinthian War, 394–387 B.C.), and Thucydides (the Peloponnesian War). The orators commemorate and praise the dead in the war and counsel the living to imitate them.

Rhetorical Purpose and Structure

The Athenian funeral orations have the primary purpose of showing the continuity between the living Athens community and the dead. Through this process, the Athenian funeral orations attempt to unify the Athens community, exhort the young, and console the adults. Because the main purpose of Athenian funeral orations is to praise the dead and to exhort and console the living, the funeral orations are consequently and naturally composed mainly of lengthy parts of encomium and consolation/exhortation common to that era.[99] These also exist in the Romans' *laudatio funebris* and

---

98. Jeal, *Integrating Theology and Ethics in Ephesians*, 34.

99. You can see the chart of comparison of the portion in the appendix: (1) Isocrates (*Evagoras*, encomium/9.12–69, consolation-exhortation/9.70–79; *Panegyricus*, encomium/15–159, exhortation/160–189); (2) Thucydides (*History of the Peloponnesian War*, encomium/XXXVI-XLII, consolation-exhortation/XLIII-XLV); (3) Pseudo-Lysias (*Funeral Oration*, encomium/3–70, lamentation-consolation-exhortation/71–80); (4)

in the Jewish funeral orations, and they function to encourage the brothers in the community. Further, Ochs correctly comments about the function of the *narratio* by saying, "The funeral speech is not an argument . . . Hearing a dramatic narrative, an audience is repositioned . . . Narratives by their nature invite participation, acceptance, and, if artfully done, some degree of identification."[100] The lengthy encomium and exhortation in the Athenian funeral orations function similarly.

Rhetorical Contents (Exordium/Encomium/ Consolation-Exhortation/Peroration)

Generally, all these Athenian funeral orations have the same content in the same order:

(a) Exordium,

(b) Encomium,

(c) Consolation/Exhortation, and

(d) Peroration.

(a) Exordium—Exordium has generally consisted of the *topoi* of the approving attitude of the law and tradition (nomos), the human being's inability of speech to match the greatness of their deeds (logos), and the proper statement about their valorous deeds (epainos). These elements in the exordium function to gain sympathy or good will from the audience.

All the Athenian funeral orators follow these *topoi* of exordium, but they sometimes change or omit one depending on the circumstances. Isocrates, Thucydides, Pseudo-Lysias, Demosthenes, and Hyperides commonly contain the *topoi* of the exordium, while Plato alone omits the commonly used general inadequacy of any human tongue to match the immortal deeds of the dead.

(b) Encomium/Epainos—This part usually fills the main and lengthy portion of the whole discourse because of the primary purpose of the funeral orations, that is, to praise the valorous deeds of the dead in the wars and

---

Plato (*Menexenus*, encomium/237b–246b, consolation-exhortation/246b–249c); (5) Demosthenes (*Funeral Speech*, encomium/4–31, consolation-exhortation/32–37); (6) Hyperides (*Oration*, encomium/6–40, consolation-exhortation/41–43); (7) Gorgias (*Fragment from a Funeral Oration*).

100. Ochs, *Consolatory Rhetoric*, 109.

to console the living. This part has the same function as the *narratio* in the epideictic rhetoric.

The encomium of the Athenian funeral oration follows the primary *topoi* of encomium of person, which is suggested by Aphthonius: γενος (the person's origin)—nation, homeland, ancestors, and parents; ανατροφη (upbringing)—habits, acquired skill, and principles of conduct; πραξεις (deeds)—(1) mind: courage and prudence; (2) body: beauty, swiftness, and strength; (3) fortune: power, wealth, and friends; (4) συγκρισις (comparison)—attributing superiority to what is being celebrated by contrast. Encomium varies amongst all the Athenian funeral orators in content and order, but there are some common topics in all speeches: praise of the ancestors, praise of Athens, and praise of the dead. Contrary to other funeral orations, Thucydides, though he begins the encomium with praise of the ancestors following the tradition, emphasizes the present greatness of the Athenians. Ziolkowski correctly points out Thucydides' intention in emphasizing this:[101]

> Thucydides seems particularly concerned in this speech with justifying the power of Athens in contemporary terms. Therefore he rushes past the ancestors and fathers in the Epainos, omitting all references to historical events. Contrary to the other funeral speeches, greater honor is given to the present than to previous generations . . . In fact, the greatest single change that Thucydides makes in the funeral tradition—the substitution of an elaborate patris for the customary genos—arises from this desire to describe the present greatness of Athens.

Pseudo-Lysias develops the encomium chronologically from ancestors (3–19), to descendents (20–66), to the dead (67–70). He maintains the continuity between the ancestors and the present ones by praising the valor of the dead. Plato also contains the *topoi* of encomium, the ancestors (origin, mother-land, upbringing, and deeds), and proclaims the continuity and identification between all generations. Demosthenes also describes the autochthony of the ancestors, the mother land, and the ancestors' deeds in war. Then, he focuses on the superior qualities of the dead in order to connect the development of Athens into a Greek superpower with the valor of the dead and ultimately with subsequent generations. Hyperides uniquely praises the general Leosthenes instead of the ancestors and the city of Athens and prepares the consolation and the exhortation to the living. Thus, through these lengthy and elaborate praises (Encomium), the orators have clear concerns of preparing the mind of the audience so they may establish continuity between ancient and present inhabitants—a continuity/

---

101. Ziolkowski, *Thucydides*, 185.

identification sustained by glorification of the recent dead as men who had lived up to the ideals of their ancestors. These lengthy and elaborate encomium are prerequisites for the consolation and exhortation to the living who must live up to the ancestors and the dead.

(c) Consolation/Lamentation-Exhortation—Through the Paramythia, the speaker attempts to alleviate the grief of the living and to give exhortation for future conduct. Further, it is intended to consolidate the community and the state of Athens, thus it takes the most crucial position of the whole rhetoric. On the list of the seven common topics for the consolation/exhortation,[102] the Athenian funeral orators put the emphasis on this part.[103]

Among the Athenian funeral orators, Thucydides (XLIII–XLV), Plato (246d–249c), Demosthenes (32–37), and Isocrates (9.70–79) mainly focus on the consolation and the exhortation to the living and thus omit the lamentation in their discourses. Particularly, Thucydides clearly expresses his intention of omitting the lamentation in his discourse from the beginning of the consolation by saying, "Wherefore, I do not commiserate the parents of these men, as many of you as are present here, but will rather try to comfort them" (XLIV). Hyperides, however, inserts a little lamentation (41a), and Pseudo-Lysias especially expresses deep lamentation (71–76); "it is natural for the living to lament and bewail them" (71). Pseudo-Lysias, however, reverses the tone from lamentation to strong consolation and exhortation (77–80) with the words "But in truth I do not know what need there is to lament so sadly . . . Therefore it is fitting to consider those most happy who have closed their lives in risking them for the greatest and noblest ends" (77, 79). Pseudo-Lysias's lamentation functions as a pre-step for emphasizing the positive effects of consolation, not as an essential part in the discourse. Thus, it is easy to conclude in the Athenians' funeral oration, the lamentation does not exist as an essential part, but just a pre-step for the strong consolation of the living. Further, the consolation and the exhortation are closely connected in unifying the community and the state of Athens.

---

102. Burgess, "Epideictic Literature," 156.

103. Thucydides: "You should follow after their manner." "Their glory survives in everlasting remembrance." "Do make these men your example."; Pseudo-Lysias: "Their lives risk them for the greatest and noblest ends." "They are immortals."; Plato: "They reach the climax for mortal men." "The gods have already hearkened unto their prayers." "Imitate the fathers."; Demosthenes: "They leave behind them the immortality of honor." "They are released from sorrows, disease of body and beyond the reach of anguish of spirit."; Hyperides: "We must take heart and restrict our grief."

(d) Conclusion/Peroration—Peroration sometimes concludes the Paramythia and repeats the consolation and exhortation. Finally, with the statement of dismissal, it ends with the prayer to the gods.

The survey of the Athenian funeral orations shows the fact that the Athenian funeral orations have a deep impact and relations with 1 Thess in terms of rhetorical exigency, rhetorical purpose and structure, and rhetorical contents. Thus, elements of epideictic funerary oratory can illuminate the language and arguments of Paul in Thessalonians.

CHAPTER 4

The Roman Oratory and the Jewish Oratory

CHAPTER 4 IS A continuation of chapter 3 in its concentration on the survey of the elements of the ancient funerary oratory. Whereas the earlier chapter was largely focused on the Athenian funeral orations, the present chapter is largely focused on the funerary elements of the Roman oratory and the Jewish oratory. Actually, the Athenian funeral oratory influenced the Roman funeral oratory, so the Roman funeral orations also developed and derived from the circumstances of war. Unlike the Athenian or Roman funeral orations, the Jewish orations derive from the circumstances of martyrdom.

The Roman Funeral Oration (2nd B. C.—4th A. D)

When compared to the Athenian funeral orations, which were delivered in front of the tomb, the Roman funeral oration (*laudatio funebris*) was delivered before the *rostra*, the forum. The Romans made a distinction between an ordinary funeral (*funus translaticium*) and the public funeral of a distinguished person (*funus indictivum*). To the latter, the people were invited by a public crier in a set form of words.[1] Furthermore, the Romans made a noisy and visual funeral procession with the funeral-bed of the deceased person reclining in the attitude of one still living (Polybius, *Hist.* VI. 53.1), the presence of a *mimus* or mummer imitating the gestures of the dead, and a train of men wearing the *imagines* or portrait-masks of his ancestors.[2] If the deceased was of illustrious rank, the funeral procession went through the forum (Dionys.iv.40) and stopped before the *rosta*, where a funeral oration (*laudatio*) of praise for the deceased was delivered. This

---

1. Sandys, *Companion to Latin Studies*, 180.
2. Sandys, *Companion to Latin Studies*, 181.

ancient practice among the Romans[3] is said by some writers to have been first introduced by Publicola, who pronounced a funeral oration in honor of his colleague Burtus (Plut. *Public.* 9; Dionys. v.17).[4]

Polybius, born c. 208 B.C., after praising the Romans' courage and spirit over the Phoenicians and Africans (*Hist.* VI. 52.1–11), describes the process of the funeral and the function of the funeral oration (*laudatio funebris*) as follows:

> Whenever any illustrious man dies, he is carried at his funeral into the forum to the so-called rostra (*Hist.* VI. 53.1) . . . a grown-up son, if he has left one who happens to be present, or if not some other relative mounts the rostra and discourses on the virtues and successful achievements of the dead . . . when the facts are recalled to their minds and brought before their eyes, are moved to such sympathy that the loss seems to be not confined to the mourners, but a public one affecting the whole people (*Hist.* VI. 53.3–4) . . . when he has finished speaking of him recounts the successes and exploits of the rest whose images are present, beginning from the most ancient. By this means, by this constant renewal of the good report of brave men, the celebrity of those who performed noble deeds is rendered immortal, while at the same time the fame of those who did good service to their country becomes known to the people and a heritage for future generations. But the most important results is that young men are thus inspired to endure every suffering for the public welfare in the hope of winning the glory that attends on brave men. (*Hist.* VI. 54.1–4)

Just as asserted above, there are two primary functions: to mark the place of the dead in the long train of descendants from a common ancestor, which is a kind of continuity between ancient origins and present times,[5] and to set in relief the dead person's lofty actions and honor in his contribution to the family glory.[6]

When compared to the Athenian branch of rhetoric (Aristotle, *Rhet.* 1358b; Quintilian, *Instit.* III, 7.1.), which concerns *laus* and does not pertain to the practical side of oratory (συμβουλευτικον) but solely to the delectation (ἐπιδεικτικον) of audience, the rhetoric in Rome differs significantly. The frequent necessity of preparing and delivering funeral orations

---

3. McGuire, "Christian Funeral Oration," xi.
4. Smith, *Dictionary of Greek and Roman Antiquities*, 559.
5. Poulakos, "Historiographies of the Tradition of Rhetoric," 178.
6. Crawford, "Laudatio Funebris," 24.

gave it some practical value.[7] Quintilian says that "Roman usage on the other hand has given it a place in the practical tasks of life. For funeral orations are often imposed as a duty on persons holding public office, or entrusted to magistrates by decree of the senate" (*Instit.* III, 7.2.). In other words, to Romans, there was something distasteful about the self-indulgence and lack of utility they attributed to Greek epideictic rhetoric.[8] In the same way, Cicero (*De Orat.* II, 84.341) evaluates the panegyric rhetoric of the Romans as follows:

> And also we Romans do not much practice the custom of panegyrics ... For the Greeks themselves have constantly thrown off masses of panegyrics, designed more for reading and for entertainment, or for giving a laudatory account of some person, than for the practical purpose of public life with which we are now concerned . . . whereas our Roman commendatory speeches that we make in the forum have either the bare and unadorned brevity of evidence (*testimonii brevitatem habent nudam atque inornatam*) to a person's character or are written to be delivered as a funeral speech, which is by no means a suitable occasion for parading one's distinction in rhetoric.

Based on Cicero's comment, in the more constructive hands of the Romans, the aspects of epideictic rhetoric could usefully be incorporated into the practical business of forensic and deliberative oratory, such as when composing character testimonials in legal defense (*Reht. Her.* 3.15; Cic. *De Orat.* 2.341, 349; Quint. *Inst.* 3.7.2).[9] Another rule for funeral oration (*laudatio funebris*) in Rome was that the delivery should be melancholy (*tristis*) and subdued (*summissa*) in contrast to other forms of panegyric (Quintilian, *Inst.* XI, 3.153).[10]

Roman funeral oration (*laudatio funebris*) consists of a recitation of the virtues of the deceased and then those of his or her ancestors. J. Hester correctly considers the function of the encomium of the deceased and of the ancestors "to bring the deeds of the deceased into association with those of the family; in that way the dead could be remembered not so much as

---

7. Crawford, "Laudatio Funebris," 22.
8. Rees, "Panegyric," 137.
9. Rees, "Panegyric," 138.

10. Quintilian says, "Consequently, in panegyric, funeral orations excepted, in returning thanks, exhortations and the like, the delivery must be luxuriant, magnificent, and grand. On the other hand, in funeral or consolatory speeches, together with most of those in defense of accused persons, the delivery will be melancholy and subdued. When we speak in the senate, it will be authoritative, when we address the people, dignified, and when we are pleading in private cases, restrained" (*Inst.* XI, 3.153).

individuals but as part of the clan or family unit whose glorious history they reflected."[11] Further, the ritual practice of exhortation and consolation, with the archiving of mask and speech, suggests the function of exhortation is to imitate virtues represented in the family history. The culture of city-state or family transcends the individual.[12]

Though there are some differences in approach among the Latin theoreticians, some points are essentially linked: "praise consists of an attribution of virtues, taken from a recognized canon, and amplified and illustrated through examples from the subject's life (and from their later reputation or legacy, if deceased)."[13] Particularly, Quintilian recommends the structure of praise in that "It has sometimes proved the more effective course to trace a man's life and deeds *in due chronological order*, praising his natural gifts as a child, then his progress at school, and finally the whole course of his life, including words as well as deeds" (*Inst.* III. 7.15, *italics* added for emphasis). Further, he deals with the effective treatment of the audience; "what most pleases an audience is the celebration of deeds which our hero was the first or only man or at any rate one of the very few to perform; and to these we must add any other achievements which surpassed hope or expectation, *emphasizing what was done for the sake of others rather than what he performed on his own behalf*" (*Inst.* III. 7.16. emphasis added).

Tacitus (*Agricola*) [M. Hutton, LCL]

Upon Domitian's death in A.D. 97, the year in which Tacitus (A. D. 55–120) was consul and delivered the funeral oration of Verginius Rufus, Tacitus felt free to record Agricola's life and achievements. It was likely finished and published in A.D. 98.[14]

(Exordium, 1–3) Tacitus says that it is customary to put down for posterity the works and ways of famous men (1). In order to gain the good-will of his audience, Tacitus attempts to narrate the lives of those who had not sought partisanship or were self-seeking, though they were already dead. Thus, Tacitus suggests the purpose of the speech, praise of the dead. "This

---

11. Hester, "Invention of 1 Thessalonians," 269.

12. Hester, "Invention of 1 Thessalonians," 269.

13. Rees, "Panegyric," 138. He concludes about the Roman funeral orations that "The Roman *laudatio funebris* may have had close similarities to the rhetoric of classical Greek panegyrics but they remained quite different in function, and therefore, ethic. The function of the panegyrical funeral speech was ritualistic, ornamental, and commemorative; the speech of pure panegyric to the living is presented in surviving Latin sources as essentially alien to Roman practice."

14. Tacitus, *Agr.* 16.

book is dedicated to the glory of my father-in-law Agricola," but "with unpracticed and stammering tongue" (3). (Encomium/Epainos, 4–42) Just as Thucydides, after shortly praising the genos (the ancestors), focuses on the present ones,[15] Tacitus also briefly praises the ancestors, "a scion of the ancient and illustrious Roman colony of Forum Julii" (4). Tacitus focuses more on Agricola's upbringing (acquired skill and principles of conduct) and deeds (mind, body, and fortune) as a soldier according to the primary topoi of encomium. According to Quintilian's rule of encomium (*Inst.* III. 7.15.), Tacitus describes Agricola's works in due chronological order: his apprenticeship to war in Britain (5), his public approval (6), and his principles of conduct. "But Agricola traced his success to the responsible general . . . he escaped envy without missing distinction . . . " (8–17) and "nor even now did he turn his success to boastfulness . . . he did not even follow up his achievement by affixing laurels to this dispatches; yet his very deprecation of glory increased his glory . . . " (18). Tacitus emphasizes what was done for the sake of others rather than what Agricola performed on his own behalf. "Yet Agricola was never grasping to take credit to himself for the achievement of others: the other, whether regular officer or officer of irregulars, found in him an honest witness to his feats" (22, Quintilian. *Inst.* III.7.16).

Regarding panegyrics of particular virtues, Cicero (*De Orat.* II, 85.346) comments as follows:

> But the most welcome praise is that bestowed on deeds that appear to have been performed by brave men without profit or reward . . . toil and personal danger supply very fertile topics for panegyric, because they admit of being narrated in a most eloquent style and of obtaining the readiest reception from the audience; for it is virtue that is profitable to others, and either toilsome or dangerous or at all events not profitable to its possessor, that is deemed to mark a man of outstanding merit.

In other words, for the Romans, the principles of panegyrics of virtue can be stated, "the greater the altruism, the greater the honor; and the wider the public affected by the altruism, the greater the admiration."[16] Tacitus praises Agricola's character during his son's death; "He took the loss neither with bravado . . . nor yet with the lamentations and mourning of a woman," (29) and praises his courage and prudence with his speech on war; "therefore not only is honorable death always better than life dishonored . . . " (33). Finally he praises Agricola's superiority through comparison; "Accordingly,

---

15. Ziolkowski, *Thucydides*, 75–77. Thucydides contrasts with the long sections on the ancestors of Lysias, Plato, and Demosthenes.

16. Ochs, *Consolatory Rhetoric*, 107.

when loss was added to loss, and every year was signalized with death and disaster, the voice of the people began to ask for Agricola's generalship: everyone compared his firmness, energy, and experience with the lethargy and panic of the generals" (41).

(Consolation of the living and exhortation/Paramythia, 43–46a) After all this, Tacitus shortly laments over Agricola's death; "The end of his life brought mourning to us, melancholy to his friends, anxiety even to the bystander and those who knew him not . . . " (43) but swiftly begins Paramythia with the statement of contrast to lamentation; "As for the man himself, though snatched away in the mid-career of his prime, he lived to a ripe old age measured by renown. The true blessings of life which lie in character he had fulfilled. What more could fortune have added to one who had been consul, and had worn the decoration of triumph?. . .Happy your fate, Agricola! Happy not only in the luster of your life, but in a timely death" (44–45).

Regarding the exhortation to the living, instead of lamenting and mourning in "womanish tears," Tacitus recommends, "Let reverence rather, let thankfulness, let imitation even, if our strength permit, be our tribute to your memory. . .so to venerate the memory of husband and of father as to ponder each word and deed within their hearts, and to cling to the lineaments and features of the soul rather than of the body" (45b-46a).

(Epilogue, 46b) In concluding Paramythia, Tacitus repeats an immortal memory and the children's heritage in the death of Agricola.

Appian (*Antony's Speech at Caesar's Funeral; Appian's Roman History* III. 2.143–148) [Horace White, LCL]

Antony's speech at Caesar's funeral was recorded by Suetonius (*Julius Caesar* 84), Cicero (*Ad Att.* 14.10.1; *Philippic* 2.89–91), Quintilian (*Institutio* 6.1.30–31), and Appian (*Appian's Roman History* III. 2.143–148). Among them, Appian attempted to comprehensively present Antony's funeral oration for Caesar by including most of Antony's speech. It seems Antony did not follow a traditional Roman funeral oration (*Laudatio Funebris*), which usually lists the origin and notable achievements of the ancestors, the deeds, and upbringing of the dead in chronological order.[17] As Cicero (*Philippic* 2.89–91) correctly pointed out, "yours (Antony's funeral oration for Caesar) was that 'pretty' laudation (*laudatio*), yours the emotional appeal (*miseratio, consolation or lamentation*), yours the exhortation (*cohortatio*)." However,

---

17. Kennedy, "Antony's Speech at Caesar's Funeral," 99–106.

Antony's funeral oration actually demonstrates the traditional elements of a Roman funeral oration.[18]

(Exordium, 143–144, 146) When Piso brought Caesar's body into the forum and placed it on the rostra, Antony was chosen to deliver the funeral oration, as a friend for a friend, a relative for a relative. First, he portrays himself as unable to be the speaker for Caesar's legacy, "It is not fitting, citizens, that the funeral oration of so great a man should be pronounced by me alone, but rather by his whole country."

(Encomium/Epainos, 144–146a) Antony praised Caesar' superiority, divine origin, and his altruism, which are the traditional elements of encomium. Antony, reading decrees of the Senate to grant honors and admiration of Caesar's merit, praised him for being "superhuman, sacred, and, inviolable, and which named him the father, or the benefactor, as the peerless protector of his country." Emphasizing his character of clemency, Antony declared "everybody else was to be held unharmed who should find refuge with him." Finally, in front of the bier, Antony marked Caesar as a celestial deity by noting his divine birth, recited his wars and his victories, and extolled each exploit as miraculous. These things demonstrated his superiority. "Thou alone hast come forth unvanquished . . . Thou alone has avenged . . . "

(Consolation/Lamentation to the living, 144b, 145b, 146b) Throughout his encomium (*narratio*), Antony found the crowds' sympathy and commotion, then he highlighted Caesar's altruism with lamentation, "Nobody who found refuge with him was harmed, but he, whom you declared sacred and inviolable, was killed, although he did not extort these honors from you as a tyrant, and did not ask for them." This reference functions as a dramatic climax to his consolation/lamentation (*miseratio*), "Let us then conduct this sacred one to the abode of the blest, chanting over him our accustomed hymn and lamentation."

(Exhortation to the living, 146b) Antony dispensed with a formal eulogy of exhortation (*cohortatio*) at the end of his funeral oration, which is common in Roman *laudatio funebris*. Instead, he wept for Caesar, recited his achievements, and finally uncovered Caesar's body and lifted his bloody clothes on the point of a spear. When the people chanted lamentations with sorrow for Caesar, Antony, using an impersonation of Caesar's voice, recounted by name his enemies and murderers saying, "Oh that I should have spared these men to slay me!" Simultaneously, a wax image of the dead Caesar was turned round and round, showing the twenty-three wounds in his body. According to Cicero, this last portion of Antony's action and impersonation of the voice of Caesar is considered to be the *cohortatio*, and this effect led

---

18. Kennedy, "Antony's Speech at Caesar's Funeral," 106.

to inciting a general riot.[19] Quintilian (*Institutio* 6.1.1–31), describing two aspects of the peroration (the emotional aspect and recapitulation), suggests two influential ways to persuade the audience. Impersonation, "fictitious speeches supposed to be uttered," may produce a greater emotional effect on the audience. Actions, as well as words, will move the heart of an audience. Quintilian takes the exemplary case of Antony's funeral oration and his actions of exhibiting the bloodstains on the purple-bordered toga of Gaius Caesar and says, "they had even seen his body stretched upon the bier; but his garment, still wet with his blood, brought such a vivid image of the crime before their minds, that Caesar seemed not to have been murdered, but to be being murdered before their very eyes." In other words, Antony's action of impersonating the voice of Caesar functioned as the peroration and the *cohortatio*, leading to the riot of people.

In summary, while Antony seems not to follow the Roman *laudatio funebris*, his funeral oration for Caesar actually does contain the traditional elements of exordium, encomium, lamentation/consolation, and exhortation to the living.

Dio Cassius (Tiberius' Funeral Oration for Augustus; *Roman History*. LVI. 34–41) [E. Cary, LCL]

Cassius Dio (A.D. 155–230) was a participant and spectator at the imperial funeral of Pertinax (A. D. 193) and records the sequence of events. His records (LXXV. 4–5) show the character and purpose of imperial funerals as follows:

> In the Roman Forum . . . upon which was set a shrine . . . surrounded by heads of both land and sea animals . . . Upon this rested an effigy of Pertinax in wax, laid out in triumphal garb . . . After this there moved past, first, images of all the famous Romans of old . . . there followed all the subject nations . . . Then came images of other men who had been distinguished for some exploit or invention or manner of life . . . When these had passed by, Severus mounted the rostra and read a eulogy of Pertinax.

In his records of Tiberius' funeral oration for Augustus (LVI. 34–41), Dio describes in detail a wax image of Augustus in triumphal garb and another upon a triumphal chariot. Behind these came the images of his ancestors

---

19. Kennedy, *Art of Rhetoric in the Roman World*, 298; Kennedy, "Antony's Speech at Caesar's Funeral," 102.

and of his deceased relatives and those of other prominent Romans, beginning with Romulus himself (34).

Concerning this connection between imperial funeral and triumphal procession, Mary Beard correctly points out that "the funeral may have been an occasion in which triumphal splendor could be called to mind and, in part, recreated long after the day of the triumph itself had passed, as with the impersonation of the ancestors of the dead man—dressed, if appropriate, in their triumphal robes."[20] Hopkins also describes the funeral procession of prominent people. Actors wore the robes and insignia of the highest office each ancestor had gained and had gold embroidery for a general who had been awarded a triumph (cf. Diodorus 31.25). They all rode in chariots, preceded by rods, axes, and other marks of public office.[21] This connection may help us understand why Paul can interweave Jesus' parousia (second coming), as a processional parousia (conquering king entering the city, or triumphal procession "with a cry of command, with the archangel's call and with the sound of God's trumpet," [1 Thess 4:16]), with discussion of death. In other words, it may be that imperial funerary motifs are present in 1 Thess' description of Christ's parousia as will be discussed later in more depth.

(Exordium, 35) Tiberius, saying in pursuance of a decree (nomos), shows his inability for funeral oration; "still I cannot feel any confidence that my abilities measure up in any wise either to your desires in the matter or to his merits." He continues with the statement, lauding "you who are thoroughly acquainted with all his achievements, who have known them all through personal experience . . . from what you yourselves know . . . by your memory of the events" (35.3–4). Tiberius attempts to gain the good will of his audience through identification on the grounds that their understanding would make them more sympathetic.

(Encomium/Epainos, 36–41.5) Complying with the rule of Quintilian, keeping "a man's life and deeds in due chronological order," (*Inst.* 7.15) Tiberius begins with Augustus' earliest manhood in his education and his courage (36.2). As customary in the delivery of the epideictic oration itself, "amplification" and "embellishment" are used to connect Augustus to Hercules; "With Hercules alone and his exploits I might compare him, and should be thought justified in so doing . . . in so far as Hercules in childhood only dealt with serpents . . . whereas Augustus, not among beasts, but among men, of his own free will, by waging war and enacting laws, literally saved the commonwealth . . . " (36.4–5). Tiberius also praises Augustus' prudence (37.2), his altruism—"From all this he derived no personal gain, but aided

20. Beard, *Roman Triumph*, 285–86.
21. Hopkins, *Death and Renewal*, 201.

us all in a signal manner" (37.3-4), his superiority, "deeds which have never been performed by any other man" (37.6), and his character of generosity and magnanimity (39.1-4). Tiberius subsequently praises Augustus' deeds of altruism for citizens (40) and with comparison highlights Augustus' altruism; "How could one forget to mention a man who in private life was poor, in public life rich; who with himself was frugal, but towards others lavish of his means; who always endured every toil and danger himself on your behalf, but would not inflict upon you the hardship of so much as escorting him when he left the city or of meeting him when he returned" (41.5).

(Consolation to the living, 41.9a) Without any lamentation, Tiberius encourages the audience to keep Augustus as "a father of the people" and to declare him "to be immortal" in their hearts.

(Epilogue, 41.9b) With exhortation to the living, Tiberius concludes "it is fitting also that we should not mourn for him, but that, while we now at last give his body back to the Nature, we should glorify his spirit, as that of a god, forever" (41.9b).

Concerning the effect of the long narrative form of praise and lack of reward in funeral orations, D. Ochs points out two main functions: the selfless acts for the greater good of a collective and the identification.[22] Just as Ochs points out the function of narrative in the Roman funeral speech, long *narratio* in funeral oration is intended to invite the participation of the audience, provide some degree of identification, and reunite the community,[23] which is the case in the *narratio* of 1 Thess 1:4—3:10. By employing long *narratio* (1:4—3:10), Paul describes his pure character in his ministry (2:1-12; 2:17—3:10) and tries to praise the Thessalonian believers' deeds (1:4-10; 2:13-16) so that he might establish the connection of the collective community to the dead and reunite the community through its relationship to the dead and to Paul himself. This process of long *narratio* functions as preparing the mind of the audience for the ensuing consolation/exhortation (4:1—5:10) to the living.

Plutarch (*Consolatio Ad Uxorem/Consolation to His Wife*) [P. H. De Lacy and B. Einarson, LCL]

Regarding the origin and function of literary forms of consolation, Martin and Philips suggest the following:

---

22. Ochs, *Consolatory Rhetoric*, 108.
23. Ochs, *Consolatory Rhetoric*, 108-9.

> In all of the works mentioned so far the consolations proper are oral, not written . . . for in Graeco-Roman literature the written word was nearly always either a representative of or a substitute for the spoken work; the conventions of written literature in organization, style, and diction rarely departed from those of spoken literature. It is likely enough that written consolations began when letter-writing became the means of communication between individuals who could not meet face-to-face . . . with the result that we cannot always be sure whether a given consolation, once written, was immediately handed to a messenger for delivery to the addressee . . . [24]

Martin's and Philips's comments describe a consolatory letter in the Greco-Roman world that contains the contents and conventions of an oral speech to the audience. In the same sense, Ochs convincingly suggests, "As travel became more commonplace individuals would be more likely to be absent when a death occurred. Similarly, as writing itself became more commonplace, written words of consolation could, and did, serve as surrogates for traditional, oral forms. Therefore, one can read consolatory literature in the same way one might read a consolatory speech."[25] In other words, consolatory letters actually follow the pattern of consolatory rhetorical speeches. In this sense, Plutarch's *Consolatio Ad Uxorem* (*Consolation to His Wife*) shows the rhetorical elements and the structure of the public funeral consolatory speech such as *captatio benevolentiae* (apology), personal exhortation, memories and encomium, contrast, further public exhortation, and peroration. Concerning the domains of the private and the public in Plutarch's *Consolatio Ad Uxorem*, Han Baltussen correctly points out that "Plutarch may be exploiting this lack of a sharp dividing line between the two domains for his own purposes, which makes this letter (whether intended or not) a public statement of a philosophical position."[26] In other words, he concludes that the function of this letter regarding Plutarch's rhetorical strategy was not only intended to advertise his family's virtuous qualities but also to be "a considered response in which his psychagogic effort aimed at his wife (private) is carefully combined with the moral responsibility he feels for his community (public)."[27] Thus,

---

24. Martin and Phillips, "Consolatio Ad Uxorem," 309–400.

25. Ochs, *Consolatory Rhetoric*, 112.

26. Baltussen, "Personal Grief and Public Mourning," 85. He insists the domains of the private and the public are not easy to define in antiquity. What is especially striking is that the two spheres were not separated as strictly as is often the case today.

27. Baltussen, "Personal Grief and Public Mourning," 87.

this seemingly personal letter contains the characters of a public funeral consolatory speech rather than a private one.

(Exordium/Apology, 608A–B) Plutarch first apologizes for writing to his wife with some delay and expresses the hope that the funeral went well in order to gain the good-will of his audience. It starts with a *captatio benevolentiae* (apology).[28] He also exhorts his wife not to wait for him on decisions she deems appropriate for making her grief more bearable, as long as it is "done without excess or superstition" (608B). Through this reminder of correct procedure (rituals) and negative elements in mourning practices (superstition), Plutarch reveals that he is not only concerned with his wife's sorrow but also encompassing considerations in the public sphere outside the circle of the family.[29]

(Encomium/Epainos, 608C–610F) Plutarch first exhorts his wife to restrain grief; "Only, my dear wife, in your emotion keep me as well as yourself within bounds" (608C–D). Then, he evokes a good memory of the precious qualities of the dead child (encomium), with the comment that "we must not sit idle and shut ourselves in, paying for those pleasures with sorrows many times as great" (608F). He praises his deceased daughter in her character and deeds, such as her mildness, good temper, kindness, and strong affection (608D). He emphasizes the results of good memory, "bringing with it joy in greater measure . . . than it brings sorrow" (608E). He moves on to the praise of his wife's exemplary behavior in light of her measured response "with decorum and in silence," (608F) expressing the right attitude of women, which should exclude the never-sated passion for lamentation and an uncomely posture (609A–C). By contrasting her deeds (sober style of living, simplicity, steadfastness in circumstances, great composure and quiet, 609C–E) with examples of bad women (an unwarranted and ungrateful grief, their mourning with wild, frenzied, and unrestricted lamentation, 609E–F, 610B–D), he exhorts that "We must, therefore, resist it [mourning/sorrow] at the door and must not let it in to be quartered on us" (610A). "Do, however, try to carry yourself back in your thoughts" (610D), and "you must not dwell upon the present tears and lamentations . . . " (611A–B). Further, the good memory and the thoughts of blessing function as antidotes to grief (610F).

(Consolation to the living, 611A–F) Finally, Plutarch ends his speech with philosophical consolation and advice, leading to the climax of the letter.[30] "Felicity depends on correct reasoning resulting in a stable habit"

28. Baltussen, "Personal Grief and Public Mourning," 80.
29. Baltussen, "Personal Grief and Public Mourning," 77.
30. Baltussen, "Personal Grief and Public Mourning," 82.

(611A). First, he consoles her through comparison; "you must not dwell upon the present tears and lamentation . . . you must rather bear in mind how enviable you still appear in their eyes for your children, home, and way of life" (611A–C). Second, it is consolation for Timoxena's present state: "If you pity her for departing unmarried and childless, you can find comfort for yourself in another consideration . . . for these are not great blessings for those deprived of them . . . That she has passed to a state where there is no pain need not be painful to us" (611C–D). Third, Plutarch demonstrates belief in the immortality of the soul, "which is imperishable, is affected like a captive bird," and suggests the soul will escape at some point and return to the better world of the Platonic Forms, "as though released from a bent position with flexibility and resilience unimpaired" (611F).

It is commonly agreed that pagan Greek and Latin consolation literature, as a whole, take a view significantly similar to the following:

> Fortune rules all and one must always be ready to meet its blows; all men are mortal; to have lived virtuously, not long, is of prime importance; time cures all ills; death gives freedom from the ravages of disease, the evils of old age, and all other misfortune; the examples of others ought to give one comfort and courage; the dead no longer suffer grief or pain; many think that there is a happy life for the soul beyond the grave; reason must temper grief; display of emotion are unmanly. These rather impersonal arguments based on reason became stereotyped.[31]

Plutarch follows the form of Greek and Latin consolation speeches (funeral orations) in the exhortations, the praise of the dead, and the good memories. Thus he receives and develops the consolatory funeral speech *topoi* in order to console his wife's sorrow and set the community rule as a public speech. In this sense, Baltussen correctly points out Plutarch's rhetorical originality:[32]

> First, how Plutarch's letter succeeds in providing sensitive advice and subtle guidance to his wife for this time of sorrow and grief, and second, how he is capable of making selective use of conventional consolatory materials and making them his own, tailored to the present situation and requirements. Plutarch's strategy

---

31. McGuire, "Christian Funeral Oration," xii–xiii. Particularly, moderation in grief should be observed, as in the face of all good or evil. Moderate behavior is especially called for from those who occupy prominent public positions. Immoderate grief is selfish, harmful, brings no advantage to either the mourner or the mourned, and dishonors the dead (Martin and Phillips, "Consolatio Ad Uxorem," 403).

32. Baltussen, "Personal Grief and Public Mourning," 91–92.

is situated within a matrix of several oppositions (life-death, mind-body, tradition-philosophy, private-public), which serve different purposes and cater to different audiences ... "priming" the addressee for the philosophical "punch line" (the climax of the speech) which defines happiness as "right thinking" ... by embedding his psychological guidance within a rhetorical framework of empathy and compassionate admonition, he remains very much aware of his grief and his responsibilities. How much of his strategy is calculated rhetoric or honest compassion is probably impossible to determine with absolute certainly.

(Epilogue/peroration, 612A–B) Plutarch ends with an appeal and exhortation to appropriate customs; "let us keep our outward conduct as the laws command, and keep ourselves within yet freer from pollution and purer and more temperate" (612B).

In summary, besides the common themes of consolatory speech, Plutarch gives his letter a rhetorical arrangement as recommended for funeral speeches by the pseudo-Dionysius's *On Epideictic Speeches*, rather than using Menander's rule. The *On Epideictic Speeches* advises encomium first, on the topics of country, family, nature, upbringing, education, and accomplishments (280). Then, it recommends the exhortatory section in public speeches. On the other hand, private speeches sometimes do not include the exhortatory section (280). In this case, Plutarch focuses on exhortation first to his wife for moderate deeds in sorrow and secondly to his potential audiences. Particularly, the consolatory topic is more essential than others. *On Epideictic Speeches* recommends the consolation but not lamentations; "We must not mourn or bewail the dead—this would not be to comfort the survivors but to increase their sorrow, and the speech would appear not to be a praise of the deceased but a lamentation ..." (281). In the consolatory section, *On Epideictic Speeches* deals with age: "if he dies young, 'the gods loved him ... and they snatched away many of the heroes of old ... not wishing them to be involved in the troubles here on earth or have their souls long buried in the body as in a tomb or prison, or be slaves to evil masters, but wishing rather to free them" (282). On the other hand, Menander suggests that in the lamentation section, "None of the various sections of the speech should be without an element of lamentation ... The expression of the lamentations must be developed in full so that the distinction of the persons concerned can be seen, while you move the listener again to lamentation. Let the encomia be your raw material for the lamentation" (*Menander the Rhetor: Division of Epideictic Speeches*. 419.20–420.5). Finally, *On Epideictic Speeches* says that, "At the end, it is essential to speak of the immortality of the soul, and to say that it is reasonable to suppose that such men are better off, because they are among the gods" (283). Plutarch deals with the immortality of the soul accordingly (611D-612B).

Plutarch (*Consolatio Ad Apollonium/A Letter of Condolence to Apollonius*) [F. C. Babbitt, LCL]

The most unique feature of this letter is the unusual frequency of quotations from many sources that it contains. There are also some striking similarities between this letter and Cicero's *Tusculan Disputations*, and these similarities derive from the same source, the works of the Academic philosopher Crantor.[33]

(Exordium and Encomium, 102.A) Sympathizing with the unexpected death of Apollonius' son, Plutarch praises Apollonium's decorous, modest, and religious character briefly.

(Consolation to the living, 102.B—121.D) Plutarch focuses mainly on consolation, with many quotations from diverse sources. His main concern is to give comfort for the mitigation of grief and the termination of mournful and vain lamentation (102.B). First of all, he recommends balanced reason and rational prudence in a time of sorrow because of the uncertainty of fortune (103.C-F) and the mortality of life and body (104.A—105.B). "For the very seed of our life, since it is mortal, participates in this causation, and from this there steal upon us defectiveness of soul, diseases of body, loss of friends by death, and the common portion of mortals" (104.C). Then Plutarch uses the poet as an example of someone extraordinarily successful in bestowing consolation: (1) death is the greatest succor from many ills, "O Death, healing physician, come" (106.C; 109.E); (2) "Living and dead are potentially the same thing" (106.E); (3) "life is a debt to destiny/death" (107.A-B) and "the indefiniteness and the brevity of life" (107.A); (4) "Socrates said that death resembles either a very deep sleep or a long and distant journey, or a sort of destruction and extinction of both the body and the soul ... for mankind the greatest of all good things" (107.D—108.F); and concluding with "it is more fitting to felicitate those ... than to pity them, as the majority do through ignorance" (107.C). Regarding an untimely death, "But he ought not to have been snatched away (αναρπαγηναι) while young," Plutarch commands the family to obey the decrees of Fate or Providence and exhorts them to minimize and put away grief and lamentation with the reason of Plato because "mourning is verily feminine and ignoble" (111.D—113.B). Plutarch finally addresses the eternity and immortality of the soul; "the departed one is now a partaker in some life more divine"

---

33. Plutarch, *Mor. II* 105–6.

(114.D, 120.A—121.D). He ends the consolation with the exhortation not to grieve "in unkempt grief (λυπαῖς) and utterly wretched mourning," (117.F—118.C) with many good examples and prayer (118.D—119.F).

(Epilogue, 121.E—122) With a repeated sympathy to Apollonius' sorrow, Plutarch exhorts him to return to reason and the natural course of life, because people offer a fitting tribute due to "Apollonium's honorable memory and to his fair fame, which will endure for time eternal," (121.E-F) and "now that he is with the gods and is feasting with them, he would not be well satisfied with your present course of life" (122).

Cicero (*Cicero's Letter to Titius; Sulpicius Rufus's Letter to Cicero*) [W. G. Williams, LCL]

These two letters show the typical forms that were recurrent in Latin consolation letters.

(*Cicero's Letter to Titius*, Exordium and Lament, XVI.1-2). Cicero shows his inability to give consolation to Titius, who had lost his children, with a deep lament.

(Consolation and Exhortation, XVI.2-6) Cicero begins by listing, as is custom, the common forms of consolation. To remember that we are human beings, born under a law of fortune, and to induce reflection on what has happened is nothing new (2). Particularly, Cicero suggests that the present plight of the state and this prolongation of the days of ruin ought to reconcile them to death (3) and that there is no evil in death, but "it should be rather regarded as deathlessness than death . . . but that he seemed to me to have been rescued by the immortal gods from all these miseries and most merciless conditions of life" (4). Cicero exhorts Titius to know that "you are bound to maintain your high character, and obey the dictates of consistency," and "it is our duty by wisdom and foresight to forestall whatever alleviation the lapse of time of itself is bound to bring us" (5-6).

(Epilogue, XVI.6) Cicero ends with some prayers.

(*Sulpicius Rufus's Letter to Cicero*, Exordium and Lament, V.1) There appear to be many similarities between Cicero's and Rufus's letters in consolatory topoi. Rufus laments over the death of Cicero's daughter, Tullia, and shows his inability to console Cicero's sorrow.

(Consolation and Exhortation, V.2-6) First, Rufus comforts Cicero in the fact that Tullia died in these troubled times, which should be a consolation (3). Further, with a vivid picture of a once great city's corruption, Rufus shows the limitation of worldly things (4). He urges Cicero to remember that "you were born a human being . . . Not so long ago there perished at one and the same time many of our famous men" (4). Then, Rufus helps Cicero remember the blessings that Tullia had in her life (5). Finally, Rufus exhorts Cicero to act in accordance with his high position and character and urges him not to forget the fact that "there is no grief that is not diminished and mitigated by the lapse of years" (6). With one last word, he urges Cicero to maintain balance and moderation.

(Epilogue, V.6) He ends with an appeal to keep admirable self-control.

In summary, between Cicero and Rufus's consolation letters, the overlapping similarities in consolatory topoi are as follows: (1) the law that we are human beings, (2) the disturbed condition of the state, which ought to reconcile a man to the loss of life, (3) time as a good consoler, (4) the exhortation to act moderately in accordance with his high character and teachings to others.[34]

Cicero (*Tusculan Disputations*) [J. E. King, LCL]

In Cicero's day, the Stoic and Epicurean schools had the most adherents in Rome. Though Cicero has strong leanings toward the Stoics, he rejects their fatalism and pantheism. Rather, Cicero himself claims to belong to the New Academy, which Plato founded. Cicero sides with Plato in this work "to believe in the pre-existence and immortality of the soul, and reject the Stoic doctrine of a limited existence after death."[35]

(Book I, *On Despising Death*) In the first book, Cicero proposes that death ought to be despised because death is not an evil (9, 24) and the fear of the lower world is a fiction (10). Regarding the questions "What is death? What is the soul?", Cicero agrees with the ancients in that "death was not annihilation obliterating and destroying all things, but a kind of shifting and changing of life . . . a guide to heaven" (27). The soul is separable from the body and mounts aloft (36–52). Thus, the soul is self-moving and immortal; "For this is the peculiar essence and character of the soul which, if it is out of all things the one which is self-moving, has assuredly not been born and is eternal" (54–55). In response to the question, "Is there then any definite sense of pain or sensation at all in the body after death?", Cicero claims that the departure takes place in a moment of time. Thus, "Death then withdraws us from evil, not from good" (83–84). Death is a sleep (92). Therefore, he exhorts to meet death calmly; "the dead were in no evil plight . . . For our own grief, and grief felt on our account, we ought to bear in a spirit of moderation, that we may not seem to be lovers of self" (111).

---

34. Fern, "Latin Consolatio as a Literary Type," 15.
35. Cicero, *Tusc.* 18.11–34.

Finally, Cicero concludes that death is a departure or a deliverance; "let us obey joyfully ... that we are being set free from prison and loosed from our chains, in order that we may pass on our way to the eternal home ... or else be free of all sensation and trouble ... let us regard it rather as a haven and a place of refuge prepared for us" (118).

(Book II, *On Enduring Pain*) Cicero proposes that pain is the greatest of evils and that to amend pain is evil (10–14). He exhorts his readers to overcome pain by virtue; "so long as honor, so long as nobility, so long as worth remain, and so long as you control yourself by keeping your eyes upon them, assuredly pain will lead to virtue and grow fainter by a deliberate effort of will" (31). Further, pain must be despised (41). By reason, pain becomes endurable (42), and the weeping of the womanish is disgraceful (55–57). Thus, Cicero concludes that though pain is evil, by virtue it becomes of trifling importance, and death is a mansion of refuge which has been prepared (66–67).

(Book III, *On the Alleviation of Distress*) In this book, Cicero deals with many kinds of distress and their alleviations. He proposes that distress is a disorder of the soul and the unsoundness of mind (7–11). He admits that even the wise man is susceptible to distress (12), but only philosophy is able to cure the soul. "Therefore let us put ourselves in the hands of philosophy for treatment" (13). Cicero lists the various opinions of the philosophers, but he sides with the New Academy and Stoics strongly; "These therefore are the duties of comforters: to do away with distress root and branch as far as possible: (1) Cleanthes—the evil has no existence at all; (2) Peripatetics—the evil is not serious; (3) Epicurus—they favor the withdrawal of attention from evil to good; (4) Cyrenaics—nothing unexpected has taken place; (5) Chrysippus—the main thing in giving comfort is to remove from the mind of the mourner the belief that he is discharging an obligatory duty to the dead" (76).

Cicero, in accordance with the Stoics, suggests remedial steps for assuaging sorrow and giving consolation: (1) to show either there is no evil or very little, (2) to discuss the common lot of life and any special feature that needs discussion in the lot of the individual mourner, (3) to show it is utter folly to be uselessly overcome by sorrow when one realizes that there is no possible advantage, (4) to understand the phrase "you are not the only one" (77, 79), (5) to know time brings alleviation but reflection is the true remedy (55–59).

Finally, Cicero concludes, "so philosophy ... did away with any mistaken idea due to any special cause ... that all distress is far remote from the wise man, because it is meaningless" (82).

Pliny the Younger (*To Calestrius Tiro*; *To Caninius Rufus*; *To Novius Maximus*) [B. Radice, LCL]

Pliny's many letters for consolation generally reflect the topoi and conventions of Latin consolation.

(*To Calestrius Tiro*, Lament, XII.1-2) When Pliny writes to Calestrius Tiro concerning the death of Corellius Rufus, he laments that Corellius died by his own wish.

(Encomium, XII.3-10) Pliny praises Corellius's good character and deeds during his life; "a good conscience and reputation, and wide influence" and his good family and many true friends. Further, he justifies Corellius's death because of his painful affliction and his long suffering in disease.

(Consolation, XII.11-12) Pliny finds some consolations in Corellius's death: (1) he had lived to the end of his sixty-seventh year, a good age; (2) he escaped from perpetual illness; (3) he left a family to outlive him and left his country in a prosperous state.

(Epilogue, XII.13) Pliny repeats his lament.

(*To Caninius Rufus*, Exordium, VII.1-2) Pliny describes how to receive the news of Silius Italiucus' death and the history of his disease.

(Encomium, VII.3-9) Pliny lists Silius's manner of life and good deeds for his praises. Silius was fortunate in life and enjoyed happiness up to the end of his days, maintaining friendships with tact and wisdom. He won fame for his conduct as governor of Asia and ranked as one of the leading citizens and consul.

(Consolation and exhortation, VII.10-15) Pliny follows the topoi of consolation as follows: Silius lives to a good age, he leaves the frailty of the human body, and the short and fleeting human life. Pliny ends his letter with an exhortation; "Since we are denied a long life, let us leave something to bear witness that at least we have lived."

(*To Novius Maximus*, Exordium, V.1) Pliny shows his grief on Gaius Fannius' death.

(Encomium, V.1-3) Pliny praises Gaius' good taste and learning, his judgment and natural intelligence, and an accurate opinion during his life.

(Lament, consolation, and exhortation, V.4-8) Pliny laments Gaius' unfinished work and that death is always sudden and cruel for those who think of posterity in their works. Life is mortal. Thus, he exhorts his friend that, "so while life lasts we must see there shall be as little as possible for death to destroy."

Seneca (*The Consolatory Letters of Seneca to Lucilius*; *The Consolatio ad Marciam*; *On Consolation to the Bereaved*) [R. M. Gummere, LCL]

These letters are all addressed to Lucilius, and Seneca writes on the many ills of life and uses philosophical precepts to comfort his friend, Lucilius, and all those suffering from similar afflictions.[36]

(*On Groundless Fears*, Ep. 13. Exordium, 1–3) Seneca begins this letter with laudation of Lucilius to prepare his mind for the following precepts.

(Consolation, 4–15) Seneca offers some safeguards, by which Lucilius may fortify himself. First, he suggests a heart of manliness because "we are in the habit of exaggerating, or imagining, or anticipating, sorrow" (5). Second, Seneca recommends for him to depend on prudence; "let prudence help you, and condemn fear with a resolute spirit even when it is in plain sight" (12).

(Conclusion/Epilogue, 16–17) Seneca concludes his letter with some comments on the foolishness of men who "lay down every day new foundations of life, and begin to build up fresh hopes even at the brink of the grave" (16).

(*On Despising Death*, Ep. 24. Exordium, 1–2) Seneca chides Lucilius for his fear of the future; "whatever the trouble may be, measure it in your own mind, and estimate the amount of your fear. You will thus understand that what you fear is either insignificant or short-lived" (2).

(Consolation, 3–25) Following some common topoi/arguments of consolation, Seneca recalls many examples to show one how to suffer well and despise death (3–11). Then Seneca asserts the philosophical precepts to despise death: (1) You were born to these perils (death); (2) Let us think of everything that can happen as something which will happen; (3) Our petty bodies are mortal and frail; (4) Death is the release from the burden of body and then there remains the better part; (5) We die every day (the death-process).[37]

(Conclusion/Epilogue, 26) Seneca concludes that all nature passes in this way, only to return.

---

36. Fern, "Latin Consolatio as a Literary Type," 34.

37. In *Ep.* 30., *On Conquering the Conqueror*, Seneca also offers similar consolatory arguments: (1) The study of philosophy prepares us to be joyful in the very sight of death; (2) Death is no evil, "death stands so far beyond all evil that it is beyond all fear of evils;" (3) Death has its fixed rule—equitable and unavoidable; (4) Do yourselves always think on death in order that you may never fear it.

(*On Grief for Lost Friends*, *Ep.* 63. Exordium, 1-2) This letter resembles the letters of Sulpicius to Cicero and of Cicero to Titius,[38] containing consolatory topoi on the death of Lucilius's friend Flaccus. Seneca shows his sympathy with Lucilius's sorrow, but in moderation; "We, however, may be forgiven for bursting into tears, if only our tears have not flowed to excess ... We may weep, but we must not wail" (1).

(Consolation and Exhortation, 2-15) According to the common topoi/ arguments of consolation, Seneca develops his consolatory arguments: (1) the good memory of the dead; (2) a certain lapse of time, "after lapse of time, every thought that gave pain is quenched, and the pleasure comes to us unalloyed", (3) life as a loan, "Fortune has taken away, but Fortune has given", (4) other friends who are left to console you, (5) death as something to be expected, (6) the mortality of all things, "not only that all things are mortal, but also that their mortality is subject to no fixed law."

(Conclusion and Prayer, 16) With a similar pattern of consolation through prayer, Seneca concludes his letter, "Let us therefore reflect . . . that we shall soon come to the goal. . .perhaps, if only the tale told by wise men is true and there is a boon to welcome us, then he whom we think we have lost has only been sent on ahead" (16). Fern correctly points out "the hope of immortality; but this hope is expressed in a vague, uncertain manner."[39] This pattern of prayer similarly appears in the funeral oration of Tacitus: "If there be any habitation for the spirits of the just; if, as wise men will have it, the soul that is great perish not with the body may you rest in peace" (*Agricola*, 46).[40]

(*The Consolatio ad Marciam*, Exordium, 1) This work of Seneca shows the most common form of the ancient consolatio in Latin, the rules of this genre, and the common topoi that were offered as solace to the bereaved.[41]

---

38. Fern, "Latin Consolatio as a Literary Type," 41.

39. Fern, "Latin Consolatio as a Literary Type," 43.

40. In *Ep.* XCIX., *On Consolation to the Bereaved*, which Seneca wrote to Marullus at the time when he had lost his little son, he also offers similar consolatory arguments: (exordium, 1-2) moderation in grief; (consolation, 3-31) examples of suffering well (3-6); death levels us, "he who is privileged to be born, is destined to die" (9); Death is not pain, but it is a mere sting (14); philosophy has done you much service (15); weep, but do not be dominated by sorrow like wise men (16-21); our shortness of life in comparison with eternity (31); (conclusion/peroration, 32) exhortation.

41. Fern, "Latin Consolatio as a Literary Type," 53. She analyzes this consolation into: (1) *an exordium*, which is followed by (2) systematic reasoning, based on the *examples of others who have grieved* and on *precepts* for the control of grief; and (3) the *peroration*, or *conclusion*. Further, Seneca's other consolatory works such as *The Consolatio ad Helviam* and *The Consolatio ad Polybium* also show the similar patterns and commonplace topoi of consolation to *The Consolatio ad Marciam*.

In this letter, the arguments are filled with common principles of Stoic philosophy.[42] Seneca praises Marcia, who lost her son, for her strength of mind and virtues proved under great trials in order to prepare her mind for the ensuing consolation.

(Consolation, 2–25) After the laudation of Marcia, Seneca develops consolatory arguments for Marcia to follow: (1) he gives two opposite examples of Octavia (negative example) and Livia (positive example)—"The greatest force in bearing adverse circumstances is equanimity of mind" (5.5); (2) there is no gain in grief (6.2); (3) there should be moderation in grief (7.1); (4) death ought not to be unexpected—"The cause of our continued lamentation is that we do not think of evils . . . He who foresees evils about to come takes away the sting from present misfortune" (9); (5) human beings are mortal (11.1–2; 17:1); (6) the remembrance of past joy can bring comfort; (7) one should follow the good examples of others who have suffered—"everywhere you will see some who have endured greater misfortunes than your own" (12.4; 13.1–3, 14, 15); (8) death is no evil—"Reflect that the dead suffers no evil . . . Death is a release from, and an end of all pain; it restores us to the peaceful rest in which we lay before we were born" (19.4–5); (9) all human works are brief and fleeting (21.1); (10) the dead are immortal—"he himself is immortal, and is now in a far better state, set free from the burden of all . . . He is complete" (24.5; 25.1).

(Conclusion and Peroration, 26) This peroration is mainly formed by the *prosopopoeia* of Cremutius Cordus,[43] who from the height of heaven looks down upon her and addresses words of comfort. By employing the *prosopopoeia* in his work, Seneca shows that this is a rhetorical work.

Galen (*On the Avoidance of Grief*) [C. K. Rothschild and T. W. Thompson, Early Christianity 2 (2011)]

Galen's work *On the Avoidance of Grief* is a letter in which he expresses how he responded to the fire that destroyed much of his library and medicines in 192 A.D. This letter shows the contents of the consolation genre in antiquity and the moral philosophy of that period.[44]

(Exordium, 1) Galen explains how he received a letter from his friend and shows which training, arguments, or teaching he never learned through encountering painful losses.

---

42. Hopkins, *Death and Renewal*, 218.
43. Fern, "Latin Consolatio as a Literary Type," 63–64.
44. Rothschild and Thompson, "Galen," 110–29.

(Narration, 2–55) Galen also explains how he suffered painful losses (2–12a), even to the most terrible loss when "hope of recovery no longer remains" (12b–14). He confesses, however, that "none of these things . . . troubled me, not even the destruction of my commentaries" (29–30) because of "fortune, in part, contributing to this and I myself, in part, contributing equally" (31). Galen, with an analogy, explains the wisdom of his not being distressed with painful losses; "rather (looks into the number of fields) sufficient to meet his own expenses, then he will bear the loss of the excess without concern" (44), instead of the insatiability (48).

(Exhortation and Epilogue, 56–84) To be free from grief, Galen exhorts that "you train the imaginative faculties of your *psyche* almost at every moment" (56) with justice and temperance. He considers all human affairs trivial and instead believes that "there is something greater and better, the good with its own nature, (the good) not defined either by the absence of pain or distress" (62). Thus, "what thought would there be for the presence or the absence of them?" (65). He concludes his exhortation with this comment: "They, therefore, fall into a most wretched life among their insatiable desires" (80) without moderation and imaginative faculties in *psyche*. Galen's exhortation follows Stoic instructions of moderation and reason in *psyche* similar to Cicero and Seneca.

Julian (*Epistle to Himerius* 69) [W. C. Wright, LCL]

Regarding the format and function of an epistula consolatoria (consolatory letter), Gregg emphasizes the similarity with the consolatory funeral oration as follows:[45]

> Whatever particular features in one of Basil's consolations might owe their existence to the fact . . . the schema, and the consolatory procedure which is at one fashioned and controlled by the schema are the products of prescribed rhetorical theory and practice. This picture gains much in the way of detail when the kindred genre, the funeral oration, as composed by the Cappadocian Fathers, is subjected to a comparable synoptic analysis . . . Bauer's research demonstrated how completely the three consolatory funeral "sermons" of Gregory are offspring, or better, blood-brothers of the paramythetic oration so wisely practiced by the rhetoricians . . . The components of the consolatory oration were seen to have "rubbed off" on the epistolary form, with the result that although we have no oration, as such, from

---

45. Gregg, *Consolation Philosophy*, 62, 66, 78.

Basil, his consolation letters reveal at certain points a thorough familiarity with oratorical practice . . . on the basis of structure and constitutive elements, as consolatory orations in miniature.

Julian's epistle to Himerius, when compared in terms of basic elements, bears a similarity to the Plutach's *Consolatio ad Uxorem*.[46]

(Exordium, 412A) With prefatory words for gaining good-will and sympathy of the audience, Julian recounts how he was unable to read Himerius's letter "without tears. . .because of your surpassing grief" (412A).

(Encomium/Epainos, 412A-B) Generally, the section of encomium occupies a lot of room in the funeral orations and consolatory letters, but in this letter, like Plutach's philosophical consolatory instructions, Julian focuses on a more lengthy consolatory story rather than the encomium section. The panegyric/encomium element of the deceased is condensed; "a young and virtuous wife . . . is prematurely snatched away (αναρπασθηναι) like a torch . . . in a little while its flame dies down" (412B). Praise of the mourning Himerius as an excellent orator, the best beloved, and as a Greek who honors true learning is also shortened (412B, 413D).

(Consolation to the living, 412C-413D) After listing the common topoi for consolation (412C), Julian offers an anecdotic story of Democritus of Abdera (the laughing Philosopher) who consoled Darius in great grief over the death of a beautiful wife (413A) with this confidence: "you will find release from your sorrow" (412D). Democritus' anecdote ends with this reproach and lesson: "Why, then, O most absurd of men, do you mourn without ceasing . . . you who cannot discover a single person of all who have ever lived who was without his share of personal sorrow?" (413C). Julian ends his consolatory oration with an exhortation; "you must find your remedy from within; for surely it would be a disgrace to the reasoning faculty" (413D). Thus, Julian's consolatory section is similar to Plutarch's philosophical one (*Consolatio ad Uxorem*). It is an evocation of the good memory of the deceased, the power of reason to assuage sorrow, the assertion of the immortality of the soul, and a concluding exhortation: "let us keep our outward conduct as the laws command, and keep ourselves within yet freer from pollution and purer and more temperate" (612B).

---

46. Gregg, *Consolation Philosophy*, 55.

Libanius (*Oration XVIII, Funeral Oration over Julian*) [A. F. Norman, LCL]

Regarding the most praiseworthy character quality for panegyric, Cicero (*de Oratore*, 2.85.346.) points out that virtue is "without profit or reward . . . profitable to others." Based on Cicero's comment about the panegyric, Ochs convincingly answers the question, "How does praise persuade?", that is, lack of reward and narrative form.[47] In other words, through the virtue of altruism, a hero who is dead persuades the audience to keep the honorable virtue for the benefit of the collective. Further, through narrative in a most eloquent style, the orator unites the community and keeps the critical virtue of continuing the collective. Thus, Ochs correctly points out the primary function of narratives in the funeral speech, which is closely related to the function of *narratio* in rhetoric.[48] In Libanius's funeral oration for Julian, he emphasizes the altruism of Julian and gives long and dramatic narratives on his deeds and exploits. Thus, this funeral oration shows the traditional function and form of a Roman funeral speech.

(Exordium, 18.1–6) According to the norm, expressing his inability to praise the greatness of Julian's deeds (18.4), he attempts to speak with praise, "the praise and narration that transmit their glorious achievements to all posterity" (18.3).

(Encomium/Epainos, 18.7–280) Wilhelm Kierdorf, in his *Laudatio Funebris*, insists that the section of encomium should contain such elements in historical order as "das Lob der Familie und der Vorfahren [praise of the family and ancestors], das Lob der Erziehung und der Lebensweise [praise of education and way of life], die lobende Aufzählung der honores [enumeration of the honorable honor], and das Lob der res gestae und virtutes [great things and virtues]."[49] First, he refers to his ancestors, his grandfather as an emperor and his father as an emperor's son (18.7), then to his education, humble mind, appearance (18.11), his superiority over others in his understanding, his perseverance (18.12), and his wisdom— "He gathered together wisdom of every kind and displayed it—poetry, oratory, the various schools of philosophy, much use of Greek and not a little of Latin . . . Athens, the home of Plato, Demosthenes and the various other branches of learning" (18.21, 28). Further, Libanius highlights his good fortune and the goodwill of the gods towards him; "It redounded more to the credit of Athens, for instance, that she gained her famous victory at

---

47. Ochs, *Consolatory Rhetoric*, 108.

48. Ochs, *Consolatory Rhetoric*, 109. He asserts that "narratives by their very nature invite participation, acceptance, and, if artfully done, some degree of identification."

49. Kierdorf, *Laudatio Funebris*, 64–79.

Marathon with the aid of Heracles and Pan than if she had done so without the gods to help her" (18.65). He also notes his courage and wisdom in his wars in the Rhine (18.39–65). Consequently, Libanius continues to praise Julian's deeds and character, which is compared to Achilles in suffering and in war (18.66–81) as well as to Constantius in suffering. Libanius praises Julian's patience (18.95) and his philosophic lament at Constantius's death (18.116). Libanius praises Julian's restoration of religion and oratory (18.121–161), his swiftness in works (18.174), and his altruism for the empire; "how much more importance he placed on its (the empire's) welfare than on his own" (18.23, 181). Finally, he highlights the wars with the Persians, Julian's genius in strategy, his courage (18.212–266), and his encouragement by deeds, not just words (18.226).

(Lament, 18.281–295) Libanius's long narration of Julian's deeds and character (body, mind, and fortune) is abruptly interrupted by the lament, "Why then, you gods and immortal powers, did you not bring it to pass? What fault had you to find in his character?" (18.281). "These hopes, and more besides, were snatched from us by a host of envious spirits . . . Not without reason, then, has the cry of lamentation re-echoed all over land and sea, and after his death men have been either glad to die or sorry to be alive" (18.282–283).

(Consolation to the living, 18.296–306) Libanius, however, drastically changes his tone and the contents of his speech in the consolatory arguments through the image of Julian himself according to the common topoi (18.296). In light of the shortness of his life, by comparing Julian to Alexander, son of Zeus, Libanius attempts to give the consolation. Further, he emphasizes the unalterable decrees of fate, the qualities and superiorities of Julian's achievements over everyone else, and the immortal memory of his fame (18.298). Finally, Libanius concludes with exhortations to the living and Julian's offspring to endure grief, the ascension to heaven, and the association with the power of the divine (18.304).

(Epilogue, 308) Libanius repeats his praise.

Dio Chrysostom (*The Twenty-Ninth Discourse: Melancomas*) [J. W. Cohoon, LCL]

Containing less philosophy when compared to Plutarch's works, *The Twenty-Ninth Discourse: Melancomas* takes the form of a funeral oration for a young boxer Melancomas, who had died very suddenly.[50]

---

50. Martin and Phillips, "Consolatio Ad Uxorem," 398–99.

(Exordium, 29.1-2) Ziolkowski enumerates the traditional features of the funeral Prooemium found in this oration: (1) a reference to the nomos, (2) a precautionary statement of the difficulty of praising the dead adequately (logos), (3) some specific statements of praise (epainos) commonly revealing the extraordinary arete (courage) of the dead and thereby justifying the speech,[51] Dio follows the traditional form of a funeral oration. Based on the works of Gregory of Nazian, Wilhelm Kierdorf asserts about the funeral Prooemium that "Nichtsdestoweniger läßt sich feststellen, daß die griechischen Leichenreden des Gregor von Nazianz stets ein Proömium haben; darin begegnen vor allem zwei Gedanken: a) der Verstorbene hat einen Anspruch auf das Totenlob, das man ihm nicht vorenthalten darf (Verpflichtungstopos/obligation topos); b) der Redner fürchtet, mit seinem Lob hinter den Verdiensten des Verstobenen zur ückzubleiben und durch seine Rede dessen Ruhm zu verkleinern (Bescheidenheitstopos mit Auxesis/auxiliary topos)."[52] Through his grief, Dio shows his friendship to Melancomas and uses the custom of the funeral speech (29.1). He expresses, however, his inability to speak a funeral oration, "incapable of speech . . . I am at the time of life . . . while their ability to speak is always less than it was . . . to speak to the best of my ability" (29.2). Dio also clearly indicates the intention of the speaker, " . . . no lengthy or studied eulogy, but praise that comes from the heart" (29.2).

(Encomium/Epainos, 29.3-18) Pseudo-Dionysius says that the funeral oration is a praise of the departed and that it must be based on the same topics as encomia (*On Epideictic Speeches.* 278). According to the primary topoi of the encomium of Aphthonius,[53] Dio orderly praises the merits of Melancomas. In the first place, Dio praises his good fortune to be born well with good parents (29.3). Then Dio praises Melancomas' surpassing physical beauty "of absolutely all those of all time who have been renowned for beauty, all those, I mean, who were born mortal," (29.4-6) and continuously praises the superiority of Melancomas' manly courage, self-control, and his power of endurance by comparing him to the ancient warriors; "Now since his was beauty of body, his was courage and a stout heart and, besides, self-control and the good fortune of never having been defeated, what man could be called happier than he" (29.7-16)? Further, in comparison to

---

51. Ziolkowski, *Thucydides*, 72.

52. Kierdorf, *Laudatio Funebris*, 59.

53. Kennedy, *Progymnasmata*, 108. Aphthonius lists the primary topoi of encomium as follows: (1) the person's origin (ancestors and parents), (2) upbringing (habits and principles of conduct), (3) deeds—(i) mind (courage and prudence), (ii) body (beauty and strength), (iii) fortune (power and friends), (4) comparison, attributing superiority to what is being celebrated by contrast.

ancient heroes such as Adonis, Phaon, Theseus, and Achilles, Dio puts the superiority over them all on Melancomas in light of both his beauty, self-control, and manly courage; "And yet for a man like him these twin virtues, courage and self-control, are most difficult to achieve" (29.17–18).

(Consolation of the living and exhortation/Paramythia, 29.19–21) Complying with the primary topoi of the consolatory section, Dio highlights Melancomas' qualitative virtues in his death, "For if the longest possible time were best for man, we might well have lamented over him in that regard; but as it is, seeing that all the life given to man is but short . . . history tell us that none of them reached a great age, neither Patroclus nor Antilochus . . . nor Memnon, nor Achilles . . . Now the gods would not have given an early death to their own children . . . if they did not consider this a good thing for mankind" (29.20). Finally, Dio exhorts the living to imitate Melancomas' blessings; "Come then, train zealously and toil hard, the younger men in the belief that this man's place has been left to them . . . " (29.21).

(Epilogue/Pero ration, 29.22) Dio repeats the remembrance of Melancomas without tears; Dio exhorts, "And as for the departed, honour him by remembrance, not by tears . . . but do you bear your grief with self-control" (29.22).

Lucian (*On Funerals*) [A. M. Harmon, LCL]

The satirist Lucian (A.D. 120–190) poked fun at "what he considers to be popular illogicality and sentimentality about contemporary burial and mourning practices, and about the alleged role and purpose of both Olympian and chthonic deities," and "Lucian ridicules the full range of Greco-Roman beliefs about the gods and death."[54] In the setting of a diatribe, there are threnody and parathrenody, such as the father's lament and the dead son's reply.[55]

(*On Funerals*, Exordium, 1) Lucian suggests the absurdities and superfluous practices of funerals and of knowledge about grieving; "they simply commit their grief into the charge of custom and habit" (1).

(Arguments, 2–24) First of all, Lucian points out their wrongful trust of Homer and Hesiod, and the other mythmakers and poetry in these matters, mistaking it for law (2–9). These beliefs lead to the foolish conclusion, "if anyone has not left a friend or kinsman behind him on earth, he goes about his business there as an unfed corpse, in a state of famine" (9). For this reason people commit vain grief and foolish funeral customs,

54. Davies, *Death, Burial and Rebirth in the Religions of Antiquity*, 132.
55. Lucian, *Lucian*, 4:111.

particularly wailing (12–14). In diatribe form, Lucian reproaches the foolishness of the mourners using the voice of the dead; "Unfortunate man, why do you shriek? Why do you trouble me?. . .Foolish man, what advantage do you think there is in life that we shall never again partake of?" (16–21). Finally, Lucian pokes fun at the funeral orations and fasting; "Some people, moreover, even hold competitions and deliver funeral orations at the monuments, as if they were pleading or testifying on behalf of the dead man before the judges down below!" (23–24). Lucian's mocking of funeral wailing and sorrow is similar to 1 Thess 4:13, "so that you may not grieve as others do who have no hope." Thus, it may be in 1 Thess 4:13 that Paul is mocking pagan mourning practices.

In this sense, G. K. Beale correctly comments that 1 Thess 4:13 should be considered to be a continuation of 4:11–12 and the exhortation of being careful as to how one behaves in public by saying, "Behaving quietly and properly also entails not grieving over the death of loved ones *like the rest of men* (i.e., the "outsiders" of 4:12), *who have no hope*."[56]]In this sociocultural context, hope in the face of death and burial will signify the symbol of the Christian community, and behavior at a funeral could be seen as an opportunity to be a good witness.[57]

(Conclusion, 24) Lucian concludes with the comment, "these things and others still more ridiculous are done at funerals, for the reason that people think death the greatest of misfortunes" (24).

Symmachus (*Letter 1.2: Symmachus' Father, Avianius, to Symmachus*) [Michele Renee Salzman and Michael Roberts, *The Letters of Symmachus: Book 1*]

In response to his son's letter, the elder Symmachus wrote epigrams on the great men of his generation with a poetic style, which are eulogies (1.2.2). Poetic eulogy was a traditional activity for Rome's elite in the fourth century,[58] and these concise eulogies (1.2.3–7) show a sample of very brief Latin eulogies of the dead. Further, it is noteworthy that this lament form bears some resemblance in the style and content to 2 Sam 1:19ff, a Jewish lamentation. From these eulogies below, it is possible to

---

56. Beale, *1 and 2 Thessalonians*, 130. It is added that the typical pagan attitude to death was that "hopes are for the living, but the ones who die are without hope"

57. Witherington, *1 and 2 Thessalonians*, 131.

58. Salzman, *Letters of Symmachus*, 11.

find the traditional senatorial values and virtues (encomium) that both Symmachi want to exemplify.[59]

Concerning Aradius Rufinus, the elder Symmachus praises his talent, his fortune, his extraordinary glory, and his deeds, "your extraordinary glory matched your prosperity to your deeds" (1.2.3; 2 Sam 1:19). Further, he calls him "one person beloved by all" (1.2.3; 2 Sam 1:23, 26). For Valerius Proculus, he praises Proculus' superiority in the dignity of his life and character through comparison with his ancestors, "Among the first men of his age, whom the glory of his ancestors did not overburden" (1.2.4; 2 Sam 1:23).

Concerning Amnius Anicius Iulianus, with poetic style Symmachus praises Amnius's eternal name and honor (1.2.5). In regard to Petronius Probianus, with a vocative "You, Probianus," he praises Probianus's modesty, happy charm, sincerity of character, and resourcefulness (1.2.6; 2 Sam 1:19, 23, 24). Finally, for Verinus, he praises highly his superiority in his eloquence, the charm of his character, and his life, "There is no further scope for virtue; for if there were, you would claim it" (1.2.7).

Between these Latin eulogies and the Jewish lamentation of 2 Sam 1:19–26, there are overlapping similarities in form and in content: the poetic lamentation, eulogy, and the praise of the character, virtue, and deeds of the dead. These facts may show the correlations and influence of the Latin eulogies and Jewish lamentation on each other. This characteristic also appears in the Jewish funeral oration of 4 Maccabees below, which contains the Hellenistic influence in form and content.

Lucretius Vespillo (*Laudatio Turiae*) [Erik Wistrand, CIL]

This funeral oration, in which a husband exalts his deceased wife's virtues and self-sacrificing love, is contained in *CIL* VI 1527, 31670, 37053 (Corpus Inscriptionum Latinarum).[60] This inscription employs the form of a *laudatio* or funeral *encomium* not actually delivered as a speech, for, throughout the funeral *encomium*, he addresses himself to the lost wife, not to an audience.[61] This inscription, however, resembles in form and function the main features of the funeral *encomium*: the *laudation* (*encomium*), *lament*, *consolation* and *exhortation*, and *epilogue with prayer*.

(Exordium) Many lines are missing in the left hand column. Thus there may be some comments as exordium.

---

59. Salzman, *Letters of Symmachus*, 11–12.

60. Wistrand, *So-Called Laudatio Turiae*, 9.

61. Fern, "Latin Consolatio as a Literary Type," 186; Fowler, *Social Life at Rome in the Age of Cicero*, 159.

(Encomium/Epainos, Left-hand column, 3-Right-hand column, 53) The *laudation*, or praise of the dead, occupies the greater part of the inscription and praises the virtues and character of the deceased wife in chronological order. The *laudation* begins with the description of horrible circumstances and of family calamity; "You became an orphan suddenly . . . when both your parents were murdered together" (Left-hand column, 3). Then, Vespillo praises examples that show the lofty spirit and courage of the deceased wife. She performed her filial duty by defending her father's will against the attempts of crafty relatives to change it (7–29), "they gave way before your firm resolution" (25). Her generosity and solicitude for the family are praised (30–52); "Why should I mention your domestic virtues: your loyalty, obedience, affability, reasonableness, industry in working wool, religion without superstition, sobriety of attire, modesty of appearance?" (30–31). Her devotion to her husband is highlighted through her submission to insults and opprobrium in order to succor her husband (Right-hand column, 2–24). He praises her actions in suffering, "you lay prostrate at his (Marcus Lepidus) feet, and you were not only not raised up but were dragged away and carried off brutally like a slave . . . your spirit was unbroken . . . although you had to listen to insulting words and suffer cruel wounds, you pronounced the words of the edict in a loud voice" (11–18). Regarding her selfless devotion to her husband, Turiae proposed to him a divorce so that he might produce a son and heir (25–53).

(Consolation to the living and exhortation, 54–59) According to the common topoi of consolation, Vespillo states, "Fate decreed that you should precede me . . . I on my part will, however, bend my way of thinking and feeling to your judgments and be guided by your admonitions" (54–55). Further, the praise which Vespillo bestowed upon the virtuous life of Turiae forms the chief assuagement of his grief; "But all your opinion and instructions should give precedence to the praise you have won so that this praise will be a consolation for me and I will not feel too much the loss of what I have consecrated to immortality to be remembered for ever" (56–57). Regarding the function of the section of consolation (54–59) and lament (60–66), Wistrand correctly points out:[62]

> This whole section is full of terms and ideas deriving from the most popular moral philosophy current at the time. Since the author clearly states that it is his wife's *iudicia* (judgment and decision), *cogitata*, *praescripta* (foreknowledge) and example (59) that he is trying to follow . . . that the remarkable unknown lady, to whom the inscription pays homage, possessed, along with her

62. Wistrand, *So-Called Laudatio Turiae*, 75.

other admirable qualities and merits, a training in philosophy, which she endeavored to put into practice.

This consolation and lament section also contains the exhortations to be imitated by the audience, which is the common topos in funeral orations.

(Lament, 60–66) "But . . . Natural sorrow wrests away my power of self-control and I am overwhelmed by sorrow. I am tormented by two emotions: grief and fear." (63–64) In the lament section, "there is the same feeling of bad conscience at not being able to maintain the tranquility of mind demanded by philosophy, especially by Stoic philosophy, and at failing to follow the authority of a respected adviser."[63] Hopkins correctly describes the social phenomenon:[64]

> According to ancient Roman ideals, men should be unmoved by personal loss, while women were allowed much greater license, though in the Twelve Tables (10.4; traditional date 451 B.C.), they were prohibited from tearing their cheeks with their nails at funerals. Later philosophical essays advise readers of both sexes against grieving too loudly, too much or too long. Such exhortations surely imply that uncontrolled or 'unseemly' mourning was widespread.

(Epilogue and Prayer, 67–69) There is repeated praise of the deceased and the prayer.

Summary and Conclusion on Romans Funeral Orations

Rhetorical Situation (Rhetorical Exigency)

Hopkins analyzes the Roman social circumstances as follows:[65]

> There can be no doubt that the Romans conquered the Mediterranean basin with carnage. And in the process, Roman armies suffered significant losses particularly in civil wars. Romans grew up in this period in the knowledge that sons would become soldiers, and face the risk of killing or of being killed. The prospect of their dying must have loomed large in their minds and in those of their families: 'Think of all those years lost by mothers and of the anxiety imposed on them while their sons are in the army' (Seneca, *Letter of Condolence to Marcia* 24).

---

63. Wistrand, *So-Called Laudatio Turiae*, 74.
64. Hopkins, *Death and Renewal*, 218.
65. Hopkins, *Death and Renewal*, 207.

Many a Roman family which sent a young son or husband as a soldier abroad never saw him again.

Under these social circumstances, the Roman funeral orations developed and derived from the circumstances of the war, like the Athenian funeral orations. For example, the imperial funeral orations of Dio Cassius (*Tiberius' funeral oration for Augustus*), Libanius (*Funeral Oration over Julian*), and Tacitus (*Agricola*) mainly deal with and praise deeds in war and console the living. Contrary to the public funeral orations of Athens, the Roman funeral orations are divided into both public and private just as Cicero (*De Orat.* II. 84. 341) comments about the funeral orations (*laudatio funebris*) in Rome.

Particularly, it is noteworthy that in this period the Latin consolatory letters, which reflect on the private funeral oration (*laudatio funebris*) while employing the epistle forms, also contain the similar structure and contents of funeral orations. For example, the consolatory letters of Plutarch, Cicero, Pliny the Younger, Seneca, and Julian reflect the structure and contents of the funeral orations (*laudatio funebris*) as follows: (1) a proem (exordium), offering some explanation of how the misfortune came to the author's notice, (2) a section of the letter constituted by eulogistic remarks (encomium) and periodic lamentations, (3) a series of consolatory arguments (consolation and exhortation), and (4) a conclusion with prayerful petitions or bits of advice to the person addressed.[66] As travel became more commonplace, individuals were more likely to be absent when a death occurred. Similarly, as writing itself became more commonplace, written words of consolation could, and did, serve as surrogates for traditional, oral forms. Therefore, one can read consolatory literature in the same way one might read a consolatory speech.[67] The written works only record, or purport to record, what was said or might have been said by the consoler to the mourners on some specific occasions.[68] In conclusion, it is manifestly shown that the Latin consolatory letters have the same functions, purpose, and content of the funeral orations, and thus, the Latin consolatory letters are deeply connected with and influenced by funeral oration.[69] Thus, while the Latin consolatory letters

---

66. Gregg, *Consolation Philosophy*, 58.
67. Ochs, *Consolatory Rhetoric*, 112.
68. Martin and Phillips, "Consolatio Ad Uxorem," 399.
69. Regarding the relationship between rhetorical theory and letter forms, F. Long correctly argues that "One concludes that the epistolary tradition represented by Pseudo-Demetrius has been shaped by Greco-Roman rhetorical theory and culture; specifically the accusing and apologetic types by forensic theory and practice . . . Whether written for the assembly or as open letters, such letters drew upon all the branches of rhetoric in their construction, most fundamentally forensic rhetoric" (*Ancient Rhetoric*

take the letter form, they actually follow patterns of consolatory rhetorical speeches and function as surrogates for oral funeral consolation.

Rhetorical Purpose and Structure

Like the Athenian funeral orations, the main functions of the Roman funeral oration (*laudatio funebris*) are to unify the Roman community, to make the audience feel the identification, and to console and exhort the living and young generations. For this main purpose, in the occasion of the public funeral orations, the encomium (*narratio*) and consolation of the Roman funeral oration (*laudatio funebris*) take the main portion of the whole discourse.[70] This is the same in the Athenian funeral oration and in the Jewish funeral orations. When compared to the structure of the Athenian, the Roman, and the Jewish funeral orations, in the consolatory letters there are mainly lengthy consolations and exhortations with a short encomium of the dead.

Rhetorical Content

Generally, the Athenian funeral orations had considerable influence on the Roman funeral orations (*laudatio funebris*) and on the consolatory letters (Cicero, Seneca, and Plutarch). Contrary to the Athenian funeral oration, which focuses only on the public sphere, Roman funeral orations were divided into both public and private funerals. Particularly, in Rome, speeches at the funerals of private individuals became common, and in these the consolatory element was more prominent.[71]

Imperial Funeral Orations—The Roman imperial funeral orations (*laudatio funebris*) take structures, rhetorical situations, and content similar to the Athenian funeral orations:

---

and Paul's Apology, 111).

70. You can see the main part of encomium and consolation in *laudatio funebris*: (1) Tacitus (*Agricola*, encomium/4–42, consolation-exhortation/43–46a); (2) Dio Cassius (*Tiberius' funeral oration for Augustus*, 36–41, consolation/41.9); (3) Libanius (*Funeral Oration over Julian*, encomium/18.7–280, lamentation/18.281–295, consolation/18.296–306); (4) Dio Chrysostom (*Melancomas*, encomium/29.3–18, consolation/29.19–21); (5) Lucretius Vespillo (*Laudatio Turiae*, encomium/left-hand column, 3-right-hand column, 1–53, consolation/54–59, lamentation/60–66).

71. Martin and Phillips, "Consolatio Ad Uxorem," 398.

(i) Exordium, (ii) Encomium, (iii) Consolation/Exhortation, and (iv) Peroration.

(i) Exordium—Generally, exordium consisted of the law and tradition (nomos) and the inability to praise the dead so they might gain the good-will of the audience.

All the Roman imperial funeral orators followed the traditional *topoi* in exordium (Appian, Dio Cassius, Libanius, Tacitus, and Dio Chrysostom).

(ii) Encomium—According to the main function of the funeral orations, encomium takes the most lengthy part in the whole oration. Just as Quintilian lists the components of encomium (*Insti.* III. 7.6–16), this part of encomium contains the events in time order, physical endowments and external circumstances, character and deeds of the dead, and superiority through comparison.

Appian and Dio Cassius describe Caesar's and Augustus' deeds in due chronological order respectively and Dio Cassius compares Augustus' education and courage to others to demonstrate his superiority (37.6). Most of all, he highlights Augustus' altruism (37.3–4; 41.5). Libanius praises the ancestors, Julian's upbringing and education, and his deeds and character in wars (18.66–81). Tacitus also contains in encomium the praise of Agricola's works in due chronological order, his altruism in wars, and he praises Agricola's superiority by comparision. Dio Chrysostom also follows similar patterns in encomium: good parents (ancestors), body, soul, and superiority by comparison. All the imperial funeral orations highlight the characteristics of altruism and courage as the most distinguished over other virtues.

Like the Athenian funeral orations, through lengthy praises and amplification in encomium, the Roman funeral orations attempt to prepare the mind of the audience to establish identification between the dead and the living. In other words, encomium as *narratio* clearly intends to establish the continuation of the collective with the dead and to unify the community through identification between the dead and itself.

(iii) Consolation/Lamentation-Exhortation—In consolation, Dio Cassius and Dio Chrysostom omit the lamentation in their funeral orations, but Libanius and Tacitus insert short lamentation into their orations.

With little lamentation, however, both Libanius and Tacitus swiftly change the tone and topic into paramythia[72] through statements of contrast

---

72. Paramythia means "consolation" and occupies the second major part of the funeral speeches, in general. Its main functions are to alleviate the grief of the living and

to the lamentation. Thus, lamentations in Roman funeral orations do not have a crucial function, but are a pre-step for consolation.

(iv) Peroration—The orators repeat the praise to the dead, or sometimes end with some exhortations to the living to imitate the dead. Particularly, Antony, omitting the overt exhortation in peroration, actually contains the exhortation to the living in the actions and impersonated voice of Caesar.

The Consolatory Letters—Though the Latin consolatory letters employ epistolary forms, their functions, strategies, and content reflect the rhetorical strategy and content of the funeral oration.

Particularly in his consolatory letters, while basing his material on traditional themes, Plutarch follows the conventional *topoi* of the funeral oration recommended by the Pseudo-Dionysius, such as exhortation, encomium of the dead, and good memories.[73] Further, in his development of the consolatory funeral speech *topoi*, Plutarch sets the community rule for the funeral as a public speech. Generally, most of the consolatory letters contain the content and structure of exordium, encomium, consolation/lamentation/exhortation to the living, and peroration. In some cases, however, there are more lengthy consolatory stories rather than a longer encomium section.

Generally, in consolation and exhortation sections there are common *topoi* as follows: "death is the greatest succor from many ills;" "life is a debt to destiny/death;" "time is a good consoler;" "it is utterly folly to be uselessly overcome by sorrow; "it is good to keep the good memory of the dead;" "death ought not to be unexpected;" "human being is mortal;" "death is no evil". These are followed by an expression of uncertainty of hope for heaven and prayer.

Between the consolatory letters and 1 Thess, there exists some overlapping similarities of content as well as manifest contrasts.

The Consolatory Letters	1 Thessalonians
The lapse of time for healing	Hope for the parousia
Release from disease	Reunion with Christ after the resurrection

to offer exhortation for future conduct such as to imitate the dead.

73. Martin and Phillips, "Consolatio Ad Uxorem," 411–12.

The Consolatory Letters	1 Thessalonians
Going to heaven (separation)	Being with Jesus forever
Uncertain hope for heaven and prayer	Certain hope for heaven and prayer

Funeral Oration as Inscription—Lucretius Vespillo (*Laudatio Turiae*), though not delivering his *laudatio* as a speech, writes in a form and function resembling the main features of the funeral oration: *laudation (encomium), lament, consolation-exhortation, and epilogue with prayer.*

Jewish Funeral Orations: 4 Maccabees

Many scholars propose some different generic labels for 4 Maccabees: development of a thesis (Stower), diatribe (Norden and Deissmann), encomium (Norden, Dupont-Sommer, and Hadas), *epitaphios logos* (Lebram), sermon (Freudenthal), or some combination of these (van Henten).[74] Lebram, Redditt, van Henten, and Avemarie, commonly show the encomiastic aspects of 4 Maccabees by drawing comparisons with the *epitaphios logos* and the Athenian funeral oration (Thucydides, Lysias, Demosthenes, Hyperides, and Plato).[75] Particularly, Paul Redditt correctly points out the genre of 4 Maccabees as follows:[76]

> These and other texts praise the martyrs for their sacrifice on behalf of their nation and homeland. Such praise occurs often in the Greek *epitaphios* . . . J.C.H. Lebram ("Die literarische Form des Vierten Makkabäerbuchs," *VC* 28 (1974)) compares 4 Maccabees with classical examples of the epitaph, showing how and why the author adopts it . . . The first part provides the basis for praise: for Plato the good birth (nobility), upbringing, and praxis of the dead; for Thucydides a historical review of past and present dangers met by martyrs. The author of 4 Maccabees is simply following the Greek epitaph when he sets the historical context of the martyrdom (chap. 4) and recounts their valiant deaths. The second part of the epitaph includes praise of the dead and encouragement to the living. The encouragement itself always contains a note of consolation and either a paraenesis or a dirge. The end

---

74. deSilva, *4 Maccabees*, xxi.
75. deSilva, *4 Maccabees*, xxii.
76. Redditt, "Concept of *Nomos* in Fourth Maccabees," 263.

of 4 Maccabees shows clear analogies to the second part of an epitaph; 17:7—18:19 especially praise the conduct of the martyrs; 18:20-21 are a dirge; 18:22-24 offer consolation by means of the eternal reward they received; and 18:1-2 are a paraenesis.

In the thought-world behind the Greek epitaph stand four motifs useful to 4 Maccabees. (1) In the Greek epitaph the Persian king is the prototype of the tyrant; in 4 Maccabees the Seleucid king plays this role. (2) The Greek epitaph often urges persons to *obey their law* rather than submit to a tyrant. 4 Macc 5:18 emphasizes this motif. (3) In the Greek epitaph the battle of the martyrs is seen as the fight for full piety; the victims of tyranny are said to be beloved by God. So also the martyrs of 4 Maccabees struggle for honor by God; piety is the basis on which and the power by which they wage their battles. (4) The Greek epitaph strongly emphasizes the difference between the temporality of the life of the dead and the eternity of their rewards, as does 4 Maccabees (18:3-4; 13:13-17).

Reflecting the common topoi of funeral oration (the language of demonstration, 1:1; 3:19; 16:2; encomium, 1:2, 10; consolation, 18:22-24; and exhortation, 18:1-2), the common arrangement of funeral oration (Exordium, 1:1-12; Propositio, 1:13—3:18; Narratio with Encomium, 3:19—17:6; Peroration with Consolation and Exhortation, 17:7—18:24),[77] the purpose of securing the audience's identification with the truth and with the nation, and the goal of evoking commitment to live in line with the proposed ethical principle, 4 Maccabees shows the characteristic of the genre of funeral oration, which is an encomium using flowery epideictic rhetoric.

(Exordium, 1:1-12) Following the topoi of the exordium of Aristotle (*Rhet.* 3.13 "in epideictic speeches . . . give the key-note") and of Quintilian (*Inst.* 4.1.5 "The sole purpose of the *exordium* is to prepare our audience . . . they will be disposed to lend a ready ear to the rest of our speech . . . by making the audience well-disposed, attentive and ready to receive instruction"), the author begins his speech: "The subject that I am about to discuss is most philosophical, that is, whether devout reason is sovereign over the emotion," (1:1) with an example of the martyred. By saying, "for me to praise for their virtues . . . I would also call them blessed for the honor . . . they became the cause of the downfall of tyranny over their nation" (1:10-11), the author shows the topoi and purpose of funeral orations. Like the funeral oration of Thucydides (*Hist.* 2.43.1-4), Dio Chrysostom (*The Twenty-Ninth Discourse: Melancomas.* 21), and Plato (*Menexenus.* 236E), the author shows his purpose "to reaffirm the

---

77. deSilva, *4 Maccabees*, xxviii-xxix.

hearer's commitment to values central to their social body, the values for which their compatriots deemed it worthy to die."[78]

(Propositio and Definition, 1:13—3:18) The author defines reason as "a mind preferring, with correct thinking, a life of wisdom" (1:15) and sets the thesis: "at that time enthroned the mind, the sacred governor . . . through the power of discernment. And to this faculty he gave the Law. Governing one's life according to the Law, the mind will rule a kingdom that is self-controlled and just and good and courageous" (2:21).

(Narratio with Encomium, 3:19—17:6) The author shows the characteristic of funeral oration in this speech through a long narration of Eleazar (5:1-6:30), the seven brothers (8:1—12:19), and the mother of the seven brothers (14:11—15:28), including encomiastic reflection (6:31—7:15; 13:1—14:10; 15:29—17:6) and a confirmation of the thesis (7:16-23).

Regarding the long narration (3:19—17:6) of this speech, deSilva correctly claims, "The lengthy narration of the brothers' martyrdoms and the author's reflection upon their achievement in their death has the potential to impact the audience quite strongly. As part of a larger kinship group . . . bounded together and 'like one another' . . . the Jewish audience could perceive the attitude, solidarity, and the mutual encouragement of the brothers."[79] In this sense, just as Ochs's assertion about the function of the long narration in the funeral oration,[80] the long narration of 1 Thess 1:4-3:10 shows similar topoi and functions as funeral oration identified in the Christian community.

With each argument finished by encomiastic speech and reflection (7:1-15; 14:2-10; 17:2-6), the author follows the pattern of narration/encomium of deeds and character found in funeral orations. It is important to note that throughout the long narration, the author employs images from the realm of athletics with the image of the "contest" (ἀγών) as a key note. Images of noble athletics (6:10, "like a noble athlete") are used in Eleazar's struggle against tyranny, and the oldest brother describes his suffering and struggle as a "contest" (9:23, τον ἀγῶνα). Further, it is clear that "it will continue to be employed throughout the remainder of the oration (12:11, 14; 13:13, 15; 16:16) . . . This is especially apt for the situation of the martyrs."[81] The word, ἀγών, generally means an athletic contest (Eur. *Or.* 847; Lucian, *Athletics.* 15; Heb 12:1). Figuratively, this word connotes "struggle/fight of

---

78. deSilva, *4 Maccabees*, 81. Lysias (*Funeral Oration* 81) also says, "So I, indeed, call them blessed in their death, and envy them . . . have left behind an immortal memory arising from their valor."

79. deSilva, *4 Maccabees*, 216.

80. Ochs, *Consolatory Rhetoric*, 109.

81. deSilva, *4 Maccabees*, 192.

suffering for the gospel" (Phil 1:30; 1 Thess 2:2) and "fight a fight, engage in a contest" (1 Tim 6:12; 2 Tim 4:7). The verb "ἄγω" is "to bring someone to trial, an accused person to court" or "of leading away to execution" (2 Macc 6:29; 7:18). Particularly, the word ἀγών in 4 Maccabees is employed in the context of martyrdom.

Paul may also use the word ἀγών in 1 Thess 2:2 in the same context. Paul's readers had received the gospel in suffering (1:6; 3:7), and some of them have already laid down their lives (4:14). Paul himself has suffered in an ἀγών "that was caused by human adversaries, while ... the ἀγών was the focal point of a battle between God and Satan (2:18; 3:5), of a battle that (Paul is sure about this at this time) was due to reach its climax before long."[82]

(Peroration with Consolation and Exhortation, 17:7—18:24) The final part of this speech contains many elements of the Greco-Roman funeral oration (*epitaphios logos*), culminating in the contest images of martyrs: the portrait, 17:7; the inscription for an epitaph, 17:8-10; the athletic image with the crowning of the fallen, 17:11-16; the attention given to rousing both pity and admiration, 17:7, 16; an exhortation, 18:1-5; a dirge, 18:20-21; a consolation, 17:11-16; 18:22-24.[83] Particularly, the part of the exhortation that evokes the audience to imitate the inheritance of the ancestors (18:1-5) has some similarity to Thucydides (*History of the Peloponnesian War*, 2.43.1-4; "you who survive ... therefore, now make these men your examples"), Isocrates (*Evagoras*, 9.80-81), Demosthenes (*Funeral Speech*, 35-37), and Dio Chrysostom (*The Twenty-Ninth Discourse: Melancomas*, 29.21, "Come then, train zealously ... ").

In summary, in respect to the rhetorical situation and purpose, the Jewish funeral oration of 4 Maccabees develops and derives from the circumstances of martyrdom. Its main function is to secure the audience's identification with the truth and with the nation, and to console and exhort the living to imitate the dead. Regarding the content and structure, it reflects the common *topoi* and arrangement of funeral oration: exordium/1:1-12, proposition/1:13—3:18, *narratio* with encomium/3:19—17:6, peroration with consolation and exhortation/17:7—18:24.

---

82. Bammel, "Preparation for the Perils of the Last Days," 99-100.

83. deSilva, *4 Maccabees*, 242; Redditt, "Concept of *Nomos* in Fourth Maccabees," 263.

Summary/Conclusion on the Roman Funeral Oration and the Jewish Funeral Oration

As stated above, both the Roman and Jewish funeral orations share the same rhetorical situation, purpose, structure, and content. They have the main function and purpose of securing the audience's identification, establishing the group identity, and consoling and exhorting the living to imitate the dead. Particularly, it is manifestly proved that the Latin consolatory letters follow the patterns of consolatory rhetorical speeches, that is, funeral oration. The Latin consolatory letters, while taking letter form, are actually influenced by funeral oration in content, structure, and purpose. They function as surrogates for funeral oratory.

The way in which the Athenian and Roman funeral orations function to unify the community through group identification and the way in which consolatory letters follow the pattern of epideictic consolation speeches will be applied to interpret 1 Thess in the subsequent chapters.

CHAPTER 5

Funeral Orations in Rhetorical Handbooks

Overview of Funeral Orations in Rhetorical Handbooks

RHETORICAL HANDBOOKS COMMONLY DEFINE epideictic rhetoric as panegyric oratory, "Praise and Censure" (Aristotle, *Rhet.* I. 9. 1; Cicero, *Rhetorica ad Herennium* III. 10 and *De Inventione* II. 177; Quintilian, *Insti.* III. 9. 1–4). There are four sub-genre of epideictic speeches from Aristotle's era: funeral oration, festal/gathering oration, paradoxical encomium, and encomium of persons (basilikos speech).[1]

Regarding the relationship between encomium and funeral orations, Aristotle is the earliest writer who defines both and comments about the overlapping extent of both. He says of encomium, "Now praise is language that sets forth greatness of virtue . . . encomium deals with achievements—all attendant circumstances, such as noble birth and education, merely conduce to persuasion" (*Rhet.* I. 9. 33). Further, in *Rhet.* II. 22. 6, Aristotle discusses the funeral oration of that time; "how could we praise them, if we did not know of the naval engagement at Salamis or the battle of Marathon, or what they did for the Heraclidae, and other similar things? For men always base their praise upon what really are, or are thought to be, glorious deeds." His comments indicate the possibility of some overlap in content between *encomium* and funeral orations.

In addition, in *Progymnasmata*, Aelius Theon (*The Exercises of Aelius Theon.* 109) claims that "*Encomion* is language revealing the greatness of virtuous actions and other good qualities belonging to a particular person. The term is now specifically applied to praise of living persons whereas praise of the dead is called an epitaphios and praise of the gods a hymn; but whether one praises the living or the dead or heroes or gods, the method of

---

1. Burgess, "Epideictic Literature," 105.

speaking is one and the same." Nicolaus the Sophist (*Preliminary Exercise of Nicolaus the Sophist.* 47) similarly defines the extent and contents of *encomium* and funeral orations. "The account of *encomion* is complicated, no longer limited to a single form (like descriptions of earlier exercises), and divided among many kinds. For speeches of arrival and addresses to officials and wedding and addresses to funeral orations, and, of course, also hymns to gods and every kind of speech of praise are listed under this species." Thus, it is possible to define the relationship and overlap between *encomion* and funeral orations.

Regarding the characteristics of *encomion*, Burgess convincingly asserts that it presents the facts "only so far as its chief aim—the glorification of the individual—may be best served. To this end facts may be selected at will, grouped in any order, exaggerated, idealized, understated, if detrimental points must be touched upon . . . The encomium is not to be made an apology . . . faults should be concealed as much as possible."[2] In this same line, Aristotle claims that "in the epideictic style the narrative should not be consecutive, but disjointed; for it is necessary to go through the actions which form the subject of the speech . . . It is only necessary to recall famous actions; wherefore most people have no need of narrative" (*Rhet.* III. 16.1–3). Theon also adds to the requirements of encomium that "one should either not mention things said against the man—for these become a reminder of his mistakes—or disguise and hide them as much as possible, lest without knowing it we create an apology instead of an encomium" (*The Exercise of Aelius Theon.* 112).

The Handbooks on Funeral Orations

Aristotle (*Art of Rhetoric*)

Though Aristotle does not separately refer to funeral oration, he is also familiar with this rhetorical genre; "as Pericles said in his Funeral Oration, that the removal of the youth from the city was like the year being robbed of its spring" (*Rhet.* I. 7. 35). Further, in II. 22. 6, he recognizes the familiar topics of the funeral oration and other panegyric orations; "How eulogize the Athenians unless we are informed of the sea-fight at Salamis, the battle of Marathon, or the exploits achieved by them on behalf of the Heraclidae and other like matters? For it is on the real or apparently honorable traits attaching to each object that all orators found their panegyrics."[3]

2. Burgess, "Epideictic Literature," 116–18.
3. Burgess, "Epideictic Literature," 105.

Aristotle classifies rhetoric into three types, corresponding to the three types of hearers: deliberative ("a judge of things to come"), forensic ("a judge of things past"), and epideictic ("the mere spectator of the ability of the speaker"). Further, though epideictic oration is appropriate to the present, "it is not uncommon, however, for epideictic speakers to avail themselves of other times, of the past by way of recalling it, or of the future by way of anticipating it" (*Rhet.* I. 3.3-4). The end of those who praise or blame (epideictic) is that which is honorable or disgraceful (*Rhet.* I. 3.6). Aristotle also claims that epideictic oration has points of agreement with deliberative; "Praise (encomium) and counsels have a common aspect" (*Rhet.* I. 9.35). In this sense, epideictic oration, including funeral oration, has the elements of advice and examples.

Aristotle asserts that in epideictic oration the most important thing is the praise of virtue and vice, of the noble and the disgraceful; "since they constitute the aim of one who praises and of one who blames" (*Rhet.* I. 9.1). The praise of epideictic oration includes not only a man or a god, but even inanimate things or ordinary animals.

First, if the noble is worthy of praise, then virtue must, of necessity, be noble, and he lists the components of virtue and his familiar topoi as follows (*Rhet.* I. 5.4; I. 9.3-25):

> Noble birth, numerous friends, good friends, wealth, good children, numerous children, a good old age; further, bodily excellence, such as health, beauty, strength, stature, fitness for athletic contests, a good reputation, honor, good luck, virtue ... The components of virtue are justice, courage, self-control, magnificence, magnanimity, liberality, gentleness, practical and speculative wisdom. The greatest virtues are necessarily those which are most useful to others, if virtue is the faculty of conferring benefits. For this reason justice and courage are the most esteemed...

Second, in the narrative, there should be the praise of actions and of moral purpose (*Rhet.* I. 9.32-34; III. 16.8):

> Since praise is founded on actions, and acting according to moral purpose is characteristic of the worthy man, we must endeavor to show that a man is acting in that manner ... one must assume that accidents and strokes of good fortune are due to moral purpose ... encomium deals with achievements ... And the narrative should be of a moral character, and in fact it will be so, if we know what effects this. One thing is to make clear our

moral purpose; for as is the moral purpose, so is the character, and for as is the end, so is the moral purpose.

Third, the speaker should employ the means of amplification and of comparison (*Rhet.* I. 9.38–41):

> We must also employ many of the means of amplification; if a man has done anything alone, or first, or with a few, or has been chiefly responsible for it; all these circumstances render an action noble . . . And you must compare him with illustrious personages, for it affords ground for amplification and is noble, if he can be proved better than men of worth. Amplification is with good reason ranked as one of the forms of praise, since it consists in superiority, and superiority is one of the things that are noble . . . since superiority is thought to indicate virtue . . . amplification is most suitable for epideictic speakers.

Fourth, the narrative pattern of epideictic discourse should be composed not historically but encomiastically (III. 16.1–3). Aristotle claims in III. 12.5–6, that the deliberative style is exactly like a rough sketch; but, the forensic style is more complete; the epideictic style is especially suited to written compositions since its function is reading. This, however, does not seem to agree with the general view, for funeral orations in the nature of panegyrics were meant to be spoken, but the proper function of an epideictic may be said to consist in reading, by being agreeable to read. Its end is to be read.[4] In other words, funeral orations were composed speeches, not given off the cuff. They were meant to be read out loud, verbatim from the written text.

Further, Aristotle adds in III. 1. 7 that "written speeches owe their effects not so much as to the sense (thought) as to the style." In other words, in written speeches, including funeral orations, the pattern of narrative in epideictic discourse should not follow logic or thought, but the style. In this sense, Aristotle pointedly asserts the following (III. 16.1–3):

> In the epideictic style the narrative should not be consecutive, but disjointed; for it is necessary to go through the actions which form the subject of the speech . . . This is why it is sometimes right not to narrate all the facts consecutively, because a demonstration of this kind is difficult to remember . . . It is only necessary to recall famous actions; wherefore most people have no need of narrative—for instance, if you wish to praise

---

4. Aristotle, *Art of Rhetoric*, 423.

Achilles; for everybody knows what he did, and it is only necessary to make use of it.

Cicero (*De Oratore*; *Ad Herennium*; *De Inventione*)

Cicero also does not deal with funeral oration separately in his handbooks of rhetoric. However, he does when comparing the Roman pattern of *laudatio funebris* to Athenian funeral orations and describes the characteristics as follows (*De Orat.* II. 84.341):

> ... and also we Romans do not much practice the custom of panegyrics ... For the Greeks themselves have constantly thrown off masses of panegyrics, designed more for reading and for entertainment, or for giving a laudatory account of some person, than for the practical purposes of public life with which we are now concerned: there are Greek books containing panegyrics of Themistocles, Aristides, Agesilaus, Epaminondas, Philip, Alexander and others; whereas our Roman commendatory speeches that we make in the forum have either the bare and unadorned brevity of evidence to a person's character or are written to be delivered as a funeral speech, which is by no means a suitable occasion for parading one's distinction in rhetoric.

Cicero describes the Romans' laudatory account of some person here to be "the bare and unadorned brevity of evidence" (testimonii brevitatem habent undam atque inornatam), emphasizing a more practical purpose rather than parading one's distinction. While pointing out differences of Roman laudations from Greek laudations, he also follows the pattern of Greek laudatory and epideictic discourse.

Cicero suggests that since epideictic includes praise and censure, the following can be subject to praise: external circumstances, physical attributes, and qualities of character (*Ad Herennium* III. 6.10). First of all, the introduction is drawn from our own person by saying "we are doing so from a sense of duty or from goodwill", from the person we are discussing by saying "we fear our inability to match his deeds with words; all men ought to proclaim his virtues; his very deeds transcend the eloquence of all eulogists", from the person of our hearers "since we are not delivering an encomium amongst people unacquainted with the man, we shall speak but briefly, to refresh their memories", or from the subject-matter itself (*Ad Herennium* III. 6.11–12). The definition and function of Cicero's introduction is the same as the introduction of a funeral oration, for the orator to gain the goodwill of the hearers.

Second, a statement of facts will depend on the circumstances either to omit or to recount, with either praise or censure, some deed of the person (*Ad Herennium* III. 6.13).

Third, it is necessary to praise (encomium) the deceased's virtues or faults of character, physical advantages, and external circumstances, observing precise sequence and chronology. Praise should be given to the subject's character as displayed in his attitude towards his own circumstances (*Ad Herennium* III. 6.13—8.15; *De Inventione* I. 34-6; II. 32-34, 59.177):[5]

(i) external circumstances: descent—the ancestors of whom he is sprung; education—being well and honorably trained throughout his boyhood;

(ii) physical advantages: merits or defects bestowed upon the body by nature like agility, strength, beauty, and health;

(iii) his virtues of character: those of wisdom, justice, courage, and temperance in all circumstances (*De Inventione* II. 53.159–54, 165).

If he is dead, what sort of death did he die and what sort of consequences followed it? This particularly applies to funeral oration. Further, beside these virtues, mercy, kindness, and fidelity are also thought to be beneficial, though not so much to their possessors as to the human race, in general (*De Oratore* II. 84.344). The most important virtues, however, are altruism and courage in misfortune, which may be gloriously expressed in funeral orations (*De Oratore* II. 85.346). (iv) The writer uses comparison to demonstrate the superiority of the subject (*De Oratore* II. 85.347-48): "And one must select achievements that are of outstanding importance or unprecedented or unparalleled in their actual character . . . a splendid line to take in a panegyric is to compare the subject with all other men of high distinction."

Fourth, the conclusion (*Ad Herennium* III. 8. 15): "Our Conclusions will be brief, in the form of a summary at the end of the discourse; in the discourse itself we shall by means of commonplaces frequently insert brief amplifications."

Finally, Cicero emphasizes an adaptation of style and pattern to the particular occasion by saying that "Although one point at least is obvious, that no single kind of oratory suits every cause or audience or speaker or occasion . . . we should choose a more copious or more restrained style of rhetoric . . . to suit the business before us" (*De Oratore* III. 55.210–12).

---

5. Cicero, *De or.* xxi.

Quintilian (*The Institutio Oratoria of Quintilian*)

Regarding the relationship between the encomium of persons and funeral orations, Burgess convincingly claims that "where a funeral oration is spoken over the body of a king, it differs from the imperial oration (encomium of persons/basilikos logos) only by the addition of the lamentation and consolation, and these are in many cases quite subordinate or much modified."[6] Though Quintilian also does not refer to funeral oration separately in *Institutio*, he demonstrates familiarity with funeral oration as genre of epideictic oration by saying that "Roman usage on the other hand has given it a place in the practical tasks of life. For funeral orations are often imposed as a duty on persons holding public office, or entrusted to magistrates by decree of the senate" (*Insti.* III. 7.2; III. 4.5; XI. 3.153). Like Aristotle, who emphasizes amplification to be suitable for epideictic speakers (*Rhet.* I. 9.38–40), Quintilian highlights the main function of encomium when he says that "Some arguments will even wear a certain semblance of defense . . . The proper functions, however, of panegyric is to amplify and embellish its themes" (*Insti.* III. 7.6). Funeral oration as an important member of epideictic orations shows this kind of amplification and embellishment in describing events and character, not depending on proof and arguments. In this sense Quintilian also defines rhetorical ornament (amplification and embellishment) as contributing to epideictic orations, particularly funeral oration, as follows (*Insti.* VIII. 3.11–12):

> To begin with the primary classification of oratory, the same form of ornament will not suit demonstrative, deliberative and forensic speeches. For the oratory of display aims solely at delighting the audience, and therefore develops all the sources of eloquence and deploys all its ornament, since it seeks not to steal its way into the mind nor to wrest the victory from its opponent, but aims solely at honor and glory. Consequently the orator, like the hawker who displays his wares, will set forth before his audience for their inspection, nay, almost for their handling, all his most attractive reflections, all the brilliance that language and the charm that figures can supply, together with all the magnificence of metaphor and the elaborate are of composition that is at his disposal.

Quintilian defines encomium as a style mainly directed at the praise of gods and men, but occasionally to the praise of animals or even of inanimate

---

6. Burgess, "Epideictic Literature," 116–18.

objects (*Insti*. III. 7.6). Among them, there is greater variety required in the praise of men, including funeral oration (*Insti*. III. 7.10–18).

First, time order:

> In the first place there is a distinction to be made as regard time between the period in which the objects of our praise lived and the time preceding their birth; and further, in the case of the dead, we must also distinguish the period following their death. With regard to things preceding a man's birth, there are his country, his parents and his ancestors . . . Other topics to be drawn from the period preceding their birth will have reference to omens or prophecies foretelling their future greatness, such as the oracle . . .

Second, physical endowments and external circumstances: "Physical accidental advantage proves a comparatively unimportant theme" (*Insti*. III. 7.12–13).

Third, character and deeds: "It has sometimes proved the more effective course to trace *a man's life and deeds in due chronological order* . . . including words as well as deeds . . . it is well to divide our praises, dealing separately with the various virtues, fortitude, justice, self-control and the rest of them and to assign to each virtue the deeds" (*Insti*. III. 7.15).

Fourth, superiority (comparison) and altruism: "what most pleases an audience is the celebration of deeds which our hero was the first or only man . . . one of the very few to perform; and to these we must add any other achievement which surpassed hope or expectation, emphasizing what was done for the sake of others rather than . . . on his own behalf" (III. 7.16).

Fifth, eulogy on funeral oration: "Children reflect glory on their parents, cities on their founders, laws on those who made them . . . Panegyrics have been composed on sleep and death" (III. 7.18, 28).

Sixth, the good will of audience (Exordium): "It will be wise too for him to insert some words of praise for his audience, since this will secure their good will, and wherever it is possible this should be done in such a manner as to advance his case" (III. 7.24).

Seventh, pattern of delivery: "in panegyric, funeral orations excepted, in returning thanks, exhortations and the like, the delivery must be luxuriant, magnificent, and grand. On the other hand, in funeral or consolatory speeches . . . the delivery will be melancholy and subdued" (XI. 3.153).

Quintilian (II. 13.2–8), however, also warns against the rigidity of rhetorical rules, and rather emphasizes the wise adaptability of an orator and rhetorical expediency as follows:

> If the whole of rhetoric could be thus embodied in one compact code, it would be an easy task of little compass; but most rules are liable to be altered by the nature of the case, circumstances of time and place, and by hard necessity itself. Consequently the all-important gift for an orator is *a wise adaptability* since he is called upon to meet the most varied emergencies ... So, too, with the rules of oratory. Is the *exordium* necessary or superfluous? Should it be long or short?...Should the statement of facts be concise or developed at some length?...The orator will find the answers to all these questions in the circumstances of the case ... For these rules have not the formal authority of laws or decrees of the plebs, but are, with all they contain, the children of expediency ... that in all his pleadings the orator should keep two things constantly in view, *what is becoming* and *what is expedient*.

Quintilian's comment indicates orators should know the varied exigencies and the rhetorical situation, and by their own discernment should wisely decide how to meet these questions in their oratory. Bitzer claims three constituents of any rhetorical situation: exigency, the audience, and the constraints.[7] Thus, among extant funeral orations of the Greco-Roman period, consolatory letters, and Jewish funeral oration, there is a vast difference in emphasis according to their own rhetorical situations, while content, structure, and purpose are similar.

Menander of Laodicea (third century A.D.)

In his treatise *Division of Epideictic Speeches*, Menander classifies epideictic speeches, which fall under the two headings of blame and praise, into twenty-three different and more detailed kinds of speeches. Among them, because of our concern for funeral orations, there are three categories related to this:

(i) The imperial oration (βασιλικος λογος), an encomium of the emperor, (ii) The consolatory speech (πάραμυθητικος), (iii) Funeral orations (επιταφιὸς).

(i) The Imperial Oration (βασιλικος λογος)

This oration consists of the three sections of prooemia (exordium/introduction), encomium/epainos, and conclusion with prayer. Prooemia

---

7. Bitzer, "Rhetorical Situation," 6.

begins with amplification; "it is hard to match" (368). After the prooemia, it is necessary to come to the encomium in this order: native country, family, birth with any divine sign (that may have occurred at the time of his birth), nature, nurture and education, accomplishmenst (qualities of character), actions in times of peace and times of war, putting war first with an emphasis on the four virtues (courage, justice, temperance, and wisdom) (369–376), fortune, and the most complete comparison of preceding reigns (377). The oration ends with a prayer beseeching God (377).

(ii) The Consolatory Speech (πάραμυθητικος λογος)

The consolatory speech has a different function from that of funeral oration but contains some similarities in content and structure. Regarding its own function, it says as follows (413.5–13):

> The speaker of a consolatory speech himself also laments and raises the misfortune to great significance, amplifying the emotion as best he can in his speech by means of the topics . . . in connection with the monody . . . the encomiastic headings (origin, nature, nurture, education, accomplishments, actions). It will not, however, preserve the sequence of the encomia, because the speaker gives the impression of being out of his mind and distracted by emotion.

Thus, the main function of this speech is emotional lamentation for the dead and, in part, the emotional consolation of the living. It is claimed that "you should divide the encomia, as has been said, into the three chronological sections," as well as various opportunities to include narratives (413.14–15; 414.7). First, the speech should express and amplify the lamentation by saying that "he was young and died prematurely, not as one would pray" (413.15–20). Second, the speaker should approach the second part of his speech, which is the consolatory part, in the following fashion: "Let me say to those of you who are parents that I am surprised it has not occurred to you to think of the words of that excellent poet Euripides . . . the dead, from trouble, relieved, we should with joy and praises hence, escort from home" (413.24–30). Third, it is necessary to philosophize in the context of human nature, generally, how the divine power has condemned men to death, how death is the end of life for all men, and how even heroes and the children of gods have not escaped it (414.5–9). Then, after this, the speaker should add something like: "I feel convinced that he who has gone dwells in the Elysian Fields, where dwell Rhadamanthus and Menelaus, and the son of Peleus and Thetis, and Memnon . . . Let us therefore sing his praises as a hero, or rather bless him as a god, make paintings of him, placate him as a superhuman being" (414.17–28).

(iii) Funeral Speech (επιταφιὸς)

Menander defines funeral speech in Athens as the speech delivered each year over those who fell in the wars. It is so called because it is spoken over the actual grave (418.5–10). He asserts that "the sophist composed orations such as would have been delivered by the polemarch, to whom this privilege is assigned at Athens. But because of the passage of time, it has come to be predominantly an encomium" (418.11–15). There is, however, another case of Thucydides who, "writing a funeral speech for those who fell at Rheitoi at the beginning of the Peloponnesian War, did not simply pronounce an encomium on the men, but made the point that they were capable of meeting death; he was cautious, however, of the topic of lamentation because of the needs of the war—it was not the orator's business (to cause) to weep those whom he was exhorting to fight. He also added the consolatory topic" (418.16–25).

Menander claims that the funeral speech delivered long after the event is a pure encomium, but "if such a speech is delivered not after a long interval, it is right to make it an encomium, but there is nothing to prevent the use of the consolatory heading at the end" (419.1–10). In the case of the emotional funeral speech, the speech should be divided according to the headings of encomia, the emotion being combined with each heading.

First, the speech should contain lamentation/exordium over the family as follows (419.10—420.5):

> Oh, how shall I share the family's grief at what has befallen? Oh, where shall I begin my lamentations?. . .You should then say that the family is a brilliant one, more splendidly glorious than any in the city: "The dead man was, as it were, a shining torch lit in that family . . . None of the various sections of the speech should be without an element of lamentation (419.20) . . . "But alas, alas! Now he has been snatched away." You should develop the other encomiastic headings in a similar way, though at the same time amplifying the lamentation . . . The expression of the lamentation must be developed in full . . . Let the encomia be your raw material for the lamentation. (420.5–9)

Second, the encomium expounds upon all the encomiastic topics (420.10—421.15):

> You should base your encomium on all the encomiastic topics: family, birth, nature, nurture, education, accomplishments. You

> should divide 'nature' into two—physical beauty and mental endowment. You should then confirm this by means of the three succeeding headings, nurture . . . education . . . and accomplishments. The most important section of an encomium, however, is that of actions, which should be placed after accomplishments (420.25) . . . After 'action' you should put in the topic of Fortune . . . wealth, happiness of children, love of friends, honor from emperors (420.30) . . . Following all this, you should put in comparisons relating to the whole subject, treating them as a separate head, but not abstaining from any comparison relating to an individual heading which it is necessary to add for the purposes of that heading. At this point you should openly take up a comparison relating to the whole subject (421.1–5)[8] . . . 'he of whom we are speaking is to be nobler than the noble or fit to rival any man of distinction—for example by comparing his life with that of Heracles or Theseus. (421.10–14) After this, insert the lamentation again as a separate section . . . Give it a special treatment . . . exciting pity and making the hearers dissolve in tears. (421.15)

Third, the speaker should include consolation and exhortation to the living (421.16–30):

> Following this section, insert the section of consolation to the whole family. 'No need to lament; he is sharing the community of the gods, or dwells in the Elysian Fields.' Divide the thoughts of these sections as follows: a separate address to the children, a separate address to the wife, first giving greater dignity to her personality, to avoid giving the impression of addressing a humble or mean person (421.20–24) . . . If the children are very young, you should deliver a speech of advice rather than of consolation, for they do not feel what has happened. Or rather, you should add to the consolation a measure of advice and counsel to the wife and children, if the children are very young; to the wife, to copy the good women of old and heroines; to the children to copy their father's virtues.

Fourth, the speech contains peroration and prayer (422); "Next praise the family for not having neglected the funeral or the preparation of the memorial. Finally, round off the speech with a prayer, asking the gods for the greatest blessings for them" (422.2–5).

Among the extant classical funeral orations at Athens, the most general and complete description of the function and content of a funeral

---

8. Quintilian, *Inst.* III.7.16.

oration may be Plato's *Menexenus* (236e); "And the speech required is one which will adequately eulogize the dead (encomium/epainos) and give kindly exhortation to the living, appealing to their children and their brethren to copy the virtues of these heroes (exhortation to the living), and to their fathers and mothers and any still surviving ancestors offering consolation (consolation to the living)." Thus, the classical funeral oration generally consists of three primary components: encomium, exhortation to the living, and consolation of the living.

In summary, Menander's handbook of funeral oration has some different components from those of the classical funeral orations. First, Menander emphasizes the section of the lamentation in every corner (419.19–20; 420.5–9; 421.15), including the consolatory speech, which also expresses and amplifies the lamentation and the emotion as far as possible in his twenty three categories of epideictic speech. Second, though Menander depends on the classical funeral oration, he makes exceptions for Thucydides' *History of the Peloponnesian War* (418.15–20) and Isocrates's *Evagoras* (419.4). Third, Menander applies more especially to a private funeral than a public one.[9] Fourth, he lists the primary topoi of encomium in detail according to the *Progymnasmata* of Aphthonius (origin, upbringing, deeds—mind, body, and fortune, comparison, epilogue with a prayer), including various opportunities to describe narratives.

In this sense, according to Meander's epideictic oration, whose important members are funeral and consolatory orations, it is probable Paul would employ common topoi of funeral oration in 1 Thess. For example: (1) Paul describes the *narratio* section with encomium in chronological order (1 Thess 1–3); (2) Paul, in his consolation to the living, claims the blessed state of the bereaved with the parousia of Christ (1 Thess 4:13—5:10), which is similar to the description of the dwelling with the gods; (3) Paul shows the wish with his prayer (1 Thess 3:11–13; 5:23–24).[10]

Pseudo-Dionysius (*On Epideictic Speeches*)

When compared with Menander, categorizing the epideictic speeches into twenty three kinds, Pseudo-Dionysius classifies epideictic speeches with only seven categories.[11] Pseudo-Dionysius begins with the inevitability of

---

9. Burgess, "Epideictic Literature," 148.

10. Witherington, *1 and 2 Thessalonians*, 107; Hughes, "Rhetoric of 1 Thessalonians," 107.

11. He lists seven epideictic speeches: (1) panegyrics, (2) procedure for marriage speeches, (3) procedure for birthday speeches, (4) procedure for the bridal-chamber

human death and funeral oration; "Nothing is certain, save that, once born, one must die, and one may not in life walk apart from trouble" (277).

Pseudo-Dionysius classifies funeral oration into both public ("the whole city and people and is spoken over the war-dead") and private funeral oration (277–78). Pseudo-Dionysius defines funeral oration as "a praise of the departed," (278) and thus concludes that "this being so, it is clear that it must be based on the same topics as encomia, viz. country, family, nature, upbringing, actions" (278).

First, comes the encomium to the dead (278–80):

> In saying of the subject's native land that it is great, famous, and old, or (maybe) the first land that came to men . . . We may indeed have something to repeat . . . 'divine' . . . When speaking of the war dead one can be lavish with these things (278–79) . . . We should proceed straight to ancestors : were they autochthonous and not incomers? (279) . . . Coming then to upbringing, in the public speeches we shall consider the form of polity—democracy of aristocracy—while in the private speeches we shall look at upbringing, education, and accomplishments. Among actions, the public speech will include deeds of war and how they died, as was done by Plato, Thucydides, and the other. On the other hand, when we speak of an individual, we shall discuss his virtue—e.g. courage, justice, wisdom.

Second, one must give the consolation and exhortation to the living (280–83)

> After this, in public speech we shall make the transition to the exhortatory part, exhorting the survivors to like deeds. This is an extensive topic. We proceed then to the consolation of the parents, both those still capable of producing children, and those past the age. This also is in Thucydides (280). In private speeches, on the other hand, we sometimes do not even include the exhortatory section . . . if the funeral speech deals with a governor or similar personality, his children should be urged to imitate their parents and aim at similar goals (280).

> The consolatory topic, however, is more essential, because we are consoling the relatives . . . We must not mourn or bewail the dead—this would not be to comfort the survivors but to increase their sorrow, and the speech would appear not to be a praise of the deceased but a lamentation, based on their

---

speech, (5) procedure for addresses, (6) procedure for funeral speeches, and (7) exhortation to athletes.

dreadful fate—but only, in the course of the consolation, give way to the survivors in their feelings, and not resist too sternly; we shall win them over more easily like this, and the speech will also contain an element of praise . . . However, since those who fall in war are alike in age . . . by saying that they died honorably for their country, and such a death is swift and not felt, and they are removed from tortures and the evils of disease; moreover they have a public burial—this is enviable also to their posterity—and their glory is undying (281).

In the case of individual, the speech will have many opportunities for consolation, arising out of the circumstances and ages of the deceased. (i) If a man dies suddenly and painlessly . . . If he dies of illness . . . if in war, 'he died fighting for his country' . . . (ii) Age: if he dies young, 'the gods loved him—for they love such—and they snatched away many of the heroes of old—not wishing them to be involved in the troubles here on earth or have their soul long buried in the body as in a tomb or prison, or be slaves to evil masters, but wishing rather to free them . . . If he has died in middle age, 'he was at the prime of his life and mental powers . . . but in his prime.' If a man has died in old age (282) . . . At the end, it is essential to speak of the immortality of the soul, and to say that it is reasonable to suppose that such men are better off, because they are among the gods (283).

Third, the style of funeral oration "should be varied, periodic in the argumentative parts, elevated and grand . . . which possess splendor and grandeur."(283)

In summary, Pseudo-Dionysius's handbook of funeral oration, when compared with Menander's, contains both similarities and differences in function and content. First, while Menander focuses on private funeral oration in his book, Pseudo-Dionysius clearly divides funeral oration into both public (in war) and private (in peace) funeral orations. Further, Menander places the public funeral oration at the beginning of every part and emphasizes its use in detail. Particularly, he refers to the classical public funeral orations of Lysias (*Funeral Oration*), Hyperides (*Funeral Speech*), Demosthenes (*Funeral Speech*), and Plato (*Menexenus*). Thus, Menander's dependence upon and relationship with the public funeral oration at Athens is shown in describing the pattern of funeral oration in his book. Second, regarding the exhortatory section after the encomium, Pseudo-Dionysius considers this "an extensive topic," on that in private speeches could be omitted. Third, Pseudo-Dionysius does not deal with epilogue and prayer, even when dealing with encomium in detail; "it is clear that it (the *epitaphios*) must be based on the same topics as encomia" (278).

Fourth, the consolatory topic is most essential, but lamentation should be removed from or minimized in these circumstances. This is the main difference between Pseudo-Dionysius and Menander concerning funeral oration. Pseudo-Dionysius clearly points out the consolatory aspect by saying, "We must not mourn or bewail the dead—this would not be to comfort the survivors but to increase their sorrow, and the speech would appear not to be a praise of the deceased but a lamentation" (281). Menander, however, urges the speaker to insert the lamentation in every corner by saying "you should develop the other encomiastic headings . . . though at the same time amplifying the lamentation (420.5) . . . After this (comparison), insert the lamentation again as a separate section . . . exciting pity and making the hearers dissolve in tears" (421.15). Actually, among the extant classical funeral orations, Gorgias, Thucydides, Plato, Demosthenes, and Hyperides omit the lamentation in their orations. Only Lysias inserts the lamentation.

Regarding this problem, Ziolkowski correctly asks this question: "for what purpose is this (combining lamentation and consolation or inserting lamentation) done?" saying:[12]

> Clearly, it is to make the consolation more effective by advancing certain "arguments" of the threnos, and then counteracting them with arguments of consolation. In this way, the suffering of the audience is not ignored, and in fact, by its recognition the consolation become more convincing. This is the significance of the "blending" of threnos and paramythia . . . The threnic phrases, on the contrary, have a subordinate and concessive effect rather than an independent and positive one. A sentence from Demosthenes (36) . . .
>
> The first half of this sentence is characteristic of a threnos . . . but the second half emphasizes the positive aspect and thus relieves the sorrow, which would be sustained in a proper threnos. This emphasis on encouragement and optimism in Demosthenes marks the section as a consolation. The mere presence of threnic phrases and commonplaces, therefore, does not necessarily indicate a threnos . . . It would be reasonable to conclude then, on the basis of the actual evidence of the speeches, the outline of Plato's Menexenus, the observations of Pseudo-Dionysius, and historical considerations, that in the classical period, at least, funeral orations normally consisted of praise of the dead and consolation of the living (by exhortation, advice and comfort).

---

12. Ziolkowski, *Thucydides*, 49–50.

In this sense, Paul, employing the motif of funeral oration in 1 Thess, denies the lamentation for the dead (4:13) and rather emphasizes the consolation and exhortation in length and in detail (4:14—5:11) in order to urge the audience to be confident in the consolation and the promise of Christ's parousia.

Polybius (*The Histories* VI. 52–54)

Polybius, when comparing Romans with Phoenicians and Africans, highlights the Romans' funeral rites and funeral orations for those who died in battle by saying, "Now not only do Italians . . . excel . . . personal courage, but by their institutions also they do much to foster a spirit of bravery in the young men. A single instance will suffice to indicate the pains taken by the state to turn out men . . . in order to gain a reputation in their country for valor" (VI. 52.10-11).

First, on the occasion of a private funeral ceremony, he is carried to his funeral into the forum (so-called rostra), then a grown son discourses on the virtues and successful achievements of the dead (VI. 53.1-2). Through this process, the multitude, "when the facts are recalled to their minds and brought before their eyes," (VI. 53.3) are moved to sympathy for the dead. Next, after the burial, they place the image of the departed in the house, a mask reproduced with remarkable fidelity to both the features and complexion of the deceased (VI. 53.4-5).

Second, on the occasion of public sacrifices, Romans display these images. When any distinguished member of the family dies, they take them to the funeral, putting them on men who seem to them to bear the closest resemblance to the original in stature. During the parade of the dead, these representatives are embroidered with gold as if the deceased had celebrated a triumph or achieved something similar. They all ride in chariots preceded by some insignia and dignity of the offices of state held by each during his life (VI. 53.8). At the rostra, they all seat themselves in a row on ivory chairs. Through the display of these images, "who would not be inspired by the sight of the images of men renowned for their excellence, all together and as if alive and breathing?" (VI. 53.10). When there is a funeral oration at the rostra (Encomium), he who makes the oration over the man about to be buried praises the dead in his deeds, then praises "the successes and exploits of the rest whose images are present, beginning from the most ancient" (VI. 54.1). The orator then gives consolation and exhortation to the living (VI. 54.2-5):

> By this means, by this constant renewal of the good report of brave men, the celebrity of those who performed noble deeds is rendered *immortal* . . . *a heritage for future generations*. But the most important result is that young men are thus inspired to endure every suffering for the public welfare in the hope of winning the glory that attends on brave men . . . many Romans have voluntarily engaged in single combat . . . setting a higher value on the interest of their country than on the ties of nature . . .

Polybius describes the characteristic of the *laudatio funebris* of the Romans as having three basic elements: (1) the visible and triumphal parade of the features of ancestors and the dead, (2) the funeral oration with encomium of ancestors and the dead, (3) the consolation and exhortation to the living, especially the young people and future generations.

Dionysius of Halicarnassus (*Roman Antiquities* 5.16.1—17.6)

Regarding the *laudatio funebris* of the Romans, Dionysius describes the death of Brutus in the war (5.16) and shows the process of a public funeral rite and public funeral oration.

First, one sees the triumphal parade of the dead (5.17.1-2):

> The bravest of the knights took up the body of Brutus and with many praises and tears bore it back to Rome, adorned with crowns in token of his superior valor . . . the consul triumphed according to the custom followed by the kings when they conducted the trophy-bearing processions and the sacrifices . . . and gave a banquet to the most distinguished of the citizens.

Second, someone gives the public funeral oration (5.17.3-6), (i) placing the body of the dead at the rostra. "But on the next day he [Valerius] arrayed himself in dark clothing, and placing the body of Brutus, suitably adorned, upon a magnificent bier in the Forum, he called the people together in assembly, and advancing to the tribunal." (ii) One gives the funeral oration; "[He] delivered the funeral oration in his honor . . . that it was an ancient custom instituted by the Romans to celebrate the virtues of illustrious men at their funeral" (5.17.3).

Third, the origin of funeral oration comes from the Romans (5.17.4-6), as Dionysius argues when he says, "yet none of them [the Greeks] makes any mention of eulogies spoken over the deceased except the tragic poets at Athens . . . But even the affair at Marathon . . . the eulogies delivered in honor of the deceased really began with that occasion—was later than the funeral of Brutus by sixteen years" (5.17.4–5).

Further, Dionysius asserts that the difference of funeral orations between the Romans and the Athenians is as follows (5.17.5–6):

> ... whereas the Athenians seem to have ordained that these orations should be pronounced at the funerals of those only who have died in war, believing that one should determine who are good men solely on the basis of the valor they show at their death ... the Romans, on the other hand, appointed this honor to be paid to all their illustrious men, whether as commanders in war or as leaders in the civil administration they have given wise counsels and performed noble deeds, and this not alone to those who have died in war, but also to those who have met their end in any manner whatsoever, believing that good men deserve praise for every virtue they have shown during their lives and not solely for the single glory of their death.

Thus, Dionysius summarizes the characteristics of Roman funeral orations as follows: (1) the triumphal parade of the dead, (2) funeral oration with encomium of virtue to the dead, (3) the broader extent of Roman funeral orations (private and public) versus Athenian funeral orations (only public).

In conclusion, it is likely Paul was exposed to the tradition set by the prominent figures of funeral orations, whether through participation in the culture or through education, (the Athenian funeral orators—Isocrates, Thucydides, Pseudo-Lysias, Plato, Demosthenes, Gorgias, and Hyperides; the Roman funeral orators—Tacitus, Dio Cassius, Libanius, and Dio Chrysostom; Jewish funeral oration—4 Maccabees), by the consolatory letters (Plutarch, Cicero, Pliny the Younger, Seneca, Galen, St. Basil, and Symmachus), or by the rhetorical handbooks (Aristotle, Cicero, Quintilian, Menander of Laodicea, Pseudo-Dionysius, Polybius, and Dionysius of Halicarnassus). All these precedents show the existence of the funeral oration genre and the power of well-arranged strategy. The next two chapters (ch. 5—6) will demonstrate how closely 1 Thess conforms to the funeral orations in terms of structure, function, and rhetorical topoi and how much 1 Thess is indebted to funeral oratory in terms of rhetorical language, exigency, and content.

CHAPTER 6

Comparing 1 Thessalonians 1–3 and Funeral Oratory

THIS CHAPTER WILL ATTEMPT to determine the parallels and similarities between 1 Thess 1–3 and the exordium and narratio of funeral orations. Just as examined previously, the extant funeral orations and the consolatory letters in the Greco-Roman era fall chiefly under four headings in this order: (1) Exordium, (2) Encomium, (3) Consolation-Exhortation, and (4) Peroration. 1 Thessalonians displays a rhetorical exigency and strategy similar to the Greco-Roman funeral orations. Particularly, Greco-Roman funeral orations (Athenian funeral orations and the Roman *laudatio funebris*) have a primary purpose of unifying the Athenian and Roman communities, identifying with the audience, and consoling and exhorting the living and younger generations. Thus, most Greco-Roman funeral orations contain the lengthy portions of encomium which have the same function as the narratio in the whole rhetorical discourse.[1] Both encomium and the narratio have the similar function of showing the character of the deceased and preparing the audience for the exhortation. As in Ephesians, which bears obvious characteristics of epideictic speech[2] and, in the *narration*, attempts to persuade the audience to move on to the behavioral goals the *exhortatio* describes,[3] Paul builds a paraclectic model in 1 Thess 1—3 (the long *nar-*

---

1. Generally, each encomium of funeral orations form 4/5 in portion: Isocrates (*Evagoras*, 9.12–69; *Panegyricus*, 15–159); Thucydides (*History of the Peloponnesian War*, XXXVI–XLII); Pseudo-Lysias (*Funeral Oration*, 3–70); Plato (*Menexenus*, 237b-246b); Demosthenes (*Funeral Speech*, 4–31); Hyperides (*Oration*, 6–40); Tacitus (*Agricola*, 4–42); Dio Cassius (*Tiberius' Funeral Oration for Augustus*, 36–41); Libanius (*Funeral Oration over Julian*, 18.7–280); Dio Chrysostom (*Melancomas*, 29.3–18); Lucretius Vespillo (*Laudatio Turiae*, 1–53); Jewish Funeral Oration (4 Macc. 3:19—17:6).

2. Jeal, *Integrating Theology and Ethics in Ephesians*, 43. He claims, since it offers quite lengthy and ornamented praise of God in chapters 1–3. Also, chapters 1–3 capture the attention and sympathy of the audience by describing their situation and status in Christ (2:1–10, 11–22).

3. Jeal, *Integrating Theology and Ethics in Ephesians*, 73.

ratio) to achieve rapport/identification with the audience and to prepare a good relationship for the following eschatological exhortation in 1 Thess 4–5. Hence, there are elements of encomium for the Thessalonian church, the martyred believers, and Paul himself (1 Thess 1–3), which conform to the exordium and narratio of funeral orations.

Discernible Disposition

Scholars have long debated the arrangement of 1 Thess. Robert Jewett offers a representative example of the views of some scholars.[4] Each of them has a unique analysis of 1 Thess. Frank Hughes labels 5:4–11 as a *peroratio* containing the exhortations with the metaphor of "light and darkness." Robert Jewett notes Paul's thanksgivings and calls 1:6—3:13 a "*narratio* of grounds for thanksgiving" (2:13 "Reiteration of thanksgiving"; 3:9–10 "Pauline thanksgiving and intercession") without *partitio*.

George Kennedy uniquely puts 2:1–8 before the *narratio* (2:9—3:13) with a title of "refutation of charges", and he labels 4:1—5:22 as a "general proposition, injunctions." Concerning this arrangement, Kennedy observes that the presence of narrative in chapters 2–3 cannot be considered a sign of judicial rhetoric, but rather as part of Paul's efforts to establish his ethos. In order to cope with the criticism in Thessalonica and his distance from the community, Paul employs 2:1–8 as a refutation of charges against himself, anticipating objections to his authority.[5] Consequently, Kennedy considers 1 Thess as basically deliberative, an exhortation to stand fast in the Lord (3:8) with specific advice for Christian life.[6]

My analysis of 1 Thess resulting from my employment of Greco-Roman funeral oration, as stated previously, exhibits the following arrangement:

I   Epistolary Prescript (1:1)

II *Exordium* (1:2–3)[7]—Reasons for thanks and obtaining the good will of the audience (exaltation)

---

4. Jewett, *Thessalonian Correspondence*, 221.
5. Kennedy, *New Testament Interpretation*, 142.
6. Kennedy, *New Testament Interpretation*, 142.
7. The problem with 1:4 is that it continues from 1:3 because 1:4 begins with a participle with cause (εἰδότες, ἀδελφοὶ ἠγαπημένοι ὑπὸ [τοῦ] Θεοῦ) as 1:3 begins with a participle with cause (μνημονεύοντες ὑμῶν τοῦ ἔργου τῆς πίστεως). Thus, grammatically, it seems to be reasonable to see the *narratio* (encomium) begins with 1:5 since it begins with "For" (ὅτι). The sentence structure seems to remain intact with this. And perhaps Paul can change the form or have a bad sentence that moves from one section to another. It is, however, probable to assert the *narratio* (encomium) begins with 1:4

III *Encomium* (*Narratio*, 1:4–3:10)—Praise of the ancestors and contemporaries

　A. 1:4–10 (Paul going to them and their imitation of Paul and Christ in suffering)

　B. 2:1–12 (Paul's ethos and his example of suffering among them)

　C. 2:13–16 (Amplification within the *Narratio*/Imitation of Judean Christians)[8]

　D. 2:17–20 (Sub-concluding section)

　E. 3:1–10 (Paul's sending of Timothy and the result of his visit)

IV *Partitio* (3:11–13) with a Prayer Pattern (*Transitus*)

V Consolation and Exhortation of Funeral Oration (4:1—5:22)

　A. 4:1–8 (Ethical exhortation/"the will of God, sanctification")

　B. 4:9–12 (Love of brothers and sisters)

　C. 4:13–18 (Exhortation concerning the Parousia/Imperial Funeral Oration Motifs)

　D. 5:1–11 (Eschatological exhortation/Imperial Funeral Oration Motifs)

　E. 5:12–22 (General Exhortation)

VI *Peroratio* and Epistolary Closing (5:23–28)

The *Exordium* (1:2–3)

According to the classical rhetoricians, particularly Quintilian (*Inst.* 4.1.5): "The sole purpose of the exordium is to prepare our audience in such a way that they will be disposed to lend a ready ear to the rest of our speech." In

---

because 1:4 begins with a disclosure formula, "For we know" (Quintilian, *Inst.* 4.2.22). From the perspective of rhetorical approach, the purpose of the *statement of facts* is not merely to instruct, but rather to persuade with some remarks: "I know that . . . " "You remember . . . " and "You are not ignorant . . . "

8. Smith, *Comfort One Another*, 79–80. In this section, Smith persuasively claims that in between the two surrounding subunits about the congregation's *ethos*, then, 2:1–12 is essentially a digressionary panegyric about the missionaries. He suggests the three subunits form a ring composition, maybe *inclusio*, with the following pattern:

　A: Laudation of the Thessalonians' mimetic endurance (1:6–10)

　B: The Missionaries' perseverance and noble intentions (2:1–12)

　A': Laudation of the Thessalonians' mimetic endurance (2:13–16)

other words, the main purpose of the *exordium* is to gain the good will of the audience (*captatio benevolentiae*). The content of the *exordium* consists of two elements: *prooemium* and *insinuatio*. Cicero (*De Inv.* 1.16.22–23) lists that, in order to get the good will of the audience, one may draw from four quarters: from one's own person (*Ab nostra persona*), from the person of the opponents (*Ab adversariorum persona*), from the persons of the jury (*Ab iudicum persona*), and from the case (*A causa*). In the case of the epideictic oratory, dealing with praise and blame, "if we refer to our own acts and service without arrogance . . . if we dilate on the misfortunes which have befallen us or the difficulties which still beset us; if we use prayers and entreaties with a humble and submissive spirit," these shall win good will from our own person (1.16.22). Point of fact, we must praise ourselves, praise our party, and present ourselves and our party as deserving of all human sympathy.[9] Additionally, if we pretend to be unprepared and incapable of speech, it shall also be helpful (Quintilian, *Inst.* 4.1.9). In a sense, the *Insinuatio* can be used as a special implementation of the *exordium*. *Insinuatio* plays an important role in having the favorable influence upon the audience's subconscious through the cunning use of psychological devices, thereby, slowly preparing the ground for winning sympathy. It also functions as the emotional devices of *benevolentia*.[10] Finally, in order to gain the good will of the audience and to make the listener responsive, the speaker enumerates the points that will be dealt with in the next part of his speech.[11]

How does Paul set up the audience for these purposes of *exordium* in 1:2–3?

First of all, Paul achieves audience responsiveness by saying a thanksgiving prayer, particularly by giving thanks to God. Through giving thanks to God in prayer, Paul obtains the personal good will of the audience and sets them before God as Father (1:2). Just as Cicero comments, "if we use prayers and entreaties with a humble and submissive spirit (1.16.22)," With a thanksgiving prayer to God, Paul gains the good will of the audience.

Second, by insinuating and foreshadowing the following topics of a "work of faith, labor of love, and steadfastness of hope" (3), Paul not only comments on these topics generally but prepares the minds of his audience to consider these topics as important matters in themselves. Cicero (*Inv.* 1.23–25) additionally comments about the *exordium*, "We shall make our audience attentive if we show that the matters which we are about to discuss

---

9. Lausberg, *Handbook of Literary Rhetoric*, 129.

10. Lausberg, *Handbook of Literary Rhetoric*, 132–33. *Captatio benevolentiae* ("fishing for goodwill") is used on Acts 24:2–8, 10b.

11. Aune, *Westminster Dictionary*, 176.

are important . . . We shall make the auditors receptive if we explain the essence of the case briefly and in plain language. . ." These elements give conviction to the speech and authrority to the speaker.

In the *partitio* (*transitus*) of 3:11–13 and *consolation/exhortation* of 4:1—5:22, the three topics of 1:2–3 (work of faith/holiness, labor of love, and steadfastness of hope) correlate thematically, and Paul clarifies and recommends these more and more.

> 3:12–13—" . . . in *love* for one another . . . your hearts in *holiness* that you may be *blameless* . . . at *the coming of our Lord Jesus* . . . "
>
> 4:3–4—" . . . the will of God, your *sanctification* . . . how to control your own body in *holiness* and honor . . . "
>
> 4:9–12—" . . . *love* of the brothers . . . taught by God to *love* . . . to do so more and more . . . "
>
> 4:13–18—". . .For the Lord himself . . . and so we will be with the Lord . . . "
>
> 5:1–11—" . . . who have no *hope* . . . Therefore encourage one another with *these words*."

Regarding the words "work of faith," on the basis of Gal 5:6, "the only thing that counts is faith working through love," and "work of faith" seems to be equal to "love" for Paul. Particularly, the word "steadfastness" of hope (τῆς ὑπομονῆς τῆς ἐλπίδος) is commonly used in the New Testament to mean the sufferings and persecutions met by Christians (Rom 5:3, ὅτι ἡ θλῖψις ὑπομονὴν κατεργάζεται; 12:12, τῇ θλίψει ὑπομένοντες; 2 Cor 6:4, ἐν ὑπομονῇ πολλῇ, ἐν θλίψεσιν; 2 Thess. 1:4, ὑπὲρ τῆς ὑπομονῆς ὑμῶν καὶ πίστεως ; 1 Pet 2:20, κολαφιζόμενοι ὑπομενεῖτε), especially in an eschatological context (Rom 8:25; 2 Cor 1:6; Mark 13:13). In fact, Paul concludes with the words of the eschatological hope of the parousia (1:10; 2:16, 19; 3:13; 4:13—5:11). Therefore, it is plausible to assert that Paul sets the eschatological context in his whole discourse from the *exordium*. In summary, the *exordium* is given as a preview of the main topics (arguments), which occurs in1:2–3.

Third, Paul's *exordium* shows the same characteristics of a funeral oration, though not the same patterns as the *exordium* of a funeral oration. Generally, the common *topoi* of a funeral oration's *exordium* consist of a precautionary statement of the difficulty of praising the dead adequately, an inability to match the deeds of the dead, and the praise of the audience in order to gain their sympathy. The *topoi*, however, depend on the circumstances and intention of the speaker. For example, contrary to other funeral orators, Hyperides (*Funeral Speech*, 2) briefly expresses his inability to speak and then focuses on the praise of the audience in order to receive their good will. In a similar context, Paul also praises the deeds and spiritual status of the audience to gain their good will (1:2–3). Thus, Paul employs a common epideictic theme to achieve a favorable relationship. Further, in 1 Thess 3:9, "How can we thank God enough for you in return for all the joy that we feel before our God because of you?" Paul expresses his inability to match their works with his speech. Indeed, Paul's *exordium* in 1:2–3 conforms to various general *topoi* of the *exordium* of epideictic oratory, including funeral oration.

The *Narratio* (*Encomium*, 1:4—3:10)

The Identity and Exigency of the Long *Narratio*

First Thessalonians displays some unique characteristics when compared with other Pauline letters. These include a repetitious reminder of Paul's first work at Thessalonica,[12] employment of collective pronouns instead of any personal or specific names,[13] and a lack of direct Old Testament quotations.[14] Most of all, 1 Thess contains the longest *narratio* (1:4—3:10) of all the Pauline letters.

Aelius Theon (*Prog.* 5.4–11) argues that narrative is a language describing things that have happened or are imagined to have happened. Consequently, there are six elements necessary to any narrative: the person, the action, the place, the time, the manner of the action, and the cause of these things (Quintilian, *Inst.* 4.2.36).[15] In the same way, Quintilian (*Inst.* 4.2.52)

12. Lührmann, "Beginnings of the Church at Thessalonica," 241. He claims that Paul refers to what they can "remember" (2:9), what they "know" (1:5; 2:1, 2, 5, 11; 3:3, 4; 4:2, 4, 5), what he had "told them beforehand" (3:4; 4:6), what they had "received" (2:13; 4:1), and what his "instructions" had been (4:2, 11). He reminded them of "the afflictions" they had to endure (1:6; 2:14; 3:3–4), and above all, again and again, he refers to his initial preaching and to their response to it (1:5, 9; 2:1, 9–12; 3:3–4; 4:1–6, 10–12).

13. Instead, Paul uses the first and second plural pronouns such as "we" (1:2, 4, 8–9; 2:1–8, 13, 17, 19–20; 3:1–3, 8–10; 4:1, 13; 5:12) and "you" (1:3, 5–8, 2:1, 5, 9–11, 14; 4:13) for the purpose of identification. Particularly, in 2:19–20, Paul highlights his identification (we) with the Thessalonian community (you) by saying, "For what is our hope . . . Is it not you? Yes, you are our glory and joy."

14. Lührmann, "Beginnings of the Church at Thessalonica," 293; Johnson, "Paul's Reliance on Scripture in 1 Thessalonians," 1. She claims that although Paul sometimes employs what seems to be recognizable biblical language and some phrases which echo the Bible in Thessalonians, nowhere does Paul directly quote Scripture as he does in other letters.

15. Kennedy, *Progymnasmata*, 28.

adds that the statement of fact (the *narratio*) will be credible in three ways: (a) "if we take care to say nothing contrary to nature"; (b) "if we assign reasons and motives for the facts on which the inquiry turns"; and (c) "if we make the characters of the actors in keeping with the facts we desire to be believed." In this context, the facts, motives, and characters described in the *narratio* make clear to some extent the rhetorical situation or exigency that prompted and generated the discourse.[16] Therefore, the *narratio* is a full description, in detail, that prepares and influences the audience in the particular direction that the speaker intends to lead them.

In addition, the three necessary virtues of the *narratio* are "brevity/ brevis, clarity/perspicua, and plausibility/narratio verisimilis, probabilis" (Rhet.Her. 1.14 *ut brevis, ut dilucida, ut very similis sit*; Cic. *Inv.* 1.28 *ut brevis, ut aperta, ut probabilis sit*; Quint. *Inst.* 4.2.31 *lucidam, brevem, verisimilem*; Vict. 16 *brevis, perspicura, probabilis*). Ultimately, each of the three virtues is connected to the goal of achieving the audience's acceptance of the narrative (*docere*), and the final aim is to obtain *persuasio* (persuasion) of the narrative's veracity, which is accomplished through plausibility (*narratio verisimilis, probabilis*).[17]

The two other virtues (brevity and clarity) are means for achieving plausibility, which is part of the ultimate goal. John O'Banion correctly grasps the heart of *narratio* and claims all appeals, even logos, are dependent upon *narratio*. For him, through lucidity, brevity, and especially plausibility, which are the key qualities of the *narratio*, the *narratio* could succeed in the "generalship" of adapting general strategy to particular cases.[18] Therefore, concerning the primary function of *narratio*, the good and skillful preparation of *narratio* with clarity, brevity, and especially plausibility can effectively elevate the veracity of the speech. O'Banion correctly asserts that *narratio* functions as a primary mode of thought and as a key to the strategy of rhetoric in actual practice. In this sense, Paul's long *narratio* (1:4—3:10), full of detail and plausibility, complies with this function, that is, the preparation for the subsequent consolation and exhortation in the mind of the audience.

In the whole rhetorical discourse, Quintilian (*Inst.* 2.1.12) highlights and considers *narratio* as the heart of rhetorical thinking. To Quintilian (*Inst.* 2.4.30–31; 2.11.7), success in persuasion was obtained by the twin arts of *continua* (continuation) and *congruens* (congruency), because the right sentiments should spring from the context. Therefore, if the speakers do not devote their attention to the actual cases, but to their isolated thoughts, the

---

16. Witherington, *1 and 2 Thessalonians*, 25.
17. Lausberg, *Handbook of Literary Rhetoric*, 140–41.
18. O'Banion, "Narration and Argumentation," 345.

speeches lack cohesion and lead to disconnection from the subject.[19] In this sense, *narratio*, which contains the statement of facts and establishes the context of the whole rhetorical discourse, reflects the urgent rhetorical exigency and intention of showing the probable facts leading toward the subsequent section of *probatio* or exhortation (consolation in funeral oration). Following it further, according to Quintilian, in order to create a powerful effect for the audience, the *narratio* should provide a "plausible picture of what occurred." Specifically, it is possible that, by being "plausible in imagination," "vehement in censure," and "vivid in description", the orator could make the "audience feel as if they were actual eyewitnesses of the scene" (4.2.123–24). Finally, the credit which accrues to the *statement of facts* comes from the authority of the speaker, and such authority derives from both "our manner of life" and "our style of eloquence" (4.2.125).[20] In the *narratio* of 1 Thess, Paul employs all of these elements and satisfies the rhetorical functions of the *narratio* throughout his whole rhetorical discourse.

At this juncture, it is worth noting that Quintilian (2.13.1–8) also suggests that the most important disposition of the orators is to show a wise adaptability to be able to meet the most varied emergencies, that is, to meet the rhetorical situation. Most rules in rhetoric are not rigid ones, but rather flexible and liable to be changed by the nature of the case and circumstances. The rhetorical situation allows the orator to decide whether to make the *exordium* necessary or superfluous, to lengthen or shorten the statement of facts, or to develop or omit other parts according to the circumstances of the case. The orators could employ and sometimes change the usual standards and rules depending on the rhetorical exigency and their own wise adaptability. The orators keep in mind the facts that highlight what is becoming and what is expedient.

Paul may have had knowledge and skill of "a wise adaptability" as a strategical rhetor, recommended by the rhetorical handbooks. Furthermore, he might have practiced this principle by adapting it to his letters through the lengthening, shortening, or omitting of some parts according to the rhetorical situations. In that case, what exigency and events would cause Paul to lengthen the *narratio* for the probability of the facts and for the preparation of the *probatio* or exhortation (consolation) in 1 Thess? Why does Paul break the rule of *brevitas* of the *narratio* and lengthen it (1:5—3:10)? Just as we examined above (chs. 2–3), the encomium (*narratio* section in funeral orations of both Athenians and Romans) usually takes the main and longest

---

19. O'Banion, "Narration and Argumentation," 335–36.
20. O'Banion, "Narration and Argumentation," 350.

part of the whole oratory.²¹ Regarding the function of the long part of the encomium (narration) in funeral orations, Ochs convincingly argues the functions and exigency of the *narratio* in funeral orations as follows:

> Cicero's pronouncement (*de Oratore*, 2.85.346) contains two clues—lack of reward and narrative form—to answer the question, "how does praise persuade?" An audience, attending to a funeral panegyric, must be made to hear a deficit . . . If a person is shown to have acted selflessly for the greater good of a collective, compensation is due. The collective, the beneficiary of the unrewarded and selfless act, is invited via the dynamic of laudation to repay, reward, or reciprocate in some way. This moral account is balanced when the audience, the affected collective, responds with admiration, esteem, heightened regard, and, possibly, a resolve to emulate. The deceased's act of selfless valor creates a moral debt on the collective, an obligation that requires fulfillment . . . In the case of a funeral, however, the hero is dead and a moral debt remains. The deceased cannot forgive the collective's liability; the collective cannot default because to do so jeopardizes the continuation of the collective itself . . . A second clue . . . "being narrated in a most eloquent style." *The funeral speech is not an argument, but a story; not reasons with proofs, but it is a dramatic form capable of containing plot, character, and actions.* Hearing a dramatic narrative, an audience is repositioned; that is, the message, in this case the panegyric, is not evaluated as are arguments or overt persuasive efforts . . . *Narratives by their very nature invite participation, acceptance, and, if artfully done, some degree of identification.* In a Roman funeral speech, then, as a part of the consolatory ritual, the narrative compliments the action and object languages whose rhetorical functions are designed to celebrate the life of the deceased and to reunite the community. It is not the deeds of the deceased that live on in the collective memory; instead, it is the virtues, the qualities of character reflected in the honored deeds of the deceased that live on.²²

Through the long encomium (narration) of funeral orations, the orators attempt to produce the continuation of the collective to the dead and to unite the community by causing identification between the dead and the community.

---

21. See notes 212 and 280 in the section of the rhetorical purpose and structure of both the Athenians' and the Romans' funeral orations.

22. Ochs, *Consolatory Rhetoric*, 108–9.

In this sense, the long *narratio* of 1 Thess reflects the similar structure, contents, and exigency of the encomium (the *narratio*) of funeral orations. There are some implications regarding the context of suffering (1:6; 2:2, 14–15; 3:3–4, 7), severe opposition from human adversaries (2:2, ἐν πολλῷ ἀγῶνι),[23] and the death of Thessalonian believers.[24] Further, it is noteworthy that in the Jewish funeral oration, 4 Maccabees, the word ἀγών ("contest," "fight a fight") is also employed to express the situation of the martyrs (12:11, 14; 13:13, 15; 16:16). In other words, Paul may employ the word ἀγών in 1 Thess 2:2 in a similar context. Between 1 Thess and the funeral oration, there is an overlapping rhetorical exigency and rhetorical purpose, that is, the suffering and death of the believers of Thessalonica, the continuation of the collective congregation to the dead, and unifying the community through their identification with the dead (rhetorical purpose).

Generally, the epideictic division always had a closer connection with deliberative than with legal oratory (Quint. *Inst.* 3.7.28; Arist. *Rhet.* 1.9.35)[25] because the same things that are usually praised are also advised.

Besides Isocrates, who was the epideictic orator *par excellence*, Gorgias suggests his own ideal form of rhetoric in *Panegyricus* 4: "I regard as the best speeches those which are on the greatest topics and which best display the speakers and profit the hearers."[26] Pursuing this further, his ideal form is a mixture of the deliberative and the epideictic, which deals with some theme of general interest that is elevated in style, preferably a speech of advice, to be treated in epideictic style.[27] Aelius Theon defines encomium as the language of revealing the greatness of virtuous actions and other good qualities, which belong to a particular person. Hermogenes comments on encomium that deeds are the most important, and the best source of

---

23. Bammel, "Preparation for the Perils of the Last Days," 100. Regarding the word ἀγῶνι, Bammel argues the context of martyrdom: "The situation is illustrated in the same verse from the viewpoint of the martyr by προπαθόντες, whereas the action of the persecutor is indicated by ὑβρισθέντες."

24. Donfried, "The Imperial Cults and Political Conflict," 222; Koester, "Imperial Ideology and Paul's Eschatology in 1 Thessalonians," 158–59; Witherington, *1 and 2 Thessalonians*, 139–40.

25. Burgess, "Epideictic Literature," 96.

26. Burgess, "Epideictic Literature," 101.

27. Burgess, "Epideictic Literature," 101–2. Gorgias, the founder of artistic prose, suggests the rhetorical devices to the epideictic literature: (1) amplification (Quintilian, *Inst.* 8.3.53); (2) brevity; (3) an answering of jest with earnest and earnest with jest; (4) teaching by example rather than by precept; (5) a style characterized by flowing expression, and rhythmic arrangement, startling figures of language, bold metaphor, and poetic epithets.

argument in encomia comes from "comparisons."[28] Further, the conclusion of encomium comes back to the hero, often with an enumeration of his qualities and deeds, ending with a prayer.[29]

In the *narratio* of 1 Thess (1:4—3:10), it is possible to find traces of epideictic rhetoric. Paul's praising of the Thessalonian believers' deeds of imitation of Paul and Christ (1:4-10; 2:13-16), the praising of his own deeds and ethos (2:1-12), Paul's exemplary care via Timothy (3:1-10), and the *partition* (3:11-13) with a prayer pattern showing the characteristic features of the *narratio* of epideictic rhetoric in 1 Thess. Most importantly, these characteristic features appear in the encomium (narration) of funeral orations. Further, the existence of the *narratio* of 1 Thess as the longest among Pauline letters shows the nature of funeral oration present in 1 Thessalonians. Funeral orations highlight *narratio* (encomium) with a lengthy section in proportion to the whole oration. The following section will attempt to show the characteristics of a funeral oration that reflect on the *narratio* in 1 Thess (1:4—3:10).

First Section of *Narratio* (1:4-10)

Paul shows the common *topoi* of *narratio* in various ways. First of all, Paul employs the appropriate words of a disclosure formula by beginning the *narratio*, "For we know . . . (εἰδότες)" (1:4). Quintilian (*Inst.* 4.2.22), emphasizing for the effect of the *statement of facts*, recommends the use of noetic expressions to prepare for the *narratio*. For example, it is effective to preface the statement with some remark such as "I know," "You remember," "You are not ignorant how this matter stands", and so on. At this moment, Paul's use of the disclosure formula with the employment of a noetic expression is appropriate in introducing narrative material according to rhetorical practice and theory.[30] Second, as described above in terms of the function of the *narratio* as a "language descriptive of things that have happened," Paul uses the past tense to describe the events, character, and deeds of the Thessalonian believers in chronological order as follows: (1:5-7, 9): "our message of the gospel came to you . . . we proved to be . . . you became <u>imitators</u> . . . in spite of persecution you <u>received</u> the word . . . you became an <u>example</u>" and "what kind of welcome we had . . . and <u>how you turned to God from idols</u>."

---

28. Kennedy, *Progymnasmata*, 50, 82.

29. Burgess, "Epideictic Literature," 130.

30. Long, *Ancient Rhetoric and Paul's Apology*, 152–53. He lists more examples in Pauline letters as follows: Gal 1:11; 1 Cor 10:1; 12:1; 2 Cor 8:1; Rom 1:13; 11:25; Phil 1:12; 1 Thess 4:13.

Quintilian (*Inst.* 3.7.15) says a narration in an epideictic rhetoric, which deals with the praise and blame of human beings, has sometimes proved the more effective course when it traces a man's life and deeds "in due chronological order." Besides, in epideictic rhetoric, the *narratio* functions "to reaffirm and remind the audience of what they already know to be true about themselves" (*Rhetorica ad Herennium* 1.8.12).[31] Through these reaffirming and reminding words, the orator could make the audience feel as if they were actual eyewitnesses of the scene described (Quint. *Inst.* 4.2.123–24). In 1 Thess, as epideictic rhetoric, Paul frequently and intentionally repeats the phrases, "just as you know," "you yourselves know," "as you know and as God is our witness," and "You are witnesses, and God also" (1:4, 5; 2:1, 2, 5, 9, 10, 11; 3:3, 4) in order to strengthen his intention and purpose through these vivid and eyewitnessing words in the *narratio*.

In the same way, in the encomium of funeral orations, there is usually praise of the ancestors, the dead, and also contemporaries in historical order. Further, the praises of physical endowments, external circumstances, character and deeds of the dead, and superiority through comparison are added here (Quint. *Inst.* 3.7.6–16). Both the Athenian and the Roman funeral orations contain these elements. Pseudo-Lysias develops the encomium chronologically from ancestors (3–9) to descendents (20–66) to the dead (67–70). Plato also praises the ancestors (their origin, mother-land, upbringing, and deeds) in the encomium, and Demosthenes praises the autochthony and deeds of the ancestors in war. Dio Cassius, Libanius, and Tacitus also contain in the encomium the praise of the ancestors and the dead in due chronological order. In comparison to others, they highlight the superiority of the ancestors and the dead over others. This element in the encomium is the same in the Jewish funeral oration.

Though the literal use of reminding languages is not always found in funeral orations, the words used still remind and reaffirm the deeds and character of the ancestors and the dead through the chronological praises. Through these lengthy and elaborate praises, the orators have intentions of preparing the mind of the audience so they might establish a sense of identification and continuity between the ancestors and the present community and live up to the ideals of their ancestors and the dead, particularly in the younger generation.

Hester, while correctly claiming the existence of the funeral oration in 1 Thess, categorizes 1 Thess 1:4–10 as *exordium*. This passage establishes the topics for amplification later in the letter as the epistolary function.

---

31. Witherington, *1 and 2 Thessalonians*, 25.

Hester asserts that, in this passage (1:4-10), there are no topics of a typical funeral oration.[32]

In the first section of *narratio* (1 Thess 1:4-10), however, there are some elements which reflect the funeral encomium of the Athenians and Romans. As Aphthonius the Sophist suggests, the primiary *topoi* of encomium, such as the person's origin, upbringing, deeds, and comparison, are the same elements in the Athenian and the Roman funeral orations. Plato, in the section of origin (γενος), praises the autochthony of the ancestors and the nurture of his mother-country (237b-246b). Tacitus also praises the ancestors, "a scion of the ancient and illustrious Roman colony of Forum Julii" (4). Particularly, when Caesar delivered the customary funeral oration from the rostra in honor of his aunt, Julia, and his wife, Cornelia, in the eulogy of his aunt, he spoke of her paternal and maternal ancestry reaching back to the immortal gods, specifically the goddess Venus.[33] In this case, a eulogy should contain the ancestor, the origin of their family, and the dead.[34] In fact, it should contain the divine origin of their ancestors and the dead.

Paul's encomium in 1 Thess contains elements similar to these of the encomiastic topics.

Firstly, in Thess 1:4 (εἰδότες, ἀδελφοὶ ἠγαπημένοι ὑπὸ [τοῦ] Θεοῦ, τὴν ἐκλογὴν ὑμῶν), Paul praises the Thessalonian believers in regard to their origin and ancestors. A. Malherbe correctly suggests that the use of ἀδελφοὶ in 1 Thess is much greater in number compared to Paul's other letters (e.g., ten times in Romans; twenty times in 1 Cor; three times in 2 Cor) and is an important part of the fictive kinship Paul develops in this letter.[35] Malherbe also argues that "kinship language" was used by other groups (for example, by mystery cults and philosophical schools), but Paul's notion was originated from Judaism, indicating "group identity or a loose sense of group kinship" (e.g., Dt. 15:3, 12; Philo, *Spec. Leg.* 2.79-80; Josephus, *Ant.* 10.201).[36] To be sure, Paul's calling to/praise of the Thessalonian believers as "beloved by God, that he has chosen you (τὴν ἐκλογὴν ὑμῶν)," through which he intended to evoke a strong sense of belonging to God,[37] indicates their divine origin and birth. According to Aristotle's definition (*Rhet.* II, 1390b, 15),

---

32. Hester, "Invention of 1 Thessalonians," 273.

33. Suetonius, *Iul.* 6.1; Suetonius, *Twelve Caesars*, 11.

34. Menander (420.10, 25) and Pseudo-Dionysius (278-79) claim in common that the encomium of funeral orations should expound all the encomiastic topics such as family, birth, nature, and accomplishments.

35. Malherbe, *Letters to the Thessalonians*, 109-10.

36. Malherbe, *Letters to the Thessalonians*, 110; Wanamaker, *Epistles to the Thessalonians*, 77.

37. Wanamaker, *Epistles to the Thessalonians*, 77.

"noble birth is a heritage of honor from one's ancestors." Just as previously discussed, the encomium of funeral oration has two chief themes: noble birth/origin and deeds. Birth/origin from God is supported by 1 Thess 1:5, "because our message . . . not in word only, but also in power and in the Holy Spirit and with full conviction."

Secondly, in vv. 6–10, Paul praises their deeds and character under past severe sufferings. Actually, in vv. 6–10, there are three main clauses (6–7, 8, 9–10) which describe their deeds and character with the aorist and the perfect tense (ἐγενήθητε, ἐξήχηται, ἐξελήλυθεν, ἔσχομεν, ἐπεστρέψατε) in the historical order.[38] This phenomenon is the same for the funeral orations of Pseudo-Lysias, Plato, Hyperides, Dio Cassius, Libanius, and Tacitus. In vv. 6–7, Paul praises the Thessalonians' deeds and the fact that they became "imitators of us and of the Lord" in the severe sufferings which resulted in "an example to all the believers." Further, in v. 8, their deeds developed in every place as well as Macedonia and Achaia. Conclusively, the last main clause of vv. 9–10 declares and praises their eschatological deeds and character by saying, "how you turned to God from idols, to serve a living and true God, and to wait for his Son from heaven." Through praises of their origin, ancestors, and deeds/character, Paul attempts to establish the continuity between ancient origins and present times, and prepares consolation and exhortation (4:1—5:22) to the recently built Thessalonian Christian community. This is the pre-requisite of funeral oration for both the Athenians' and the Romans' funeral orations.

Regarding vv. 4–10, there have been some debates about the epistolary analysis. Jan Lambrecht attempts to subsume 1 Thess 1–3 under a thanksgiving period or a triple period (thanksgiving: 1:2–10; 2:13–16; 3:9–10) on the basis of epistolary analysis.[39] For the epistolary analysis, the thanksgiving foreshadows the central themes and issues to be developed in the body of the letter as well as the letter's style and character. Paul Schubert defines the thanksgiving's function as foreshadowing the central themes and issues to be developed in the body of the letter along with the letter's style and the degree of intimacy.[40] To them, it seems that vv. 2–10 foreshadows the whole letter as follows: (a) vv. 5, 9a foreshadows the opening of 2:1–12 (εἴσοδον); (b) vv.

---

38. Quintilian's assertion about a narration in an epideictic rhetoric (*Inst.* 3.7.15), "Praise awarded to character is always just . . . It has sometimes proved the more effective course to trace a person's life and deeds in due chronological order," correctly conforms here in this passage.

39. Lambrecht, "Thanksgivings in 1 Thessalonians 1–3," 135–62.

40. Schubert, *Form and Function of the Pauline Thanksgivings*, 77; Peter O'Brien also concludes that the thanksgiving introduces and indicates the main themes of the letters (*Introductory Thanksgivings in the Letters of Paul*, 15).

6–7 foreshadows suffering with joy in 2:14; 3:1–5; (c) v. 9b "how you turned to God from idols, to serve a living and true God" foreshadows the life-style changes in 4:1–12; and (d) vv. 3, 10 "hope in our Lord" and "to wait for his Son from heaven" foreshadows Christ's return in 4:13–18; 5:1–11.

In the ancient letters, however, two verses are about the normal length of a wish prayer and the thanksgiving section. This approach splits the whole discourse into smaller units without any whole unity. A further problem of the epistolary analysis is that it does not recognize the signals and characteristics of *narratio* in rhetorical discourse, which are reflected in 1:4–10. Particularly, this section contains elements of funeral oration like the origin of praise and deeds so that the orator might have the total persuasive effect in the following consolation and exhortation section (4:1—5:22).

Another approach to vv. 1:4–10 is to consider 1 Thess as a "paradoxical encomium" of epideictic rhetoric. W. Wuellner attempts to identify 1 Thess as a "paradoxical encomium" by asserting that Paul employs a special kind of exordium in 1 Thess, known as *insinuatio*.[41] Wuellner takes the first *oxymoron* in 1:6 ("much affliction with joy") as the central word for all discourse, which stands in paradoxical contrast to "full conviction." Further, he claims that 1:9–10 should be read as the unfolding of the central "theme," the "*propositio*," which concludes the exordium and introduces the subsequent argument (2:1–3:13; 4:1—5:22).[42]

Wuellner's assertion is correct in the perspective of his categorizing of 1 Thess as a branch of epideictic rhetoric. The rest of his assertion, however, has some problems.

In the first place, he unconvincingly asserts that Paul uses *insinuatio* as a special kind of exordium. For example, it is clear that Paul employs *insinuatio* as a special kind of exordium in Rom 1:16–17, "to the Jew first and also to the Greek," which already "hints at the gauntlet he intends to throw down in chapters 9–11." Through this *insinuatio*, Paul prepares rapport with his audience to demonstrate his *refutatio* of Gentile misunderstandings, the climax of his discourse in chapters 9–11.[43] In 1 Thess, however, it is not possible to see the exordium as *insinuatio* for the subsequent *refutatio*/arguments in the whole discourse because 1:4—3:10 is *narratio* for identification with the audience while 4:1—5:10 is consolation/exhortation for the living and not intended for argumentative purposes. Here, Paul directly describes

---

41. Wuellner, "Argumentative Structure of 1 Thessalonians," 106. He adds that the *insinuatio* type of exordium is held appropriate when the credibility of the case under discussion is rated as paradoxical, highly problematic as to its plausibility or cultural/social acceptability, or aptness.

42. Wuellner, "Argumentative Structure of 1 Thessalonians," 118, 128–34.

43. Witherington, *Paul's Letter to the Romans*, 17, 236–79.

their spiritual deeds and character in severe suffering with hope and the specific problem of death, not hinting at the upcoming *refutatio* or climax. Rather, this section of 1:4–10 is a *narratio* of funeral oration, describing their origin and deeds with praise.

In the same way, the origin and purpose of the genre of paradoxical encomium are different from the rhetorical exigency of 1 Thess. Historically, the paradoxical encomium originated from a mere display of ingenuity, which mainly has the connotation of comedy. Moreover, its other chief motive is the desire to startle others by a simple exhibition of wit in order towin applause and admiration. In a sense, it is a way of demonstrating the sophistic ability in extravagant form to make the worse reason appear to be the better one.[44] This trend is evident in the extant paradoxical encomium in Lucian's *Encomium of Muia* and *Encomium on the Fly*, Alcidamas' *Encomium on Death* and *Encomium of Poverty*, and Polycrates' encomia on mice, pots, counters, and salt with a cynic source and method.[45] Paul's letter of 1 Thess, however, has no hints of a cynic source or a euphemistic way of stating the events. Paul deals with the real problems of death and martyrdom of the Thessalonian believers and actual consolation/exhortation.

Finally, Wuellner's assertion of 1:9–10 as the thesis for the ensuing discourse is also not entirely convincing. Of course, 1:9–10 functions as the partial conclusion of the first *narratio*, that is, praise of their spiritual origin, deeds, and character. His assertion that 1:9–10 forms the thesis, however, overlooks the whole structure and the rhretorical exigency/situation of 1 Thessalonians. Particularly, by neglecting the elements of double consolation and exhortation in 4:18 ("So console one another with these words") and 5:11 ("Therefore console/encourage one another . . ."), which reflect the *topoi* of funeral oration, he misses Paul's main concerns and the rhetorical exigency of 1 Thess. Hence, his analyses derive from a misunderstanding of the rhetorical genre and exigency.

Third, this section (1:4–10) functions as the *initium narrationis*. The *narratio* is divided into three stages (*initium*, *medium*, and *finis*) in order to make the phenomena apparent (Cicero, *Inv.* 1.20). Quintilian (*Inst.* 4.2.129–31) suggests the essential elements for the beginning of the *narratio*. The statement of facts should always begin with reference to some person. For example, if that person is on one's side, one must praise him, but if he is on the side of one's opponents, one must abuse him. Sometimes, it is useful to introduce and praise him with circumstances such as his father's character, reputation, and birth, to support his fame and merits.

44. Burgess, "Epideictic Literature," 157–58.
45. Burgess, "Epideictic Literature," 163–66.

Paul's *narratio* (1:4–10) conforms to this rule by praising the people with their origin, birth, deeds, and character through hyperbole. This *initium narrationis* often increases into an ekphrastic digression, which is the graphic, often dramatic, visual description of any person or experience.[46] The main content of longer digressions is an epideictic description (2:1–12), and "the emotional digression creates an atmosphere favorable to one's party for the compelling effect of the *argumentatio*: the emotional concluding digression of the *narratio* represents, so to speak, a new *exordium* just before the *argumentatio*."[47] Therefore, Paul's first section of *narratio* in 1:4–10 naturally connects to a digressional praise of himself in 2:1–12, preparing for the compelling effect of the consolation and exhortation in 4:1—5:22.

For this purpose, Paul reminded them of the works of God (1:5 "not in word only, but also in power and in the Holy Spirit"), his preaching, and their response (1:5, 9 " . . . what kind of persons we proved to be among you for your sake . . . what kind of welcome we had among you, and how you turned to God from idols"), and he praised their origin and the suffering they endured (1:6 "in spite of persecution you received the word with joy").

In summary, as mentioned previously, the final aim is to achieve persuasion of the narrative's veracity, which is attained through plausibility (*probabilis*). Paul attempts to achieve this goal in their minds and shows the concrete facts of the past in Thessalonica by praising their origin, deeds, and character, and reminding them of God's works with words of remembrance (1:4–5). These *topoi* reflect on the encomium of funeral orations. Through this process of encomium, Paul establishes rapport with the audience and finds identification with the Thessalonian community in order to offer consolation and exhortation in 4:1—5:22.

Second Section of *Narratio* (2:1–12)

Survey of Study in 2:1–12

In the *narratio*, there is a distinct account of facts, persons, times, and places related in a positive way (Quint. *Inst.* 4.2.36), and there is a stress on conveying the mental attitudes and motives of the one who is speaking or writing (Aristotle. *Rhet.* 3.16.10; Quint. *Inst.* 4.2.52). Further, the orator makes the audience feel as if they are actual eyewitnesses of the scene (Quint. *Inst.* 4.2.123–24) by employing various reaffirming and reminding words.

---

46. Lausberg, *Handbook of Literary Rhetoric*, 143–44, 159, 496.
47. Lausberg, *Handbook of Literary Rhetoric*, 159.

Just as Lausberg's assertion that the *initium narrationis* usually develops into an ekphrastic digression,[48] the digression of Paul's autobiography (2:1–12) conforms to these *topoi* of epideictic *narratio*. Theon and Menander speak of the great freedom allowed in applying rhetorical precepts, and the subject and circumstances must determine the prominence of the various *topoi*.[49]

At this juncture, it is important to survey the history of debate concerning to the questions, "What is the function of Paul's autobiographical statements in 1 Thess 2:1–12?" and "What are the rhetorical *topoi* of 1 Thess 2:1–12?" The thematic and logical approach, the epistolary approach, and the mirror-reading approach commonly assert that this section is Paul's defense against specific opponents, inward or outward. Just as discussed in chapter 1, F. C. Baur and the Tübingen school consistently interpreted Paul as combating Judaizers. Schmithals considered Paul's autobiography in 1 Thess 2:1–12 as an apology against "Gnostic libertinism." Christopher L. Mearns claimed that Paul had been charged by opponents with error because he had changed his teaching from a realized eschatology to a futuristic eschatology after leaving Thessalonica. Identifying the opponents against Paul in 1 Thess 2:1–12, Horbury considers 1 Thess 2:1–12 as a "defense against a charge of false prophecy" which was made by Jews.[50]

The epistolary approach asserts that the thanksgiving section of the letter (1:2–10) typically functions to foreshadow the central concerns of the letter as a whole, and the length and apparent defensive tone of 1 Thess 2:1–12 would seem naturally to defend Paul's character and integrity. In final consideration, it is not difficult for Paul to present a lengthy defense at the beginning of the letter-body (2:1—5:22).

All of these approaches can be summarized through employing a mirror-reading approach. Mirror-reading is a kind of methodology in the task of historical reconstruction. Moises Silva defines the concept of mirror-reading, particularly in Pauline letters, as reading between the lines of the text because of lack of explanation about the circumstances. Thus, mirror-reading attempts to approach the text for what it reflects about the original situation, not so much for what it says.[51] John Barclay also affirmatively recommends the employment of mirror-reading in Pauline letters if it could help us reconstruct the historical situation and make sense of difficult statements in the text.[52] In the same way, he concludes that this method can be

---

48. Lausberg, *Handbook of Literary Rhetoric*, 143–44, 159, 496.
49. Burgess, "Epideictic Literature," 121.
50. Horbury, "1 Thessalonians 2:3," 492–508.
51. Silva, *Explorations in Exegetical Method*, 103–4.
52. Barclay, "Mirror-Reading a Polemical Letter," 79–86.

legitimately used, on the condition that the conclusions derived from this method honor the relevant criteria, which is suggested by his own assertion in a footnote.[53] He also suggests, however, the dangerous pitfalls of such an enterprise including *undue selectivity, over-interpretation, mishandling polemics,* and especially *latching onto particular words and phrases* as direct echoes of the opponents' vocabulary, which may lead one to hang a whole thesis on frail pretexts.[54]

For example, Weima, employing the epistolary and mirror-reading methodology, attempts to prove Paul's apologetic defense against specific opponents in 1 Thess 2:1-12 through showing witness language (2:5, 10), legal-like language (2:4, "God who examines (δοκιμάζοντι) our hearts"), a very heavy concentration of antithetical statements (vv. 1-2, 3-4, 4b, 5-7a, 8b), and an appeal to firsthand knowledge.[55] His problem is, however, that he latches onto particular ostensible Pauline self-defense words and tones and ignores the warnings against mirror-reading. In addition, he neglects the rhetorical *topoi* and signals in this passage such as epideictic rhetoric, particularly funeral oration. G. Fee also, disagreeing with Malherbe's rhetorical approach in this section, argues with mirror-reading that "we will better understand Paul if we see him as indeed using language from the philosophers; but . . . he is here adapting to express his concerns in a very real historical situation, where some from the pagan population were using Paul's 'escaping town' so quickly as fodder against the believing community."[56] His approach also focuses on "historical plausibility," which is one of the factors for the employment of mirror-reading, neglecting the rhetorical exigency and *topoi* of epideictic rhetoric.

In contrast, Abraham Malherbe's article ("'Gentle as a Nurse': The Cynic Background to 1 Thess ii") dramatically changed the situation by showing the possible Cynic background of 1 Thess 2:1-12. Malherbe argued that the apostle in 2:1-12 is not defending himself against actual accusations, and the function of 2:1-12 is not apologetic but paraenetic as a model for Thessalonian believers. Malherbe developed the earlier claims of Martin Dibelius ("Wandering sophists, Cynic philosophers") concerning the Cynic background of 1 Thess 2:1-12, especially highlighting the striking parallels in language and thought between Paul and Dio Chrysostom (Dio

---

53. Barclay, "Mirror-Reading a Polemical Letter," 84-85. He offers seven criteria for a legitimate use of mirror-reading: (1) Type of Utterance; (2) Tone; (3) Frequency; (4) Clarity; (5) Unfamiliarity; (6) Consistency; (7) Historical Plausibility.

54. Barclay, "Mirror-Reading a Polemical Letter," 79-80.

55. Weima, "Function of 1 Thessalonians 2:1-12," 119-21; "An Apology for the Apologetic Function," 73-99.

56. Fee, *First and Second Letters to the Thessalonians*, 56.

Chrysostom, *The First Discourse on Kingship-The Fourth Discourse on Kingship* [Cohoon, LCL]).[57] Finally, Marlherbe supposed that Paul, in 2:1-12, was not exactly defending himself against actual accusations, because "Dio was not responding to any specific statements that had been made about him personally."[58] He concludes that there is no evidence in this letter for Paul to make a personal apology, because, like a philosopher, Paul also describes his works and ministry in Thessalonica through negative and antithetic terms under the same context of Dio's work.[59]

George Lyons, stressing the importance of the imitation theme in 1 Thess, points out that the autobiographical remarks in 1 Thess, particularly 2:1-12, serve as parenetically reminding Paul's converts of the Christian ethical values as embodied in the ethos of their *typos*.[60] Consequently, Paul's autobiographical remarks are employed as exemplary to imitate rather than apologetic because Paul's autobiographical remarks in 2:1-12 have clear direction for achieving the ethical purpose, that is, encouraging his suffering converts in Thessalonica. Clearly, he does not intend to work toward selfish ends (self-defense against actual opponents).[61] Moreover, regarding the historical reconstruction of opponents in the Pauline letters, he refutes the assumptions of the technique known as mirror-reading.[62]

Abraham Smith also correctly grasps the function of 2:1-12 as a digressionary panegyric about the missionaries in terms of rhetorical perspective. Like a traditional antithetical style of speaking among philosophers, Paul's autobiographical reference of 2:1-12 is neither a self-defence nor a mirror image, which indicates the mirror-reading of Paul's opponents, but rather another portrait of the congregations' *ethos*.[63]

In the same sense, Franz Laub, while criticizing F. C. Baur's and Schmithals's assertion of the existence of opponents in 2:1-12, correctly claims Baur wrongly pushes the Corinthian situation into 1 Thess 2:1-12 ("sondern es werde ihm die korinthische Situation untergeschoben"). In 2 Cor, some overlapping accusations with 1 Thess 2:1-12 exist from the opponents of Paul (cf. 2 Cor 12:16-17 especially; also 4:2; 6:8; 7:2). The threat of a false teacher, however, is in 1 Thess 1:5—2:12 without acknowledgement,

57. Malherbe, "'Gentle as a Nurse,'" 216.
58. Malherbe, "'Gentle as a Nurse,'" 217.
59. Malherbe, "'Gentle as a Nurse,'" 217.
60. Lyons, *Pauline Autobiography*, 221.
61. Lyons, *Pauline Autobiography*, 219.
62. Lyons, *Pauline Autobiography*, 75-76.

63. Smith, *Comfort One Another*, 78-79. See also his dissertation "The Social and Ethical Implications of the Pauline Rhetoric in 1 Thessalonians" (Vanderbilt, 1990), 85, 132-36.

while Paul shows his arguments in Gal and 2 Cor clearly. Furthermore, in 1 Thess, Paul's main concern is for his fledgling community, not for defense of his integrity and position. Neither libertinistic tendencies (4:3-8), Gnostic hostility (4:11-12; 5:11-12), nor Gnostic rejection of the resurrecton of the dead and spiritualized Parousia (4:13—5:11), but rather in 2:1-12, Paul reminds and recommends his ministry and works to encourage and establish a good relationship with the Thessalonian fledgling community.[64]

D. W. Palmer compares the items in Paul's ostensible self-defense with those in Cynic diatribes and concludes that just as these philosophers were not necessarily defending themselves against specific charges, neither was Paul.[65] Steve Walton correctly asserts "The antithetical style used in 2:1-12 does not necessarily mean that the views on the 'not' side actually exist: opponents are an unnecessary hypothesis."[66] I also agree with the position of the denial of self-defense in 1 Thess 2:1-12, which has been discussed. Yet, I assert that 1 Thess 2:1-12 is the panegyric digression, which is intended to establish rapport and identification with the Thessalonian Christian community.

Just as Lausberg suggests (*initium narrationis*),[67] Paul freely applies some *topoi*. Paul's character and deeds in his autobiographical section of 2:1-12 embody many of these traits and content. Like the first section of *narratio* (1:4-10), Paul appropriately uses noetic expressions in the beginning (2:1 "You yourselves know"). Furthermore, it is noteworthy that Paul particularly emphasizes the dramatic and visual description of anything with ekphrastic witness language in 2:1-12, which indicates his strategical intention. Paul concentrates his ekphrastic remembrance and witness languages in this section among the whole discourse as follows: 2:1 - "You yourselves know"; 2:2 - "as you know"; 2:5 - "As you know and as God is our witness"; 2:9 - "You remember"; 2:10 - "You are witnesses, and God also"; and 2:11 - "As you know." These might conform to the function of ekphrastic digression in epideictic rhetoric. Paul also shows personal character (2:2, 7 "courage . . . in spite of great opposition" and "gentle among you"), deeds, and motives (2:3-7) with some metaphors (2:7, 11 " . . . like a nurse . . . like a father"). Most of all, Paul uses several contrasts which attribute superiority to himself over others (2:2-6, 9).

---

64. Laub, *Eschatologische Verkündigung und Lebensgestaltung nach Paulus*, 133-36.
65. Palmer, "Thanksgiving, self-defense, and exhortation," 23-31.
66. Walton, "What has Aristotle to do with Paul?," 229-50.
67. Lausberg, *Handbook of Literary Rhetoric*, 143-44, 159, 496.

In the perspective of the structure of the *narratio* (partly 1:4–2:16), Paul's autobiographical panegyric of 2:1–12 is surrounded by two subunits (1:4–10; 2:13–16) as follows:[68]

A: Laudation of the Thessalonians' mimetic endurance (1:4–10)

B: The Missionaries' perseverance and noble intentions (2:1–12)

A': Laudation of the Thessalonians' mimetic endurance (2:13–16)

It is noteworthy to question, "Why does Paul employ this kind of self-praise as a digression (2:1–12) surrounded by two subunits of laudation of the Thessalonians in suffering (1:4–10; 2:13–16)?" Paul's aim in this process of self-praise is to produce the continuation of the collective to the dead and to unite the community by causing an identification between the dead and the community, including himself, with a long encomium of funeral oration. In addition, through this process, Paul prepares the mind of the audience and establishes rapport with the community for consolation and exhortation in 4:1—5:11.

Actually, two subunits (1:4–10; 2:13–16) reflect the context of severe suffering and persecution, and even the martyrdom of the believers. Paul praises the Thessalonians for their imitation of the Lord and Paul himself in spite of persecution (ἐν θλίψει πολλῇ, 1:6). The Lord was killed by the Jews (2:15) and Paul had been opposed and suffered in great opposition (ἐν πολλῷ ἀγῶνι, 2:2). Their evidences of suffering are their acts of "how you turned to God from idols, to serve a living and true God," (1:9) and of their eschatological hope of "to wait for his Son from heaven" (1:10).

In addition, the subunit of 2:13–16 shows clearer evidence of their sufferings and develops the motif of martyrdom of the believers (2:15) by repeating similar content. Indeed, the subunit of 2:13–16 contains more, clearer, and developed content than the subunit of 1:4–10, though both of them have similar content and structure (1:5–6, 9–10; 2:13–14, 15–16):

1:5–6	2:13–14
"our message . . . not in word only, but also in power And in the Holy Spirit . . ." (5) " . . . imitators of us and of the Lord, for in spite of persecution . . . " (6)	" . . . the word of God . . . not as a human word . . . but God's word . . . " (13) " . . . imitators of the churches of God . . . for you suffered . . . " (14)

68. Smith, *Comfort One Another*, 79–80.

1:9-10	2:15-16
"... how you turned to God from idols, to serve a living and true God," (9)	"... who killed both the Lord Jesus and the prophets... they displease God..." (15)
"... to wait for his Son... who rescues us from the wrath that is coming." (10)	"... they... filling up the measure of their sins; but God's wrath has overtaken them at last." (16)

Particularly, it is possible to assert in the second subunit (2:13–16) that Paul praises, first of all, Christ who was martyred by the Jews and who comes to raise the dead. Simultaneously, according to 2:14–15, "... for you suffered... from the Jews, who killed both the Lord Jesus and the prophets...," Paul praises the prophets who were killed and implicitly praises the suffering Thessalonian believers and the dead Thessalonians as the prophets were praised. Consequently, Paul praises the martyred Jesus, prophets, and also martyred believers of the Thessalonian church implicitly. In addition to this, the words employed in 1 Thess 3:2-3 are strikingly similar to those used in the Jewish apocalyptic texts: στηρίξαι (to strengthen)—σαίνεσθαι (be shaken)—θλίψεσιν (persecutions),[69] which reflect the context of martyrdom and suffering.

Between these surrounding contexts of suffering and martyrdom (1:4–10; 2:13–16; 3:2–3), Paul employs digressional and ekphrastic self-praise in 2:1–12, and also shows his suffering (2:2, ἐν πολλῷ ἀγῶνι), deeds, and character in his ministry so he might establish rapport with the Thessalonian believers and make the continuation/identification among the dead, the Christian community, and Paul himself. Through this process, Paul prepares the audience and sets the spiritual ground for his consolation and exhortation in 4:1—5:11.

The *narratio* of a funeral oration normally begins with the description of ancestors, noble birth, native land and soil, education and upbringing, and the deeds and courage of the dead in battle. The Athenian orators (Isocrates, Thucydides, Pseudo-Lysias, Plato, Demosthenes, and Gorgias, Hyperides) and Roman orators (Tacitus, Dio Cassius, Libanius, Dio Chrysostom) commonly dealt with these topics, though these elements of encomium could be changeable depending on the orators' intention and focus. Regarding the elements of encomium in funeral oration, Pseudo-Dionysius, in his rhetorical handbook (*On Epideictic Speeches*, 275–80), suggests three essential elements to be dealt with. Firstly, when speaking of war, the dead can be lavished with praise of his native land. Secondly, if there is some story of fame about an

---

69. Bammel, "Preparation for the Perils of the Last Days," 97.

individual—that his fathers and ancestors were distinguished—a brief praise of these may also be given, explaining their public and private character, and any other acts or deeds they performed. Thirdly, the orators should look at upbringing, accomplishments, and deeds.

Hester asserts that because Paul is the progenitor to the Thessalonian church and its believers, Paul cannot use the typical commonplace elements when talking about ancestors or family of the Thessalonians. Specifically, according to Hester, Paul suggests himself and his companions as examples of virtue as ancestors to the Thessalonian believers.[70] Hester's assertion that Paul himself might be suggested as an ancestor to Thessalonian church believers could be possible in the newly established community of the Thessalonian church.

Beyond this, however, Paul's autobiographical self-praise has a unique function of identification with the Thessalonian church believers. Thucydides (*History of the Peloponnesian War*), when compared with other extant funeral orators both in Athens and Rome, has the unique arrangement of encomium. Thucydides, while beginning the encomium with a short praise of the ancestors (36.1), dramatically switches his emphasis and praise to the contemporary warriors (the present generation), "And not only are they worthy of our praise, but our fathers still more . . . we now possesses and bequeathed it, not without toil, *to us who are alive today. And we ourselves here assembled, who are now for the most part still in the prime of life, have further strengthened the empire in most respects* . . . But I shall first set forth by what sort of training *we have come to our present position . . . of what manner of life our empire became great . . .* " (36.2–4) Thucydides' encomium seems to be the opposite of Pseudo-Dionysius's suggestion above. However, regarding the difference of Thucydides' from other orators, Ziolkowski correctly says "greater honor is given to the present than to previous generations . . . Thucydides was much more interested in describing Athens's superiority than the later speakers were." Intentionally, he increases the effectiveness of his praises by presenting them in the first person plural, consequently establishing identification with his audience and provoking participation directly in his glorification of Athens.[71] In the same way, in 1 Thess 2:1–12, Paul praises himself for establishing the continuity and identification with the Thessalonian community, which are under suffering, martyrdom, and persecution, rather than only praising himself as an ancestor to the Thessalonian believers.[72]

70. Hester, "Invention of 1 Thessalonians," 275.
71. Ziolkowski, *Thucydides*, 185–87.
72. 1 Thess 2:1–12 is surrounded between the praise of the Thessalonians' suffering,

In addition, the plural pronouns in 1 Thess support this aspect as funeral oration. Just as Thucydides highlights the first person plural "we" in his discourse, 1 Thess contains Paul's similar use of this language for the purpose of identification and continuity between Paul and the Thessalonian community. This phenomenon is manifest in 1 Thess compared to other Pauline letters as follows:[73]

> Paul employed first and second person pronouns (mostly plural) almost exclusively throughout 1 Thessalonians. In the sections and places at which he praised the Christian attributes of the believers, he addressed them in second person plural. In section in which he spoke of his own ministry, he employed first person plural consistently... In this regard, 1 Thessalonians and even 2 Thessalonians tend to be unique among Paul's letters. In polemics, for example, in Galatians, Paul almost always employs the first person singular. It could be that the plural is more the language of exhortation and praise... It is significant, however, that Paul was interested in divine community building, and these first person plurals highlight the need for the involvement of all in mutually growing conviction and excitement.

In summary, beyond Hester's assertion about 2:1–12 that Paul shows himself as ancestor, in 2:1–12 there exists Paul's other rhetorical strategy. In other words, 2:1–12 focuses on and shows the praise of himself and of the Thessalonica believers in the present so that he might establish the identification between himself and the Thessalonica believers and prepare their mind for the consolation and exhortation in 4:1–5:11. This parallels Thucydides' funeral oration in encomium focusing on the present and living Athenians' superiority over ancestors of the past.

The Elements of Funeral Oration in 2:1–12

THE REPETITIVE AND LENGTHY AMPLIFICATION IN CONTENT AND STRUCTURE 2:1–12

It is noteworthy that F. F. Bruce analyzes 2:1–12 into three subsections: (1) The Missionaries' Visit (2:1–4); (2) The Missionaries' Behavior (2:5–8);

---

martyrdom, and persecution (1:4–10; 2:13–16). Thus, the context of 1 Thess 2:1–12 is the continuation of these two subunits (1:4–10; 2:13–16) and the identification with those two.

73. Olbricht, "Aristotelian Rhetorical Analysis of 1 Thessalonians," 234.

and (3) The Missionaries' Example (2:9-12).[74] Grammatically, 2:1-12 mainly consists of three main clauses (1-4, 5-8, 9-12) commonly utilizing the conjunction γάρ This means that there are some close connections among these three sections together, not separate ones. Wanamaker correctly comments that the real emphasis in 2:1-12 is on the nature of Paul's ministry in Thessalonica, while the γάρ of 2:1 appears to offer an explanation about the themes in 1:5, 9.[75]

Additionally, between 1:4-10 and 2:13-16, and between 2:5-8 and 9-12, repetitions are developed through amplification of the content.

2:5-8	2:9-12
"As you know and as God is our witness" (5)	"You are witness, and God also" (10)
"... have made demands (δυνάμενοι ἐν βάρει)" (7a)	"... not burden (μὴ ἐπιβαρῆσαί)" (9b)
"But... gentle... like a nurse tenderly caring" (7b-8) (ἤπιοι ἐν μέσῳ ὑμῶν, ὡς ἐὰν τροφὸς θάλπῃ)	"like a father... urging, encouraging" (11-12) (ὡς πατήρ...παρακαλοῦντες, παραμυθούμενοι)

Furthermore, repetitive comparison/contrast in 2:1-2, 3-4, and 5-8 (οὐ...ἀλλὰ), function by emphasizing and reminding the audience of the positive deeds and character of Paul.

These repetitive and confirming patterns conform to the panegyric rhetoric, particularly to funeral oration. Epideictic rhetoric triggers the remembrance of fundamentals with amplifications and embellishments, as well as the use of a good deal of repetition for emphasis.[76] Quintilian emphasizes the proper function/purpose of panegyric is amplification and embellishment of its themes (*Inst.* 3.7.6). In the same way, these repetitive amplifications and embellishments in content and structure (1:4-10//2:13-16; 2:5-8//9-12) show the fact that 1 Thessalonians is epideictic rhetoric, neither apologetic forensic nor deliberative rhetoric.

It could be argued that other forms of forensic and deliberative rhetoric use the same methods as epideictic rhetoric. However, the main function and purpose of forensic rhetoric is formal proof and deliberative rhetoric with the main function of being "expedient or useful" at a future time (Aristotle, *Rhet.* 1.3.4). Quintilian's *Institutio Oratoria* undertakes a broad treatment of amplification (8.4—9.2.4). He suggests methods of amplification

---

74. Bruce, *1 and 2 Thessalonians*, 23-39.
75. Wanamaker, *Epistles to the Thessalonians*, 91.
76. Witherington, *1 and 2 Thessalonians*, 22-23.

such as the comparison between words of stronger definition (8.4.2), augmentation of one step or several (8.4.3–9), comparison (8.4.9–14), accumulation of words and sentences identical in meaning (8.4.26–27), and figures of repetition "to fix one point in the mind of the audience by repetition" (9.2.4).[77] Epideictic rhetoric, mainly associated with amplification rather than a series of arguments to prove a thesis statement, "is rather dedicated to amplifying, expanding, and expounding on certain key ideas and themes that are already familiar and accepted."[78]

Paul develops the content of 1:5–6 and 1:9–10 in relation to the content of 2:13–14 and 2:15–16, each through repetitive amplification and augumentation. Further, he emphasizes his own superiority over others in character, works, and values through the repetitive comparison/contrast in 2:1–2, 3–4, and 5–8. Finally, he repeats and develops the content and values of 2:5–8 in 2:9–12 by figures of repetition to fix one point in the mind of the audience through repetition. This is not merely redundancy, but functions to explain and emphasize the main issue and values adequately and accurately. Therefore, Paul's use of the repetitive and amplified nature in 1 Thess 2:1–12 is an intentional rhetorical topoi of epideictic rhetoric to increase his audience's adherence to the familiar values. Perelman correctly points out the function of amplification in epideictic rhetoric that "the argumentation in epideictic discourse sets out to increase the intensity of adherence to certain values . . . The speaker tries to establish a sense of communion centered around particular values recognized by the audience, and to this end he uses the whole range of means available to the rhetorician for purposes of amplification and enhancement."[79] In other words, Paul's use of epideictic rhetoric in 1 Thess is mainly intended to establish and increase the audience's adherence and identification of Paul with the Thessalonian community, which is under persecution and death.

Regarding the repetitive amplification of encomium in funeral oration, Menander (*Division of Epideictic Speeches—The Funeral Speech*, 420) suggests that after praising nature (physical beauty and mental endowment), it should be confirmed and amplified by the three succeeding headings of nurture, education and accomplishments. Through this amplification, the hero can be described as being ahead of his contemporaries and being superior over others. Through detailed, repetitive praises and the lengthy encomium (*narratio*) the orators trigger remembrance for fundamental and

---

77. Watson, "Amplification Techniques in 1 John," 101–3.
78. Witherington, *New Testament Rhetoric*, 226–27.
79. Perelman and Olbrechts-Tyteca, *New Rhetoric*, 51.

praiseworthy characteristics so they might set the foundation of the consolation and exhortation.

Among the extant funeral orations, Thucydides praises Athens as a model of democracy and stresses their superiority in the land because of the training, education, deeds, and courage of the dead using repetitive embellishments. Pseudo-Lysias, with a lengthy mythical and historical narrative, develops the encomium chronologically according to three divisions such as ancestors, descendants, and the dead.[80] The Athenian and Roman orators in funeral oration commonly employed the lengthy and repetitive amplification in encomium so they might establish the continuity and identification between the dead, the living, and all generations.

In the same way, Paul employs repetitive and lengthy *narratio* (1:4-10//2:13-16; 2:5-8//2:9-12) for his self-praise so he might establish continuity and identification between himself and the Thessalonian community. With this process, like the Thessalonian believers under severe suffering and death, Paul attempts to identify himself with them in the same suffering. Furthermore, Paul employs a triple-repetitive metaphor to amplify his character in his ministry. The rhetorical function of Paul's triple-repetitive metaphor in the *narratio* (2:1-18) is to magnify and emphasize his character to establish a good relationship with the Thessalonian community. All three metaphors use kinship language (2:7-8—gentle /a nurse; 2:11—a father; 2:17—orphans) and demonstrate the character of his ministry, placed at the end of each unit (2:2-8, 9-12, 17-20). In addition, these metaphors share a similar structural pattern which ends with the purpose/result clause (phrase) in each unit as follows:

Contrast clause	7a ἀλλὰ ἐγενήθημεν νήπιοι ἐν μέσῳ ὑμῶν 7b ὡς ἐὰν <u>τροφὸς</u> θάλπῃ τὰ ἑαυτῆς τέκνα·
Result clause	8 οὕτως ὁμειρόμενοι ὑμῶν εὐδοκοῦμεν μεταδοῦναι ὑμῖν οὐ μόνον τὸ εὐαγγέλιον. . . ἀλλὰ καὶ τὰς ἑαυτῶν ψυχάς,
Comparative clause	11 καθάπερ οἴδατε ὡς ἕνα ἕκαστον ὑμῶν ὡς <u>πατὴρ</u> τέκνα ἑαυτοῦ
Participle/manner	12 παρακαλοῦντες ὑμᾶς καὶ παραμυθούμενοι καὶ μαρτυρόμενοι

---

80. Plato, Demosthenes, Dio Cassius, Tacitus, and Dio Chrysostom also repeatedly praise the ancestors and the dead in chronological order or by repetitive comparison.

Infinitive/purpose	εἰς τὸ περιπατεῖν ὑμᾶς ἀξίως τοῦ Θεοῦ τοῦ καλοῦντος ὑμᾶς εἰς τὴν ἑαυτοῦ...
Participle/cause	17a Ἡμεῖς δέ, ἀδελφοί, <u>ἀπορφανισθέντες</u>...ὥρας προσώπῳ οὐ καρδίᾳ,
Resut clause	17b περισσοτέρως ἐσπουδάσαμεν τὸ πρόσωπον ὑμῶν ἰδεῖν ἐν πολλῇ ἐπιθυμίᾳ.

The most striking rhetorical feature of the *narratio* (2:1–18) is its repetitiveness in amplifying Paul's character discussed above. Paul's character is remolded and amplified through a triple-metaphor (a gentle nurse, a father, and orphan) to prepare their minds for receiving the consolation and exhortation (4:1—5:10). Additionally, Paul employs the same repetitive amplification in consolation and exhortation in 4:13–18 and 5:1–11, which ended with the same consolation and exhortation ("Therefore comfort one another...") as well as in 1:4–10//2:13–16 and in 2:5–8//2:9–12. All of these characteristics indicate 1 Thess contains elements of a funeral oration throughout.

The Repetitive Contrast/comparison in Character and Deeds in 2:1–12

Paul shows another example of repetitive amplification in 2:1–12 by employing repeated contrast/comparison so he might attribute superiority to himself over others. Regarding the function of contrast/comparison in encomium, Aphthonius clearly expounds that after praising the person's origin, upbringing, and deeds, a comparison serves as attributing superiority to what is being celebrated by contrast.[81] According to him, the main function of the contrast/comparison in encomium is to give superiority to those who are praised. Between 1 Thess 1–3 and 1 Cor 1–4, there is some similarity in context and rhetorical exigency. Charles Wanamaker claims in 1 Cor 1–4, particularly 1:21–25, that Paul uses an associative argument with a radical contrast of human wisdom to God's wisdom. Through the antithesis between divine wisdom and human wisdom, Paul emphasizes the manner of his founding proclamation of Christ crucified with the demonstration of the Spirit and power. In this way, Paul's position of spiritual superiority and dominance in his relation with the Corinthians is repeatedly

---

81. Kennedy, *Progymnasmata*, 108; Burgess, "Epideictic Literature," 120.

emphasized through 2:1—3:3.[82] In 1 Thess 2:1–12, Paul shows the superiority of his character and deeds over those who were compared by contrast, and also emphasizes the work of the Holy Spirit (1:5).

Lausberg claims that in the body of the *narratio* (*narrationis medium*), repetition can be used in content or in words. Repetition is for reinforcement, generally with emotional emphasis, but it is also exploited intellectually and the repetition of the word's meaning with a change of the word's form serves to reinforce the *voluntas* (will) behind the statement in the interest of *amplification* and because of their effect of emotive intensification.[83]

Through repetition of contrast, Paul amplifies and intensifies the Thessalonian believers' favor and identifies himself with them.

2:1-2	οὐ κενὴ γέγονεν	ἀλλὰ . . . ἐπαρρησιασάμεθα <u>ἐν τῷ θεῷ</u>
2:3-4	οὐκ ἐκ πλάνης οὐδὲ ἐξ ἀκαθαρσίας οὐδὲ ἐν δόλῳ	ἀλλὰ . . . δεδοκιμάσμεθα <u>ὑπὸ τοῦ θεοῦ</u>
	οὐχ ὡς ἀνθρώποις ἀρέσκοντες	ἀλλὰ <u>θεῷ τῷ δοκιμάζοντι</u>
2:5-7	οὔτε γάρ ποτε ἐν λόγῳ κολακίας ἐγενήθημεν	ἀλλὰ ἐγενήθημεν ἤπιοι. . .ὡς ἐὰν
	οὔτε ἐν προφάσει πλεονεξίας	τροφὸς θάλπῃ τὰ ἑαυτῆς τέκνα·
	οὔτε ζητοῦντες ἐξ ἀνθρώπων δόξαν, οὔτε ἀφ' ὑμῶν οὔτε ἀπ' ἄλλων	
2:8	οὐ μόνον τὸ εὐαγγέλιον τοῦ θεοῦ	ἀλλὰ καὶ τὰς ἑαυτῶν ψυχάς

In these repeated contrasts (οὐ. . .ἀλλὰ), there is one similarity in the ἀλλὰ clauses where God is commonly the main subject or character (2:2b, 4a, 4b, ἐν τῷ θεῷ, ὑπὸ τοῦ θεοῦ, θεῷ). However, in 2:5–7, Paul uses the ἀλλὰ clause in "we were gentle" instead of God or God's character. Moreover, in this section, Paul contrasts three οὔτε clauses to one ἀλλὰ clause. This may suggest gentleness as a character of God, while Paul emphasizes his gentleness in comparison to God and Paul's superiority in character and deeds over others' flattery, greed, and praise from mortals. Particularly, B. Rigaux brands the pattern of "οὐκ. . . οὐδὲ. . . οὐδὲ" in 2:3 as "a gradation"[84] for the climax of the opposite character of the subject, which appears in Paul's character in 2:4. In Mark 13:32, Matt 24:36, and John 1:13, 25, there are similar constructions of gradation for the climax of the opposite character (Περὶ δὲ τῆς ἡμέρας ἐκείνης ἢ τῆς ὥρας οὐδεὶς οἶδεν, οὐδὲ οἱ ἄγγελοι

---

82. Wanamaker, "Socio-Rhetorical Analysis of 1 Cor. 4:14—5:13," 342–43.

83. Lausberg, *Handbook of Literary Rhetoric*, 145, 274, 293. He shows some examples of repetition such as repetition of the same words, *reduplication*, *gradatio*, and repetition at a distance.

84. Rigaux, *Les Épitres aux Thessaloniciens*, 407.

ἐν οὐρανῷ οὐδὲ ὁ Υἱός, εἰ μὴ ὁ Πατήρ). Actually, in 2:4, Paul, shows his God-proven character ("but just as we have been approved by God"; ἀλλὰ καθὼς δεδοκιμάσμεθα ὑπὸ τοῦ Θεοῦ), emphasizing his reflective image of God's character. In other words, after the rhetorical negation in 2:3, Paul begins 2:4 with a reference to his vocation from God through the positive contrast.[85] Therefore, though it seems to be embarrassing, Paul uses the verb "δοκιμάζω" in 2:4,[86] Paul climaxes his image of God's character through borrowing the verb "δοκιμάζω" from Jer 12:3; 11:20; and 17:10.[87]

Among the rhetorical handbooks, when Quintilian lists the elements of encomium, this part of encomium contains: the events in chronological time order, physical endowments and external circumstances, character and deeds of the dead, and superiority through comparison (*Inst.* 7.6-16). Plutarch also offers self-praise with the use of contrast in order to obtain approval from the audience (*On Inoffensive Self-Praise*, 541.E-F). Particularly, in his handbook Menander emphasizes the element of contrast/comparison in the encomium of funeral oration (*The Funeral Speech*, 420.25—421.14). Through the contrast/comparison with others, the orator highlights the character and attributes of the superiority of the character to the subject of praise.

It is noteworthy that among the extant funeral orations, most orators commonly employ the *topos* of contrast/comparison in encomium so they might highlight and apply superiority to the character and deeds of the subject of praise. Isocrates (*Evagoras*, 9.12-65, *Panegyricus*, 23-25) praises Evagoras' body, mind, and the greatness of his deeds by using comparison. Thucydides (*History of the Peloponnesian War*, 39.1—41.1-5) praises Athens as a model of democracy, stressing their superiority. Plato (*Menexenus*, 238-39c, 242e), Demosthenes (*Funeral Speech*, 15-18), and Hyperides (*Oration*, 10-14, 20-23, 33, 35) in common praise Athens's valor and the superior qualities of the dead by comparison and contrast.[88]

Just as discussed previously, among the extant examples of funeral orations, Paul's repetitive contrast/comparison in his character and in the deeds of his ministry at the Thessalonica church (2:1-12) function to highlight his

---

85. Wikenhauser and Kuss, *Der Erste und Zweite Brief an die Thessalonicher*, 127.

86. Masson, *Les Deux Épitres de Saint Paul aux Thessaloniciens*, 27.

87. Rigaux, *Les Épitres aux Thessaloniciens*, 411; Masson, *Les Deux Épitres de Saint Paul aux Thessaloniciens*, 27.

88. Tacitus (*Agricola*, 41), Julius Caesar (Suetonius, *The Deified Julius*, VI), Dio Cassius (*Roman History* 36.4-5), Plutarch (*Concolatio Ad Uxorem/Consolation to His Wife*, 609E-F, 610A-D), Libanius (*Funeral Oration over Julian*, 18.12-95), and Dio Chrysostom (*The Twenty-Ninth Discourse: Melancomas*, 29.7-18) all stress superiority of the subject over others through the repetitive contrast/comparision in their funeral orations.

superiority over others, particularly showing the element of encomium of funeral oration. It is noteworthy that Thomas Olbricht concludes that Hebrews most resembles a funeral oration of classical Greece in light of structure, content, and purpose. Supporting this claim, he offers a variety of topoi of funeral oration in Hebrews such as the origin of divine descent (Heb 1:4; 2:9, 11) and an exhortation to emulate the heroes at the end of the oration (Heb 7, 13). Most significantly, he emphasizes "comparison and contrast in setting forth the superiority of Christ as the mode of amplification" as the convincing evidence of his assertion that Hebrews reflects a funeral sermon structure.[89] In this sense, it may be probable that Paul employs the repetitive comparison/contrast in the *narratio* (encomium) of 2:1–12 that he might show his superiority over others, and that he might establish the ground for exhorting the Thessalonian believers in 1 Thess chapters 4–5.

Paul also employs the repetitive comparison/contrast of the Thessalonian community with others to establish the superiority of the Thessalonian community over outsiders throughout 1 Thess. First, Paul contrasts the Thessalonian community (1:9–10, ". . . how you turned to God from idols, to serve a living and true God . . . to wait for his Son . . . the wrath that is coming") with the Jews (2:15–16, ". . . who killed both the Lord Jesus and the prophets . . . but God's wrath has overtaken them at last"). Second, in consolation and exhortation Paul sharply contrasts the Thessalonian believers with other Gentiles (4:5b, "the Gentiles who do not know God"; 4:12a, "outsiders"; 4:13, "as others do who have no hope"). Third, in 5:3–9, particularly in 5:4–5, 8a, Paul recognizes the Thessalonian believers as "children of light and children of the day . . . belong to the day," constrasting them with outsiders ("in darkness . . . of the night or of darkness"). Through these repetitive comparison/contrasts, Paul also attempts to show the superiority of the Thessalonian community over others, which reflects the characteristics of funeral oration.

Another important factor, which deserves attention, is the characteristic of "altruism" in Paul's character found in 2:1–12. Altruism is commonly emphasized as the character to be praised most in funeral oration. Quintilian (*Inst.* 3.7.16) highlights two main elements in the panegyric which we should bear in mind:] (a) what most pleases an audience is the celebration of deeds which our hero was the first or only man, or at any rate one of the very few to perform; (b) in addition, we must insert any other achievements, which surpassed hope or expectation, particularly focusing on what was done for the sake of others rather than what he performed on his own behalf, that is, altruism (Cicero (*De Orat.* II.85.346). Both Quintilian and

---

89. Olbricht, "Hebrews as Amplification," 375–87.

Cicero commonly emphasize the element of altruism in encomium as the most valuable virtue of the subject. In the same way, Ochs's principles concerning the praise of virtue in funeral oration are in accord with both of them that "the greater the altruism, the greater the honor; and the wider the public affected by the altruism, the greater the admiration

Dio Cassius (*Roman History*, LVI.37.3-4, 40.3, 41.5) highlights Caesar's altruism in his character and deeds using contrast (μὲν. . .δὲ), which parallels 1 Thess 2:1-12, as follows:

> From all this he derived no personal gain, but aided us all in a signal manner . . . Furthermore, he did not take away from them the right to cast lots . . . but even offered them additional prizes as a reward for excellence . . . nor did he do away with their privilege of voting, but even added safeguards for their freedom of speech . . . *How could one forget to mention a man who in private life was poor, in public life rich; who with himself was frugal, but towards other lavish of his means; who always endured every toil and danger himself on your behalf, but would not inflict upon you the hardship of so much as escorting him when he left the city or of meeting him when he returned.*

Paul's self-praise in 2:1-12 may finally lead to his altruistic character, which is the main element of the narratio in the funeral oration of the Romans. Through employing the repetitive contrast/comparison, ultimately Paul emphasizes his character of altruism toward the Thessalonian believers in his ministry, which reflects the elements of funeral oration: his boldness to exhort them (2:1-2), God-pleasing appeal rather than human-pleasing language (2:3-4), his pure motive, like a nurse and a father, not burdening any of them but rather for the Thessalonian community (2:5-7, 12), and Paul's determination to share even "our own selves," which shows sacrificial models of deeds as well as the gospel of God (2:8). Through showing this altruism, Paul attempts to establish his identification with the Thessalonian believers to establish a rapport with his audience, to console and exhort them in 4:1—5:11. Indeed, with his repetitive emphasis in content and structure (1:4-10//2:13-16; 2:5-8//2:9-12) and his emphasis on altruism through the repetitive contrast/comparison (2:1-12, 3-4, 5-7, 8), Paul employs the *topoi* of encomium in funeral oration so he might establish the identification and grounds for the consolation and exhortation in 4:1—5:11.

The Suffering and Persecution Context in 2:1–12

Throughout 1 Thess, it is clear some distinguishing expressions, which indicate the context of suffering and persecution, are diffused at every corner. Paul praises the Thessalonian believers' enduring faith under the suffering and persecutions through repeating the strong suffering words "θλῖψις" (1:6; 3:3-4, 7; Matt 24:21; Acts 11:19; Rom 5:3b; 12:12; 2 Cor 6:4; 8:2; 2 Thess 1:4; Rev 1:9; 2:9, 22; 1 Macc 9:27). In various ways he connotes their suffering (2:14) and employs encouraging words to overcome suffering (3:2-3, εἰς τὸ στηρίξαι ὑμᾶς. . .τὸ μηδένα σαίνεσθαι ἐν ταῖς θλίψεσιν ταύταις). In addition, he manifestly describes Jesus' death (2:15, ἀποκτεινάντων Ἰησοῦν) and even the death of Thessalonian believers (4:13, περὶ τῶν κοιμωμένων). Finally, he decribes how to experience his own suffering with words of suffering (2:2, 15, ἐν πολλῷ ἀγῶνι). Actually, the Thessalonian believers received the Gospel in θλῖψις (1:6; 3:7), and some of them had already died in suffering and persecution (4:14). Paul himself had suffered much by human adversaries while the ἀγών (struggle and battle) was the focal point of a battle between God and Satan (2:18; 3:5), which will be due to reach its climax before long.[90]

Actually, Paul describes his spiritual battle in Thessalonica: "but though we had already suffered and been shamefully mistreated at Philippi, as you know, we had courage in our God to declare to you the gospel of God in spite of great opposition" (2:2, ἀλλὰ προπαθόντες καὶ ὑβρισθέντες. . .ἐν πολλῷ ἀγῶνι). The word ἀγών literally refers to a place of contest and any kind of conflict, and ἀγωνίζομαι means "to carry on a conflict, contest, debate or legal suit." In metaphorical uses of Hellenistic Judaism, there are many examples of the use of this imagery and terminology of the arena in relation to the heroic struggle, which the pious has to go through in this world (Stauffer, *TDNT* 1: 135–36).[91] Though some scholars consider the word ἀγών in 2:2 as internal effort,[92] Best, Marshall, and Wanamaker

---

90. Bammel, "Preparation for the Perils of the Last Days," 99–100.

91. Stauffer comments further that the Hellenistic virtue of struggling and the Jewish type of a martyr fighting unto death seem to come together in the picture of the divine warrior Job as sketched in the Testamentum Iobi. Thus, literature of this kind obviously helped in large measure to fix the sense and application of avgw/n and its derivatives in early Christianity.

92. Rigaux, *Les Épitres aux Thessaloniciens*, 404–5. Rigaux suggests the evidence for his assertion that the context of 1 Thessalonians makes a happy contrast with the sufferings of Philippi. Acts 17:1–9, however, shows the context of continuous external sufferings in the Thessalonian church. Dibelius, Dobschütz, and Knabenbauer have the same position as Rigaux, while De Wette, Lünemann, Lightfoot, Milligan, Schmidt, and Weiss agree with the position of external persecutions.

commonly interpret the phrase "in spite of great opposition" (ἐν πολλῷ ἀγῶνι) as meaning a life-and-death struggle against external conflict and circumstances.[93] Malherbe also considers *thlipsis* in 1:6 (ἐν θλίψει πολλῇ) and the "great opposition (ἐν πολλῷ ἀγῶνι)" in 2:2 mental distress or "an inward struggle . . . the distress and anguish of heart," rather than external dangers that Paul and the Thessalonian believers faced.[94] However, Paul's severe suffering and his ministry against antagonism reflect on 1:6 (ἐν θλίψει πολλῇ), 2:13–17 (ὅτι τὰ αὐτὰ ἐπάθετε καὶ ὑμεῖς . . . τὸν κύριον ἀποκτεινάντων Ἰησοῦν καὶ τοὺς προφήτας), 3:1–5 (τὸ μηδένα σαίνεσθαι ἐν ταῖς θλίψεσιν ταύταις), and Acts 17:5–7, 13–14. V. Pfitzner, who rightly understands Paul's ἀγῶν motif as his eschatological view and dimension to these sufferings, defines Paul's use of ἀγῶν motif in 1 Thess 2:1–2 as the military image to fight against external opposition including suffering, as well as in Phil 1:27–30; 4:3 and Col 1:28—2:2.[95] In other words, Paul's use of ἀγῶν motif is a description and characterisation of his eschatological life of faith to fight against external persecution and suffering.[96]

It is noteworthy that Stauffer classifies the thought motifs of the words ἀγῶν and ἀγωνίζομαι in the New Testament into five motifs.[97] Dio Chrysostom also employs this word to illustrate the severe struggle of the athletes who strove for noble achievements like the Homeric heroes (*The Second Discourse on Kingship*, 18).

As discussed above, Paul's use of the word ἀγῶν in various ways, shows the context of suffering and persecution and of his suffering for his Christian communities. For example, in Col 1:29—2:2, Paul struggles with all his passion (ἀγωνιζόμενος κατὰ τὴν ἐνέργειαν) for his communities (ἡλίκον

---

93. Best, *Commentary on the First and Second Epistles to the Thessalonians*, 91–92; Marshall, *1 and 2 Thessalonians*, 63–64; Wanamaker, *Epistles to the Thessalonians*, 93.
94. Malherbe, *Paul and the Thessalonians*, 47–48.
95. Pfitzner, *Paul and the Agon Motif*, 157–58.
96. Pfitzner, *Paul and the Agon Motif*, 190–93.
97. Stauffer, *TDNT* 1:136–139: (a) First, the thought of the goal which can be reached only with the full expenditure of all our energies (Col 1:29; 1 Tim 6:12; 2 Tim 4:7–8); (b) The struggle for the reward does not demand only full exertion but a rigid denial (1 Cor 9:25; 1 Tim 4:7 ff); (c) The thought of the antagonists, obstacles, dangers and catastrophes through which the Christian must fight his or her way (1 Thess 2:2; Heb 11:33; Jude 3); (d) The sharpest form of ἀγῶν, which the person who is faithful to God must undergo on earth, is the battle of suffering fulfilled in martyrdom, a familiar Jewish concept (1 Tim 6:11–12; Heb 10:32–33; 11:33; 4 Macc 15–17); (e) The supreme goal for which we fight and suffer is not our salvation alone; it is for the salvation of many (altruism). Paul's struggle is for his communities (Col 1:29—2:2; 4:12–13; Phil 1:27ff; Rev 15:30; 4 Macc.).

ἀγῶνα ἔχω ὑπὲρ ὑμῶν καὶ τῶν ἐν Λαοδικίᾳ), not just for himself (altruism). Then Paul offers the exhortation for the community (2:16-4:6).

Hebrews 10 displays a context full of suffering and persecution (10:32b-33). With many examples of heroes in faith, the author offers the eschatological exhortation for the community (12-13). In the same way, in Phil 1:27-30, Paul uses the image of avgw/n along the lines of the martyr theology of later Judaism by saying, "οὐ μόνον τὸ εἰς αὐτὸν πιστεύειν ἀλλὰ καὶ τὸ ὑπὲρ αὐτοῦ πάσχειν, τὸν αὐτὸν ἀγῶνα ἔχοντες οἷον εἴδετε ἐν ἐμοὶ" (29-30, TDNT 1:139). Paul also offers the exhortation for the Christian community.

In 4 Maccabees, there are many examples of the word ἀγών, which is used in the context of suffering and death for the community. In 9:23, the first brother encourages the rest to fight a sacred fight for piety by saying, "Do not leave the ranks of my contest." In the seventh brother's contest of 12:11-14, he rebukes and fights a sacred fight by saying "were you not ashamed ... to murder his servants and torture the athletes (ἀγωνιστὰς) of piety?" In the encomium of the seven brothers of 13:13-15, it is said: "Let us not fear the one supposing to kill, for great is the soul's contest (ἀγών) and the peril in eternal torment ... " In the mother's counsel of 16:12-16, the mother calls her children who were already murdered by tyranny, "O children, it is a noble contest (ἀγών) ... contend (ἐναγωνίσασθαι) eagerly on behalf of the ancestral law." In the enumeration of the martyrs' achievement and exhortation to the hearers in 17:11-16, it is praised, "For ... truly a divine contest (ἀγών) ... Eleazar was competing first (προηγωνίζετο), and the mother of the seven children was contending, and the seven brothers were competing (ἠγωνίζοντο) ... Reverence for God conquered, crowning her own athletes."

In the same context, Paul's use of the word ἀγών in 1 Thess 2:2, "in spite of great opposition," shows the context of suffering and persecution and of his suffering for his Christian community in Thessalonica (2 Cor 7:4-7, ἀλλ' ἐν παντὶ θλιβόμενοι· ἔξωθεν μάχαι, ἔσωθεν φόβοι). Through his ministry in Thessalonica under the context of suffering and persecution, Paul attempts to show his altruism for the community and further establish identification with the suffered and persecuted believers so that he might prepare the audience for the consolation and the exhortation in 4:1—5:11. Paul's use of the word ἀγών here is manifestly intentional to show this context. Therefore, Paul's panegyric digression of self-praise (2:1-12) functions as a continuation and identification with 1:4-10 and 2:13-16, which emphasize the suffering and persecution of the Thessalonian believers.

Then, what forms of the suffering and persecution does it take in 1 Thess? Some scholars see it as economic and social rejection and exclusion.[98] Simultaneously, it could be also possible with the physical suffering and persecutions. At this juncture, it is noteworthy that the context of suffering and persecution in 2:2 (2:1–12) can be supported from the social perspective of Thessalonica. K. Donfried's question, "What situation/s is Paul referring to with his several references to affliction and suffering in 1 Thess (1:6; 2:14; 3:3–4)?" suggests or concludes the possibility of death of the believers through suffering and persecutions. On the basis of Bruce's assertion about the possibility of the martyrdom of the Thessalonian believers (Acts 17:9),[99] he suggests three pieces of evidence for this assertion: (a) The use of κοιμαομαι in Acts 7:60, "fell asleep (died)", which describes the martyrdom of Stephen, is remarkably connected to 1 Thess 4:13 "about those who have died" (περὶ τῶν κοιμωμένων); (b) In 2:14–16, the phrase "became imitators of God's churches" involves the dimension of death; (c) 1 Thess 1:6–8; 2:2 have a parallel context with Philippians 2:17, which connotes the martyrdom of both Paul and the congregation of Philippi.[100]

W. H. C. Frend also suggests the probability of death for the Thessalonian believers in light of the whole context of 1 Thess. Paul assures them to have hope of sharing in Christ glory on the last trump, though they would suffer and even be put to death on earth as "imitators of us and of the Lord" (1 Thess 1:6).[101] E. A. Judge, with his study of the decrees of Caesar at Thessalonica, suggests a probable assertion for the reference of the decrees of the emperor in Acts 17:7b, "They are all acting contrary to the decrees of the emperor, saying that there is another king named Jesus." In order to offer specific evidence for the suffering and deaths of Thessalonian believers, he lists two kinds of decrees and oaths, which were declared at that time. Firstly, he offers the Caesarian edict about the ban on prediction and prophesy, which was reinforced and elaborated upon by Tiberius.[102] Secondly, he

---

98. Nicholl, *From Hope to Despair in Thessalonica*, 158–66; Russell, "Idle in 2 Thess.," 105–13; Winter, "'If a Man Does Not Wish to Work,'" 303–15.

99. Bruce, *Acts of the Apostles*, 327–28. He claims that from 1 Thess 2:13–14 and 3:3, it is probable that the Jews continued to organize persecution against the Thessalonian believers; perhaps those who "fell asleep" so soon (1 Thess 4:13) were victims of this persecution.

100. Donfried, "Imperial Cults of Thessalonica and Political Conflict in 1 Thessalonians," 221–22.

101. Frend, *Martyrdom and Persecution in the Early Church*, 83.

102. Judge, "Decrees of Caesar at Thessalonica," 4. "But as for all the other astrologers and magicians and such as practiced divination in anyway whatsoever, he put to death those who were foreigners and banished all the citizens that were accused of still employing the art at this time after the previous decree (*dogma*) by which it had been

lists "The Oath of Paphlagonia," which embraced Roman and non-Roman alike in the same obligation:

> I swear . . . that I will support Caesar Augustus, his children and descendants, throughout my life, in word, deed and thought . . . that in whatsoever concerns them I will spare neither body nor soul nor life nor children . . . that whenever I see or hear of anything being said, planned or done against them I will report it . . . and whomsoever they regard as enemies I will attack and pursue with arms and the sword by land and by sea.[103]

Judge correctly concludes the decrees of the emperor in Acts 17:7b are likely related to the Caesarian decree and oath, which is discussed above. Consequently, the gospel and ministry of Paul and his coworkers at the Thessalonica church would oppose these decrees and oath, and consequently cause suffering and the death of the Thessalonian believers. Indeed, it is probable the description of the ministry of Paul and his coworkers in 2:1–12 may contain the context of suffering and persecution.

H. L. Hendrix, who studies the history of honors given to the Romans by inhabitants of Thessalonica during the second and first centuries B.C.E. and the first century C.E., concludes that between the Thessalonians and Romans there existed a close relationship in many aspects. Hendrix concludes:

> Thessalonica, like other Greek cities . . . publically honored local and foreign individuals who distinguished themselves in furthering the city's interests. As Romans became increasingly important in Thessalonican affairs, they became the objects of a distinct system of honors . . . Honors for the gods and Romans benefactors expressed a hierarchy of benefaction extending from the divine sphere into human affairs. While Roman benefactors were granted awards appropriate for human beings, their honors . . . involved recognition of those deities responsible for the continued well-being of the city.[104]

For this conclusion, he offers some evidence to show the close relationship between Thessalonica and Rome, such as the construction of the "temple of Caesar" at Thessalonica and the city's honorific coinage with Julius *Theos* and games. Furthermore, Thessalonica added Augustus, his divine father and his successors, to the honors granted "the gods and Roman

---

forbidden to engage in any such business in the city . . . (Dio 57.15.8)."
103. Judge, "Decrees of Caesar at Thessalonica," 6.
104. Hendrix, "Thessalonicans Honor Romans", 336–37.

benefactors" and "Roma and Roman benefactors."[105] He then goes on rightly to stress that "the Imperator's priest assumes priority, the priest of 'the gods' is cited next followed by the priest of Roma and Roman benefactors."[106] Just as asserted by Hendrix above, the social and religious background between Rome and Thessalonica during the 2nd and 1st centuries B.C. and the 1st century A.D. shows the strong influence of Rome on Thessalonica. This fact may prove Acts 17:7 is under the influence of the Caesarian decree and oath. It could be summarized that Paul's context of suffering and persecution reflects "physical suffering . . . a series of episodes of suffering probably caused by persecution," and also economic social pressures.[107]

Quintilian, pointing out *narratio* to be at the heart of rhetorical thinking, asserts narration as one of the "weapons which we should always have stored in our armoury ready for immediate use as occasion may demand" (2.1.12). Particularly, to affect change of mind, the *narratio* should provide "a plausible picture of what occurred," that the orator could make the "audience feel as if they were actual eyewitnesses of the scene" (4.2.123–24). Quintilian asserts that *narratio* succeeded only to the degree of the authority of the speaker, and that authority derives from two sources: "our manner of life" and "our style of eloquence" (4.2.125).[108] Through the witness and context of his own suffering and persecution (2:1–12), Paul intentionally seeks to change their minds and prepares them for the following consolation and exhortation (4:1—5:11). In other words, through his manner of life under suffering and persecution, Paul identifies himself with the suffering Thessalonian believers (1:4–10 and 2:13–16) to unify the community and establish an identification between the dead and the community and between himself and the living Thessalonian community. Paul's employment of *narratio* by identifying with the Thessalonians believers may reflect funeral oration in a rhetorical situation and with a rhetorical purpose.

Textual Criticism of 1 Thess 2:7 as "Gentle"

For a long time, there has been a controversial debate about the two possible readings in 1 Thess 2:7, that is, *gentle* (ἤπιοι) and *infants* (νήπιοι). But these days, the pendulum is definitely swings in support of the reading of "gentle." Many commentators and most English translations accept the reading of

---

105. Hendrix, "Thessalonicans Honor Romans," 298–99, 308.
106. Hendrix, "Thessalonicans Honor Romans," 312.
107. Witherington, *1 and 2 Thessalonians*, 42–43.
108. O'Banion, "Narration and Argumentation," 333–50.

"gentle" (ἤπιοι).¹⁰⁹ The reason many commentators accept this usage is because some internal evidence exists to support the reading of "gentle." Furthermore, "gentle" can be strongly supported by the classical rhetorical approach. Clearly, the reading of "gentle" shows the influential evidence for Paul's self-praise to identify with the audience in Thessalonica.

The 27th edition of the Novum Testamentum Graece takes the reading of 'infants' (νήπιοι), supported by strong external evidence, such as P⁶⁵ ℵ* B C* D* F G I 104* *pc* it. Of course, the reading of "gentle" (ἤπιοι) is weak in external evidence (ℵ² A C² D² *Majority*). In terms of date, the oldest Greek witnesses all utilize νήπιοι (P⁶⁵: 3rd century, Sinaiticus ℵ* and Vaticanus B: 4th century, Ephraemi Syri Rescriptus C* and Claromontanus D* and Washingtonensis I: 5th century), and yet the reading ἤπιοι is supported by Alexandrinus A (5th century). Furthermore, in terms of text type and geographic distribution, the reading νήπιοι occurs in the majority of Alexandrian and Western texts, and is supported by Old Latin and Clement (P⁶⁵).¹¹⁰ In this case, the reading νήπιοι is strong in external evidence because the reading νήπιοι is supported by ℵ* B D*.

In textual criticism, the external evidence is an important factor to take into account. There are, however, some other crucial elements besides external evidence. The scholars who take the reading ἤπιοι usually have used four strong arguments. Among them, the first two are related to "transcriptional probabilities,"¹¹¹ and the last two deal with "intrinsic probabilities."¹¹²

---

109. Many commentators, for example, B. Rigaux, E. Best, F. F. Bruce, T. Holtz, F. Laub, I. H. Marshall, W. Marxsen, L. Morris, C. A. Wanamaker, E. J. Richard, M. W. Holmes, A. J. Malherbe, take sides with the reading of "gentle", and also AV, RV, RSV, NRSV, NEB, NIV, NASB, NAB, NJB, REB, and Phillips take the same position. But only the American Bible Society (1995) chooses "children."

110. Scholars who regard the Proto-Alexandrian text-type and the Western text-type as independent will view the agreements between the two as multiple attestation. (Sturz, *Byzantine Text-Type and New Testament Textual Criticism*, 130). The criterion of multiple attestation does not always indicate originality and can sometimes be explained as the accidental agreement of scribal tendencies, but if a reading is attested in multiple independent witnesses, it has a good claim to being prior to other attested readings, other factors being equal. Metzger also preferred the agreement of the Proto-Alexandrian and the Western text-type to any other combination of witnesses (Shin, "Search for Valid Criteria in Textual Criticism," 21).

111. Shin, "Search for Valid Criteria in Textual Criticism," 30–45. He suggests the elements of Transcriptional Probabilities as follows: The Principle of Explainability, Dissimilarity to Scribal Tendencies, Tendencies of Linguistic Alteration (Septuagintalisms, The Less Polished Reading, The Less Familiar Reading), Tendencies of Theological Alteration, Scribal Mistake, The More Difficult Reading, Conflation.

112. Shin, "Search for Valid Criteria in Textual Criticism," 49–52. He suggests the elements of Intrinsic Probabilities as follows: The Style of the Author, Coherence with the Immediate Context.

Firstly, νήπιοι is the result of dittography.[113] For example, F. F. Bruce insists "the variant νήπιοι, 'infants,' is well attested, but is due probably to dittography of the final letter of ἐγενήθημεν."[114] Secondly, νήπιοι is a common term replacing the rare ἤπιοι. Marshall claims that scribes, either intentionally or accidentally replaced the rare term ἤπιοι with the more common and familiar word νήπιοι by saying, "there can, however, be little doubt that the less-attested reading is correct; the rare word was replaced by a more familiar one."[115] From J. J. Griesbach's theory,[116] this assertion seems to be correct. Thirdly, νήπιοι is always used pejoratively by Paul. For example, Delobel claims Paul uses νήπιοι in an exclusively negative way, so he would not have used this term to refer to himself in 1 Thess 2:7, by saying, "Paul uses the image of 'babe' for the Christians in their early-Christian or even pre-Christian situation, i.e., with a somewhat unfavorable connotation."[117] Therefore, in this passage, Paul would not use the negative connotation toward himself. Fourthly, νήπιοι creates the problem of a mixed metaphor. For this, Bruce Metzger rightly stresses, if Paul violently diverts in the same sentence from a reference to himself as babe to the image of a mother-nurse, it must be unreasonable and almost absurd.[118] Against this, some scholars assert the double metaphor of "infants" and "nursing mother" is clearly the more difficult reading, *lectio difficilior*.[119] In addition to this, pious scribes might have replaced "infants" with the smoother and more laudatory "gentle."[120] This assertion, however, is slightly arbitrary because from the perspective of the rhetorical approach of 1 Thess 2:5–8 ("gentle . . . like a nurse") and 2:9–12 ("like a father . . . "), they are repetitive and confirming patterns which conform to the panegyric rhetoric, particularly also with funeral oration.

---

113. Repeating "a letter, a syllable, a word, a group of words or even part of a sentence."

114. Bruce, *1 and 2 Thessalonians*, 31.

115. Marshall, *1 and 2 Thessalonians*, 70; Metzger also accepted that scribes might "replace an unfamiliar word with a more familiar synonym" (Metzger, *Text of the New Testament*, 210.

116. Griesbach, "Prolegomena": "The more unfamiliar reading is preferable to that which contains nothing unfamiliar."

117. Delobel, "One Letter Too Many in Paul's First Letter," 128.

118. Metzger, *Text of the New Testament*, 231.

119. " . . . if one among those is more obscure, others being more intelligible, then surely the obscure one can be credited as being genuine . . . " (Clericus, "De Emendatione locorum corruptorum," 389). Griesbach (in 1796) adopted this criterion and preferred the apparently unintelligible reading, which has a "deep meaning" (Shin, "Search for Valid Criteria in Textual Criticism," 40).

120. Weima, "'But We Became Infants Among You,'" 554.

In addition to these positive assertions for the reading of "gentle," the extant discourses of Dio Chrysostom (40–120 A. D. *The First-Fourth Discourse on Kingship*) and Plutarch (45–120 A.D. *De Se Ipsum Citra Invidiam Laudando-On Praising Oneself Inoffensively*) show clear evidence of Paul's use of the word "gentle" in his self-praise. Dio Chrysostom, when addressing the subject of kingship, emphasizes the most important character of kingship as the "gentleness of a good shepherd" (*The First Discourse on Kingship*, 13, 17, 20) by saying, "He is addressed as 'King' because of his dominion and power; as 'Father,' I ween, on account of his solicitude and *gentleness*" (*The First Discourse on Kingship*, 40). Also, Chrysostom wrote, "he would surely have chosen the lion for his simile and thus have made an excellent characterization. No, his idea was to indicate *the gentleness of his nature and his concern for his subjects* . . . when a wild beast appears, not fleeing but fighting in front of the whole herd . . . to save the dependent multitude from dangerous wild beasts" (*The Second Discourse on Kingship*, 6, 67–69) and "if he lacks even *the quality of a good shepherd*" (*The Third Discourse on Kingship*, 40–41). "Homer seems to answer this very question clearly also when in commending some king he calls him a 'shepherd of people.' For the shepherd's business is simply to oversee, guard, and protect flocks" (*The Fourth Discourse on Kingship*, 44–45).

In contrast, Dio Chrysostom rejects the character of flattery, love for money, and reputation by saying, "all who act deliberately do so either for money, for reputation, or some pleasurable end, or else, I suppose, for virtue's sake . . . Furthermore, flattery seems neither reputable nor honorable . . . flattery will be found to be the meanest . . . Flatterers, therefore, do much more harm than those who debase the coinage" (*The Third Discourse on Kingship*, 14–17; *The Fourth Discourse on Kingship*, 10, 15–16, 33). Finally, Dio Chrysostom offers the image of a nurse and the gentleness of a good shepherd by saying, "do you believe that he means that kings are nourished by Zeus as by a nurse, on milk and wine and various foods, and not on knowledge and truth? . . . Then Diogenes told it to him with zest and charm, because he wanted to put him in a good humor, just as nurses, after giving the children a whipping, tell them a story to comfort and please them" (*The Fourth Discourse on Kingship*, 41–42, 74). Indeed, in Dio Chrysostom's discourses, the image of a nurse and the gentleness of a good shepherd are closely related, just as Paul describes himself to be gentle like a nurse in 1 Thess 2:7.

Plutarch (*On Praising Oneself Inoffensively*) also suggests the positive effect of self-praise in discourse. He claims the statesman could venture on self-glorification, "not for any personal glory or pleasure, but when the occasion and the matter in hand demand that the truth be told about himself

... especially when by permitting himself to mention his good accomplishment and character he is enabled to achieve some similar good" (539.E). For this purpose, he offers two major avenues to earn the audience's approval toward his discourse. Firstly, he suggests the blending of praise for himself with the audience together, leading to the identification and conciliation with the hearers as follows (542.B-D):

> ... by most harmoniously blending the praise of his audience with his own he removed the offensiveness and self-love in his words ... For in this way the hearers, taken off guard, accept with pleasure the praise of the speaker, which insinuates itself along with the praise of themselves; and their delight in the rehearsal of their own successes is followed at once with admiration and approval of him ... In this way they conciliate the hearer and draw his attention to themselves; for although they are speaking of another, he at once recognizes in the speaker a merit that from its similarity deserve the same praises.

In the same way, Paul intentionally places his own self-praise in 1 Thess 2:1–12, which is sandwiched between both the praise of the Thessalonian believers (1:4–10; 2:13–16). By harmoniously blending the praises of his audience (1:4–10; 2:13–16) with his own (2:1–12), he removed offensiveness but could lead to the identification and approval between them. Actually, Paul praises them in terms of God's choice (1:4), their imitation of God and Paul (1:6), their act of turning to God from idols and of waiting of Jesus (1:9–10), and their imitation to the church of God, denoting death (2:14) with his own self-praise. Naturally, they could listen to Paul's praise of himself with pleasure and agreement, which insinuates itself along with the praise of themselves. In final consideration, it is possible to praise himself as "gentle ... as a nurse," not debasing himself by referencing "infants or children" in 2:7.

Secondly, Plutarch suggests self-praise to contain the intention of exhortation and model for the audience as follows (544.D–F):

> It is not enough, however, to praise ourselves without giving offence and arousing envy ... not merely to be intent on praise, but to have some further end in view. Consider first, then, whether a man might praise himself to exhort his hearers and inspire them with emulation and ambition ... For exhortation that includes action as well as argument and presents the speaker's own example and challenge is endued with life: it arouses and spurs the hearer, and not only awakens his ardor and fixes his purpose, but also affords him hope that the end can be attained and is

not impossible...to the young examples close at hand and taken from their own people ... to be their model.

In the same context, 1 Thess 2:1–12 contains Paul's intention to exhort his audiences and inspires them to imitate his own example. In 1 Thess 2:1–12, Paul offers his self-praise to the Thessalonian believers in the context of suffering and martyrdom so he may establish the continuation and identification between himself and the Thessalonian believers. Furthermore, he proceeds to offer himself as the example and model to imitate (2:2–5) in light of his courage (boldness), pure motives, gentleness like a nurse, and blamelessness in ministry like a father. This intention is also reflected on the imitation language in 1:6; 2:14. Consequently, he could prepare their minds for the consolation and exhortation in 1 Thess 4:1—5:11. This is the same pattern of the funeral oration of the Athenians and the Romans just as discussed previously. Therefore, his self-praise of "gentle ... as a nurse" can function as an exhortation, not a debasing reference to himself as "infants."

6.4 Third Section of *Narratio* (2:13–16; Amplification within the *Narratio*)

As discussed above, two subunits (1:4–10; 2:13–16) reflect the context of severe suffering and persecution, and even martyrdom of the Thessalonian believers. Particularly, the subunit of 2:13–16 contains clearer and more developed content compared to the subunit of 1:4–10.

It is noteworthy to find the matching points between 1:4–10 and 2:13–16. First of all, in 2:13–16, Paul repeatedly references the manner of "receiving the word of God, not as a human word but as God's word" (2:13; in 1:5 "in power and in the Holy Spirit and with full conviction"). However, in 2:13, the subject is the Thessalonian believers ("you received ... you accepted") while in 1:5, it is Paul and the missionaries ("our message of the gospel came to you"). Consequently, the emphasis is put on the praise of the Thessalonian believers rather than Paul and his coworkers. Besides that, Paul repeatedly emphasizes their imitation of suffering like the churches in Judea (2:14). In 1:6, their imitation is of "us and of the Lord" in the persecution. Paul praises Christ who was martyred by the Jews along with the prophets who were killed by them. Paul consequently praises the Thessalonian believers by saying "for you ... became imitators ... for you suffered the same things," which implies the act of martyrdom of the Thessalonian believers.

At this juncture, it is helpful to note Paul's two rhetorical devices with the intention of encomium. First, Paul develops the Thessalonian believers' faith in a progressive manner. Specifically, in 2:13-16, Paul emphasizes the Thessalonian believers' acts of receiving the word of God instead of Paul and his coworkers' acts. Just as Lausberg points out, one of the primary functions of repetition is for reinforcement with addition of emotional emphasis,[121] it is through this developed repetition in the *narratio* that he reinforces the Thessalonian believers' favor.

Second, Paul employs amplification of the praising of the Thessalonian believers. Some scholars have considered 2:13-16 as an interpolation.[122] All arguments for the interpolation of 1 Thess 2:13-16 can be summarized in two primary ways: (1) the structural argument, namely that of 2:13-16, does not fit into the flow of the letter, and (2) the anti-Jewish argument, namely that Paul's assertions in this periscope, are inconsistent with his assertion about the Jews in Rom 9-11. However, K. P. Donfried correctly answers the problems of these assertions. Like J. C. Beker's assertion of "the characteristically Pauline interaction between coherence and contingency,"[123] Paul's coherent theology can be comprehended, only when we fully understand the contingent situation of each Pauline audience.[124] T. Holtz correctly claims and proves Paul's consistency in his theology between Romans 9-11 (esp. 11:15, 25-32) and 1 Thess 2:13-16. In Romans 9-11 Paul shows the eschatological fate of the people of promise, Israel; in 1 Thess 2:15-16 Paul attacks the historic, contemporary Jews who are the active opponents of the gospel. This fact is demonstrated in his use of the aorist "ἔφθασεν δὲ ἐπ' αὐτοὺς ἡ ὀργὴ εἰς τέλος," which is not prophetic speech that prefigures the future, but the already-come event ("Der Aorist ist keine prophetische Redeweise, die die Zukunft vorwegnimmt, um die Sicherheit ihres Eintreffens darzustellen").[125] The passages do not talk about the final judgment but temporal judgment, though the conversion of Jews should be vindicated only through the faith of Jesus.[126] In this sense,

---

121. Lausberg, *Handbook of Literary Rhetoric*, 274. Quintilian (*Inst.* 9.3.28) suggests the function of the repetition by saying that "these figures and the like, which consist in change, addition, omission, and the order of words, serve to attract the attention of the audience and do not allow it to flag."

122. (a) Pearson, "1 Thessalonians 2:13-16"; (b) Boers, "Form Critical Study of Paul's Letters," 140-58; (c) Koester, *History and Literature of Early Christianity*; (d) Okeke, "1 Thess 2:13-16."

123. Beker, *Paul the Apostle*, 34-35, 92.

124. Donfried, "Paul and Judaism," 253.

125. Holtz, *Der erste Brief an die Thessalonicher*, 108.

126. Kümmel, "Die Probleme von Römer 9-11," 251-52. Concerning Rom 9:6a

Holtz rightly interprets the word "εἰς τέλος" as "completely," "entirely," and "in full measure," not the time sense of "finally" ("Judgment has totally fallen upon them"). Therefore, 1 Thess 2:13–16 cannot be attributed to the interpolatore.[127] Rather, as Donfried correctly asserts, Paul uses 1 Thess 2:13–16 as amplification in order to meet the particular rhetorical situation of the Thessalonian community. In other words, Paul rhetorically employs this comparison of 2:13–16 for the encomium of the Thessalonian believers to praise and encourage according to the contingent rhetorical situation, that is, death and martyrdom of the Thessalonian believers, particularly utilizing an epideictic one.

Indeed, it is more reasonable for Paul to use "amplification" (αὔξησις) in rhetorical exigency here. "Amplification" is a broad term covering various methods of promoting, or conversely, denigrating any given matter. These methods may be considered the most suited to epideictic rhetoric since the subject matter here is not in dispute. Anaximen Lampsac. *Rh.* 3 lists seven methods of αὔξησις as follows:

1. Enumeration of good things that arose because of x (Arist. *Rh.* 1.9.38)
2. Comparison with a previous favorable judgment (Arist. *Rh.* 1.9.39)[128]
3. Contrasting the proposition to the least of those things in the same class (Arist. *Rh.* 1.9.39)[129]
4. Mention of the opposite to discredit something
5. Arguing that x acted intentionally
6. Building up a series of logically related comparisons
7. Consideration as to whether it is better to show x as a whole or in parts (Arist. *Rh.* 1.7.31)[130]

---

and 11:23–26, he says "viel eher läßt das Glaubenspostulat 9:6a zu Beginn der ganzen Erörterung vermuten, daß Paulus die Hoffnung auf eine Rettung seines Volkes nicht aufgegeben hatte und von Anfang an durch seine Ausführungen diese Hoffnung begründen wollte."

127. Holtz, *Der erste Brief an die Thessalonicher*, 107–12; Holtz, "Judgment on the Jews and the Salvation of All Israel," 284–94. He also asserts "Der Aspekt der zeitlichen Endgültigkeit ist in dem eschatologischen Begriff ὀργή bereits enthalten."

128. "And you must compare him with illustrious personages, for it affords ground for amplification and is noble, if he can be proved better than men of worth. Amplification is with good reason ranked as one of the forms of praise, since it consists in superiority, and superiority is one of the things that are noble" (Arist. *Rh.* 1.9.39).

129. "That is why, if you cannot compare him with illustrious personages, you must compare him with ordinary persons, since superiority is thought to indicate virtue" (Arist. *Rh.* 1.9.39).

130. Anderson Jr., *Glossary of Greek Rhetorical Terms*, 26. Quintilian (*Inst.* 8.4.3)

In this case, Paul employs the amplification of (2)-(4) in order to discredit the Jews compared to the churches in Judea and their imitators, the Thessalonica believers. Also, through this amplification, Paul praises them and emphasizes their faith while suffering so he might establish grounds for the consolation and exhortation in 1 Thess 4:1–5:11. Finally, through this process Paul attempts to help the Thessalonian believers grasp the history of the persecution and suffering, which is worthy for them to endure, so they might find their position in salvation history.

Final Section of *Narratio* (2:17–3:10; Paul's Continuing Encomium of His Deeds)

In this section, Paul continually narrates his own motives of his deeds, which is the main element of encomium in funeral oration for the Thessalonian believers with the metaphor of orphans (2:17b) so he might gain the mind of the audience and identify with the Thessalonian believers. Just as Quintilian recommends the chronological description in epideictic rhetoric, which is the same in funeral oration, "Praise awarded to character is always just . . . It has sometimes proved the more effective course to trace a person's life and deeds in due chronological order" (*Inst.* 3.7.15). This section is described in chronological order. Particularly, Paul employs an *inclusio* structure between 3:2 (". . . to strengthen and encourage you for the sake of your faith") and 3:10 ("and restore what is lacking in your faith").

Regarding this section of 2:17—3:13, Robert Funk identifies it as an "apostolic parousia." He defines an "apostolic parousia" to be a section of the body of the letter when Paul is particularly concerned to make his presence felt, either by means of the letter itself, reference to his emissary, or mention of a future visit. Funk identifies some passages in Pauline letters which pertain to "apostolic parousia:" Rom 15:14–33; Phlm 21–22; 1 Cor 4:14–21; 2 Cor 12:14—13:13; 1 Thes 2:17—3:13; Phil 2:19-24; and Gal 4:12-20. Analyzing Rom 15:14–33 as a model case for apostolic parousia, he suggests five major units of an apostolic parousia: (1) Paul's letter-writing activity and purpose (15:14–15a); (2) Paul's relationship with his letter's recipients (15:15b–21); (3) plans for paying a visit (15:22–28); (4) invocation of divine approval and support for the visit (15:29–32a); (5) benefits of the impending visit (15:32b–33).[131] He insists apostolic parousia in Paul's letters could function as an indirect threat to recipients (1 Cor 4; 2 Cor 12:14ff; Phlm

---

also lists the main four elements of amplification: incrementum (augmentation), comparatio (comparison), ratiocination (reasoning), and congeries (accumulation).

131. Funk, "Apostolic Parousia," 249–68.

22). Finally, he concludes by saying, "All of these (i.e., references to either the writing of the letter, the sending of his emissary or his own impending visit) are media by which Paul *makes his apostolic authority effective* in the churches. The underlying theme is therefore the apostolic parousia—*the presence of apostolic authority and power*."[132]

As Funk asserts in 1 Thess 2:17—3:13, there is an element of eagerness to see (2:17b), a dispatch of an emissary (3:2-5), an an invocation of the recipients' benefits (3:10b-11) as found in Rom 15:14-33. It is difficult, however, to define whether the apostolic parousia can be appointed to be a distinct epistolary unit like an opening, thanksgiving, and an ending, as Funk asserts above. First of all, elements of apostolic parousia are not always similarly used and placed in various passages (Rom 15:14-33; Phlm 21-22; 1 Cor 4:14-21; 2 Cor 12:14—13:13; 1 Thess 2:17—3:13; Phil 2:19-24; and Gal 4:12-20). Neither the forensic rhetoric of 2 Cor 12:14—13:13[133] nor the deliberative rhetoric of Gal 4:12-20 contain invocation and prayer, and the apostolic parousia passages are not positioned in the same way and at the specific place. Secondly, apostolic parousia passages usually function as a way to assert authority and power, even with an indirect threat (1 Cor 4; 2 Cor 12:14; Phlm 22), but in 1 Thess 2:17—3:13 there is no indirect threat or authority. Instead, the lavish language of a friendly relationship and praise, which are characteristic of epideictic rhetoric, is utilized (2:19-20, "hope or joy or crown of boasting . . . you are our glory and joy."; 3:7-10, " . . . during all our distress . . . How can we thank God . . . for all the joy . . . Night and day we pray most earnestly . . . "). Thirdly, 1 Thess 2:17—3:13 functions to explain the deeds of human beings in the present, while 2:1-12 demonstrates the deeds of the past, rather than the fixed form of emissary-sending and impending visit. Quintilian, suggesting a narration in an epideictic rhetoric, shows this characteristic, "It has sometimes proved the more effective course to trace a person's life and deeds in due chronological order" (*Inst. Or.* 3.7.15).

Just as Quintilian's assertion of the orator's wise adaptability, " . . . the all-important gift for an orator . . . to meet the most varied emergencies . . . the children of expediency . . . what is becoming and what is expedient" (2.13.2-8) in 1 Thess 2:17—3:13, Paul may employ the rhetorical strategy

132. Funk, "Apostolic Parousia," 249, emphasis mine.

133. Long, *Ancient Rhetoric and Paul's Apology,* 178-97. Long helpfully asserts that 2 Cor 10:1—11:15 (*refutatio*) and 11:16—12:10 (self-adulation) demonstrate the characteristic of forensic rhetoric in 2 Corinthians. Further, it is reasonable that 12:11—13:10 should be called to be *peroratio* rather than a fixed form of apostolic parousia because it contains self-reflective contents, amplification (appeals to emotions), and recapitulation of the arguments of 2 Corinthians.

and languages according to the rhetorical genre and rhetorical situation in which he encounters his Thessalonian audiences. In this sense, it is more convincing that 2:17—3:10 would be the continuation of 2:1-12 in the *narratio* of an epideictic rhetoric because the theme of friendship, which dominates 2:17—3:10, "leads to the deep pathos with which Paul writes regarding his relationship with the Thessalonians."[134] Through this process of *narratio*, which creates a rhetorical situation for his core consolation and exhortation in 4:1—5:11, Paul prepares the minds of the Thessalonians and establishs the ground for his continuing consolation and exhortation.

From the rhetorical perspective, this section displays *narration* (encomium) to gain the favor of the audience. Particularly, in funeral oration of epideictic rhetoric, the long encomium functions to establish an identification with the audience for the following section of consolation and exhortation. In the section of *narratio* (encomium) in funeral oration, the orator normally praises himself and the audience through identifying, not exerting his apostolic authority or power over the audience. Further, the honorific prayer of 3:11-13 is a normal part of epideictic rhetoric, particularly in funeral oratory, and it also functions to establish "rapport with the audience" so they might be disposed to accept the following consolation and exhortation, that is, as "the *transitus*" and "a new *exordium*."[135]

Therefore, this section of *narratio* (encomium) of the funeral oration is used to identify and to confirm the favorable relationship with the orator and the audience for the following consolation and exhortation. In this sense, Hester correctly points out in 2:17 the word ἀπορφανισθέντες (ἀπορφανίζω, a *hapax legomenon* meaning "make an orphan," or here "made orphans by separation") implies separation based on the death of parents, thus situating (identifying) Paul in the Thessalonian believers' community.[136]

Among the extant funeral orations, the orphan image is familiar with the funeral orators. Plato (*Menexenus*, 249), in the consolation section of funeral oration, employs this word by saying, "the City . . . endeavoring to render them as little conscious as possible of *their orphaned condition*." Lysias (*Funeral Oration*, 71-72, "left their own children orphans"), Demosthenes (*The Funeral Speech*, 35-37, "orphaned of a father"), and Libanius (*Funeral Oration over Julian*, 621, "orphaned children"), when emphasizing the duty of the living, use this orphan image.

---

134. Wanamaker, *Epistles to the Thessalonians*, 119.

135. Witherington, *1 and 2 Thessalonians*, 27, 101-2.

136. Hester, "Invention of 1 Thessalonians," 277; D. F. Watson describes this word as "a word used of children robbed of parents or parents robbed of children" ("Paul's Appropriation of Apocalyptic Discourse," 69).

From this rhetorical context, Paul's use of the word ἀπορφανίζω which may not be accidental, but was used intentionally to imply his identification with the Thessalonian believers' sorrow in suffering and in the death of their church members. Point in fact, this section of 2:17—3:10 functions as the continuing *narratio* for his praise and identification with the audience. Moreover, Paul's tone in this section is not authoritative over the Thessalonian believers, which is asserted on an "apostolic parousia," but with an earnest (2:17b; 3:10 "we longed with great eagerness to see you face to face"; 3:1a "Therefore when we could bear it no longer") and encomiastic tone (2:19 "For what is our hope or joy or crown of boasting ... Is it not you?"; 3:7 "For this reason ... during all our distress and persecution we have been encouraged about you through your faith").

In addition to these, Paul continually praises his deeds for the Thessalonian believers, particularly the pure motive for his deeds: 3:1b-5, "we sent Timothy ... to strengthen and encourage you for the sake of your faith ... somehow the tempter had tempted you and that our labor had been in vain."; 3:9-10, "How can we thank God enough for you ... Night and day we pray most earnestly that we may see you face to face and restore whatever is lacking in your faith." Menander (420.20-25) and Cicero (*De Orat.* II, 85.346) highlight the pure motive (altruism) of deeds in panegyrics and in funeral oration. Quintilian (*Inst.* 4.2.52) also emphasizes the three essential factors of *narratio* as the facts, character, and motives. As related to Ochs' comments, "the greater the altruism, the greater the honor; and the wider the public affected by the altruism, the greater the admiration,"[137] Paul's description of his deeds in 2:17—3:10, which emphasizes his motive of altruism for the Thessalonian believers, reflects the encomium of funeral oration. In final analysis, this section of 2:17—3:10 functions as an encomium of his deeds so he might establish the identification with the Thessalonian believers for the following section of consolation and exhortation (chs. 4-5).

Summary of *Narratio* (Encomium) in 1:4—3:10 (Elements of Funeral Oration)

Quintilian, who considers narration "the most important department of rhetoric in actual practice" (2.1.10), asserts that to affect a change of mind, the *narratio* should provide "a plausible picture of what occurred" through " ... anything more plausible in imagination, more vehement in censure or more vivid in description" (4.2.123, 125). This process will lead the audience to feel "as if they were actual eyewitnesses of the scene" (4.2.123). Further,

---

137. Ochs, *Consolatory Rhetoric*, 107.

the credit of the *statement of facts* (*narratio*) will increase to the degree of authority of the speaker and such authority will come from "our manner of life" and "our style of eloquence" (4.2.125).

Quintilian notes that without a developed sense of *narratio*, a speech "composed of disconnected passages . . . must necessarily lack cohesion" (2.11.7) and the *narratio* should function as "connecting links" to connect a particular commonplace with the "subject" in the whole speech (2.4.30). For this function, the orator should have a sense of how to determine what was relevant to say, that is, "wise adaptability" (2.13.2) needed to meet the most varied emergencies (2.13.2).[138]

On the basis of the contents of *narratio* (encomium) discussed above, it is possible to assert that Paul employs the elements of the *narratio* in 1 Thess 1:5—3:10 with some overlapping elements found between 1 Thess 1:5—3:10 and funeral oration.

First of all, both contain the long *narratio* (encomium) which narrates, in chronological order, the facts, character, and motives of deeds.[139] In funeral oration, by narrating the long encomium of the ancestors, the dead, and contemporaries, "narratives by their very nature invite participation, acceptance, and, if artfully done, some degree of identification."[140] In the same way, Paul, employing the long encomium of himself and the Thessalonian believers, establishes the ground to unify the community and identify with the audience to prepare the mind of the audience for the following section of consolation and exhortation (4:1—5:11). Just as funeral oration mainly works for character, not for reasons with proofs, Paul attempts to accomplish identification through the narration, namely to shape his character and console the Thessalonians in the *narratio*.

Second, both show similar content for the encomium (*narratio*) just as listed on the handbook of funeral oration in chronological order: country, family, birth, nurture, education, and accomplishments (deeds). In funeral oration, deeds and the origin of ancestors, the dead, and the contemporaries exist. In 1 Thess 1:5—3:10, Paul suggests he and the Thessalonian community are ancestors and particularly emphasizes the function of

---

138. O'Banion, "Narration and Argumentation," 336–39.

139. Generally, each encomium of funeral orations form 4/5 in portion: Isocrates (*Evagoras*, 9.12–69; *Panegyricus*, 15–159); Thucydides (*History of the Peloponnesian War*, XXXVI-XLII); Pseudo-Lysias (*Funeral Oration*, 3–70); Plato (*Menexenus*, 237b-246b); Demosthenes (*Funeral Speech*, 4–31); Hyperides (*Oration*, 6–40); Tacitus (*Agricola*, 4–42); Dio Cassius (*Tiberius' Funeral Oration for Augustus*, 36–41); Libanius (*Funeral Oration over Julian*, 18.7–280); Dio Chrysostom (*Melancomas*, 29.3–18); Lucretius Vespillo (*Laudatio Turiae*, 1–53); Jewish Funeral Oration (4 Macc. 3:19—17:6).

140. Ochs, *Consolatory Rhetoric*, 109.

the contemporaries (himself and the Thessalonian community) following Thucydides, who highlights praise of the present generation rather than the ancestors and the dead.

Third, both of them contain reaffirming and reminding language for the vivid expression (*enargeia, ekphrasis*), which is characteristic in the *narratio* of epideictic rhetoric (Quintilian, 4.2.123). For example, in this sense, Hyperides (*Funeral Speech*, 4-5) states: "for my listeners will be no random audience but the persons who themselves have witnessed the actions of these men." Paul also intentionally and frequently employs reminding language and vivid expressions, "you yourselves know" and "You are witnesses, and God also" (1:4, 5; 2:1, 2, 5, 9, 10, 11; 3:3, 4).

Fourth, both reflect the context of suffering and death in tone and content. 1 Thess 2:1-12 is sandwiched between 1:5-10 and 2:13-16, which show the context of suffering and death. Following this further, the words ἀγῶν and ἀπορφανίζω may imply the context of suffering and death, and the words employed in 1 Thess 3:2-3 are strikingly similar to those used in the Jewish apocalyptic texts: στηρίξαι (to strengthen)—σαίνεσθαι (be shaken)—θλίψεσιν (persecutions), which reflect the context of suffering and death.

Fifth, both have the repetitive amplification in structure and contents, which is characteristic in epideictic rhetoric (funeral oration). With repetitive amplification, embellishments in content and structure (1:4-10//2:13-16; 2:5-8//9-12), and the triple-repetitive metaphor (2:7-8, 11, 17), Paul amplifies his character in ministry to prepare the minds of the audience for receiving the consolation and exhortation (4:1—5:10).

Sixth, both contain the repetitive contrast/comparison in character and deeds, which functions to put superiority on the subject. Just as the extant funeral orations commonly employ the repetitive contrast in encomium to highlight the superiority of the character, Paul also uses the contrast of his character in 2:1-2, 3-4, 5-7, and 8 repeatedly.

Seventh, with shepherding language ("gentle [ἤπιοι] . . . as a nurse" [2:7]) and with a sandwiched pattern of both the praises of the Thessalonian believers (1:4-10; 2:13-16) and of his own self-praise (2:1-12), Paul establishes an identification between himself and the Thessalonians to prepare their minds for the consolation and exhortation (4:1—5:11).

182   THE RHETORICAL APPROACH TO 1 THESSALONIANS

Transitus with the Prayer Pattern (3:11–13)

It is recommended a break between the end of the narrative and the beginning of the argumentation be avoided.[141] In this case, this core part of the *partitio* can be expressed at the end of the *narratio* as a *propositio*, where it appears as a summary of the *narratio*. Also, this section serves as a bridge to the exhortations and consolations in 4:1—5:11. In other words, the wish prayer, the *transitus* between the *narratio* and the exhortation (consolation), could function as a new *exordium* which again establishes rapport with the audience and prepares their minds to accept the following exhortations.[142]

It is pointed out, the encomium's conclusion comes back to the hero, often with an enumeration of his qualities and deeds, ending with a prayer.[143] Menander (*Division of Epideictic Speeches*, 377.25–30), in the imperial oration (*Basilikos Logos*), comments, " . . . you must utter a prayer, beseeching God . . . " Where a funeral oration is spoken over the body of a king, it differs from the imperial oration (*Basilikos Logos*) by the addition of the lamentation and consolation with exhortation, and these are in many ways flexible depending on the case.[144] In the same way, Menander (*Division of Epideictic Speeches*, 422.1–4), in the funeral oration (*Epitaphios*), says: "Finally, round off the speech with a prayer, asking the gods for the greatest blessings for them."

To be sure, honorific prayers are frequently used in epideictic rhetoric, particularly in funeral orations, and they usually take the form of appealing "to the deity to act in some way to strengthen the audience, especially if they are suffering loss or suffering in some other way."[145] In this sense, Paul's prayer in 1 Thess 3:11–13 precisely complies with the *topoi* of funeral oration because the community of the Thessalonian believers are suffering loss and death.[146]

141. Lausberg, *Handbook of Literary Rhetoric*, 159.
142. Witherington, *1 and 2 Thessalonians*, 101–2.
143. Burgess, "Epideictic Literature," 130; Kennedy, *Progymnasmata*, 108.
144. Burgess, "Epideictic Literature," 130.
145. Witherington, *1 and 2 Thessalonians*, 27.
146. Among the extant funeral oration, some kinds of honorific prayers are familiar with the orators. Plato (*Menexenus*, 244.A, 247.D), in encomium and consolation (exhortation), employs the honorific prayers. Plutarch (*Consolatio Ad Apollonium*, 119.A) comments on Xenophon's example and prayer for his son, "I prayed to the gods, not that my son should be immortal or even long of life . . . but that he should be brave and patriotic." Seneca (*On Grief for Lost Friends*, Ep. 63.16) ends his consolatory rhetoric in letter with prayer, and Tacitus (*Agricola*, 46) also says the prayer "If there be any habitation for the spirits of the just . . . may you rest in peace . . . " Libanius (*Funeral Oration over Julian*, 624) says, "before now people have offered up prayers to him also

In conclusion, in *exordium* (1:2-3) and in *narratio* (1:4—3:10), following the elements and conventions of funeral oration, Paul attempts to persuade the recipients of Thessalonica and strives to establish ground and identify with the audience so that he might make the audience responsive to the consolation and exhortation (4:1—5:11). In other words, Paul's long *narratio* functions to shape the character of the author and to console the Thessalonians. Furthermore, according to *topoi* of funeral oration, the author ends with a prayer (3:11-13), foreshadowing what is to come in 4:1—5:11. Chapter 6 will attempt to find the parallels between funeral oration and 1 Thess, particularly consolation and exhortation, which mainly indicate the rhetorical situation and the rhetorical purpose of 1 Thess.

..." Lucretius Vespillo (*Laudatio Turiae*, 67–69), in epilogue, ends with repeated praise of the deceased and a prayer.

CHAPTER 7

Comparing between 1 Thessalonians 4–5 and Funeral Oratory

THE PRECEDING ANALYSIS OF the *exordium* and *narratio* (encomium) of 1 Thess shows the *topoi* of funeral oration in Greco-Roman and Jewish cultures. Just as the encomium of funeral oration is commonly long, Paul intentionally employs long *narratio* (encomium) and the language of reaffirming and reminding within the context of death and martyrdom. Further, he follows the *topoi* of funeral oration such as the repetitive amplification and the repetitive contrast/comparison. Through this process of the *exordium* and *narratio* (encomium), Paul attempts to establish rapport with the audience and to identify with the Thessalonian community so he might offer consolation and exhortation in 4:1—5:11.

In the same way, R. Jeal, who considers the book of Ephesians to fit the genre of "sermon," rightly points out the function of the *exordium* and *narratio* (encomium) in epideictic rhetoric. According to Jeal, the actual connection between Ephesians chapters 1–3 (the *exordium* and *narratio*) and 4—6 (the exhortations) happens through the unique rhetorical effect of the *exordium* and *narratio*. Just as the author intends and presents in the *exordium* and *narratio*, the minds of the recipients are developed and are meant to have been so favorably persuaded and prepared to move on to the behavioral goals the exhortation describes.[1] In other words, the function of the *exordium* and *narratio* in epideictic rhetoric is to establish rapport with the audience so they might practice the behavior the exhortation calls for.

René Kieffer also correctly grasps the function of 1:2—3:13 (*narratio* or *encomium*) as "la longue *captatio benevolentiae*," which prepares the readers' minds for the eschatological consolation/exhortation in 4:13–18a.[2] Paul strengthens them in the Gospel (2:1–12; 2:17—3:13) and praises their models of faith (1:7; 2:14–16) to prepare their minds and identify with them

1. Jeal, *Integrating Theology and Ethics in Ephesians*, 177–78.
2. Kieffer, "L'eschatologie en 1 Thessaloniciens," 211.

for the following exhortation. Paul's employment of praise and blame in *narratio* shows this letter to be the epideictic genre. In funeral oration there is the unique effect of inviting participation, acceptance, and identification by hearing the long and dramatic encomium (*narratio*).[3]

The goal of this chapter is to show the parallels and similarities in content, structure, and *topoi* between funeral oration of the Greco-Roman culture and 1 Thess 4–5. Particularly, by comparing the *topoi* and concentrating on 4:13—5:11, it will be shown how the *topoi* of 4:13—5:11 are related to funeral oration and how 4:13—5:11 fits the rhetorical situation of funeral oration.

Paul's prayer of *transitus* consists of three petitions for the Thessalonian believers, which foreshadow what is to come in 4:1—5:11 (consolation and exhortation), so they function as a new *exordium* which establishes an identification with the audience. C. Wanamaker analyzes 3:11-13 in three petitions: (1) Paul's desire to visit the Thessalonians (v. 11); (2) Paul's hope that their Christian love would increase (v. 12); (3) his concern that they should persevere until the parousia of Christ (v. 13). Then he asserts the implicit parenetic character of the last two petitions (2) and (3) serve as transitions to the themes of holiness or Christian ethical behavior (4:1-12; 5:13-22) and the parousia (4:13-5:11).[4] His problem, however, is that he skips an important petition of v. 11, which also contains the implicit parenetic character. In other words, the petition of 3:11 should be related to 4:1-8 because the petition of 3:11, "may God . . . direct our way to you," equals Paul's moral instruction in 4:1-8, "sanctification, holiness in sexual conduct." Unlike Funk's assertion, my assertion is that 2:17—3:10 is not a travelogue or apostolic parousia, and 3:11 is also not merely a travelogue to express Paul's desire or schedule to visit the Thessalonians. Instead, it is a prayer for the Thessalonians to restore their faith with instruction for moral conduct (4:1-8). Thus, 3:11 may mean "May God direct our way (of moral conduct) to you." Paul employs the verb (κατευθύνω) from the wisdom tradition in which prayer is offered for the direction of one's moral path or ways.[5] For example, in the prayer of Ps 118:5 (LXX), "O that <u>my ways may be steadfast</u> in keeping your statutes!" (ὄφελον <u>κατευθυνθείησαν αἱ ὁδοί μου</u> τοῦ φυλάξασθαι τὰ δικαιώματά σου) uses the words "κατευθυνω" and "ὁδος" to direct moral conduct and ways of ethical living. Further, in 3:11 and 3:13, the name of God and Lord Jesus overlaps "God and Father himself

---

3. Ochs, *Consolatory Rhetoric*, 109.

4. Wanamaker, *Epistles to the Thessalonians*, 140.

5. Long, "From Epicheiremes to Exhortation," 29. This meaning is seen in Ps 118:5 (LXX) and Prov 4:26 (Ps 5:9; 36:23; 118:133; Prov 9:15; 29:27) and in the New Testament with reference to moral conduct (Luke 1:79; 2 Thess 3:5).

and our Lord Jesus." These names are commonly employed in 4:1-8 [God (x5); Lord Jesus (x3)] and in 4:13-18 [God (x2); Lord Jesus (x8)].

3:11—"... may God ... direct our way to you."   4:1-8—Holiness ("sanctification")

3:12—"... may the Lord ... abound in love ... "   4:9-12—Love ("... taught by God")

3:13—"blameless ... at the coming of our Lord"   4:13-5:11—Hope of Jesus' Parousia

In the prayer of *transitus* of 3:11-13, which foreshadows the upcoming consolation and exhortation in 4:1—5:11, it actually consists of two main clauses of voluntative optative (vv. 11-12) and an articular infinitive of purpose/result (v. 13) as follows:

> Main clause 11Αὐτὸς δὲ ὁ Θεὸς καὶ Πατὴρ ἡμῶν καὶ ὁ Κύριος ἡμῶν Ἰησοῦς <u>κατευθύναι</u> τὴν ὁδὸν ἡμῶν πρὸς ὑμᾶς·
>
> Main clause 12 ὑμᾶς δὲ ὁ Κύριος <u>πλεονάσαι καὶ περισσεύσαι</u> τῇ ἀγάπῃ εἰς ἀλλήλους καὶ εἰς πάντας,
>
> καθάπερ καὶ ἡμεῖς εἰς ὑμᾶς,
>
> Art.Inf: Purpose/Result 13 <u>εἰς τὸ στηρίξαι</u> ὑμῶν τὰς καρδίας ἀμέμπτους ἐν ἁγιωσύνῃ
>
> ἔμπροσθεν τοῦ θεοῦ καὶ πατρὸς ἡμῶν
>
> <u>ἐν τῇ παρουσίᾳ τοῦ κυρίου ἡμῶν Ἰησοῦ</u>
>
> μετὰ πάντων τῶν ἁγίων αὐτοῦ. [ἀμήν]

This structure, two voluntative optative clauses (vv. 11-12), functions to lead to the result or the purpose of v. 13, "... strengthen ... that you may be blameless ... at the coming of our Lord Jesus." Consequently, it may be proper that Paul's focus of prayer, consolation, and exhortation is highlighted in v. 13 and 4:13—5:11.

Handbook of Funeral Oration (Consolation and Exhortation)

Menander Rhetor (*Division of Epideictic Speeches*) considers the consolatory speech and the funeral speech separately, though both contain overlapping elements. Regarding the consolatory speech, he claims the speaker also laments the fallen and raises the misfortune to great significance, amplifying the emotion with the impression (II, 413.5-15). He suggests three essential elements for the consolatory speech:

1. You should divide the encomia into the chronological sections (413.15);
2. After having amplified the lamentation as far as possible, the speaker should approach the consolatory part (413.25–30);
3. For advice, it is good to philosophize on human nature generally, how death is the end of life for all men and how the change from this life is perhaps to be preferred, "I feel convinced that he who has gone dwells in the Elysian Fields ... he is living now with the gods, travelling round the sky" (414.5–22).

In the consolation and exhortation of funeral orations, Menander, in the same way, recommends emphatically a lament for the departed, "None of the various sections of the speech should be without an element of lamentation ... " (419.10—420.4). After this, he inserts the section of consolation to the whole family, "No need to lament; he is sharing the community of the gods" (421.15–25). Finally, there should be a speech of advice (exhortation) rather than of consolation; to the children, to replicate their fathers' virtues (421.26–30). Pseudo-Dionysius (*On Epideictic Speeches*) also contains the similar *topoi* to Menander regarding the consolation and exhortation by saying, "After this (encomium) ... to the exhortatory part, exhorting the survivors to like deeds ... " (280). Contrary to Menander, however, Pseudo-Dionysius omits the lamentation section, but emphasizes the consolatory topic, which is manifest in Thucydides: "The consolatory topic, however, is more essential ... *We must not mourn or bewail the dead—this would not be to comfort the survivors but to increase their sorrow*, and the speech would appear not to be a praise of the decreased but a lamentation ... " (281). Finally, at the end, it is essential "to speak of the immortality of the soul ... because they are among the gods" (283).

In the next part, I will explore how the *topoi* of funeral oration (consolation/exhortation) appear in 1 Thess 4–5, and how it fits the rhetorical situation for the Thessalonian church.

First Exhortation–Call to a Life of Holiness (4:1–8)

Concerning Paul's exhortation in 4:1—5:22, Laub correctly grasps the purpose of 1 Thessalonians to build an eschatological community and classifies both 4:1–12 and 5:12–22 as exhortations to the fledgling community. But he considers 4:13—5:11 Paul's attempt at problem-solving the fate of the dead and the time of the Parousia.⁶ He, however, neglects the rhetorical approach of funeral oration, which shows 4:13-18 to be consolation to the dead and 5:1-11 to be the exhortation for the living.

Paul uses the disclosure formula to open each exhortation (4:1-8 "Λοιπὸν οὖν"; 4:9-12 "Περὶ δὲ"; 4:13-18 "περὶ τῶν κοιμωμένων"; 5:1-11 "Περὶ δὲ τῶν χρόνων καὶ τῶν καιρῶν"). In 4:1-12, the religious and moral exhortation, Paul employs the essential rhetorical quality of the O. T., in which the ethos is strengthened and accompanied by the pathos. "Le rappel de l'autorité divine et de celle du Christ (4:1-2, 8-9; the ethos) y est renforcée par l'évocation du judement final (5b; the pathos)."⁷

Looking back to the *transitus* with prayer (3:11-13), holiness (4:1-8; sanctification, blamelessness before God) and the hope for the Parousia (4:13-18) are intertwined together because holiness is the pre-requisite (cause) for the Parousia of Jesus (effect). Just as discussed, the structure between vv. 11-12 and v. 13 is organized with the climax in v. 13 (Jesus' Parousia), which indicates the purpose/result of vv. 11-12. The exhortation of vv. 11-12 (4:1-8, 9-12) functions as the pre-requisite for the eschatological Parousia of Jesus and for the eschatological Christian community, which was newly established.

Therefore, it is possible for Paul to form the *inclusio* structure between holiness (4:1-8) and hope for the Parousia (4:13-18) in order to emphasize the holiness of the eschatological Thessalonian community. Paul spends more time exhorting them on holiness (4:1-8) and the hope for the Parousia (4:13—5:11) than on love for one another (4:9-12). Further, he concludes each argument of holiness (4:1-8) and of hope for the Parousia (4:13—5:11) with a strong recommendation: "Therefore (τοιγαροῦν) whoever... rejects not human... but God (οὐκ...ἀλλὰ)..." (4:8), "Therefore encourage... (Ὥστε παρακαλεῖτε)" (4:18), and "Therefore encourage... (Διὸ παρακαλεῖτε)" (5:11). In contrast, Paul simply praises their continuing love for others (4:10). Clearly, then, Paul recognizes the problems in their faith to be lacking holiness and hope for the Parousia of Christ and attempts to establish the eschatological Christian community.

---

6. Laub, *Eschatologische Verkündigung und Lebensgestaltung nach Paulus*, 123-32.

7. Kieffer, "L'eschatologie en 1 Thessaloniciens," 211; Kennedy, *Classical Rhetoric*, 121. Kennedy claims that authority is analogous to ethos in classical rhetoric, and ethos is bolstered by something like pathos by the fears of future punishment or hopes of future reward.

Second Exhortation—Love for One Another (4:9-12)

This section is continually developed on the prayer found in 3:12, "may the Lord ... abound in love," for the newly established Christian community of Thessalonica. Regarding the connection between 4:9-10 and 11-12, G. Beale claims though there seems to be no logical link, Paul likely intends to achieve the same purpose or result in 4:12: "that your daily life may win the respect of outsiders and so that you will not be dependent on anybody." Finally, Beale concludes that this section functions as a good witness to the unbelieving world.[8] Charles Masson also asserts similarly Paul helped them as new converts to live in a manner worthy of God (2:12), and that naturally, in 4:12, Paul emphasizes their public functions to outsiders by saying, "Et il importe singulièrement que *ceux du dehors* ne soient pas éloignés de l'Evangile et de l'Eglise par les fautes et les inconséquences des chrétiens."[9] Consequently, v. 12 contains the context of funeral ritual.

Paul employs two voluntative optative clauses (3:11-12), and finally uses the infinitival purpose/result of 3:13 for the climax. In the same way, in this section, after using several infinitival commands in 4:10-11, he finally employs the climax clause of purpose/result in 4:12. Certainly, Paul's focus on exhortation is largely highlighted on 4:12, "so that you may behave properly toward outsiders and be dependent on no one."

Main clause	[10] Παρακαλοῦμεν δὲ ὑμᾶς, ἀδελφοί,
Inf/Command	περισσεύειν μᾶλλον,
Inf/Command	[11] καὶ φιλοτιμεῖσθαι ἡσυχάζειν
Inf/Command	καὶ πράσσειν τὰ ἴδια
Inf/Command	καὶ ἐργάζεσθαι ταῖς [ἰδίαις] χερσὶν ὑμῶν, καθὼς ὑμῖν παρηγγείλαμεν,
Final clause (purpose/result)	[12] ἵνα περιπατῆτε εὐσχημόνως πρὸς τοὺς ἔξω καὶ μηδενὸς χρείαν ἔχητε.

It is noteworthy that Paul, in both exhortations of 4:1-8 and 9-12, commonly employs similar expressions, which distinguish the Thessalonian Christian community from others, "like *the Gentiles* who do not know God" (4:5b, καθάπερ καὶ τὰ ἔθνη τὰ μὴ εἰδότα τὸν θεόν) and as they "behave properly toward *outsiders*" (4:12a, περιπατῆτε εὐσχημόνως πρὸς τοὺς ἔξω). Paul's intention of both exhortations toward the newly

---

8. Beale, *1-2 Thessalonians*, 126-27.
9. Masson, *Les Deux Épîtres de Saint Paul aux Thessaloniciens*, 52.

established Christian community is to distinguish them from the pagan world and outsiders, and to establish a firm identity and unity as the chosen, eschatological community. In the same light, the main purpose of the consolation/exhortation in funeral oration is to exhort the audience to have a firm identity, unity as a community separated from outsiders, and to imitate the dead in their future life.

Besides that, Paul's claim to "*behave properly* (περιπατῆτε εὐσχημόνως) toward outsiders" (4:12a) reflects the language of funeral orations when it is recommended to the audience and the living. Garry Wills, who shows how Abraham Lincoln used Greek funeral oratory to craft his Gettysburg Address, claims the prose form of Greek funeral oration, including bald and astringent speech, is for "a transition from family mourning to the larger community's sense of purpose."[10] Greek funeral oration has the purpose of challenging the living community to struggle to contain individual sorrow so that one may express it publically and collectively and to take up the task left by the dead just as Lincoln said in his Gettysburg Address, "It is altogether fitting and proper that we should do this . . . to the great task remaining before us."[11] Particularly, Lincoln's employment of the "right and fitting" formula is found in Greek funeral orations, which command the proper attitude of the living and the community: Thucydides puts individual tragedy in a larger pattern of ordered things, "I shall speak first of our ancestors, for it is *right* and at the same time *fitting* . . . such words as I had that were *fitting*" (2.36.2; 2.46.1). Plato (*Menexenus*) says, "of whom it is *right and proper* that we should make mention first and celebrate their valor" (239d3). Hyperides also recommends, for the living, "While praise is *due* to Athens for her policy . . . Leosthenes must *have first claim* (δίκαιον) upon our gratitude for ever."

Lysias says, "we must *needs* (αναγκη) follow our ancient customs"- (81).[12] Finally, Demosthenes (*The Funeral Speech*, 35) employs this language in his consolation/exhortation, which is similar to 1 Thess 4:12b, "*behave properly*"(περιπατῆτε εὐσχημόνως) by saying, "While it is perhaps difficult to mitigate the present misfortunes by the spoken word, nevertheless *it is our duty to endeavor* to turn our minds to comforting thoughts, reflecting that it is *a beautiful thing* . . . to be seen *enduring* their affliction *more decorously (properly) than the rest of mankind* (δεῖ. . .καλόν εστι τα δείν εὐσχημονεστερον τῶν αλλῶν. . .)." These expressions indicate proper

---

10. Wills, *Lincoln at Gettysburg*, 53. He suggests for his assertion Thucydides's words "Your individual lamenting done, depart" (2.46.2).

11. Wills, *Lincoln at Gettysburg*, 53–54.

12. Wills, *Lincoln at Gettysburg*, 273.

behavior and attitude toward outsiders beyond the boundaries of a funeral oration's context. Indeed, Paul may intentionally echo the Greek funeral oration formula of "proper and fit," particularly Demosthenes' when he says, "enduring . . . more properly (decorously, εὐσχημονεστερον) than the rest of mankind," and when he says, "behave properly (περιπατῆτε εὐσχημόνως) toward outsiders" in 4:12b. In the following passage of 4:13—5:11, I will continue to explore the elements of funeral oration on the basis of the assertion discussed above.

Third Exhortation/Consolation—The Hope for the Parousia (4:13-18)

Just as asserted, the third exhortation/consolation is foreshadowed in the *transitus* prayer of 3:13, which shows that Paul's focus of prayer and of consolation and exhortation climaxes at 3:13 and 4:13—5:11. This assertion is also supported by some literary features reflected in verse 13, which contains the disclosure formula. Paul employs the disclosure formula, which usually indicates the new topic, "You know that . . . " (2:1; 4:1-2, 9, 11). In 2:1, Paul begins his panegyric digression with the words "You yourselves know . . . " and in 4:1-2, he also says, " . . . as you learned from us . . . for you know what instruction . . . " Also, in 4:9, 11, Paul begins with the same pattern: "Now concerning love . . . for you yourselves have been taught by God . . . "

In contrast to this normal form of a disclosure formula, however, Paul employs a distinctive emphatic (double-negative) disclosure formula by saying, "But we do not want you to be uninformed . . . about those who have died" (4:13). This emphatic formula indicates Paul's intention to show and teach a new topic, which is not yet known to them. Paul's exhortation may be climaxed in this section of 4:13-18.

Regarding the relationship between 4:11-12 and 13-18, G. Beale correctly grasps Paul's consolation and exhortatation (4:13—5:11) are closely connected with Paul's last admonition in 4:11-12, not two distinct exhortations. Christians should behave properly before the unbelieving world in order to be good witnesses, because behaving quietly and properly also comprises not grieving over the death of loved ones *like the rest of men* (i.e., the "outsider" of 4:12), *who have no hope*.[13] This passage reflects the funeral context and funeral oration. Thus, it is probably right to claim that this exhortation, "so that you may behave properly toward outsiders . . . so that you may not grieve as others do who have no hope" (4:12-13), indicates having an awareness of how one behaves at a public funeral before non-Christians

---

13. Beale, *1–2 Thessalonians*, 130.

because their behavior may "count in this category and should be seen as an opportunity to be a good witness."[14]

Beale's assertion correctly reflects the social and cultural context because it is said, "hopes are for the living, but the ones who die are without hope" (Theocritus, *Idyll* 4.42).[15] Though there was classical literature, philosophy, and Greek-Latin epitaphs implying belief in immortality, the prevalent concept about death was the complete hopelessness, the end of hope, which was reflected in the epitaphs in the Greek-Latin era. Greek-Latin epitaphs express desolation before the utter finality of death, an eternal separation, and particularly a feeling of hopelessness: "All of us who have died and gone below are bones and ashes: there is nothing else" (*Epigrammata Graeca* 646). "Death is the final depth to which all things sink, rich and poor, brute and man (*EG* 459) . . . This harsh tomb has received you, to take your final sleep in the gloomy dust (*EG* 101)."[16] A feeling of hopelessness is manifestly expressed by jingles, half-prose, half-verse in epitaphs: "I, Nicomedes, am happy. I was not, and I became, I am not, and nothing hurts me (*EG* 595) . . . I was not and I came to be; I am not; I don't care" (*non fui, fui, memini, non sum, non curo. Inscriptiones Graecae* 14; *Corpus Inscriptionum Latinarum* 13).[17]

From this observation, it could be probable that 4:13—5:11 contains the funeral context and through the funeral oration, Paul attempts to console and exhort the Thessalonian believers to act differently from outsiders. Through this, they could become a good witness to outsiders. Moreover, Paul, in three exhortations within 4:1—5:11 (4:1-8; 4:9-12; 4:13—5:11), commonly employs some expressions, which sharply contrast the Thessalonian believers: "the Gentiles who do not know God," (4:5b) "outsiders (4:12a)," and "as others do who have no hope" (4:13, οἱ λοιποὶ οἱ μὴ ἔχοντες ἐλπίδα). By contrasting those without hope with the Thessalonian believers, Paul differentiates them from pagan attitudes and unifies the Thessalonian believers into the newly chosen Christian community with a new collective identity. This is the same as a funeral oration in purpose and function.

Paul's main topic in 1 Thess is the theme of hope of Jesus' parousia and suggests that hope at every partial conclusion such as 1:3, 10; 2:12, 19; 3:13; 4:13—5:11; and 5:23. In the same way, in 4:13b, the words "so that you may

---

14. Witherington, *1 and 2 Thessalonians*, 131.
15. Beale, *1-2 Thessalonians*, 130.
16. Lattimore, *Themes in Greek and Latin Epitaphs*, 74-82.
17. Lattimore, *Themes in Greek and Latin Epitaphs*, 84. This expression was simply abbreviated n f f (m)n s n c. It could be interpreted as, "First I was nothing, then I became something, now I am nothing again; and being nothing, I do not care."

not grieve as others do who have no hope," function as Paul's main concern which he deals with in 1 Thess.

Given the Thessalonian church's rhetorical exigencies, and the form, content, and function of funeral oration in antiquity, it is probable Paul employs the purpose and topics of funeral orations in order to solve the present Thessalonian church's problems. Encountering the growing persecutions, suffering, and even death/martyrdom of members, the Thessalonian believers needed encouragement and Paul needed a rhetorical strategy to answer these problems, especially the reality of death/martyrdom problem.

For this, Paul employs the common rhetorical aspects of funeral oration: exordium, encomium, and *transitus* of prayer. With the long encomium (*narratio*) of himself and the Thessalonian believers, Paul establishes identification with the Thessalonian believers who are under suffering and death, so he might prepare their minds for the following consolation and exhortation. Through the employment of the funeral oration, Paul praises the dead and plants the hope of Jesus' parousia and eternal life, consoling and exhorting the Thessalonians to live their lives in the eschatological era (4:13—5:11). I also agree with Beale's assertion that 4:13–18 reflects the funeral context of Paul's era. Paul's use of funeral language such as τῶν κοιμωμένων ("those who have died") and μὴ λυπῆσθε ("not grieve") supports the evidence for his employment of *topoi* in funeral oration.

From a cultural and social perspective, Lucian (*On Funeral*, 11–24) shows the reality of a funeral in that era and ridicules the full range of Greco-Roman beliefs concerning death:

> Then they bathe them . . . crowning it with pretty flowers . . . clothed in splendid raiment . . . Next come cries of distress, wailing of women, tears on all sides, beaten breasts, torn hair, and bloody cheeks . . . while he, all serene and handsome and elaborately decked with wreaths, lies in lofty, exalted state, bedizened as for a pageant . . . The father utters strange, foolish outcries . . . "Dear child . . . dead, bereft away . . . leaving me behind all alone" . . . Regarding grave-mounds, pyramids, tombstones, and epitaphs . . . are they not superfluous and akin to child's play? Some people, moreover, even hold competitions and deliver funeral orations at the monuments, as if they were pleading or testifying on behalf of the dead man before the judges down below! As the finishing touch to all this, there is the funeral feast, and the relatives come in, consoling the parents of the departed . . . that these things and others still more ridiculous are done at funerals. . .

This implies that during his time, there was a prevalent phenomenon of grief and sorrow in the funeral ceremony saying, "hopes are for the living, but the ones who die are without hope" (Theocritus, *Idyll* 4.42).

It is noteworthy that the theme of not grieving the dead is common in consolatory literature and funeral oration.

Paramythia in Roman funeral orations and consolatory literature

Plutarch	*Consolatio Ad Uxorem* (609E–F, 610A–D, 611F); *Consolatio Ad Apollonium* (111.D–113.B, 114D, 120.A–121D, 117.F–118.C)	Recommending not to grieve (an unwarranted grief, their wild mourning, and unrestricted lamentation). "We must resist sorrow at the door ... in unkempt grief and utterly wretched mourning."
Cicero	*Tusculan Disputations*; *On Despising Death*	With the Stoics, he consoles the grieving not to grieve.
Seneca	*On Grief for Lost Friends*; *The Consolatio ad Marciam*; *On Consolation to the Bereaved*	With philosophical concepts, he recommends not to grieve because humans were born to die.
Tacitus	*Agricola*, 43–46a	"though snatched away ... What more could fortune ... decoration of triumph?"
Libanius	*Oration XVIII, Funeral Oration over Julian*, 18.281–306	After a lamentation (18.281–296), he drastically changes his tone and content into the consolatory *topoi*.
Dio Cassius	*Roman History: Tiberius' Funeral Oration for Augustus*, 41.9a	Without any lamentation, Tiberius encourages the audience to keep the immortality in their hearts.
Dio Chrysostom	*The Twenty-Ninth Discourse: Melancomas*, 29.19–21	Without any lamentation, he highlights the consolatory *topoi*.

In this sense, paramythia in Roman funeral orations and consolatory literature (consolation) not to grieve is at least reminiscent of 1 Thess 4:13–18, where Paul urges the Thessalonians not to grieve (μὴ λυπῆσθε) for the dead in Christ since they will rise from their graves at the Parousia.[18] At this juncture, it is worth noting, the main topos in the consolation of funeral

---

18. Martin and Phillips, "Consolatio Ad Uxorem," 413.

oration is to not grieve for the dead. Among the extant funeral orations of Athens, except Lysias, Gorgias, Thucydides, Plato, Demosthenes, and Hyperides, all omitted the threnos (lamentation) in their orations but focused on epainos and paramythia.[19]

Paramythia in Athens funeral orations

Thucydides	*History of the Peloponnesian War*, 43–45	He does not contain any hint of lamentation for the dead, rather, it is full of consolation for the dead.
Plato	*Menexenus*, 246d–249c	In his consolation, he urges the living not to lament. In Plato's case, the emphasis of consolation rather than lamentation is more directive with a more direct imperative with χρη (must, ought).
Demosthenes	*Funeral Speech*, 32–37	He praises the glory of death, the immortality of honor without any hint of lamentation for the dead.
Hyperides	*Oration*, 41–43	He puts the emphasis on the consolation, "we must restrict our grief as best we may."
Pseudo-Lysias	*Funeral Oration*, 71–80	With some lamentation, Lysias makes a drastic change from lamentation to consolation. Though he takes a different pattern, he also puts an emphasis on the consolation rather than lamentation.[20]

In addition to these, in the Jewish funeral oration of *4 Maccabees* (16:1—17:6, *The Mother's Praiseworthy Response and Counsel*), after seven sons' death there is no lamentation, but rather praise and consolation/exhortation, " . . . not bewail with the dirge . . . cease to be grieved" (16:22). Additionally, in *peroration* with consolation/exhortation (17:7—18:5), the

---

19. As discussed, Plutarch, Cicero, and Seneca also prohibited lamentation and rather focused on praise for the fallen and the exhortation and consolation to the citizens.

20. Ziolkowski, *Thucydides*, 49. It makes the consolation more effective by advancing a certain "argument" of the lamentation, and then counteracting them with arguments of consolation.

author praises and consoles the audience (17:15–16; 18:23–24). In the Jewish funeral oration, there is also no hint of lamentation for the dead, but rather praise and consolation with the hope of glory.

Just as discussed in both the consolatory literature and funeral oration, particularly in funeral oration, from the perspectives of the rhetorical situation and of the rhetorical structure, the emphasis is put on the consolation and exhortation rather than lamentation. Mainly, the lamentation is omitted. In the case of the funeral oration of Athens, the orators delivered the speech at the beginning of the war, or during and after the war. If they lamented those who died in the war, that would have discouraged the audience and hindered them from continuing the war. In the case of the Jewish funeral oration of *4 Maccabees*, with a lengthy narration of the brother's martyrdom and the author's praise upon achievement, the Jewish audience could have perceived the attitude of solidarity with brothers and sisters, namely the identification of the Jewish community. Furthermore, it is natural with a lengthy encomium and consolation to not include any lamentation, "Even if they experience some measure of loss on account of their adherence to the Jewish way of life, the audience is also 'not to be grieved,' for the rewards of covenant loyalty far outweigh any disadvantages they might experience here" (16:12).[21]

Contrary to Menander Rhetor (*Division of Epideictic Speeches*, 419.10), Pseudo-Dionysius, omitting the lamentation section, rather puts emphasis on the consolatory topics because mourning and bewailing the dead does not comfort the survivors, but multiplies their sorrow (281). In 1 Thess 4:13–18, Paul's rhetorical situation and rhetorical purpose are similar to the Athenian funeral oration and Jewish funeral oration. Paul also employs this *topos* of consolation/exhortation with different content, not employing the lamentation for the dead because they are also under severe suffering and even death/martyrdom. Through a lengthy narration (encomium) of Paul and the Thessalonian believers (1:4—3:10), Paul establishes rapport (identification) with the audience so he might prepare their minds for the following consolation/exhortation (4:13—5:11). Consequently, he begins his consolation for the dead with the words "so that you may not grieve as others do who have no hope" (4:13b).

The content of his consolation for the dead, however, is drastically different from the Athenian or Jewish funeral oration. In 4:13b, the words "others who have no hope," have the same indication as the words, "the Gentiles who do not know God" (4:5b), and the feelings "toward outsiders" (4:12). In

---

21. deSilva, *4 Maccabees*, 216, 239.

other words, these terminologies are used as boundary-defining by Paul.²² Through these different expressions, Paul sets a clear boundary between the Thessalonian Christian believers and the Gentiles and outsiders. In Eph 2:12b, Paul also claims that "[you Gentiles were] having no hope and without God in the world" (ἐλπίδα μὴ ἔχοντες καὶ ἄθεοι ἐν τῷ κόσμῳ).²³ The reason the Thessalonian believers are also "not to be grieved," is that the faith and hope for the rewards of death far outweigh any disadvantages they might experience here, even death. Therefore, Paul gives the reason "not to be grieved," by saying, "for since we believe that Jesus died and rose again, even so, through Jesus, God will bring with him those who have died" (4:14). Through this consolation, Paul encourages the newly founded church who has been attacked and has suffered death/martyrdom so he might strengthen and confirm their unity/identity. This is the main purpose and content for the consolation/exhortation of funeral oration.

Imperial Funerary Motifs in 1 Thess 4:13–18

Just as discussed, it is possible to find some overlapping connections between imperial funerary triumphal procession and Jesus' Parousia from the perspective of socio-cultural exploration. Particularly, these connections may explain why Paul can interweave "Jesus' Parousia" (second coming) as a processional parousia (the image of conquering general entering the city or the image of triumphal procession "with a cry of command, with the archangel's call and with the sound of God's trumpet" [1 Thess 4:16]) with the discussion of death. Actually, Paul was probably aware of the recent triumphal processions in Rome by Germanicus Caesar in A.D. 17, Caligula in A.D. 40, and Claudius in A.D. 43. From the founding of Rome until the reign of Vespasian there were more than 320 such triumphal processions.²⁴ Paul was likely familiar with the triumphal processions in his period and their cultural implications. In the following section, I will show imperial funerary motifs present in 1 Thess 4:13–18 with the description of Christ's Parousia.

Roman Imperial Funeral Procession

In Roman imperial funeral processions, there are various images and messages delivered to the people of Rome. Mary Beard correctly describes the

22. Trebilco, *Self-Designation and Group Identity in the New Testament*, 77–90.
23. Wikenhauser and Kuss, *Der Erste und Zweite Brief an die Thessalonicher*, 182.
24. Aus, *Imagery of Triumph and Rebellion in 2 Corinthians 2:14–17*, 1–2.

image and the hidden-purpose/intention of the imperial funeral procession, implying the triumph of death, as follows:

> An obsession with the connection between the triumph and the games has tended to obscure *the links between the triumph and another great ceremonial procession in Roman culture*—known by convenient, if misleading, shorthand as *the aristocratic funeral... Certainly, some elements of triumphal practice have been found in funeral processions.* Dionysius of Halicarnassus himself observed, in his account of the *pompa circensis*, that a strand of ribaldry and satire was shared by all three of circus, funeral, and triumphal parades: men dressed as satyrs or Sileni, dancing and jesting, in both circus procession and funeral, the satiric songs of the soldiers in triumph. Some have tried to argue from this for a common ancestry for all three pompae: Greek roots, as Dionysius himself would predictably have it, or an Etruscan inheritance, as some of his modern successors would prefer.[25]

In this comment, Beard asserts the hidden or manifest connections between a Roman imperial funeral and the triumphal practice. She continually describes Augustus's triumphal funeral rituals for supporting her assertion as follows:

> My concern is not so much with these overlaps between the two processions (triumphal processions and funeral processions) but *with their interrelationship at a broader cultural and ideological level.* We have already noted the links between imperial triumphal and apotheosis, monumentalized in the Arch of Titus with its echoes between the more-than-human status of the triumphing general and the deification of the emperor on his death. The logic of that connection had an even bigger impact on early imperial ritual culture. This is strikingly evident not only in the strange story of Trajan's posthumous triumph (when an effigy of the already deified emperor was said to have processed in the triumphal chariot) but also in the arrangement made for the funeral of Augustus.
>
> On that occasion, one proposal was that the cortège should pass through the *porta triumphalis*; another, that the statue of Victory from the senate house should be carried at the head of the procession; another, that placards blazoning the titles of laws Augustus had sponsored and peoples he had conquered should be paraded, too. Dio, reflecting the logic even if not the more sober facts, claims that the cortège did indeed pass through

---

25. Beard, *Roman Triumph*, 284, emphasis mine.

the triumphal gate, that the emperor was laid out on his bier in triumphal costume, and that elsewhere in the procession there was an image of him in a triumphal chariot. *The triumph here was providing a language for representing (even if not performing) an imperial funeral and the apotheosis that the funeral might simultaneously entail.*[26]

Finally, she concludes about these connection and the effects that "the funeral may have been an occasion in which triumphal splendor could be called to mind, in part, recreated long after the day of the triumph itself had passed, as with the impersonation of the ancestors of the dead man—dressed, if appropriate, in their triumphal robes."[27]

In the same way, Penelope Davies explores the Roman imperial funerary monuments and asserts the similar conclusion that the funerary monuments of the Roman emperors arose to establish a firm foundation and the continuation of the Roman empire safely with the image of triumphal achievements. Furthermore, the functions of an imperial tomb and funeral ritual were to justify the deceased emperor's apotheosis so as to promote the dynasty by highlighting the triumphal image of apotheosis.[28] Davies concludes many of the emperors who designed funerary monuments emphatically and intentionally included a visual representation of highpoints from their respective *res gestae*; further, they selected for their tomb bivalent architectural types, referring both *"to death and to triumph."*[29]

Davies's conclusion from the exploration of Roman emperors' monuments is that the death and the triumphal images are closely connected. Beard also claims there is a connection between an imperial funeral and the triumphal practice and apotheosis. Supporting this assertion, the triumphal image was closely linked with death and imperial funeral procession. Some extant works describe the funeral procession and exhibit the cultural resonance of this connection.[30] Seneca (*To Marcia on Consolation* 3.1–2) described the death of Livia's son Drusus, Augustus's stepson, on the campaign into Germany and emphasized the triumphal funeral procession, " . . . crowds poured forth . . . escorting the funeral train all the way to the city, made it seem more like a triumph." Plutarch (*Philopoemen* 21.2–3) also expressed the similar cultural concept when he described the death of the Achaean general, Philopoemen, and the return of his body

26. Beard, *Roman Triumph*, 285, emphasis mine.
27. Beard, *Roman Triumph*, 285–86.
28. Davies, *Death and the Emperor*, 49–67.
29. Davies, *Death and the Emperor*, 67–68.
30. Beard, *Roman Triumph*, 286.

to Megalopolis. Philopoemen's body was burned and sent home. Above all, his funeral procession was "not in loose or promiscuous order, but with a blending of triumphal procession and funeral rites." Both of those cases display the close connection between the funeral procession and the triumphal image culturally and ideologically.

It is noteworthy that Polybius (*The Histories of Polybius* 53–54), while describing the procession of an imperial funeral, uniquely points out the results and function of the Roman funeral procession, " . . . but the most important result is that young men are thus inspired to endure every suffering for the public welfare in the hope of winning the glory that attends on brave men." Consequently, it may be asserted that the funeral oration and the funeral procession are intended to speak "to the living about the living" in the role of exemplum[31] rather than the memorial to the dead.

Extant Works of Roman Imperial Funeral Procession

At this juncture, the extant works of the description of actual imperial funeral processions adds some information about my thesis. Imperial funerals followed a standard pattern, starting in the Roman Forum and moving in solemn procession to the Campus Martius, a mile to the north-west. Then the ceremony, up to the moment of cremation, was rooted in the traditions of the Roman nobility: the display of the body (or effigy), the ancestral masks, the funeral oration and the cremation were all standard practices.[32]

Cassius Dio (*Roman History* LVI.34–42) describes the funeral procession of Augustus together with Tiberius' funeral oration as follows:

> Then came his funeral. There was a couch made of ivory and gold and adorned with coverings of purple and gold. In it his body was hidden . . . but a wax image of him *in triumphal garb* was visible. This image . . . still another *upon a triumphal chariot*. Behind these came the image of his ancestors . . . and those of other Romans . . . and *all the nations he had acquired, each represented by a likeness which bore some local characteristic, appeared in the procession* . . . Afterwards (after Tiberius' funeral oration) the same men as before took up the couch and *carried it through the triumphal gateway* . . . When the body had been placed on the pyre in the Campus Martius . . . and they cast upon it *all the triumphal decorations* . . . and lighted the pyre from beneath.

---

31. Davies, *Death and the Emperor*, 49, 73.
32. Price, "From noble funerals to divine cult," 56–105.

So it was consumed, and an eagle released from it flew aloft, appearing to bear his spirit to heaven. (emphasis mine)

His description highlights the triumphal scene of Augustus through the imperial funeral process. Cassius Dio (A.D. 155–230, LXXV.4.2—5.5), however, being a participant and spectator at the imperial funeral of Pertinax, records the sequence of events in more detail:

> In the Roman Forum a wooden platform . . . In it there was placed a bier of the same materials . . . Upon this rested an effigy of Pertinax in wax, laid out *in triumphal garb* . . . After this there moved past, first, images of all the famous Romans of old . . . singing a dirge-like hymn to Pertinax . . . there followed *all the subject nations* . . . Behind these were the cavalry and infantry in armor, the race-horses, and all the funeral offerings . . . Following them came an altar gilded all over and adorned with ivory . . . Severus mounted the rostra and read a eulogy of Pertinax . . . Finally, when the bier was about to be moved . . . All the rest of us, now, marched ahead of the bier . . . and in this order we arrived at the Campus Martius. There a pyre had been built in the form of a tower having three stories and adorned with ivory and gold as well as a number of statues, *while on the very summit was placed a gilded chariot that Pertinax had been wont to drive* . . . The emperor then ascended a tribunal . . . The magistrates and the equestrian order . . . Then at last the consuls applied fire to the structure, and when this had been done, an eagle flew aloft from it. Thus was Pertinax made immortal. (emphasis mine)

When we compare the extant works of an imperial funeral procession and funeral oration, they commonly share the topic of triumphal images of the dead.

Cassius Dio (LVI.34-42) (Augustus funeral)	Cassius Dio (LXXV.4.2—5.5) (Pertinax funeral)	Polybius (VI.52-54)	Dionysius of Halicarnassus (the death of Brutus: 5.16-17)
Wax image in triumphal garb, upon a triumphal chariot. Parade of all the nations he had acquired, carrying it through the triumphal gateway.	Wax image in triumphal garb, parading all the subject nations and funeral offerings. A gilded chariot that Pertinax had been wont to drive.	the parade of the dead embroided with gold, celebrating a triumph, riding in chariots preceded by some insignia, dignity.	the triumphal parade with adorned with crown, conducting the trophy-bearing processions, the sacrifies, and a banquet.

Triumphal Image of Jesus' Parousia

Before analyzing the content and aspects of Paul's consolation in 4:13–18, I want to suggest Paul's reason and thought for employing the image (metaphor) of triumphal procession at this point. When dealing with the destiny and sorrow of the dead for the Thessalonian believers, Paul interweaves Jesus' Parousia as a processional parousia with the discussion of death. Paul describes Jesus' Parousia (second coming) as a processional parade with the image of a conquering general entering the city and with the image of a triumphal procession "with a cry of command, with the archangel's call and with the sound of God's trumpet" (1 Thess 4:16). It is clear that Paul employs "les phénomènes auditifs et visuels . . . aux 4:15–17" to make a strong impression on readers,[33] particularly in the Roman context. Actually, in the Roman imperial the power of images is effectively realized in various ways, not only in "works of art, buildings, and poetic imagery, but also religious ritual . . . state ceremony, the emperor's conduct and forms of social intercourse,"[34] even in the funeral procession with images and masks (Dio Cassius 56.34). The Roman imperial broadly created visual imagery for implanting a visual impression on people and made a new visual language such as with "Peace and Security" (1 Thess 5:3). In this sense, the power of visual images may be familiar to the Thessalonian people because they are clients of the Roman economy and politics. Paul may know well this phenomenon and naturally evoke some visual images with the readers from verses 15–17. Just as the Roman imperial funeral procession interweaves the imperial funeral procession as a processional parade with the triumphal image and the apotheosis of the emperor, Paul also employs the triumphal image of Jesus' Parousia with a discussion of the death of some of the Thessalonian believers.

Actually, in his other letters Paul frequently employs the image of the triumphal procession of Christ for explaining his ministry and Jesus' victory. In 2 Cor 2:14–16, "God, who in Christ always leads us in triumphal procession . . . For we are the aroma of Christ to God among those who are being saved and among those who are perishing; to the one a fragrance from death to death, to the other a fragrance from life to life," Paul describes his and his co-workers ministry by employing "the images of triumphal processions and the sacral use of incense, perhaps at such processions" (cf. Josephus *War* 7.72).[35] In this triumphal procession metaphor, God plays

---

33. Kieffer, "L'eschatologie en 1 Thessaloniciens," 214.
34. Zanker, *Power of Images in the Age of Augustus*, 1–4, 213.
35. Keener, *1–2 Corinthians*, 164.

a role of triumphant general who leads Paul in a triumphal procession of eternal life with Christ. In the Roman triumphal ceremony, the triumphal procession was divided into three parts. The first included the spoils, the golden crowns of conquered peoples, and the captives in chains in front of the general's chariot. The second part was the group around the general himself riding a special horse-drawn chariot and the final part was made up of the victorious soldiers.[36] Most captives led in triumphal procession were killed after the procession, but paradoxically Paul, though being the conquered slave exposed to public ridicule and death (his suffering for the gospel), will be the joyful participant in Christ's triumphal celebration, his resurrection.[37] Art from Hellenictic and Roman times shows the metaphorical portrayal of an epiphany procession of deity as a triumphal procession. Depending on this, Paul may emphatically demonstrate that his ministry and himself join to the epiphany type "triumphal procession" rather than to the procession of death.[38] In the same way, in 1 Thess 4:13–18, the martyred Thessalonian believers and the living, though being despised and suffering under the outsiders who have no hope, paradoxically will join the triumphal procession of Christ's Parousia, his resurrection and eternal life over death. Through the triumphal processional image (metaphor), Paul intends to console/exhort them and implant this hope and new perspective.

Furthermore, in Eph 4:7–8, Paul also employs the image of the victorious king's triumphal procession when he explains the bestowing of gifts by the ascended Christ. By quoting Ps 68:17–24 at Eph 4:7–8, "With mighty chariotry, twice ten thousand, thousands upon thousands . . . You ascended the high mountain, leading captives in your train and receiving gifts from people (68:17–18)," Paul describes God as the victorious king who leads his captives in triumphal procession to the temple mount. Paul applies this image to Christ's ascension because in Jesus' exaltation Paul found the eschatological fulfillment of this triumph of God.[39] When God raised Jesus from the dead and seated him at his right hand in the heavenly places (Eph 1:20–22), Paul envisioned the image of the victorious king's triumphal procession of Psalm 68:18. By showing Christ's supremacy over the powers of evil through leading captives to Jesus' exaltation, Paul brings further comfort to the readers in their spiritual warfare with the hosts of darkness.[40]

36. Beard, *Roman Triumph*, 81–82.

37. Keener, *1–2 Corinthians*, 164; Long, *Ancient Rhetoric and Paul's Apology*, 166; Matera, *II Corinthians*, 70–73; Martin, *2 Corinthians*, 46; Williamson, "Led in Triumph," 317–32.

38. Duff, "Metaphor, Motif, and Meaning," 85, 88, 92.

39. O'Brien, *Letter to the Ephesians*, 288–89.

40. O'Brien, *Letter to the Ephesians*, 289; Hoehner, *Ephesians: An Exegetical*

Paul would have been familiar with the image of a triumphal procession due to his experience with the Roman triumphal procession and from the Old Testament. Thus, it is probable that when he describes Christ's triumphal Parousia by employing the image of the victorious king's triumphal procession, there is an overlap between the death of Thessalonian believers and Jesus' triumphal second coming (Parousia). Through this image, Paul implants Jesus' triumphal second coming for the dead into the heart of the living (1 Thess 4:13–18) to help them keep this hope and console/exhort them.

Concerning the hidden word in 1 Thess 4:13–18, particularly 4:16–17, Poul Nepper-Christensen claims the most obvious parallels to 1 Thess 4:16–17 is to be found in John 11:25–26, and further, in 1 Cor 15:51–52.[41] According to him, between 1 Thess 4:16–17 and John 11:25–26 there is an overlapping context, because in John 11:25–26, Jesus talked with Martha about the death of Lazarus and the living who believe in him. In this sense, he correctly claims that "wir haben hier also ein klares Auferstehungswort und dazu ein ebenso klares Worte in derselben Reihenfolge wie in 1 Thess 4:16–17."[42] Though he asserts the hidden and overlapping word between 1 Thess4:16–17 and 1 Cor 15:51–52, however, there are some different rhetorical emphases between them. In 1 Cor 15:51–52, Paul proves the certainty of the resurrection of the dead in body by answering the doubtful question, "now if Christ is proclaimed as raised from the dead, how can some of you say there is no resurrection of the dead?" (1 Cor 15:12). In other words, between 1 Cor 15 and 1 Thess 4:13–18 there exists a different rhetorical function. In 1 Thess 4:13–18, Paul emphasizes Jesus' triumphal image of parousia over death by employing the Roman triumphal image of the funeral procession and funeral oration beyond just the certainty of the resurection of the dead (1 Cor 15). Consequently, in 1 Thess 4:13–18, Paul may implant the hope of Jesus' triumphal Parousia to them and console to overcome their sorrow.

Additionally, Willi Marxsen claims Paul's thought about the resurrection of the dead developed from the fledgling-understanding in 1 Thess 4:13–18 to the full-understanding in 1 Cor 15. For example, in 1 Thess 4:13–18 there is no knowledge of Jesus' first fruits of those who have died (1 Cor 15:20). Marxsen concludes, "Ich meine aber, die Texte zeigen, daß die Entwicklung vom 1 Thess zu dem (einige Jahre später geschriebenen) 1 Kor geht."[43] Both Nepper-Christensen and Marxsen, however, neglect Paul's

---

Commentary, 529–30.

41. Nepper-Christensen, "Das verborgene Herrnwort," 136–65.

42. Nepper-Christensen, "Das verborgene Herrnwort," 151–52.

43. Marxsen, "Auslegung von 1 Thess 4:13–18," 28–29. Marxsen's developmental approach, however, is similar to John Drane's idea movement from thesis (Galatians) to antithesis (1 Corinthians) to synthesis (Romans) over time (*Paul: Libertine or Legalist?*),

strategic employment of rhetorical function in 1 Thess 4:13–18, particularly funeral oration. Joël Delobel correctly claims that while in Thessalonica as well as in Corinth, Paul was faced with the issue of the fate of deceased Christians, there were the basic differences in the *Sitz-im*-Leben,[44] that is, the differences in rhetorical exigency and situation. In 1 Thess 4:13–18, Paul uses Jesus' triumphal image of parousia over death by employing the Roman triumphal image of funeral procession and funeral oration, not showing the overlapping or developmental thoughts of 1 Corinthians 15. The contingent atmospheres and rhetorical situation of Paul's audience may best explain the differences of eschatological and rhetorical emphasis between 1 Thess 4:13–18 and 1 Cor 15.

Three Ways of Referring to Jesus' Triumphal Parousia

Jesus' triumphal Parousia (triumphal procession) is described by three propositional phrases, but referring to the same sound and event.[45] Paul says, do "not grieve as others do who have no hope" (4:13b) because Jesus' second coming will be a triumphal processional parousia, "For the Lord himself, with a cry of command, with the archangel's call and with the sound of God's trumpet (ἐν κελεύσματι, ἐν φωνῇ ἀρχαγγέλου καὶ ἐν σάλπιγγι θεοῦ), will descend from heaven" (4:16). In 1 Thess, the Parousia is always connected to the Kyrios title (Im 1 Thess ist die Parusie immer mit dem Kyrios-Titel verbenden; 2:19; 3:13; 4:14; 5:23).[46] Wikenhauser and Kuss correctly grasp the meaning of v. 16 that as "war Gott auch Subjekt in v. 14 beim Heraufführen der Entschlafennen mit Jesus," even in v. 16 God is "Subjekt und Initiator der Auferstehung (resurrection) der Toten und der Entrückung (rapture) aller in die Sphäre Gottes."[47] Rigaux also agrees with the position that God is the subject of v. 16.[48] This assertion can be proved by the words, "with the sound of God's trumpet" (16b).

The first of three phrases, which describe the various aspects of Jesus' parousia, is "with a cry of command." The word κελεύσμα has the detailed meaning of "the command of a deity," "call and summons," and "the call

---

and Hans Hüber's developmental ideas of Paul from negative view in Galatians to a more moderate view of the law in Romans (*Law in Paul's Thought*).

44. Delobel, "Fate of the Dead According to 1 Thess 4 and 1 Cor 15," 340–47.

45. Bruce, *1 and 2 Thessalonians*, 101.

46. Wikenhauser and Kuss, *Der Erste und Zweite Brief an die Thessalonicher*, 184. This is the same in 1 Cor 16:22 (Maranatha: Komm, Herr!) and Rev 22:20.

47. Wikenhauser and Kuss, *Der Erste und Zweite Brief an die Thessalonicher*, 184.

48. Rigaux, *Les Épitres aux Thessaloniciens*, 542–43.

for the rowers on a ship."⁴⁹ It is probable that Christ's cry of command is directed to the dead, whom he calls to the resurrection through the voice of the archangel and the trumpet of God.⁵⁰ It is, however, not clear how to distinguish the various aspects of Jesus' parousia. Rather, the κελεύσμα, φωνη and σάλπιγξ are all signals for the resurrection and an accompanying mark and intimation of the end.⁵¹

Particularly, it is noteworthy that the third event to mark Jesus' Parousia as a triumphal processional parousia is "the sound of God's trumpet." In antiquity the trumpet was not used much as a musical instrument; its main use was to give signals and it strengthened the war-cry of the soldiers. Apart from the military's use of trumpets, they were used in various occasions such as shepherds gathering flocks, the sign at the beginning of a trial, the sign of ordering silence before prayer, and the beginning of athletic contests. Particularly, in the Greek and Roman period, they are mentioned in *both mourning processions and triumphs*. "At the head of the procession to the grave of those who fell at Plataeae marched the trumpeter who blew the war signal (Plut. Aristides, 21.3). Originally the task of mourning music was to secure for the dead a friendly welcome among the gods of the underworld . . . In Sen. Apocolocyntosis, 12.1 we read in an account of the burial of Claudius that many trumpeters made such music that the deceased could hear. A Roman relief has a vivid depiction of a funeral procession with its musicians. The triumph, too, was opened by trumpeters."⁵² Appian also describes how a magnificent procession accompanied Sulla's embalmed body to Rome with a trumpet call. While his embalmed body rested on a gilded couch on a chariot, standard-bearers and lictors led the procession, and after the body trumpeters, dancers, mimes, and armed soldiers followed. Finally, the cortège passed beneath the city gates, the trumpeters moved to the front, and there was intoning dirgeful music to herald their arrival.⁵³

On the contrary, the trumpet in Judaism functions both as the mark of the visible appearance of God (Theophanies, Zech 9:14; Exod 19:19, "The voice of the trumpet sounded long") and as the eschatological Day of the Lord (the Last Judgment, Isa 27:13; Joel 2:1; Zech 9:14; Zeph 1:14-16; 4 Esd 6:23 "The trumpet will sound out loud, and all men will hear it suddenly and quake"; *Apoc. Mos.* 22, "When we heard the archangel's trumpet, we said: Lo, God comes to Paradise to judge us"; *Pss. Sol.* 11:1, "God will take

---

49. Schmid, in Kittel and Friedrich, *TDNT* 3:656-57.
50. Wanamaker, *Epistles to the Thessalonians*, 173.
51. Schmid, in Kittel and Friedrich, *TDNT* 3:658.
52. Friedrich, in Kittel and Friedrich, *TDNT* 7:74-75.
53. Davies, *Death and the Emperor*, 8.

a great horn in his hand . . . he will blow it and its note will go from one end of the earth to the other. At the first blast the whole earth shakes; at the second the dust is sifted out; at the third the bones are brought together; at the fourth the limbs are warmed; at the fifth their skin is put on; at the sixth the spirits and souls enter their bodies; at the seventh they come to life and stand on their feet in their clothes, as it is said: The almighty Yahweh will blow the horn" (Zech 9:14; *TDNT* 7.80–84)).

Actually, Paul is describing the entrance liturgy of the triumphal king based on Ps 24:7–10, "lift up your head, O gates! And be lifted up, O ancient doors! Then the King of glory may come in . . . Who is the King of glory?. . .The Lord, mighty in battle."[54] A procession of the Ark, which symbolized God's triumphal presence, marked the arrival and return of the victorious warrior king to his people,[55] so then the gates/doors of the temple are invited to lift up their heads with the obedience to their triumphant king. In this passage, Paul employs "the sound of God's trumpet" because the trumpet is the instrument of the herald, commanding the attention of the watchman on the wall and the watchtower. Just as Ps 24:7–10 celebrated and hoped the arrival/return of the triumphant king, Jesus, who was celebrated by his resurrection from the dead, will be welcome by his people through his ultimate and triumphant Advent, his Parousia. In 1 Thess 4:16–17, Paul says, with the sound of God's trumpet "the dead in Christ will rise first. Then we who are alive . . . will be caught up in the clouds together." Through his triumphant Parousia, the triumphant king, Jesus will sound God's trumpet for waking his people, the dead, and the living, like commanding the attention of the watchman of the city. Then, he will be welcomed ("lift up your head," εἰς ἀπάντησιν) by his people.

In the New Testament, the trumpet serves as the triumphal and eschatological signal, which appears in Matt 24:31 (gathering his elect from the four winds with as loud trumpet call) and Rev 8:2–13; 9:13–14; 11:14–15 (seven angels with the trumpets). Particularly, in 1 Cor 15:51–52, Paul reveals God's mystery of the transformation of the living and the raising of the dead, "We will not all die, but we will all be changed, in a moment, in the twinkling of an eye, at the last trumpet. For the trumpet will sound, and the dead will be raised imperishable and we will be changed." Therefore, the trumpet originally signals the eschatological return of Christ and the judgment of God. Also, for the Thessalonian believers who suffer and encounter the sorrow of death, the last trumpet sound indicates Jesus' triumphal

---

54. Witherington, *1 and 2 Thessalonians*, 138.
55. Craigie, *Psalms 1–50*, 214; Kraus, *Psalms 1–59*, 312–16.

procession over death and God's hope for the raising of the dead and the transforming of the living.

In summary, it is possible to say the trumpet has the double image with both the mournful funeral procession and God's triumphal parousia (triumphal Ark procession, eschatological judgment) for his people's resurrection. With the trumpet image, Paul employs the funeral motif of a trumpet in Greco-Roman culture, but simultaneously reverses it with Jesus' triumphal processional parousia, particularly the triumphal entrance of warrior king in Ps 24:7–10. This is in line with the fact that Paul implants Jesus' triumphal Parousia for the dead into the hearts of the living with the overlapping image of the trumpet (the mournful funeral and the triumphal procession of Christ's Parousia). Furthermore, just as Beard claims that in the Roman imperial funeral procession, "some elements of triumphal practice have been found in funeral processions," Paul interweaves the triumphal image of Christ's Parousia into the funeral ritual and the death of his people.

The Funerary Language of "ἁρπαγησόμεθα ἐν νεφέλαις" ("will be snatched in the clouds" 4:17) and the Triumphal Language

Another symbolic funerary language, which provokes the image of funeral procession, is "ἁρπαγησόμεθα ἐν νεφέλαις" ("will be snatched in the clouds" 4:17). Paul employs the funerary language for the expression of the funeral context, but reverses it into the triumphal image of Christ. In vv. 16b-17a, Paul describes the order of the resurrection (the dead first and then the living) and how both of them meet the Lord, "and the dead in Christ will rise first. Then we who are alive, who are left, will be caught up in the clouds ["ἁρπαγησόμεθα ἐν νεφέλαις"] together with them to meet the Lord in the air." The verb ἁρπαζω literally and symbolically means "to take something forcefully or rapaciously," "to steal," and "to denote the rapture of visions" (Foerster, *TDNT* 1.472). First of all, the verb ἁρπαζω is employed in the Scripture with the negative meaning such as found in Matt 12:29 ("plunder his property"), 13:19 ("the evil one snatches away what is sown in the heart"), and John 10:28–29 ("No one will snatch them out of my hand"). On the contrary, it is also used in the positive sense of the mighty operation of God in Acts 8:39 ("the Spirit of the Lord snatched Philip away"), Jude 23 ("save others by snatching them out of the fire"), and Rev 12:5 ("the child was snatched away and taken to God and to his throne"). Paul uses it as he discusses his rapture to heaven (2 Cor 12:2, 4; "was caught up to the third heaven"), nowhere else.[56] In addition, in the apocalyptic writings, the verb

---

56. Rigaux, *Les Épitres aux Thessaloniciens*, 545.

ἁρπάζω is employed for the description of the ascent into the heavens (3 Bar. 2:1; 1 En. 39:3; 2 En. 3:1).

It is noteworthy, however, that the verb ἁρπάζω is predominantly used in secular works in the context of the funeral procession and death. Particularly, among the extant consolatory literatures, Plutarch (*Consolatio Ad Apollonium*, 111.D–113.B, 117.B–C) expresses thoughts about an untimely death, "But he ought not to have been snatched away (αναρπαγηναι) while young... they deplore his being snatched from their arms... they deplore his death, saying, 'He was snatched away.'" Julian (*Epistle to Himerius* 69, 412B), St. Basil (*Epistle to Nectarius*, 412B), Lucian (*On Funerals*, 12–14), and Libanius (*Funeral Oration over Julian*, 18.282) also employ the similar expression about death with the verb "ἁρπάζω."[57]

Additionally, the examples of the verb ἁρπάζω in the funeral context are frequently found in relation to themes of death in Greek and Latin epitaphs.

EG 125, 170; SEG 8, 473–75, 502a	"Malice suddenly snatched (ἥρπασεν) Panathenius away from life, but it left him dwelling among the immortals." "With libation and sacrifice glorify Isidora, who was snatched away by the nymphs..."
MAMA 3, 556; EG 526, 1–3; IG 12, 9, 293,3; SEG 8, 378; IG 5, 1, 1186, 1	"Some sorcerer snatched him away from mortal men... the *daemones* snatched me away from life." "... fate, eternal death, snatched (ἥρπασεν) you away untimely... with Hades has snatched him... At fifteen the grievous thread of the *Moirai* snatched you away."
SEG 1, 464, 3; 8, 484; EG 174	"Death snatched (ἀφήρπασεν) away the finest flower of your lovely youth." "And even if fate snatched (ἥρπασεν) her away, it did not conquer her, for though dead she is not the only one who has died."

Just as explored above in the extant consolatory literature, in funeral oration and in Greek and Latin epitaphs, the verb ἁρπάζω is mainly employed to express the death and the power of death in the context of funeral rituals. Paul, however, in 4:17, uses the verb ἁρπάζω with some twist in meaning and perspective. Though Paul employs the funerary word "ἁρπάζω" he inverts this symbolic word of death into the triumphal and hopeful word of resurrection through the Lord's Parousia. In other words, while the word "ἁρπάζω" usually indicates death and separartion from the

---

57. The expressions of "snatched away (αναρπασθηναι) like a torch", "these hopes were snatched from us by a host of envious spirits", and "dead, reft away [snatched away]" are common to them.

living, Paul conversely uses it to denote association with the Lord and the living.[58] It is probable that Paul might have seen or read the contemporary inscriptions of the tombs in the death-prevalent culture of Greco-Roman socities. He likely saw the hopeless attitude of the pagan societies toward death and sought to employ a reversal on the symbolic expression of death "ἁρπαζω" into a hopeful and triumphal meaning.

To support this argument, the pagan expression of "ἁρπαζω" is mainly used in the past tense, which indicates the doomed destiny and despair concerning death, including a few present tense uses as discussed above. Paul, however, employs the expression of "will be caught up" with the future passive tense "ἁρπαγησόμεθα" in 4:17. When Paul employs the word "ἁρπαγησόμεθα" in 4:17 with the future passive tense, he emphasizes the result of an association with the Lord and the living (4:17b, "πάντοτε σὺν κυρίῳ ἐσόμεθα"; 5:10, "ἅμα σὺν αὐτῷ ζήσωμεν"). In other words, Paul emphasizes the hopeful future of the believers and the dead together, and replaces the hopeless condition of the pagans with the hope of salvation, "obtaining salvation through our Lord Jesus Christ" (5:9b). Further, just as Paul employs "in Christ <u>always</u> (<u>πάντοτε</u>) leads us in triumphal procession" (2 Cor 2:14a) in order to show God's eternal triumph over the contemporary Roman emperor,[59] he intentionally and emphatically communicates "so we will be with the Lord <u>forever</u> (<u>πάντοτε</u>)" (1 Thess 4:17b) to show that Jesus' parousia will bring an eternal reunion with the Lord and the dead over a contemporary segregation through death.

Between the consolation to the dead (4:13–18) and the exhortation to the living (5:1–11), there exists some overlapping and developed content and structure.

4:16b–17a "... will be caught up ... with them"	5:9 "... destined not for wrath ... but salvation"
17b "so we will be with the Lord ..."	10 "we are awake or asleep we may live with him"
18 "Therefore encourage one another"	11 "Therefore encourage one another and build up each other"

Instead of the doomed destiny of death, Paul highlights the triumphal victory and future salvation found in 4:17b and 5:10. In 5:10, the tense is a subjunctive aorist ("ζήσωμεν") as a purpose clause but is parallel with 4:17b "so that whether we are awake or asleep we may live with him" (5:10), which

---

58. Malherbe, "Exhortation in First Thessalonians," 238–56.
59. Aus, *Imagery of Triumph and Rebellion in 2 Corinthians 2:14–17*, 8–9, 82.

functions as the future context. Furthermore, Paul intentionally relates to and develops the preceeding passage 4:13–18 (the destiny of the dead and the consolation) to 5:1–11 (the exhortation to the living) with the expressions "we are awake" (the living) and "asleep" (the dead) so that he might establish the continuation and identification between the dead and the living. Therefore, in the pagan funeral oration the expression of "ἁρπαζω" functions as the eternal separation and the doomed destiny of the dead, but Paul shifts it into eternal salvation and a hopeful future of being with Jesus. Consequently, with this symbolic word ἁρπαζω, Paul deals with the destiny and sorrow of the dead and ultimately interweaves Jesus' triumphal Parousia as a processional parousia with the discussion of death.

In addition, the funerary language of the orphaned condition (Plato, *Menexenus* 249a "endeavoring to render them as little conscious as possible of their orphaned (ορφανιαν) conditions"; Demosthenes, *Funeral Speech*, 35–37, "It is painful for children to be orphaned (ορφανοις) of a father") is converted emphatically into the unity of both the dead and the living through Jesus' Parousia, "we who are alive . . . will be caught up . . . together with them" (ἅμα σὺν αὐτοῖς ἁρπαγησόμεθα, 1 Thess 4:17a). The force of the preposition σὺν is strengthened by the preceding ἅμα.[60]

Finally, the subjects of the verb ἁρπαζω in consolatory literature and epitaphs in Greek and Latin are mainly death, malice, the *daemones*, fate/eternal death, and *Moira* with Hades. These snatched the mortal one under the earth. Paul, however, employs the divine passive in 4:17 "ἁρπαγησόμεθα" with the subject of God so both the living and dead might be caught up into the air. The funeral language of the pagan society ("ἁρπαζω") is employed to express the extreme sorrow of the power of death to snatch the dead from under the earth and eternal separation. To the contrary, Paul transforms the meaning and uses the expression "ἁρπαζω" to indicate God's divine action while showing God's work to release the dead to the air (heaven) and for an eternal life/union. Indeed, Paul inverts sorrow into hope of reunion and the power of death into the triumphal victory of life through Jesus' triumphal Parousia.

Garry Wills, who claims Abraham Lincoln employed Greek funeral oratory in his Gettysburg speech, particularly Pericles's famous funeral oration, asserts nothing marked Greek literature more than its use of the polarizing particles μεν and δὲ. Particularly, the characteristic

organization of Greek prose by polarities, namely the broad contrast, is prevalent in all the surviving Epitaphioi.[61] For example, the extant Greek

---

60. Bruce, *1 and 2 Thessalonians*, 102.
61. Wills, *Lincoln at Gettysburg*, 55–56.

funeral oratory expresses the polarities by means of contrasts of "mortal and immortal,"[62] "Athenians and others,"[63] "word and deed,"[64] "teachers and taught,"[65] "past and present,"[66] and "life and death."[67]

Wills concludes that Abraham Lincoln used the funerary contrast motifs in his Gettysburg speech.[68] In the same way, Paul also employs the funerary contrast motifs in 1 Thess 4:13-18 in various ways. First of all, he contrasts the Thessalonian believers with "the Gentiles who do not know God . . . outsiders" (4:5, 12), and "others . . . who have no hope (4:13)." He also contrasts the mortality of the dead against the immortality of resurrection, "the dead in Christ will rise first . . . and so we will be with the Lord forever" (4:17). He contrasts those who grieve over the dead against those who hope for Jesus' Parousia, "Therefore comfort one another with these words" (4:18). He contrasts death to the resurrection and life, "we who are alive . . . will be snatched up in the clouds" (4:17). With the expression of "ἁρπάζω," he contrasts the snatching of the dead under the earth with the releasing to the air. Finally, he contrasts the dead in Christ with those living so that the living (the present) might have the power and example from the dead (ancestors, the past). Thus, Paul's consolation/exhortation in 1 Thess 4:13-18 contains the funerary contrast motifs which are prevalent in the extant Greek funeral oratory. Paul's use of pagan funerary language "ἁρπάζω" and

---

62. The lives of the soldiers were short, but their honor and fame will live forever (Thucydides, *History* 1.43.2-3; Plato, *Menexenus* 247d5-6; Lysias, *Lysias,* 80-81; Demosthenes, *Funeral Speech,* 32-34; Hyperides *Funeral Speech* 28).

63. Athenians differ from all others in their death (Thucydides *History* 2.40-41; Plato, *Menexenus* 238c-239b; Lysias, *Lysias,* 17-18; Demosthenes, *Funeral Speech,* 23; Hyperides *Funeral Speech* 8-9).

64. It is hard to fit poor words to the heroes' great deeds (Thucydides *History* 2.35; Plato, *Menexenus* 236d, 246a, 247e; Lysias, *Lysias* 1-2, 19; Demosthenes, *Funeral Speech* 1-2, 12, 35; Hyperides *Funeral Speech* 1-2).

65. By their death, they teach others to live, making their city a training for the whole civilized world (Thucydides *History* 2.40-41; Plato, *Menexenus* 238c-239b; Lysias, *Lysias* 17-18; Demosthenes, *Funeral Speech* 23; Hyperides *Funeral Speech* 8-9).

66. The mythical exploits of the ancestors are poised against those of the present heroes, and thus produces the continuity and power from the past (Thucydides *History* 2.40-41; Plato, *Menexenus* 239-45; Lysias, *Lysias* 20; Demosthenes, *Funeral Speech* 7-24; Hyperides, *Funeral Speech* 3).

67. Wills, *Lincoln at Gettysburg,* 56-57.

68. Wills, *Lincoln at Gettysburg,* 58-59. He suggests examples for this conclusion: (1) "those who here gave their lives:" "shall not perish from the earth;" (2) separating America from other nations; (3) "what we say here:" and "what they did here;" (4) "the great task remaining . . . the unfinished work."

of the funerary contrast motifs in 4:13–18, indicate the fact that 4:13–18, as consolation, contains and reflects elements of funeral oration.

The Collective and Funerary Language of "We"

Regarding the characteristics of funeral orations in the Greco-Roman era, Ochs highlights the collectivism as the most important one, which causes the relationship of an individual to the collective. Certainly, consolation for the collective should take precedence over consolation for the immediate and most closely related survivors.[69] Through this collective "we" in funeral oration, the orator can produce unity and an identification with the community to persuade them to imitate the dead.

With a comparison of both Pericles's funeral oration and Lincoln's speech at Gettysburg, Wills also reaches the same conclusions about the collective "we" of funeral oration. The Greek orator, most often, employs the plural "we" (ἡμεῖς) of all the citizenry, not referring to himself. This is the same as Lincoln's speech at Gettysburg. Furthermore, the Greek dead are not referred to by name, but instead they are usually called just "these (men)." In Lincoln's speech, the names of the dead were substituted with the expression of "what they did here" or of "these dead."[70] Both Pericle's funeral oration and Lincoln's speech at Gettysburg commonly employ the collective expression following the principle of funeral oration to produce the identification and unity of the community.

Nicole Loraux also points out the same purpose of funeral oration as follows:

> To praise any Athenians in Athens amounts, then, to praising *the* Athenians, all Athenians, dead and alive, and above all "we who are still living," those who coincide with the city's present: such is the scarcely veiled purpose of the funeral oration exposed by Plato in the *Menexenus* . . . the epitaphioi, dominated by *the rule of anonymity*, give the citizens no other name than that of Athenians, no other glory but *a collective one* . . . as we have seen, the mythical exploits are attributed to the Athenian community in combat, and the synoecist Theseus has no place in *an oration that ignores individuals*.[71]

---

69. Ochs, *Consolatory Rhetoric*, 85–86.
70. Wills, *Lincoln at Gettysburg*, 53.
71. Loraux, *Invention of Athens*, 2, 43, 277. Emphasis mine.

Hence, in funeral oration, through the employment of collectivism, particularly in consolation and exhortation, the orator has the effect of including the living in the glory and in the exploitation of the dead. The orator has the task of persuading the living to imitate the deeds and value of the dead for the unity of the community.

Among the extant funeral orations, Thucydides (*History of the Peloponnesian War*) in Pericles's speech, distinctively employs the collective language "we": "we now possess and bequeathed . . . And we ourselves here assembled . . . we have come to our present position" (36.3–4). "We live under a form of government . . . we are ourselves a model" (37.1).[72] Lysias (*Funeral Oration*, 75–77), in consolation, associates himself with the collective mourning through "we" language. Plato (*Menexenus*, 243d, 247d) also, in his consolation and exhortation for the living, employs the collective language "we".

Paul's employment of the collective language "we" in 4:13–18 also indicates the funeral context and emphasizes collectivism, which is distinctive in funeral oration, particularly in consolation and exhortation. With the use of the first person plural "we" language, not individual language, Paul associates himself and the living with the dead (martyrdom), thus including the audience directly in the glory of Christ' Parousia together. Richard Ascough, who examines the social context of Paul's eschatological description in 1 Thess 4:13–18, claims that in the first century A.D. the burial function of associations was so pervasive in the Greco-Roman period and that the death and burial provided the opportunity for community definition and for a community/group identity. Paul particularly gave the community-building discourse through the pervasiveness of death in 1 Thess 4:13–18.[73] Just as "the role associations played in the burial and memorial . . . cannot be separated from their sense of group identity, nor from the sense of identity that individuals would gain within the group . . . to reunite all the surviving members of the group . . . also with the deceased."[74] Paul may use funeral language for community-building purposes with the hope of Jesus' Parousia through the

---

72. "Moreover, we have provided for the spirit . . . We are also superior to our opponents in our system" (38.1; 39.1). "For we are lovers of beauty yet with no extravagance . . . and we Athenians decide . . . we stand in sharp contrast to most men . . . and therefore we shall be the wonder . . . we shall need no Homer to sing our praise" (40.1, 2, 4; 41.4).

73. Ascough, "Question of Death," 509–30. He asserts in antiquity many people were members of one or more voluntary associations, which were generally categorized into religious associations, professional associations, and funerary associations. For many people in the Greco-Roman world, associations provided opportunities for seeking personal and corporate meaning for one's life.

74. Ascough, "Question of Death," 518, 520.

death (martyrdom) of Thessalonian church members. As a new association/community founded on turning to God from idols (1:9b), but a fledgling phase of the Thessalonian Christian community, for a community-cohesion purpose, Paul employs funeral language/oration and hope of reunion of the living and the dead. In other words, through the death of church members, Paul strategically uses the social context of death and burial association and attempts to establish community cohesion and identity with the assurance of salvation and the hope of Jesus' Parousia.

Actually, reflecting this social context and rhetorical situation, in 4:13–18, Paul employs the collective language "we" six times: 4:13, 14, 15 (x2), 17 (x2). Paul's use of the first plural "we," however, is interchangeable among the speaker(s), the collective living, and both the living and the dead. In vv. 13, 14, 15a, Paul uses "we" as the speaker(s), being separate from the audience, "we do not want you . . . we believe . . . we declare to you." In vv. 15b, 17a, however, the first plural "we" is used as the collective for the living, "we who are alive, who are left." Finally, in 17b, Paul employs the first plural "we" as the union of both the living and the dead. Having said the coming of the Lord from heaven would include a summons to the dead in Christ to rise first, Paul now proceeds to connect those who are resurrected with those who remain alive at the time of Jesus' Parousia,[75] "together with them we will be caught up on clouds to meet the Lord in the air; and so we will be with the Lord forever" (ἅμα σὺν αὐτοῖς ἁρπαγησόμεθα ἐν νεφέλαις εἰς ἀπάντησιν τοῦ κυρίου εἰς ἀέρα· καὶ οὕτως πάντοτε σὺν κυρίῳ ἐσόμεθα.). With the rule of anonymity, Paul calls the Thessalonian Christian community the collective "we," according to the funerary collective language. Also, through this employment of "we," Paul includes the audience and himself in the glory of Jesus' Parousia with the dead in Christ together. Consequently, it is probable that Paul establishes the community cohesion and identity, apart from pagan associations, others, and the Gentiles (4:5, 12, 13) through employing funeral language/oration and context, urging the living to imitate the dead. This community is with the assurance of salvation from God's upcoming wrath (1:10; 2:16) and with the hope of Jesus' Parousia (1:10; 4:5b, 13; 5:6a, 23).

The Funerary Language of Immortality and Consolation (4:17b-18)

In the perspective of the Greco-Roman funeral context, Menander Rhetor, in his handbook on consolatory speech (413.5–414.30) and funeral speech

---

75. Wanamaker, *Epistles to the Thessalonians*, 174.

(418.5—422.4), recommends inserting the dwelling of the dead with the gods as follows:

> ... he has escaped the pains of life. Then again: 'I feel convinced that he who has gone dwells in the Elysian Fields, where dwell Rhadamanthus and Menelaus ... Or rather perhaps he is living now with the gods, travelling round the sky and looking down on this world ... For the soul, being kin to the divine and coming down from on high to earth ... Let us therefore sing his praises as a hero, or rather bless him as a god ... placate him as a superhuman being (414.14-26) ... Following this section (the lamentation), insert the section of consolation to the whole family, 'No need to lament; he is sharing the community of the gods, or dwells in the Elysian Fields.' (421.15-16)

Pseudo-Dionysius, in his handbook of funeral speeches, after consolation, recommends to insert the fact, "At the end, it is essential to speak of the immortality of the soul, and to say that it is reasonable to suppose that such men are better off, because they are among the gods" (*On Epideictic Speeches*, 283). Lysias (*Funeral Oration*, 77–81), in consolation, shows the exemplary *topoi* of the Athenian funeral oration, particularly the immortality of the dead: "because of their valor they are lauded as immortal. Their immortality left behind an immortality memory in the future." In the same way, the Romans' funeral oration and consolatory literature also have a similar *topoi* in consolation such as the hope of immortality in the future: death is the release from the burden of body and then there remains the better part.[76] Moreover, just as in imperial funerals " ... an eagle released from it flew aloft, appearing to bear his spirit to heaven ... Then at last the consuls set fire to the structure, and when this was done, an eagle flew aloft from it. Thus was Pertinax made immortal" (Dio Cassius, *Roman History*

---

76. Particularly, in both the Athenians' and the Romans' funeral oration and consolatory literature, there is a common feature of the dead dwelling with the gods in immortality. Demosthenes (*The Funeral Speech*): " ... them to be now seated beside the gods below ... in the islands of the blest" (34). Hyperides (*Funeral Speech*): " ... those of the so-called demi-gods" (35). Libanius (*Funeral Oration over Julian*): "So obviously has he ascended to heaven and has partaken of the power of the divine by the will of the gods themselves" (18.304). Dio Cassius (*Roman History*): "you finally made him a demigod and declared him to be immortal ... as that of a god, for ever" (41). Cicero (*Tusculan Disputations*): " ... let us regard it rather as a haven and a place of refuge prepared for us" (I.XLIX.118). Plutarch (*A Letter to Apollonius; Consolation to His Wife*): " ... the condition after the end of life is the same as that before birth (108D, 109F) ... Whereas the soul that tarries after its capture but a brief space in the body before it is set free by higher powers proceeds to its natural state" (611).

LVI.42.3; LXXV.4.2—5.5), it signifies the flight of the emperor's spirit upwards to the heavens with the gods.[77]

Regarding the Greco-Roman consolatory works, however, Fern rightly points out the problem about the hope of immortality, that their hope of immortality is generally represented in a vague and uncertain pattern.[78] Specifically, the hope of immortality is not certain, but expressed vaguely in their mind. For example, Tacitus (*Agricola*) prays for the spirit of Agricola with a weak attitude by saying, "If there be any habitation for the spirits of the just; if, as wise men will have it, the soul that is great perish not with the body, may you rest in peace" (46). Seneca (*On Grief for Lost Friends*) also expresses his hope but a vague one for immortality, "Let us therefore reflect . . . perhaps, if only the tale told by wise men is true and there is a bourne to welcome us, then he whom we think we have lost has only been sent on ahead" (16).

In 1 Thess 4:16–17, Paul declares the destiny of the dead and the living at Jesus' Parousia, that the dead in Christ will rise first and then we who are alive will be caught up in the clouds to meet the Lord. Then Paul concludes, "and so we will be with the Lord forever" (17b). Paul clearly proclaims that both the dead and the living together will dwell with the Lord (a dwelling place) and dwell with the Lord forever (immortality). Indeed, Paul follows the conventional *topoi* of funeral oration and consolatory literature. Paul, however, inverts the uncertainty of hope in immortality and the dwelling place of a secular funeral oration into the certainty of hope of immortality in Christ's Parousia. Therefore, Paul is indebted to the funeral oration in 1 Thess, but inverts the content and the order.

In 4:18, Paul concludes the passage of 4:13–17 with the exhortation: "Therefore encourage one another with these words" (Ὥστε παρακαλεῖτε ἀλλήλους ἐν τοῖς λόγοις τούτοις.). The particle Ὥστε functions here to draw out the conclusion from the facts discussed in vv. 13–17 and to introduce some exhortation for the future. The verb παρακαλέω ("comfort") is the conventional word for the consolation/exhortation part of the funeral oration and consolatory. The funeral orations commonly end with the comforting and exhorting words for the community and family. Thucydides (43–45), Pseudo-Lysias (77–80), Plato (246d–249c), Demosthenes (32–37), Hyperides (41–43), Dio Cassius (41.6, 9), and Libanius (18.296–306) all end their orations with comforting words. The consolatory literature mainly contains the comforting words of the conventional *topoi* discussed above.

Paul's concluding exhortation to "comfort one another" is indebted to the conventional *topos* of funeral oration and consolatory literature. Paul's

---

77. Davies, *Death, Burial and Rebirth in the Religious of Antiquity*, 143.
78. Fern, "Latin Consolation as a Literary Type," 43.

exhortation, however, is drastically contrasted with a secular one such as a 2nd century A.D. letter of consolation (P.Oxy. 115). This letter, written by a woman named Irene, who lost her son, is addressed to a couple, Taonnophirs and Philo, whose son has just died. After praising their faithful works for their son, she comforts these grieving parents by saying, "But nevertheless, one is able to do nothing against such things. Therefore, comfort yourselves." Irene's comforting words are an attempt to combat the hopelessness and despair for the future after the death of a loved one. This is similar to the vague, uncertain manner for the hope of a dwelling place after death in Tacitus (46) and Seneca (*On Grief for Lost Friends*, 16), which are discussed above.

Paul's comforting words, however, with certainty are based on the triple-source of consolation, which also show the characteristics of epideictic rhetoric, that is, repetitive amplification. The first consolation Paul offers is the Lord's death and resurrection (14) and the word of the Lord, "we who are alive, who are left until the coming of the Lord, will by no means precede those who have died" (15). Jesus' resurrection and God's promise, "God will bring with him those who have died" (14b), will be the source of consolation concerning the immortality of the dead. The second developed consolation Paul offers is the hope of parousia that the Lord himself will descend from heaven with a cry of command, with the archangel's call, and with the sound of God's trumpet (16). Through Jesus' Parousia and the hope of the immortality of the dead (16b), the first consolation is strengthened and amplified. After this, the living will be caught up in the clouds together with them to meet the Lord in the air (17a). Finally, the promise, "so we will be with the Lord forever" (17b), confirms the consolation of the immortality of the dead and the certainty of being with the Lord forever. To support this, grammatically, each verse (14–16) explains the reason for consolation beginning with the causal clause:

Causal/logical clause	14 εἰ γὰρ πιστεύομεν ὅτι Ἰησοῦς ἀπέθανεν καὶ ἀνέστη...
Causal clause	15 Τοῦτο γὰρ ὑμῖν λέγομεν ἐν λόγῳ κυρίου, ὅτι ἡμεῖς...οὐ μὴ φθάσωμεν τοὺς κοιμηθέντας· οἱ ζῶντες οἱ περιλειπόμενοι εἰς τὴν παρουσίαν τοῦ κυρίου
Causal clause	16 ὅτι αὐτὸς ὁ κύριος καταβήσεται ἀπ' οὐρανοῦ ἐν κελεύσματι, ἐν φωνῇ ἀρχαγγέλου καὶ ἐν σάλπιγγι θεοῦ,

A third consolation is the triumphal image of Jesus who will descend from heaven with a triumphal procession (16b, "with a cry of command, with the archangel's call and with the sound of God's trumpet") over death. Paul interweaves Jesus' Parousia with the image of a conquering general who enters the city through triumphal procession to implant the message of Jesus' triumph over death and the certainty of immortality. Jesus' triumphal image with the triumphal procession might give consolation to the Thessalonian believers who lost community members and to provide an understanding of death and the new situation of the Kingdom of God.[79] This repetitiveness in consolation is similar to the case of Paul's repetitive amplification with metaphors in 2:1–18 (*narratio*), which also demonstrates the feature of epideictic rhetoric, particularly funeral oration. In the consolatory speech of epideictic rhetoric in John 13–17, the most striking rhetorical feature of the unit is its repetitiveness of consolation as epideictic rhetoric. The first consolation of the coming of the Holy Spirit (John 14:15–21) is amplified and developed in the second consolation of Jesus' coming again (16:16).[80] In the same sense, the amplification and the repetitiveness of consolation in 1 Thess 4:13–18 shows its feature of epideictic rhetoric, that is, funeral oration. In Isa 40–66, God comforts God's people and promises their restoration on that day, the eschatological day. Isaiah repeatedly employs the words "comfort, comfort my people" (Isa 40:1; 49:13; 51:3, 12, 19; 52:9; 54:11; 57:18; 61:2; 66:13 (x3)) with God's promise and hope of victory. In conclusion, Paul's comforting words in 4:18 stand in sharp contrast to the secular comforting words due to God's own words and the hope of Jesus' Parousia. Though Paul employs the *topoi* of funeral oration, he inverts the content with certainty of immortality of the dead through Jesus' Parousia.

Reverse of Order in the Funeral Procession with Triumphal Procession

In 1 Thess 4:13–18, Paul employs the image of Jesus' triumphal procession for expressing Jesus' parousia, which is discussed above. The triumphal image of Jesus' parousia procession is overlapped with the imperial funeral procession, which demonstrates the triumphal images during the procession. In the same sense, just as the Roman imperial funeral procession interweaves itself as a processional parade with the triumphal image and the apotheosis of the emperor, Paul also uses the triumphal image of Jesus' parousia with a discussion of the death of the Thessalonian believers.

79. Hester, "Invention of 1 Thessalonians," 270.
80. Kennedy, *New Testament Interpretation*, 73–85.

The Thessalonian church members consisted of mainly the converted Gentiles, who were not familiar with the O.T. Therefore, when being compared to other Pauline letters, it is natural there is not any direct quotation from the O.T., though Paul shows some indirect allusions. To them, the word "Parousia" can be techically connected to the Greco-Roman context. In the Hellenistic context, the Parousia indicates an imperial visit, or the visit of a sovereign or high official such as Germanicus, Ptolemy Philometor and Cleopatra Ptolemy or the king of Chrysippus.[81] These Parousias are accompanied by ceremonial speeches, presents, horses and chariots, improvement of roads, gold crowns, and most of all, it inaugurates a new era by the date of the Parousia or the consecratio of one day (On inaugure une nouvelle ère par la date d'une parousie ou par la consécration d'un jour).[82] In the same way, Jesus' triumphal Parousia inaugurates a new era to both the dead and the living.

At this juncture, it is noteworthy that Paul reverses the direction and order of the funeral procession through Jesus' triumphal procession in 1 Thess 4:13–18. The funeral procession starts from inside the city and progresses to the cemetery outside the city, which shows the segregation of life and the end of life. Jesus' triumphal procession began outside the city and went into the city, which indicates a new era of Jesus' eternal reign with life for both the dead and the living and an eternal feast with the triumphal Lord.

In description of Athens's funeral procession, Loraux shows the route taken by the cortège from the ekphora (transport of the coffin to the cemetery) before entering the cemetery, Kerameikos. Though the precise location of the prothesis is unknown (exposure and lamentation of dead), it is likely the remains of the dead were exposed in the Agora. Then the cortège of citizens and strangers, in which the Athenian army, in full array, occupied the place of honor, moved toward the Dipylon. After passing through the Dipylon (beside Sacred Gate), the cortège entered the Kerameikos on the road to the Academy.[83] Thucydides (*History of the Peloponnesian War*, II.XXXIV.1–8) also points out the place of the public sepulcher "which is situated in the most beautiful suburb (The Outer Cerameicus/Kerameikos, just outside the Dipylon gate) of the city; there they always bury those fallen in war . . . delivers over them an appropriate eulogy." Just as described above, the Athenian funeral procession starts from inside the city to outside the city, outside the Sacred Gate and Dipylon, the Outer Cerameicus/Kerameikos.

---

81. Rigaux, *Les Épitres aux Thessaloniciens*, 198.
82. Rigaux, *Les Épitres aux Thessaloniciens*, 198–99.
83. Loraux, *Invention of Athens*, 20.

In the case of the Roman funeral procession, for the élite, the body was transported to the Forum for the delivery of a eulogy. Cemeteries were located outside the walls of Roman towns, thus it was illegal to bury or cremate a body within a town or city in the Roman world (extramural burial).[84] A more common honor was burial in or close to the *pomerium*, a narrow strip of land, and thus the majority of burials took place beyond this *pomerium*.[85] In the case of imperial funerals, which followed a standard pattern, they started in the Roman Forum and moved in solemn procession, passing through the triumphal arch to the Campus Martius, a mile to the north-west.[86] From the Forum, the body was taken to be buried outside the boundary (*pomerium*) of Rome, the Campus Martius, which was ideal for imperial funerals. It was still technically outside the *pomerium*, but it was also a place of great civic importance.[87]

In the same way, the Roman funeral procession and burial also follow the same pattern of the Athenian procession, that is, from inside the city to outside the city, outside the boundary (*pomerium*) and the Campus Martius. After the burial of the dead, the dead and the living were symbolically united on the ninth-day's feast and at subsequent festivals, such as the annual festivals of the *Parentalia* and the *Lemuria*.[88] At the *Parentalia* and on other days, relatives traditionally visited the graves and had a meal at the graveside. The dead were thought of as being present at these feasts. For example, an inscription from the city of Rome contained the expression of the hope that the couple whom it commemorated would "come in good health to the funeral feast and enjoy themselves along with the everybody else" (*CIL* 6.26554).[89] Through these feast, the living and the dead were closely related.

On the contrary, in 1 Thess 4:13–18, Paul reverses the direction and the meaning of the funeral procession through Jesus' triumphal Parousia. Jesus will descend from heaven (4:16a), which is outside the city. In the cemetery outside the city, the dead in Christ will rise first (4:16b) with Jesus' triumphal Parousia through the herald of archangels' trumpets. For a visual image to support this event, it is proved archaeologically that "everywhere in ancient Greek cities, the cemeteries line the main roads leading into the city, often for miles."[90] Then, we who are alive, who are left, will be caught

84. Hope, *Roman Death*, 74, 154–55.
85. Hope, *Roman Death*, 155.
86. Price, "From noble funerals to divine cult," 59.
87. Price, "From noble funerals to divine cult," 68.
88. Hope, *Roman Death*, 86, 99–102.
89. Hopkins, *Death and Renewal*, 233.
90. Koester, "Imperial Ideology and Paul's Eschatology in 1 Thessalonians," 160.

up in the clouds together to meet (εἰς ἀπάντησιν) the Lord in the air (17a). Clouds, as a sign of God's presense, become connected not only with the ascension of Christ (Acts 1:9), but also with his future return, an image that can be traced ultimately to Daniel's vision of "one like a son of man coming with the clouds of heaven" (7:13).[91] The term ἀπάντησιν evokes the image of a Greco-Roman formal reception as it is a technical term referring to the civic custom of a Hellenistic formal reception. This word ἀπάντησιν refers to the custom of sending a delegation of leading officials outside the city to welcome the royal person or dignitary into the city or community for his official visit with great tribute and honor to that person.[92] Koester correctly observes that Paul, in his own language, describes the coming of the Lord ("parousia") like the coming of a king or Caesar in order to highlight the preparedness of the whole Thessalonica community, the joint presence of those who are still alive and those who have died, to meet Jesus' second coming.[93] Assuredly, it is correct to assume that through these analogies, in association with the term παρουσία and ἀπάντησιν, Paul pictures the Lord Jesus as the king escorted on the remainder of his journey to earth by his royal chosen people, that is, both those newly raised from the dead and those who have remained alive.[94] Through this process, both the dead and the living together, who are prepared for the Parousia, will meet Jesus and escort him into the city. It is there that they will feast with Jesus (*CIL* 6.26554; the annual festivals of the *Parentalia* and the *Lemuria*), "and so we will be with the Lord forever" (4:17b).[95]

Fourth Exhortation to the Living (5:1–15)

The extent of the passage concerning the consolation and exhortation, which constitutes the main part of funeral oration after the encomium of the dead,

---

91. Witherington, *1 and 2 Thessalonians*, 137; Wanamaker, *Epistles to the Thessalonians*, 175.

92. Witherington, *1 and 2 Thessalonians*, 138; Peterson, in in Kittel and Friedrich, *TDNT* 1:380–81.

93. Koester, *Paul and his World*, 59.

94. Bruce, *1 and 2 Thessalonians*, 103.

95. Concerning the main background of feast with Jesus (4:17b), it may also be possible that the Jewish Messianic banquet is rooted in Isaiah 25–26 (25:6–9; 26:1 "... On this mountain the Lord of hosts will make for all people a feast of rich food, a feast of well-aged wines ... And he will destroy ... the shroud ... the sheet ... he will swallow up death forever. Then the Lord God will wipe away the tears from the faces ... It will be said on that day ... On that day this song will be sung in the land of Judah ... "). Actually, Paul's use of apocalyptic language (5:4–8) reflects this background and also resurrection is a Jewish concept.

extends from 4:13-18 to 5:1-11. Though it seems 5:1-11 deals with the new topic of "the times and the seasons" through the opening disclosure formulae Περὶ δὲ (5:1), both passages are closely connected in function, content, and structure. This close connection between both passages also reflects the features of the epideictic rhetoric, particularly funeral oration, in light of amplification and embellishment.

I argued in chapter 5 that between 1:4-10 and 2:13-16 and between 2:5-8 and 9-12 repetitions are developed through amplification, which show the genre of epideictic rhetoric; likewise, between 4:13-18 and 5:1-11, amplification and embellishment are developed in many ways. Gerhard Friedrich, by saying "1 Thess 5:1-11 stammt nicht von Paulus, sondern von einem Späteren, der die Anschauung des Apostels von der unmittelbar bevorstehenden Parusie, die dieser noch selbst erleben wollte, apologetisch korrigiert und zu den Fragen, die durch die ausgebliebene Parusie entstanden sind, Stellung nimmt," shows the evidence for the interpolation, that is, the inconsistency between 4:13-18 and 5:11.[96] Particularly, he concludes that 5:10 would be a direct correction of 4:15 ("5:10 wäre dann eine direkte Korrektur von 4:15") because of the failed Parousia viewpoint of the interpolator.[97]

There is, however, clear consistency of thought between 4:13-18 and 5:1-11 in light of the rhetorical approach. First of all, Johanson, while asserting the delimitation and coherence of 4:13—5:11, shows some evidence of the striking similarities in content and structure between both 4:13-18 and 5:1-11: Both passages commonly deal with the Parousia of Christ; both passages fomally close with the exhortation "comfort one another" (4:18; 5:11); both contain the references of "those who have fallen asleep . . . the dead in Christ . . . we who are alive . . . we will be with the Lord forever," (4:13, 15, 16, 17) which are echoed in the following passage in the wordplay of "whether we are awake or asleep we may live with him" (5:10); both passages make abundant use of apocalyptic motifs; both passages emphasize the boundary/identity between the Thessalonian believers and "others who have no hope" (4:13, οἱ λοιποὶ οἱ μὴ ἔχοντες ἐλπίδα) and "as others . . . asleep" (5:6, ὡς οἱ λοιποί).[98] In other words, through repetition and amplification, which are characteristic of epideictic rhetoric, Paul develops and connects his message of 4:13 with 5:1-11. Secondly, there are also differences of function between both passages. Though 4:13-18 focuses on

96. Friedrich, "1 Thessalonicher 5:1-11," 288-315.
97. Friedrich, "1 Thessalonicher 5:1-11," 314.
98. Johanson, *To All the Brethren*, 118-19; Plevnik ("1 Thess 5:1-11," 71-90) and Collins (*Studies on the First Letter to the Thessalonians*, 154-72) similarly assert the coherence of 4:13—5:11.

the fate of the dead in Christ's Parousia, 5:1–11 deals with the fate and the attitude of the living until Jesus' Parousia. In other words, while 4:13–18 focuses on the consolation to the dead, 5:1–11 mainly consists of exhortations to the living (5:6, 8) rather than consolation. Though both passages are closely connected and developed, they have different rhetorical functions and content, that is, the exhortation to the living rather than consolation to the dead in funeral oration. Actually, Paul emphasizes the attitude of the living and exhortation in 5:1–11 instead of focusing on time sequence Friedrich asserts. 5:10 should not be contrasted with 4:15 because the main point of both 4:15 and 5:10 is to reassure the readers that both the living and the dead will share in the life to come.[99] In the following sections, I will show the rhetorical characateristics of funeral oration in 5:1–11, just as I have shown the topoi of funeral oration in 4:13–18.

The Exhortation, Closely Connected with the Consolation (5:1–11)

As the authors of the handbook of funeral orations, Menander the Rhetor and Pseudo-Dionysius commonly suggest authors insert words of exhortation to the living after the consolation. Menander says, "if the children are very young, you should deliver a speech of advice . . . to the children to copy their father's virtues" (II, 421.26–30). Pseudo-Dionysius, after showing the list of encomium of the dead, recommends one makes the transition to the exhortatory part, "exhorting the survivors to like deeds . . . his children should be urged to imitate their parents and aim at similar goals" (280). Polybius, when describing the funeral procedure and speech, highlights the goal of exhorting the young generation to imitate the dead ancestors by saying, "there could not easily be a more splendid sight for a young man who aspires to fame and virtue . . . the glory . . . handed down as a model to future generations" (*The Histories of Polybius* 54). On the basis of these sources, it should be emphasized that words of exhortation to the living are essential in funeral oration.

Actually, the examples of extant funeral orations show the close connection between the consolation and exhortation to the living, that is, to the whole community. Among the Athenian funeral orations, except Lysias, most focus on the consolation and then on the exhortation to the community while omitting the lamentation. Furthermore, both the consolation and exhortation have one goal of unifying the community and the state of Athens. Isocrates (*Evagoras*, 9.80–81), Thucydides (43–45), Plato (248b–249c),

---

99. Wanamaker, *Epistles to the Thessalonians*, 33.

Demosthenes (35–37), and Hyperides (31) commonly contain the exhortation to a future conduct and the injunction to imitate one's ancestors.[100] Particularly, Plato shows a good model of exhortation by using the expression of the direct imperative as well as some exhortation to imitate the city's ancestors. After some exhortations, Plato employs more direct imperatives with χρη (must, it ought) for a more forceful effect.[101]

The extant Roman funeral orations, like the Athenian funeral orations, show a similar pattern of exhortation as a crucial part of funeral orations. Tacitus (45b–46a), Dio Cassius (41.9b), Libanius (18.304), and Dio Chrysostom (29.21–22) commonly contain the exhortation to the living as the vital part of their funeral orations. The consolatory letters, which follow funeral oration patterns, also contain the exhortation to the living as an important part (Cicero, *Tusculan Disputations*, 111, 118; Pliny the Younger, *To Caninius Rufus*, VII.10–15; Seneca, *On Grief Lost Friends*, Ep. 63, 16; Julian, *Epistle to Himerius* 69, 413D). Plutarch (*Consolation to His Wife*) contains the exhortation, "let us keep our outward conduct as the laws command . . . (612A-B)" as well as the commandment, "you must not dwell . . . lamentation . . . you must rather bear" (611A–C).

Jewish funeral oration, 4 Maccabees, derives from the circumstances of martyrdom and its main function is to secure the audience's identification to the nation and exhort the living to imitate the martyrs. 4 Maccabees (18:1–5) also contains the exhortation and commandment to the living as an essential part of it: "O Israelites, children descended from the seed of Abraham, obey this law and fulfill your religious duty." Therefore, just as Thucydides concludes Pericle's funeral oration with an exhortation to the hearers to inspire them with the greatness of the dead (II, XLIII, 43), and Dio Chrysostom closes his eulogy for Melancomas with an exhortation to the hearers to seek the same distinction; funeral oration (eulogy) is intended

---

100. The words of exhortation to the living are as follows: Isocrates ("to incite you to strive . . . but as at present so in the future to pay heed to yourself and to discipline your mind . . . of all your ancestors"); Thucydides ("you who survive should resolve . . . Do you, therefore, now make these men your examples"); Plato ("first and last and always, in every way to show all zeal . . . I myself, on their behalf, entreat the children to imitate their fathers"); Demosthenes ("it is a beautiful thing to be the heir of a father's fame"); and Hyperides (" . . . strive themselves to take as an example these men's lives").

101. Plato's model of both the exhortation and the commandment with direct imperatives ("you must practice it in union with valor" (246e); "you must be consoled . . . must not weep" (247c); "we should exhort the city" (248d); "you must bear your misfortune" (249c)) is similar to 1 Thess 5:1–11, which contains exhortations and concludes with an imperative of commandment.

to rouse the hearers to emulation, encouraging them to the same virtues of the dead for the same honor.[102]

Therefore, this shows exactly why exhortations should follow consolation in epideictic rhetoric, particularly in funeral oration. It is a rhetorical convention being followed. In addition, this also shows how a speech of praise and blame (epideictic rhetoric) could and should include ethics and exhortation. One of the main goals of epideictic rhetoric is to excite admiration of someone and to unify the whole community that it might offer the exhortation (ethics) to future conduct and the value of the community. The exhortation to the community is an essential part of funeral oration, and this is shown in 5:1-11 (the exhortation to the living community) after the consolation (4:13-18).

In the same way, 1 Thess 5:1-11 demonstrates the topoi of exhortation in funeral oration, which is closely connected to the consolation of 4:13-18. When compared to the consolation of 4:13-18, 5:1-11 shows some examples of the exhortation of funeral oration. First of all, 5:1-11 mainly consists of four emphatic and hortatory subjunctives to recommend and exhort the living Thessalonian community as well as the imperative of v. 11: "So then let us not fall asleep (μὴ καθεύδωμεν) as others do, but let us keep awake and be sober (ἀλλὰ γρηγορῶμεν καὶ νήφωμεν) ... let us be sober (νήφωμεν), and put on the breastplate of faith and love ... the hope of salvation" (5:6, 8). The hortatory subjunctive is commonly used to exhort one's associates, "to urge some one to unite with the speaker in a course of action upon which he has already decided."[103] Paul's use of the hortatory subjunctive in his letters is employed mainly in the hortatory section at the conclusion of his discourses to urge his readers to imitate or to unite with him (Rom 5:1; 13:12-13; 1 Cor 15:32; Gal 5:25, 26; 6:9; Eph 4:15; Phil 3:15). Particularly, Rom 13:11-14 has striking similarities to 1 Thess 5:1-11 in light of the eschatological situation (13:11, "what time it is ... the moment for you to wake from sleep"//5:1, "concerning the times and the seasons"), apocalyptic language (13:12a, "the night is far gone, the day is near"//5:4-8, "children of light and children of the day ... not of the night or of darkness"), the hortatory subjunctives (13:12-13, "let us then lay aside ... let us live honorably"//5:6, 8), and the conclusion with an imperative (13:14, "put on the Lord ... make no provision for the flesh"//5:11, "encourage one another and build up each other"). Furthermore, as discussed above, Plato (*Menexenus*) and Plutarch (*Consolation to His Wife*) employ direct

---

102. deSilva, *4 Maccabees*, 253.

103. Wallace, *Greek Grammar beyond the Basics*, 464; Chamberlain, *Exegetical Grammar of the Greek New Testament*, 83.

imperatives as well as some exhortation to imitate their ancestors. In 1 Thess 5:1–11, as the exhortation in funeral oration, Paul also employs a direct imperative (5:11) as well as four hortatory subjunctives to the living (5:6, 8).

Secondly, Paul's use of apocalyptic language (5:4–8) in his exhortation to the living reflects his rhetorical purpose and strategy in 5:1–11, that is, a group cohesion/identification of the funeral oration. Just as Thucydides and Dio Chrysostom close their funeral oration with an exhortation to the hearers for the cohesion/identification of the community, Paul also employs the apocalyptic languages for the cohesion/identification of the Thessalonian community. In other words, Paul's use of an apocalyptic perspective and language in 5:1–11 is intended to meet (console) the need of the Thessalonian believers' suffering and martyrdom, and to enhance cohesion/identification of the Thessalonian community. In this sense, Jörg Baumgarten, who considers 1 Thess 4:13—5:11 to be the largest of the three apocalyptic examples of Paul (1 Cor 15; Rom 8; 1 Thess 4:13–5:11), correctly regards 1 Thess 4:13—5:11 as the center of 1 Thessalonians while relating it also to 1:9–10; 2:19; 3:13; 5:23. According to him, because of futuristic-apocalyptic teachings and hope, 1 Thess 4:13–5:11 can function as "real consolation (echte Trost-Funktion)" to the audiences (1 Thess 4:13—5:11; Rom 8:18ff; 1 Cor 15:12–57).[104] Therefore, 5:1–11 functions well to console the audience with its futuristic-apocalyptic languages and perspective, particularly with its consolation/exhortation of the funeral oration.

Wayne Meeks, surveying Paul's use of an apocalyptic perspective and language in his letters, surmises a variety of functions of apocalyptic language in the lives of the congregation:

1. To emphasize and legitimize boundaries between Christian groups and the larger society

2. To enhance internal cohesion and solidarity

3. To provide sanctions for normative behavior

4. To warrant innovations over and against Jewish norms and structures from which Christianity emerged

5. To resist, on the other hand, deviant behavior that led to the disruption of the Christian community

6. To legitimize the leadership of Paul and his associates against challenges

7. To justify radical interpretations of scripture and tradition[105]

---

104. Baumgarten, *Paulus und die Apokalyptik*, 56–58, 230–35.

105. Meeks, "Social Functions of Apocalyptic Language in Pauline Christianity," 700. Koch (*Rediscovery of Apocalyptic*, 18–35) and Vielhauer ("Introduction to Apocalypses

Particularly, through the metaphor of two ages and two societies in 1 Thess, Paul emphasizes the group's distinctiveness (#1) and then naturally flows into internal cohesion and solidarity of the Thessalonian community (#2).[106] Meeks' assertion explains well why Paul employs the apocalyptic language and what his rhetorical situation and strategy are in 5:1-11, because in many respects apocalyptic language and perspective originate from a theology of martyrdom.[107] Specifically, in 5:3-9 Paul clearly demonstrates the group cohesion/identity through antithesis with exhortation, which is also an apocalyptic language:

A: Main clause	3a ὅταν λέγωσιν Εἰρήνη καὶ ἀσφάλεια...ἐπίσταται ὄλεθρος
B: Emphatic Future Negation (Constrast)	3b οὐ μὴ ἐκφύγωσιν
	4-5 ὑμεῖς δέ, ἀδελφοί, οὐκ ἐστὲ ἐν σκότει φωτός ἐστε καὶ υἱοὶ ἡμέρας.
(Hortatory Subjunctives)	6 ἄρα οὖν μὴ καθεύδωμεν ὡς οἱ λοιποί, ἀλλὰ γρηγορῶμεν καὶ νήφωμεν.
B': Main clause	7 Οἱ γὰρ καθεύδοντες νυκτὸς καθεύδουσιν· καὶ οἱ μεθυσκόμενοι νυκτὸς μεθύουσιν·
(Contrast) (Hortatory Subjunctive) (Circ. Part/Means)	8a ἡμεῖς δὲ ἡμέρας ὄντες
	8b νήφωμεν ἐνδυσάμενοι θ ὥρακα πίστεως καὶ ἀγάπης καὶ περικεφαλαίαν ἐλπίδα σωτηρίας
A': Main Clause	9 ὅτι οὐκ ἔθετο ἡμᾶς ὁ θεὸς εἰς ὀργὴν ἀλλὰ εἰς περιποίησιν σωτηρίας διὰ τοῦ κυρίου...

B and B' use antithesis (constrast) and exhortation to distinguish the Thessalonian community from others (5:6a) who serve idols (1:9b), who are Gentiles and outsiders who do not know God (4:5b, 12a), and those who grieve death without hope (4:13). These antitheses and exhortations function to enhance the group cohesion/identity of the Thessalonian community and overcome the present suffering and martyrdom with the apocalyptic perspective. Rigaux, who examines the structure and Paul's redaction of 5:1-10, asserts that this passage can be divided into three parts (1-3; 4-8a; 8b-10) and that each section has its own distinctive theme (la jour du seigneur; la vigilance; l'existence chrétienne).[108] In light of the

---

and Related Subjects") also similarly outlines the basic components of apocalyptic.

106. Meeks, "Social Functions," 689-94.
107. Beker, *Paul the Apostle*, 136.
108. Rigaux, "Tradition et Rédaction dans 1 Th. V. 1-10," 320-35.

exhortation of funeral oration, however, he ignores the rhetorical function of this passage, particularly the exhortation for group cohesion through contrast against outsiders. Paul, in this passage, focuses on the exhortation of 3b-8 with the repeated pattern (main clause/contrast/hortatory subjunctive) to exhort the Thessalonian Christian community (B and B'). Particularly, 8b cannot be separated from 8a because, grammatically, 8a (contrast) should be followed by 8b (hortatory subjunctive with circumstantial participle of means) as the same pattern of B (3b-6). Furthermore, Rigaux considers 5:11 as "une repetition et un élargissement" relating to all 4:13—5:10 and as a general conclusion of 4:13—5:10.[109] Both 4:13-18 and 5:1-11, however, have their own rhetorical functions such as consolation and exhortation. It is better to consider 5:11 as amplification and embellishment of 4:13-18 following consolatory literature/funeral oration rather than the general conclusion of 4:13—5:10.

In this sense, Paul's use of apocalyptic language in 1 Thess fits the rhetorical situation of the Thessalonian church, which needs to have a new perspective of death/martyrdom and a strong group boundary and internal identity. Furthermore, with inclusio A and A', Paul encourages and confirms their destiny of not being for wrath, but of obtaining salvation through Christ (5:9). Their destiny is opposite to that of the outsiders who will receive God's coming wrath (1:10; 2:16) and who will not escape sudden destruction (5:3). Paul emphasizes not only the solidarity of the Thessalonian community in the eschatological sense but also its unqualified vindication (1:10; 5:9-10) and the honor of the dead/martyrdom.[110]

In the same sense, funeral oration's rhetorical situation and purpose fit Paul's use of apocalyptic language in 5:1-11. Ochs correctly claims the main rhetorical situation and function of funeral oration/ritual as follows:

> Funeral rituals also contain symbolic behaviors that redirect the participant's future...Death is a dramatic event calling forth not the forms of reasoned argument but rather dramatic forms of narrative, poetry, and theater ... *these forms persuade in the sense that the moral behavior of the characters in a drama offers the participating audience models for believing and acting, for assimilating values, and for living one's life.*
>
> The symbolic behaviors in a funeral ritual that affect participants' future lives can be best labeled *epideictic* ... its identifying ethos circumscribing and, to a considerable extent, controlling those who participate in the occasion ... Hearing the deceased

---

109. Rigaux, "Tradition et Rédaction dans 1 Th. V. 1–10," 321.
110. Cranford, "Pagan Ethics and the Rhetoric of Separation."

praised can stir a resolve to emulate and imitate. *Moving in unison with other participants one is compelled to accept the fact that each person is not only separate and individual but also united in a bond of community.* The ritual provides opportunities for social interaction . . . The epideictic ceremony of the ritual clearly functions to influence the future lives of the participants.[111]

According to Ochs, both funeral oration/ritual and apocalyptic languages have a common purpose/function and rhetorical situation. Both have the function of persuading to imitate the model under suffering (#3). Both also have the same rhetorical situation of enhancing internal cohesion and unity in a bond of community (#1 and #2). In 1 Thess 5:1-11, Paul strategically and intentionally employs apocalyptic language in his exhortation to the living in funeral oration. Through using apocalyptic language, Paul encourages the living believers to have a new apocalyptic perspective on death/marthydom to overcome the present suffering/martyrdom and sorrows. In addition, he persuades them to imitate the model of the suffering one (5:6, 8) so the fledgling community of the Thessalonian church might have different boundaries from others (1:9b; 4:5b, 12a, 13; 5:6a), enhance internal cohesion/solidarity in a bond of community, and finally share the hope and goal for obtaining salvation through Jesus, avoiding God's coming wrath (1:10b; 2:16; 5:9). In this sense, Paul's use of funeral oration with apocalyptic language/perspective fits the Thessalonian church's rhetorical situation.

Thirdly, with the parallel expression in content and structure between 4:16b-18 and 5:9-11, Paul reemphasizes and amplifies the exhortation to the living. Paul employs the parallel expression in the consolation and the exhortation to the living as follows:

4:16b-17a " . . . will be caught up . . . with them"	5:9 " . . . destined not for wrath . . . but salvation"
17b "so we will be with the Lord . . . "	10 "we are awake or asleep we may live with him"
18 "Therefore encourage one another"	11 "Therefore encourage one another and build up each other"

Although there are differences in the introducing conjunctions (4:18, Ὥστε παρακαλεῖτε ἀλλήλους ἐν τοῖς λόγοις τούτοις.; 5:11, Διὸ παρακαλεῖτε ἀλλήλους καὶ οἰκοδομεῖτε εἰς τὸν ἕνα, καθὼς καὶ ποιεῖτε. , two concluding conjuctions share the same function, which concludes with the preceeding

111. Ochs, *Consolatory Rhetoric*, 31–32 (emphasis is mine).

content (4:13-17; 5:1-10). The distinct differences include the addition of the new command (5:11b, οἰκοδομεῖτε εἰς τὸν ἕνα) and the comparative clause (5:11c, καθὼς καὶ ποιεῖτε). In other Pauline letters, Paul mainly uses the verb "οἰκοδομεω" figuratively to build up, complete, and strength the symbolic Christian church (Rom 15:10; 1 Cor 8:1; 10:23; 14:4; Gal 2:18). This may mean that in the exhortation to the living (5:1-11), Paul emphasizes the command and edification to the living congregation (the Thessalonian church) to build each other up. This exhortation/command to the living community is essential after the consolation in funeral oration. Michel (*TDNT* 5:140) correctly points out that the word "οἰκοδομεω" in the NT is used to connote "an apocalyptic and Messianic concept" (Matt 16:18; Mark 14:58; Acts 15:16) through the Parousia, which denotes the eschatological act of Christ to build the future temple and the new community. Particularly, in 1 Thess 5:11, with the addition of the word "οἰκοδομεω" Paul connotes the exhortation of the individual to edify the whole community and highlights the responsibility of all church members to build up the church.[112] In other words, the main goal of 1 Thess 5:11 is focused on the exhortation of the church members to build up the whole community as an eschatological new community. It is probable that with the repetitive amplification (4:18; 5:11), Paul emphasizes the function of the whole community/church to build each other up, which is essential to the exhortation to the living in funeral oration.

The Exhortation to the Living (5:1-11)

Compared to 4:13-18 which demonstrates the consolation concerning the dead, 5:1-11 functions to show the exhortation to the living while both are being connected and developed together.

Plato (*Menexenus*) highlights the main tasks of funeral oration as both eulogy to the dead and exhortation to the living by saying, "and the speech required is one which will adequately eulogize the dead and give kindly exhortation to the living, appealing to their children and their brethren to copy the virtues of these heroes . . . any still surviving ancestors offering consolation" (236e). Among various elements of funeral oration (the person's origin/ancestors, upbringing, deeds, consolation, and exhortation), however, the funeral orators developed these themes by altering the order or emphasis and contracting, even omitting this or that according to "a co-ordinated vision rather than mechanical formulae."[113]

---

112. Michel, in Kittel and Friedrich, *TDNT* 5:138-41.
113. Wills, *Lincoln at Gettysburg*, 60.

In this sense, while other funeral orators in Athens adequately eulogized the dead and the ancestors, Thucydides (*History of the Peloponnesian War*, II, 36) focuses his oration on his own generation and their deeds rather than the ancestors and the dead by saying:

> I shall speak first of our ancestors . . . And not only are they worthy of our praise, but our fathers still more; for they, adding to the inheritance which they received, acquired the empire we now possess and bequeathed it . . . to us who are alive today. And we ourselves here assembled, who are now for the most part still in the prime of life, have further strengthened the empire in most respects . . . But I shall firt set forth by what sort of training we have come to our present position . . .

By altering the emphasis from the ancestors to his present generation and omitting the lamentation in his funeral oration, Thucydides intends to meet the rhetorical situation under the ongoing war. Wills, who shows the evidence of Abraham Lincoln's use of Greek funeral oratory to address his audience at Gettysburg, asserts that Lincoln particularly employs Thucydides' oration and models the rhetorical situation. Just as Pericles rejected the notion that his ancestors had done more than his own generation (II, 36), Lincoln's funeral speech also highlights the exhortation to the living/survivors rather than the dead and the ancestors by saying, "it is for the living, rather, to be dedicated to the unfinished work . . . It is rather for us to be here dedicated to the great task remaining before us."[114] Just as Pericles, at the end of the speech dismissed mourners with stern rebuke, "Your individual lamenting done, depart (II, 46.2)," Lincoln also exhorts the living/survivors without any lamentation but with the challenge of the moment; " . . . for us to be here dedicated to the great task remaining before us . . . that we here highly resolve that these dead shall not have died in vain."[115]

In the same way, if Lincoln can use Greek funeral oratory, particularly Thucydides, to address his audience to meet their rhetorical situation, Paul could also employ similar topoi of the funeral oratory. Firstly, as both Pericles and Lincoln have the same rhetorical situation, that is, during a war that is not yet finished, Paul also has the same rhetorical situation[116] to meet the spiritual needs of the Thessalonian believers who are now

---

114. Wills, *Lincoln at Gettysburg*, 52–62.

115. Wills, *Lincoln at Gettysburg*, 52, 61.

116. There is really clear war language in 1 Thessalonians: (1) 5:8b " . . . and put on the breastplate of faith . . . for a helmet the hope of salvation."; (2) the Jewish apocalyptic language in 3:2–3 [στηρίξαι (to strengthen)—σαίνεσθαι (be shaken)—θλίψεσιν (persecutions)]; (3) the future battle in 4:16 " . . . with the sound of God's trumpet . . . "

suffering persecution, martyrdom, and Satan's attack (1:6; 2:14–16, 18; 3:3–5; 4:13a). Secondly, as both Pericles and Lincoln reject lamentation with a stern air of rebuke, Paul also differentiates between the Thessalonian community and others who have no hope by saying, "you may not grieve" (4:13b). Thirdly, both Pericles and Lincoln do not refer to the dead by name but by the group community, just as Loraux describes the epitaphios as "an oration that ignores the individual."[117] Likewise, Paul does not name the dead and instead employs group language, "those who have died" and the first plural of "we" (4:13—5:11), which functions to enhance group identification, including Paul himself, in the Thessalonian community. Furthermore, Paul's concluding exhortation/command in 5:11 adds "build up each other" and "encourage one another." Through this, Paul emphasizes the community of the Thessalonian church, not the individual, which indicates the character of his funeral oration.

Finally, as both Pericles and Lincoln praise and emphasize the present generation/the living and their remaining work to be done, Paul also emphasizes the living, including Paul himself and the living Thessalonian believers. Paul praises the living, the present generation of Thessalonian believers (1:4-10), himself, and his coworkers (2:1—3:10) instead of praising the dead and the ancestors. Furthermore, in his consolation to the dead (4:13-18), Paul highlights the status and future mission by giving four exhortations (5:1-11), particularly using a war metaphor: "put on the breastplate of faith and love, and for a helmet the hope of salvation" (5:8). Paul commands the Thessalonian community as children of light and children of the day (5:5) to do the remaining work with an apocalyptic perspective toward death and an apocalyptic hope of parousia, being differentiated from the outsiders and others who have no hope.

The Power of Images

As discussed, in the consolation of 4:13-18, Paul employs Roman triumphal images in funeral oration and the funeral procession/ritual to console the Thessalonian believers, overlapping them with Jesus' triumphal Parousia. Actually, the triumphal arch is generally held to be a creation of the Romans and becomes an integral part of the city, functioning to serve as an entrance to monumental zones. From the regional catalogues, there exist 36 triumpahl arches in Rome.[118] In this sense, the Thessalonian believers may be familiar with the Roman culture of triumphal images and Paul may use

117. Loraux, *Invention of Athens*, 277.
118. Maso, *Rome of the Caesars*, 45.

these triumphal images to console the Thessalonian believers by comparing them to Jesus' triumphal Parousia.

In the same way, Paul may also use the powerful Roman images of "peace and security" to exhort the Thessalonian believers and confirm their apocalyptic status. In 5:1-3, when explaining the times, the seasons, and the day of the Lord, Paul warns that "when they say, 'There is peace and security,' then sudden destruction will come upon them, as labor pains come upon a pregnant woman, and there will be no escape" (5:3). Traditionally, the phrase "peace and security" has been understood as a quotation of O.T. prophetic warnings (Jer 6:14; Ezek 13:10; Mic 3:5), particularly Gordon Fee concluded that Paul is quoting from the prophetic tradition, "especially Jeremiah 6:14, Paul reaffirms the constant danger in which the unbeliever lives."[119] Connected with the preceding consolation of 4:13-18 where Paul employs the cultural and Roman triumphal images, however, the assertion that Paul's exhortation to the living in 5:1-11 contains the imperial Roman propaganda image of "peace and security" (5:3) is more convincing.[120] Furthermore, the Thessalonian believers mainly consisted of Gentile believers who were familiar with the Roman culture, so it is probable that there are no direct OT quotations. Paul already employed the Roman imperial funeral motifs (4:13-18; triumphal procession of Caesar or a general) and the term ἀπάντησιν (the image of a Hellenistic formal reception). These facts support Paul's use of the Roman images of "peace and security." Frend, who asserts the probability and context of martyrdom in 1 Thess, correctly points out that in 5:3 Paul attacks *Pax et Securitas*, the "programme of the early Principate" (imperial Roman propaganda) under an apocalyptic context.[121] Concerning the apocalyptic context of 5:3, Rigaux correctly notes that "'Destruction subite' est concomitante avec la proclamation par certains de 'paix et sécurité'" which is abundantly demonstrated in Qumran and Daniel.

---

119. Fee, *First and Second Letters to the Thessalonians*, 189; Beale (*1 and 2 Thessalonians*, 142–43) also suggests other allusions reflecting Jer 6 in 1 Thess 5:3: (1) the sound of a trumpet signals the visitation of God (6:1, 17); (2) the sudden report of calamity for Jerusalem (6:24); (3) the sudden coming of the destroyer (6:26). Joel R. White recently asserted that it is undeniable that *pax* played an important role in the propaganda of the Roman Empire from the time of Augustus onward, but a strong emphasis on *securitas* was a later development, which postdated Paul's reference to "peace and security" by at least 15 years ("'Peace and Security,'" 382–95).

120. Donfried, "Cults of Thessalonica and the Thessalonian Correspondence," 344: he suggests other political terms which Paul uses before 5:3 such as παρουσία, ἀπάντησις, and κύριος; Koester, "Imperial Ideology and Paul's Eschatology in 1 Thessalonians," 162; Gaventa, *First and Second Thessalonians*, 70; Green, *Letter to the Thessalonians*, 233–34; Witherington, *1 and 2 Thessalonians*, 146–47; Weima, "'Peace and Security,'" 331–59.

121. Frend, *Martyrdom and Persecution in the Early Church*, 83, 96.

Furthermore, Paul's use of the impersonal word "ὅταν λέγωσιν" (when they say) in 5:3 is similar to the repetitional use of the impersonal word in Luke 17:26-27 (Matt 24:37-39) "ἤσθιον, ἔπινον" (they were eating and drinking), "qui son tune caractéristique du style apocalyptique."[122] In this sense, it is probable that Paul employed the Roman propaganda image of "peace and security" by means of apocalyptic language in order to strengthen his exhortation in 5:1-11.

Zanker, who discusses the overwhelming power of images in the age of Augustus, shows that the Roman emperors used all kinds of images such as works of art, buildings, poetic imagery, state ceremony, and the emperor's conduct in order to create a visual impression for imperial Roman propaganda. Through constant repetition and the combination of new symbols and highlighted images, "even the uneducated viewer was indoctrinated in the new visual program."[123] Among them, the image of "peace and security" was a prevalent one in the Roman society for political propaganda. Numismatic, monumental, and inscriptional evidences, are full of themes of peace accomplished through military victory and of security given to the people under the rule of the Roman emperors.[124]

The phrase "peace and security" (5:3) is an allusion to the Roman imperial propaganda, with which the Thessalonian believers would be familiar. Paul employs this imperial propaganda to warn strongly against those who trust in the Roman imperial power. For this purpose, Paul employs apocalyptic language and a perspective toward the death/martyrdom in 5:1-11, contrasting the children of light and the children of darkness (5:4-8). Though Jesus' Parousia is still the topic of 5:1-11, the focus is rather on the need to be prepared for its sudden and unexpected arrival, not on the event of Jesus' Parousia itself.[125] Antithetical pairing (5:4-8) is a rhetorical tool of apocalyptic discourse that enhances group identity and internal cohesion.[126] As discussed, both funeral oration/ritual and apocalyptic language/perspective have common purposes and rhetorical situations, that is, to enhance group identity and to strengthen internal cohesion. In 5:3, Paul warns against those who trust in the Roman imperial propaganda, which seems to give peace and security but brings sudden destruction upon them. By contrast, in 5:5, 8a, Paul defines the Thessalonian community under suffering and death/martyrdom to be "children of light and children of the

---

122. Rigaux, "Tradition et Rédaction dans 1 Th. V. 1-10," 322-25.
123. Zanker, *Power of Images*, 3, 112.
124. Weima, "'Peace and Security,'" 331-59.
125. Watson, "Paul's Appropriation of Apocalyptic Discourse," 74.
126. Watson, "Paul's Appropriation of Apocalyptic Discourse," 75.

day" and to belong to "the day" so they will obtain salvation through Jesus, not being destined for wrath (5:9). Therefore, as the community of light and day, they should not fall asleep as others who trust in the imperial propaganda like outsiders (4:5,13) but keep awake, be sober, and put on the breastplate of faith and love, and for a helmet put on the hope of salvation (5:6, 8). By employing imagery (metaphor) of warfare and soldiers in 5:8 (the breastplate and a helmet), Paul strengthens and exhorts the Thessalonian community to become like soldiers of the triumphant Christ. According to funeral orations' exhortation *topoi*, Paul ends the exhortation (5:1–11) with "encourage one another" (5:11a), which is repetitive and similar to the 4:18 consolation. This repetitive and concluding exhortation (5:11a) indicates the fact that both 4:13–18 and 5:1–11 are written under the same context and the passage of 5:1–11 is the developed amplification of 4:13–18, which is the characteristic of epideictic oration, particularly funeral oration. Most intriguingly, he adds the developed exhortative command of "build up each other" (5:11b)" to (5:11a) "encourage one another." Paul's additional exhortative command (5:11b) functions to strengthen the internal cohesion of the apocalyptic community and complies with the Thessalonian community's rhetorical situation. In this sense, Paul employs the apocalyptic language to meet the rhetorical situation of the Thessalonian community which encourages and exhorts them to imitate the martyrs and to enhance internal cohesion of the apocalyptic community with the hope of Jesus' Parousia. In this sense, Paul's discourse in 5:1–11 shows the exhortation to the living as the apocalyptic community and reflects funeral oration in light of its contents, structure, and purpose.

Continuing Exhortation to the Community (5:12–15)

This last part of the exhortation functions to teach a fledgling community how to treat leaders (12–13) and community members (14–15). Franz Laub, who examines 1 Thess from the perspective of Paul's eschatological proclamation to build community, considers 5:12–22 as one block of the "fundamentals of community life." He correctly points out that Paul gives a loose juxtaposition of specific individual warnings, which is primarily aimed at the orderly coexistence in the community because this section derives its basic idea from this congregational life of 5:11, to "exhort and build up each other."[127] Among the warnings, it is noteworthy that in 5:14a, Paul urges the Thessalonian believers "to admonish the idlers" (νουθετεῖτε τοὺς ἀτάκτους),

---

127. Laub, *Eschatologische Verkündigung und Lebensgestaltung nach Paulus*, 50, 69–70.

which is clearly connected to and developed with 2 Thess 3:6–15, particularly 3:6, 7, 11 (ἀτάκτως περιπατοῦντος…οὐκ ἠτακτήσαμεν…περιπατοῦντας ἐν ὑμῖν ἀτάκτως). The word ἀτάκτως derives from the verb τασσω, "to give instructions as to what must be done," "to order" (BDAG 991). Therefore, in 2 Thess 3:6, ἀτάκτως περιπατοῦντος refers to the pattern of their lives which implies "disorderly and rebelliously." Beverly Gaventa introduces the problem in that, even though the refusal to work seems to be the major issue, the word ἀτάκτως connotes "something other than sloth," namely, "a sense of insubordination that results in disorderliness" including a refusal to work.[128] Therefore, the word ἀτάκτως indicates the one who not only acts idly but also intentionally does not obey the traditions from Paul. In the same sense, the same meaning in 2 Thess 3:6 can apply to 1 Thess 5:14a "to admonish the idlers" (νουθετεῖτε τοὺς ἀτάκτους). In 2 Thess 2:1, 8–9, Paul tries to correct the Thessalonians' misunderstandings concerning matters of eschatology.[129] Although Paul does not explicitly make a direct connection between eschatology and the problem of idleness in this passage, it is because of their unjust suffering that the eschatology must have affected the believers.[130] Many commentators address this problem of the eschatological background.[131] Actually, the juxtaposition of topics occurs in chapter 2 (the Day of the Lord) and chapter 3 (the treatment of idleness), just as the problem of idleness (1 Thess 4:11–12; 5:14) is extended with the topic of Christ's return (4:13—5:11). Therefore, in 1 Thess 5:14a, Paul deals with the problem of the rebellious idlers in the Thessalonian church and also tries to protect the church from being contaminated by the rebellious idlers from an eschatological perspective.

In 5:14b, various encouragements toward the community members, "encourage the fainthearted, help the weak, be patient with all of them," are crucial in funeral orations so that they might strengthen and enhance the cohesion and identity of community.

---

128. Gaventa, *First and Second Thessalonians*, 128.
129. Witherington, *Paul Quest*, 142–44.
130. Carson and Moo, *Introduction to the New Testament*, 546.
131. Best, *First and Second Epistles to the Thessalonians*, 334; Bruce, *1 and 2 Thessalonians*, 209; Gaventa, *First and Second Thessalonians*, 129; Beale, *1–2 Thessalonians*, 249–51; Menken, *2 Thessalonians*, 129; Morris, *First and Second Epistles to the Thessalonians*, 251; Whiteley, *Thessalonians*, 108; Hoekema, *Bible and the Future*, 153; Ridderbos, *Paul*, 511.

Peroratio (5:16–22) and Wish Prayer/Closing (23–28)

A peroration (epilogue) is usually composed of four parts: to dispose the hearer favorably or unfavorably; to amplify key concerns; to excite the emotions of the hearer; and to recapitulate (Aristotle, *Rhetoric* 3.19.1; *Rhet. ad Her.* 2.20.47–49). Particularly, in peroration of epideictic or funerary rhetoric the audience would expect a final harangue that would comply with the conciliatory and exhortative tone of such rhetoric and focus on the the community.[132] In addition, in funeral orations, epilogue contains an appeal to others to imitate heroes' virtues and ends most appropriately with a prayer: "you must utter a prayer, beseeching God that the emperor's reign may endure long, and the throne be handed down to his children and his descendents [Menander, *The Imperial Oration*, 377,28–29] . . . Finally, round off the speech with a prayer, asking the gods for the greatest blessings for them" (Menander, *The Funeral Speech*, 422,3–4).

In 1 Thess 5:16–24, there appears to be conformity with the content and tones of epideictic and funeral orations. 1 Thess 5:16–18 consists of three commands (16–18a) and a statement (18b), and these commands are directed to the community, not to the individuals. Paul addresses the community in the 2nd person plural (χαίρετε, προσεύχεσθε, εὐχαριστεῖτε, εἰς ὑμᾶς) and these commands function as the boundary marker of Christian community against others, Gentiles, and those who have no hope, "for this is the will of God in Christ Jesus for you" (18b).

Furthermore, Paul employs strong and repeated hyperbolic expressions at every outset of imperative, "always," "constantly," and "in all things," (Πάντοτε, ἀδιαλείπτως, ἐν παντὶ), which are characteristic of epideictic rhetoric in closing. In the funeral oration of Plato (*Menexenus*), there are similar consolatory tones in consolation/exhortation/peroration with the repeated hyperbolic expressions. For children, it is commanded that "do ye make it your endeavor, *first and last and always, in every way to show all zeal that you may exceed . . .* " (247a) (πρωτὸν καὶ ὑστατὸν καὶ διὰ παντὸς πάσαν πάντως προθυμιαν πειρᾶσθε εχειν. . . ὑπερβαλεισθε. . .). These hyperbolic expressions are characteristic of the closing and strong exhortation in funeral oration.

The Thessalonian community must rejoice always (5:16) despite the afflictions, suffering, and even death from the hands of their own compatriots (2:14). They must pray constantly as a significant sign of those who "turned to God from idols, to serve a living and true God" (1:9). Finally, they must give thanks in everything because ingratitude to God is

---

132. Witherington, *1 and 2 Thessalonians*, 164.

characteristic of the pagan world (Rom 1:21) and of "the Gentiles who do not know God" (4:5). Paul claims this is the will of God in Christ for you, the chosen Thessalonian Christian community, contrary to the outsiders and those who have no hope. In addition, for the establishment of the fledgling Thessalonian community, Paul continually repeats two negative commands (5:19–20), which warn against the rejection of Spirit-inspired prophecy, and three positive commands (5:21–22), which ask them to test everything and to hold fast to what is good.

Finally, Paul ends his discourse with prayer (5:23), which is proper to funeral orations. His prayer for the Thessalonian community can be summarized into two topics: sanctification and blamelessness of the Thessalonian community with the hope of the coming of the Lord Jesus Christ. This prayer corresponds to the *transitus* prayer of 3:11–13, particularly 3:13, in content and structure. As discussed before, the themes of the sanctified living of God's people (3:13; 4:3–4, 7–8) and the hope of Christ's Parousia (1:3, 10; 2:19; 3:13; 4:13—5:11) are interwoven throughout 1 Thess like threads. As part of an eschatological community, Paul prays for the Thessalonian community regarding their identity and cohesion with an eschatological hope wherein Paul employs the funeral oration's purpose and topoi in 1 Thess.

Conclusion of Consolation/Exhortation in 4:1—5:28 (Elements of Funeral Oration)

Based on the contents of consolation/exhortation discussed above, it is probable to find some overlapping elements between 1 Thess 4:1—5:28 and funeral oration. First of all, both Menander the Rhetor and Pseudo-Dionysius, in their handbooks of funeral oration, commonly recommend consolation and exhortation after the encomium as essential in funeral oration. In 1 Thess 4:1—5:28, Paul employs the topoi, contents, structure, and purpose of the consolation/exhortation in funeral oration and follows the Greco-Roman funeral oration after the encomium/narratio of 1 Thess 1:4—3:10. Secondly, Paul's main topic in 1 Thess is the hope of Jesus' Parousia, which appears at every partial conclusion (1:3, 10; 2:12, 19; 3:13; 4:13—5:11; 5:23). Encountering sufferings and even death/martyrdom, the Thessalonian believers need to be encouraged and Paul employs the rhetorical strategy of funeral oration to answer their problems through the hope of Jesus' Parousia. Thirdly, Paul intentionally and repeatedly uses separating/boundary language between the pagan world and the fledgling Thessalonian Christian community such as "the Gentiles" (4:5b), "outsiders" (4:12), and "others who have no hope" (4:13b) in order to differentiate them from the pagan world and unify the Thessalonian believers into a new community with a new identity. This is similar to funeral oration in purpose through the unique effect of inviting participation, acceptance, and finally introduces some degree of identification and the unification in the community against the outsiders. Fourthly, the theme of not grieving the dead is a main idea in consolatory literature and funeral oration in the Greco-Roman world as seen in Plutarch, Cicero, Seneca, Thucydides, Plato, Demosthenes, and Hyperides. This is the same in the Jewish funeral oration. Though Pseudo-Lysias and Dio Cassius employ lamentation in their orations, both of them drastically begin Paramythia with a statement contrasting lamentation. In 1 Thess 4:13-18, Paul's rhetorical situation and rhetorical purpose are similar to Athenian funeral oration and Jewish funeral oration, "so that you may not grieve as others do who have no hope" (4:13b). Fifthly, Paul employs Roman imperial funerary motifs in 1 Thess 4:13-18 because there are some overlapping images in both Roman imperial funerary motifs and 1 Thess 4:13-18. Just as the Roman imperial funeral procession interweaves the imperial funeral procession as a processional parade with the triumphal image and the apotheosis, Paul similarly uses the triumphal image of Jesus' Parousia while discussing the death of some of the Thessalonian believers. Sixthly, Paul's use of funerary language with some twists in meaning and purpose illustrates that Paul employs topoi and the purpose of funeral oration in 1 Thess with such examples as "snatching",, funerary contrast motif, and the collective and funeral language of "we" (4:13, 14, 15 (x2), 17 (x2)). Seventhly, Paul employs the funerary language of immortality and consolation in 1 Thess 4:17b-18 with certainty through the hope of Jesus' Parousia while the pagan immortality and comforting words are vague and without certainty. This phenomenon appears in his description of reverse order in the funeral procession through the triumphal procession. Eighth, Paul's use of rhetorical strategy (amplification/embellishment) in 4:13-18 and 5:1-11 shows the characteristics of epideictic rhetoric, particularly funeral oration. Furthermore, the exhortation to the living in 5:1-11, which is particularly emphasized here, compares to Thucydides's funeral oration. In 1 Thess 5:1-11, particularly the emphasis is placed on the living to outline how they should live as a collective community with apocalyptic themes and languages. Finally, Paul's use of prayer in the epilogue also agrees with the topoi of funeral oration because in encomium and funeral oration, the epilogue contains an appeal to others to imitate heroes' virtues and ends most appropriately with a prayer.

In conclusion, in light of topoi, structure, content, and the purpose of funeral oration, 1 Thess 4:1—5:28 has some convincing parallels to funeral oration discussed previously. Therefore, it is logical to conclude that Paul may employ the elements of funeral oration in 1 Thessalonians in order to meet the Thessalonian community's rhetorical situation. This fact also sheds light on Paul's intention and use of rhetorical strategy to encourage the Thessalonian fledgling community in 1 Thessalonians.

CHAPTER 8

Conclusion

THE PRESENT DISSERTATION IS an attempt to show the fact that Paul employs elements of epideictic funerary oratory to persuade his audience in writing 1 Thess, though it is not a funeral oration, and that elements of epideictic funerary oratory illuminate the language and arguments of Paul in 1 Thess. In chapter one of this dissertation we examined the history of interpretation for 1 Thess. Through examining key advocates of the thematic and doctrinal approach, the epistolary approach, and the mirror-reading approach, we discovered that each of them has some critical problems. F. C. Baur and the Tübingen school argued that the 1 Thess church was under the control of Judaizers, but there is no evidence of central issues of Judaism. Walter Schmithals continually sees the apostle fighting off Gnostic intruders from his newly founded congregation, but there is no evidence of dualism or a docetic view of Christ. The epistolary approach has also been overly formalistic and the comparative basis of that activity has been too narrowly focused on the nonliterary papyrus letters of the past. Thus, the epistolary approach is unable to deal with the issues of intention and meaning, and can only address the fragments of the epistolary elements. Robert Jewett has argued that certain members of the Thessalonian church radicalized some of Paul's teaching, which resulted in the problems of libertinism and idleness, and then afterwards he employed a social-scientific approach to understanding the Thessalonian church and proposed a "millenarian" situation.

Recently, concerning the specific genre of 1 Thess, Juan Chapa, Stowers, and Abraham Smith have suggested a consolation letter pattern for 1 Thess. They found the overlapping parallels of consolatory topics between the letter of consolation in the Greco-Roman world and 1 Thess, and attempt to identify the pattern of 1 Thess. I found, however, that 1 Thess is beyond just a consolation or a consoling letter. I found, rather, that these conclusions and approaches above derive from negligence and ignorance of the clear rhetorical signals and epideictic nature of this material.

In light of this, I propose the best solution for a clear interpretation of 1 Thess is to take into account the particular elements of the funeral oration, which is one of the main types of epideictic speech. Subsequently, I endeavored to substantiate this in a number of ways through the following chapters.

In chapter two, I surveyed the pagan philosophy of death, focusing on Epicurean and Stoics, and found their limitation of hope after death. Thus, while employing the rhetorical elements of the ancient funeral orations, Paul made a strong contrast against pagan thought. Paul's theology of death is the hope of the living reuniting with the dead, and the new creation in Christ with his triumphant parousia. This survey of the philosophy of death in the 1st century foreshadows and supports the thesis in light of social circumstances.

First of all, in chapter three, I attempted to categorize the rhetorical genre of 1 Thessalonians into epideictic rhetoric in order to consolidate my assertion. Mitchell asserts the genre designation must precede the compositional analysis so the arrangement can be investigated concerning its appropriateness to that species. Before analyzing the structure and arrangement in order to consolidate my assertion, it is crucial to know the rhetorical need and what the rhetorical exigency is in writing this letter. I found 1 Thess displays many elements of epideictic rhetoric as found in funeral orations: amplification and embellishment with the hypobole (1:8; 5:16–22), the ongoing stress on anamnesis, an epideictic contrast between praiseworthy and blameworthy behavior, the prayer (3:11–13), and the consolation and exhortation at the end of 1 Thess.

In addition to defending my position on the basis of the rhetorical genre and the rhetorical exigency, I have also attempted to show the kind of rhetorical situation that works, the rhetorical purpose that exists, and the kind of rhetorical content found in the extant Athenian funeral orations (5th–4th B.C.). This exploration in proto-typical and exemplary funeral oration actually shows a variety of evidence which supports my assertion that 1 Thess employs elements of funeral oration in terms of funeral language, the rhetorical exigency and purpose, and the rhetorical content and order. The rhetorical exigency in the Athenian funeral speech derives from the commemoration of those who had fallen in battle for their country. In terms of rhetorical purpose, the Athenian funeral orations have the primary purpose of showing the continuity between the living Athenian community and the dead. Through this, the Athenian funeral orations attempt to unify the Athenian community and exhort the young to imitate the dead and console the adults. Finally, all the Athenian funeral orations have the same content in the same order: (a) Exordium, (b) Encomium, (c) Consolation/

Exhortation, (d) Peroration. Particularly, the lengthy and elaborate praises in encomium (*narratio*) prepare the mind of the audience for the consolation and exhortation to the living and function to establish a continuity/identification between the dead and the living. Without any lamentation, except Pseudo-Lysias, all orators focus on the consolation and exhortation to the living. Pseudo-Lysias's lamentation, however, actually functions as a pre-step for emphasizing the positive effects of consolation. Thus, the Athenian funeral orations have the primary purpose to console and exhort the living, which is reflected in 1 Thess 4:13b. Finally, the Athenian funeral orations end with wishful prayers.

After exploring the exemplary funeral orations in Athens, I continually examined the Roman funeral orations/the Latin consolatory letters, and Jewish Funeral orations (Chapter 4). I found that under the influence of the Athenian funeral orations, the Roman funeral orations develop and derive from the circumstances of the war like the Athens funeral orations, while the Romans made a noisy and visual funeral procession. In addition, both had the strikingly similar parallels in terms of the rhetorical purpose and the rhetorical content and order. It is noteworthy that I found, in the Latin consolatory letters, reflection on the private funeral oration (*laudatio funebris*), which also contain similar structure, purpose, and content of funeral orations, while employing the epistle forms. Therefore, as writing became more commonplace, written words of consolation could, and did, serve as surrogates for oral funeral orations. Through this process, I have shown how consolatory letters follow the pattern of epideictic consolation speeches and how I can apply this fact readily to 1 Thess in the subsequent chapters (5-6). I argued that the Jewish funeral oration 4 *Maccabees*, while developing from the circumstances of martyrdom, functions to secure the audience's identification to the nation and to console and exhort the living to imitate the dead.

These elements in the funeral orations are further evidenced by analysis of rhetorical handbooks in that period (ch. 5). Among them, I focused on both Menander of Laodicea (*Division of Epideictic Speeches*) and Pseudo-Dionysius (*On Epideictic Speeches*). I found that though both of them have common factors, Pseudo-Dionysius claimed that the consolatory and exhortatory topics as most essential, and lamentation should be removed from or minimized in the circumstances, while Menander emphasized lamentation in funeral oration. In this sense, I argued that Paul, employing the motive of funeral oration in 1 Thess, denies lamentation for the dead (4:13), and rather emphasizes the consolation and exhortation in length and in detail (4:14—5:11) so that he might urge the audience to be confident in the consolation and promise of Christ's Parousia. Finally, I concluded that Paul might understand the convincing evidence and precedence set by the prominent figures of funeral orations (the Athenian funeral orations, the Roman funeral orations, and the Jewish funeral oration), the consolatory letters, and the rhetorical handbooks. All these precedents show the existence of the funeral oration genre and the power of the well-arranged strategy in that period.

On the basis of the exploration on the extant ancient funeral orations and on rhetorical handbooks, I demonstrated how closely 1 Thess conforms to the funeral orations in terms of structure, function and purpose, and rhetorical topoi, and how much 1 Thess is indebted to funeral oratory in terms of rhetorical exigency and content in the following two chapters (chs. 6–7).

In chapter 6, I endeavored to find and show the elements of encomium regarding the Thessalonian church, the martyred believers, and Paul himself (1 Thess 1–3), which conform to the exordium and narratio of funeral oration. Through this process, I concluded Paul builds a paraclectic model in 1 Thess 1–3 (the long *narratio*) to achieve rapport/identification with his audience and to prepare a good relationship for the consolatory and eschatological exhortation in 1 Thess 4–5. Particularly, I argued that as examined in chapters 3–4, the encomium in funeral orations takes the main and longest part of the whole oratory. In the *narratio* of 1 Thess (1:4—3:10), it is possible to find a number of traces of epideictic rhetoric. Paul's praising of the Thessalonian believers' deeds of imitation of Paul and Christ (1:4–10; 2:13–16), the praising of his own deeds and ethos (2:1–12), Paul's exemplary care via Timothy (3:1–10), and *partition* (3:11–13) with a prayer pattern show the characteristic features of the *narratio* of epideictic rhetoric in 1 Thess. Most importantly, these characteristic features appear in the encomium (narration) of funeral orations. Further, the uniquely long *narratio* of 1 Thess shows the characteristics of the funeral oration of 1 Thess, since funeral oration highlights *narratio* (encomium) with the lengthy part of a whole oration.

Additionally, to support my assertion of the elements of the funeral oration in 1 Thess 1–3, I found other overlapping elements between 1 Thess 1:5—3:10 and funeral oration. Both contain the reaffirming and "reminding language", which is characteristic in *narratio* of epideictic rhetoric (funeral oration). Both reflect the rhetorical exigency of death and martyrdom in tone and content with a *transitus* prayer pattern (3:11–13). Both have the repetitive amplification in structure and content (1:4–10//2:13–16; 2:5–8//2:9–12) and repetitive contrast (comparison) in charcter and deeds, which functions to put superiority on the subject (2:1–12). Just as Ochs convincingly argues the functions and exigency of the *narratio* in funeral oration "narratives by their very nature invite participation, acceptance, and, if artfully done, some degree of identification," Paul, employing the elements of funeral oration in *narratio* (1:5—3:10), establishes the ground and identifies with the audience so that he might prepare the mind of the audience for the following parts of consolation and exhortation (4:1—5:11).

In chapter 7, I continually endeavored to find the overlapping elements and topoi between funeral oration and 1 Thess 4–5, particularly consolation and exhortation, which mainly reflect the rhetorical situation and the rhetorical purpose of 1 Thess. The Athenian and Roman funeral orations, as well as the Jewish funeral oration, emphasize the consolatory topics omitting lamentation; 1 Thess 4:13–18 displays Paul's rhetorical situation and purpose, that is, consolation to the living.

In order to support my assertion, I argued nine topics in 1 Thess 4:1—5:28, which overlap with topoi of funeral oration. Firstly, in 1 Thess 4:1—5:28, Paul employs the topoi, contents, structure, and purpose of the consolation/exhortation in funeral oration and follows the Greco-Roman funeral oration after the encomium of 1 Thess 1:4—3:10. Secondly, with the hope of Jesus' Parousia (1:3, 10; 2:12, 19; 3:13; 4:13—5:11; 5:23), Paul attempts to encourage the Thessalonian believers who encounter suffering and even death/martyrdom. For this, Paul employs the rhetorical strategy of funeral oration to answer their problems. Thirdly, Paul intentionally uses boundary languages ("the Gentiles," "outsiders," and "others who have no hope") between the pagan world and the fledgling Thessalonian Christian community. Funeral oration also has the unique purpose and function of inviting participation, acceptance, and finally identification and unity of the community from the outsiders. Fourth, Paul's emphasis of "so that you may not grieve as others do who have no hope" (4:13b) demonstrates his rhetorical situation and purpose because the theme of not grieving the dead is the main content and purpose in consolatory literature and funeral oration in the Greco-Roman world. Fifth, Paul employs Roman imperial funerary motifs particularly in 1 Thess 4:13–18 to highlight Jesus' triumphal images of Parousia. When consoling the sorrow of the dead, Paul interweaves Jesus' Parousia as a processional parousia with the discussion of death. By employing the triumphal image of Jesus' Parousia as compared with the Roman imperial funerary motif, Paul implants Jesus' triumphal second coming into the hearts of the living so they might keep their hope. Sixth, Paul's use of funerary language ("snatching"), funerary contrast motif, and the collective language of "we" illustrates the fact that Paul employs topoi of funeral oration in 1 Thess. Seventh, Paul employs the funerary language of immortality and consolation in 1 Thess 4:17b-18 with certainty through the hope of Jesus' Parousia. Eighth, Paul's use of rhetorical strategy in 4:13–18 and 5:1–11 (amplification and embellishment) demonstrates well the characteristics of funeral oration. Particularly, 5:1–11 and 12–15, which is the exhortation to the living, shows exactly why we should get exhortations following consolation in epideictic rhetoric. In addition, this also shows how a speech of praise and blame could and should include ethics and exhortation. In the same way, 1 Thess 5:1–11 demonstrates the topoi of exhortation in funeral oration, which is closely connected to the consolation of 4:13–18. Finally, Paul's use of prayer in epilogue also comports with the topoi of funeral oration. Through this evidence above, I concluded Paul may employ the elements of funeral oration in 1 Thess to meet the Thessalonian community's rhetorical situation. In addition, I argued that this fact also sheds light on Paul's intention and rhetorical strategy to encounter the Thessalonian fledgling community in 1 Thess.

Succinctly and simply put, Paul employs elements of epideictic funerary oratory to persuade the audience by writing 1 Thess, though it is not a funeral oration. Elements of epideictic funerary oratory illuminate the language and arguments of Paul in the epistle. For his rhetorical purpose and rhetorical situation, Paul intentionally lengthens the encomium (*narratio*) to establish the continuity and identification with the audience according to the example of the ancient funeral oration. Moreover, after the encomium, following the ancient funeral oration, he emphasizes the consolation to the dead and living, and finally highlights the exhortation to the living, the Christian community, to imitate the dead. Therefore, Paul's rhetorical strategy, purpose, and content in 1 Thess conform to the topoi and the rhetorical situation and purpose of the ancient funeral orations in the Greco-Roman world.

In closing, I contend that Paul employs elements of epideictic funerary oratory to persuade his audience in writing 1 Thess. I recognize the relatively small range of this study. However, it is my hope that this thesis contributes to approaching Pauline's other letters with a specific genre of rhetoric; e.g. funeral oration of epideictic rhetoric. Consequently, I propose investigating in greater depth how the theme of funeral oratory could be applied in Pauline's other letters, and in general letters, would prove fruitful. Moreover, it would be worth exploring how the genre of funeral oratory originated, developed, and related among the Athenians, the Romans, and Jewish funeral oration. More broader and deeper research of ancient funeral oratory resources could be also worth investigating. Finally, it would also be worth exploring more how Paul employs methodological synthesis or discord between rhetorical approach and epistolary approach in 1 Thessalonians.

Bibliography

Achtemeier, Paul J. "Omne Verbum Sonat: The New Testament and the Oral Environment of Late Western Antiquity." *Journal of Biblical Literature* 109 (1990) 3–27.
Amador, J. D. H. *Academic Constraints in Rhetorical Criticism of the New Testament: An Introduction to a Rhetoric of Power*. Journal for the Study of the New Testament: Supplement Series 174. Sheffield: Sheffield Academic Press, 1999.
Anderson, R. D., Jr. *Ancient Rhetorical Theory and Paul*. Leuven: Peeters, 1999.
———. *Glossary of Greek Rhetorical Terms*. Leuven: Peeters, 2000.
Aristotle. *The "Art" of Rhetoric*. Translated by John H. Freese. Loeb Classical Library. Cambridge, MA: Harvard University Press, 1926.
———. *Rhetoric*. Translated by W. Rhys Roberts. New York: Modern Library, 1954.
———. *Topica*. Translated by H. Tredennick and E. S. Forster. Loeb Classical Library. Cambridge, MA: Harvard University Press, 1960.
Ascough, Richard S. "A Question of Death: Paul's Community-Building Language in 1 Thessalonians 4:13–18." *Journal of Biblical Literature* 123 (2004) 509–30.
Aune, D. E. *The New Testament in its Literary Environment*. Library of Early Christianity 8. Philadelphia: Westminster, 1987.
———. *The Westminster Dictionary of New Testament and Early Christian Literature & Rhetoric*. Louisville: Westminster John Knox, 2003.
Aus, Roger D. *Imagery of Triumph and Rebellion in 2 Corinthians 2:14–17 and Elsewhere in the Epistle: An Example of the Combination of Greco-Roman and Judaic Traditions in the Apostle Paul*. Lanham, MD: University Press of America, 2005.
Baltussen, Han. "Personal Grief and Public Mourning in Plutarch's *Consolation to His Wife*." *American Journal of Philology* 131 (2009) 67–98.
Bammel, E. "Preparation for the Perils of the Last Days: 1 Thessalonians 3:3." In *Suffering and Martyrdom in the New Testament*, edited by William Horbury and Brian McNeil, 91–100. Cambridge: Cambridge University Press, 1981.
Barclay, John. "Mirror-Reading a Polemical Letter: Galatians as a Test Case." *Journal for the Study of the New Testament* 31 (1987) 73–93.
Basil. *The Letters I*. Translated by R. J. Deferrari. Loeb Classical Library. Cambridge, MA: Harvard University Press, 1926.
Bauckham, R. *The Fate of the Dead: Studies on the Jewish and Christian Apocalypses*. Leiden: Brill, 1998.
Baumgarten, Jörg. *Paulus und die Apokalyptik: Die Auslegung apokalyptischer Überlieferungen in den echten Paulusbriefen*. Wissenschaftliche Monographein zum Alten und Neuen Testament 44. Neukirchen-Vluyn: Neukirchener, 1975.

Baur, F. C. *Paul the Apostle of Jesus Christ, His Life and Work, His Epistles and His Doctrine: A Contribution to the Critical History of Primitive Christianity.* Edited by E. Zeller. Translated by A. Menzies. Edinburgh: Willians and Norgate, 1875.

Beale, G. K. *1–2 Thessalonians.* Downers Grove, IL: InterVarsity, 2003.

Beard, Mary. *The Roman Triumph.* Cambridge, MA: Belknap, 2007.

Beker, J. Christiaan. *Paul the Apostle: The Triumph of God in Life and Thought.* Philadelphia: Fortress, 1980.

Best, E. *The First and Second Epistles to the Thessalonians.* Peabody, MA: Hendrickson, 1972.

Betz, Hans Dieter. *Galatians: A Commentary on Paul's Letter to the Churches in Galatia.* Philadelphia: Fortress, 1979.

Bitzer, Lloyd F. "The Rhetorical Situation." *Philosophy and Rhetoric* 1 (1968) 1–14.

Boers, Hendrikus. "The Form Critical Study of Paul's Letters: 1 Thessalonians as a Case Study." *New Testament Studies* 22 (1975–1976) 140–58.

Bruce, F. F. *1 and 2 Thessalonians.* Waco, TX: Word, 1982.

———. *The Acts of the Apostles.* London: Tyndale, 1956.

———. "St. Paul in Macedonia." *Bulletin of the John Rylands University Library of Manchester* 61 (1979) 339.

Burgess, T. C. "Epideictic Literature." PhD diss., The University of Chicago, 1902.

Burke, Kenneth. *A Rhetoric of Motives.* Berkeley: University of California Press, 1969.

Burtt. *Minor Attic Orators, Volume II: Lycurgus. Dinarchus. Demades. Hyperides.* Cambridge, MA: Harvard University Press, 1954.

Carson, D. A., and Douglas J. Moo. *An Introduction to the New Testament.* 2nd ed. Grand Rapids: Zondervan, 2005.

Chamberlain, William D. *An Exegetical Grammar of the Greek New Testament.* Grand Rapids: Baker, 1979.

Chapa, Juan. "Consolatory Patterns?: 1 Thess 4:13–18; 5:11." In *The Thessalonian Correspondence*, edited by Raymond F. Collins, 220–28. Bibliotheca ephemeridum theologicarum lovaniensium 87. Leuven: Leuven University Press, 1990.

———. "Is First Thessalonians a Letter of Consolation?" *New Testament Studies* 40 (1994) 150–60.

Chase, J. Richard. "The Classical Conception of Epideictic." *The Quarterly Journal of Speech* 47 (1961) 293–300.

Cicero. *De Oratore* I-II. Translated by E. W. Sutton and H. Rackham. Loeb Classical Library. Cambridge, MA: Harvard University Press, 1960.

———. *De Inventione.* Translated H. M. Hubbell. Loeb Classical Library. Cambridge, MA: Harvard University Press, 1942.

———. *Tusculan Disputations.* Translated by J. E. King. Loeb Classical Library. Cambridge, MA: Harvard University Press, 1927.

[Cicero.] *Ad C. Herennium De Ratione Dicendi (Rhetorica ad Herennium).* Translated by H. Caplan. Loeb Classical Library. Cambridge, MA: Harvard University Press, 1954.

———. *Letters to Atticus* III. Translated by E. O. Winstedt. Loeb Classical Library. Cambridge, MA: Harvard University Press, 1918.

———. *Letters to His Friends* I. Translated by W. Glynn Williams. Loeb Classical Library. Cambridge, MA: Harvard University Press, 1927.

Clericus, Ioannes. "De Emendatione locorum corruptorum." In *Ars Critica*, vol. 2, 3–401. Amsterdam: apud Georgium Gallet, 1699. First printing 1697.

Collins, R. F. *Studies on the First Letter to the Thessalonians*. Bibliotheca ephemeridum theologicarum lovaniensium 66. Leuven: Leuven University Press-Peeters, 1984.
Craigie, Peter C. *Psalms 1–50*. Word Biblical Commentary 19. Waco, TX: Word, 1982.
Cranford, Michael. "Pagan Ethics and the Rhetoric of Separation: A Sociological and Rhetorical Context for 1 Thessalonians 4:1–5:11." Unpublished paper.
Crawford, O. C. "Laudatio Funebris." *The Classical Journal* 37 (1941–1942) 17–27.
Cumont, Franz. *After Life in Roman Paganism*. New Haven, CT: Yale University Press, 1922.
Davies, Jon. *Death, Burial and Rebirth in the Religions of Antiquity*. New York: Routledge, 1999.
Davies, Penelope J. E. *Death and the Emperor: Roman Imperial Funerary Monuments from Augustus to Marcus Aurelius*. Cambridge: Cambridge University Press, 2000.
Delobel, J. "The Fate of the Dead According to 1 Thess 4 and 1 Cor 15." *The Thessalonian Correspondence* 13 (1990) 340–47.
———. "One Letter Too Many in Paul's First Letter? A Study of (ν)ήπιοι in 1 Thess 2:7." *Louvain Studies* 20 (1995) 128.
Demosthenes. *Funeral Speech*. Translated by N. W. and N. J. Dewitt. Loeb Classical Library. Cambridge, MA: Harvard University Press, 1949.
deSilva, David A. *4 Maccabees: Introduction and Commentary on the Greek Text in Codex Sinaiticus*. Septuagint Commentary Series. Leiden: Brill, 2006.
Dill, Samuel. *Roman Society from Nero to Marcus Aurelius*. London: Macmillan, 1905.
Dio Cassius. *Roman History*. Translated by E. Cary. 9 vols. Loeb Classical Library. Cambridge, MA: Harvard University Press, 1917–1927.
Dio Chrysostom. *Dio Chrysostom*. Translated by J. W. Cohoon. 5 vols. Loeb Classical Library. Cambridge, MA: Harvard University Press, 1932–1951.
Dionysius of Halicarnassus. *Critical Essays* I. Translated by Stephen Usher. Loeb Classical Library. Cambridge, MA: Harvard University Press, 1974.
———. *Roman Antiquities*. Translated by E. Cary. 7 vols. Loeb Classical Library. Cambridge, MA: Harvard University Press, 1940–1950.
Donfried, Karl P. "The Cults of Thessalonica and the Thessalonian Correspondence." *New Testament Studies* 31 (1985) 336–56.
———. "The Imperial Cults and Political Conflict in 1 Thessalonians." Pages 215–23 in *Paul and Empire*. Edited by R. A. Horsley. Harrisburg: Trinity, 1997.
———. "Paul and Judaism: 1 Thessalonians 2:13–16 as a Test Case." *Interpretation* (1984) 242–53.
Donfried, Karl P., and I. Howard Marshall. *The Theology of the Shorter Pauline Letters*. Cambridge: Cambridge University Press, 1993.
Doty, W. G. *Letters in Primitive Christianity*. Philadelphia: Fortress, 1973.
Drane, John. *Paul: Libertine or Legalist?* London: SPCK, 1975.
Duff, P. B. "Metaphor, Motif, and Meaning: The Rhetorical Strategy behind the Image 'Led in Triumph' in 2 Corinthians 2:14." *Catholic Biblical Quarterly* 53 (1991) 79–92.
Fee, Gordon D. *The First and Second Letters to the Thessalonians*. New International Commentary on the New Testament. Grand Rapids: Eerdmans, 2009.
Ferguson, Everett. *Backgrounds of Early Christianity*. 2nd ed. Grand Rapids: Eerdmans, 1993.
Fern, Mary Edmond. "The Latin Consolatio as a Literary Type." PhD diss., Saint Louis University, 1941.

Findlay, G. *The Epistles of Paul the Apostle to the Thessalonians*. Cambridge, MA: Harvard University Press, 1904.
Fowler, W. W. *Social Life at Rome in the Age of Cicero*. New York: Macmillan, 1909.
Frend, W. H. C. *Martyrdom and Persecution in the Early Church*. Oxford: Alden, 1965.
Friedrich, G. "1 Thessalonicher 5:1–11, der apologetische Einschub eines Späteren." *Zeitschrift für Theologie und Kirche* 70 (1973) 288–315.
Funk, R. W. "The Apostolic Parousia: Form and Significance." In *Christian History and Interpretation: Studies Presented to John Knox*, edited by W. R. Farmer et al., 249–68. Cambridge: Cambridge University Press, 1967.
———. "The Form and Function of the Pauline Letter." In *SBL Seminar Papers*, 8. Missoula: Scholars, 1970.
———. *Language Hermeneutic and the Word of God*. New York: Harper and Row, 1966.
Gaventa, B. R. *First and Second Thessalonians*. Louisville: John Knox, 1998.
Goulder, M. D. "Silas in Thessalonica." *JSNT* 48 (1992) 87–106.
Green, G. L. *The Letter to the Thessalonians*. Grand Rapids: Eerdmans, 2002.
Gregg, Robert C. *Consolation Philosophy: Greek and Christian Paideia in Basil and the Two Gregories*. Patristic Monograph 3. Cambridge: Philadelphia Patristic Foundation, 1975.
Griesbach, Johann Jacob. "Prolegomena." In *Novum Testamentum Graece*, vol. 2, iii–cxxxii. 2nd ed. London: Elmsly, 1796.
Harris, W. V. *Ancient Literacy*. Cambridge, MA: Harvard University Press, 1989.
Heath, J. M. F. "Absent Presences of Paul and Christ: *Enargeia* in 1 Thessalonians 1–3." *Journal for the Study of the New Testament* 32 (2009) 3–38.
Hendrix, Holland L. "Thessalonicans Honor Romans." PhD diss., Harvard University, 1984.
Hengel, Martin, and R. Deines. *The Pre-Christian Paul*. Valley Forge, PA: Trinity Press International, 1991.
Hester, James D. "The Invention of 1 Thessalonians: A Proposal." In *Rhetoric, Scripture and Theology: Essays from the 1994 Pretoria Conference*, edited by Stanley E. Porter and Thomas H. Olbricht, 251–79. Journal for the Study of the New Testament: Supplement Series 131. Sheffield: Sheffield Academic Press, 1996.
Hinks, D. A. G. "Tria Genera Causarum." *The Classical Quarterly* 30 (1936) 170–76.
Hoehner, Harold Walter. *Ephesians: an Exegetical Commentary*. Grand Rapids: Baker Academic, 2003.
Hoekema, A. A. *The Bible and the Future*. Grand Rapids: Eerdmans, 1982.
Holmes, Michael. *1 and 2 Thessalonians*. Grand Rapids: Zondervan, 1998.
Holtz, Traugott. *Der erste Brief an die Thessalonicher*. Evangelisch-katholischer Kommentar zum Neuen Testament 13. Zürich: Benziger, 1986.
———. "The Judgment on the Jews and the Salvation of All Israel: 1 Thess 2:15–16 and Rom 11:25–26." In *The Thessalonian Correspondence*, edited by Raymond F. Collins, 284–94. Leuven: Leuven University Press, 1990.
Hope, Valerie M. *Roman Death*. New York: Continuum, 2009.
Hopkins, Keith. *Death and Renewal*. Cambridge: Cambridge University Press, 1983.
Horbury, William. "1 Thessalonians 2:3 as rebutting the charge of false prophecy." *The Journal of Theological Studies* 33 (1982) 492–508.
Hüber, Hans. *The Law in Paul's Thought*. Edinburgh: Clark, 1978.

Hughes, Frank W. "The Rhetoric of 1 Thessalonians." In *The Thessalonian Correspondence*, edited by Raymond F. Collins, 94–116. Bibliotheca ephemeridum theologicarum lovaniensium 87. Leuven: Leuven University Press, 1990.

———. "The Social Situations Implied by Rhetoric." In *The Thessalonians Debate: Methodological Discord or Methodological Synthesis?*, edited by Karl P. Donfried and Johannes Beutler, 241–54. Grand Rapids: Eerdmans, 2000.

Hyperides. *Funeral Speech*. Translated by J. O. Burtt. Loeb Classical Library. Cambridge, MA: Harvard University Press, 1954.

Isocrates. *Isocrates*. Translated by G. Norlin and La Rue van Hook. 3 vols. Loeb Classical Library. Cambridge, MA: Harvard University Press, 1928–1945.

Jamieson, K. H., and K. K. Campbell. "Rhetorical Hybrids: Fusions of Generic Elements." *Quarterly Journal of Speech* 68 (1982) 146–57.

Jeal, Roy R. *Integrating Theology and Ethics in Ephesians: The Ethos of Communication*. Lewiston: The Edwin Mellen, 2000.

Jervis, Ann L. *The Purpose of Romans: A Comparative Letter Structure Investigation*. Journal for the Study of the New Testament: Supplement Series 55. Sheffield: JSOT, 1991.

Jewett, Robert. *The Thessalonian Correspondence: Pauline Rhetoric and Millenarian Piety*. Philadelphia: Fortress, 1986.

Johanson, Bruce C. *To All the Brethren: A Text-Linguistic and Rhetorical Approach to 1 Thessalonians*. Stockholm: Almqvist & Wiksell International, 1987.

Johnson, E. Elizabeth. "Paul's Reliance on Scripture in 1 Thessalonians." *SBS Conference* (2009) 1–20.

Judge, E. A. "The Decrees of Caesar at Thessalonica." *The Reformed Theological Review* 30 (1971) 1–7.

Juel, Donald H. *A Master of Surprise: Mark Interpreted*. Minneapolis: Fortress, 1994.

Julian. *Julian*. Translated by W. C. Wright. Loeb Classical Library. Cambridge, MA: Harvard University Press, 1923.

Kaye, B. N. "Eschatology and Ethics in 1 and 2 Thessalonians." *Novum Testamentum* 17 (1975) 47–57.

Keener, Craig S. *1–2 Corinthians*. NCBC. Cambridge: Cambridge University Press, 2005.

Kennedy, George A. *The Art of Persuasion in Greece*. Princeton: Princeton University Press, 1963.

———. *The Art of Rhetoric in the Roman World: 300 B.C.–A.D. 300*. Princeton: Princeton University Press, 1972.

———. *Classical Rhetoric and Its Christian and Secular Tradition from Ancient to Modern Times*. Chapel Hill: The University of North Carolina Press, 1980.

———. "The Genres of Rhetoric." *Handbook of Classical Rhetoric in the Hellenistic Period 330 B.C.—A.D. 400*, edited by S. E. Porter, 43–50. Leiden: Brill, 1997.

———. *New Testament Interpretation through Rhetorical Criticism*. Chapel Hill, NC: University of North Carolina Press, 1984.

Kennedy, George. "Antony's Speech at Caesar's Funeral." *Quarterly Journal of Speech* 54 (1968) 99–106.

Kennedy, George A., trans. *Progymnasmata: Greek Textbooks of Prose Composition and Rhetoric*. With introductions and notes. Atlanta: Society of Biblical Literature, 2003.

Kieffer, René. "L'eschatologie en 1 Thessaloniciens dans une Perspective Rhétorique." In *The Thessalonian Correspondence*, edited by Raymond F. Collins, 206–19. BETL 87. Leuven: Leuven University Press-Peeters, 1990.

Kierdorf, Wilhelm. *Laudatio Funebris: Interpretationen und Untersuchungen zur Entwicklung der römischen Leichenrede*. Meisenheim am Glan: Hain, 1980.

Kittel, Gerhard, and Gerhard Friedrich, eds. *Theological Dictionary of the New Testament*. Translated by Geoffrey W. Bromiley. 10 vols. Grand Rapids: Eerdmans, 1964–1976.

Koch, Klaus. *The Rediscovery of Apocalyptic: A Polemical Work on a Neglected Area of Biblical Studies and Its Damaging Effects on Theology and Philosophy*. Studies in Biblical Theology 2/22. London: SCM, 1972.

Koester, Helmut. *History and Literature of Early Christianity II*. Philadelphia: Fortress, 1982.

———. "Imperial Ideology and Paul's Eschatology in 1 Thessalonians." In *Paul and Empire: Religion and Power in Roman Imperial Society*, edited by R. A. Horsley, 158–66. Harrisburg: Trinity, 1997.

———. *Paul and his World: Interpreting the New Testament in its Context*. Minneapolis: Fortress, 2007.

Kraus, Hans-Joachim. *Psalms 1–59: A Continental Commentary*. Translated by Hilton C. Oswald. Minneapolis: Fortress, 1993.

Kümmel, Werner G. "Die Probleme von Römer 9–11 in der Gegenwärtigen Forschungslage." In *Heilsgeschehen und Geschichte* 2, edited by Erich Grässer and Otto Merk, 13–33. Tübingen: Laupp & Göbel, 1978.

Lambrecht, J. "Thanksgivings in 1 Thessalonians 1–3." In *The Thessalonian Correspondence*, edited by R. F. Collins, 183–205. BETL 87. Leuven: Leuven University Press-Peeters, 1990.

———. "Thanksgivings in 1 Thessalonians 1–3." In *The Thessalonians Debate: Methodological Discord or Methodological Synthesis?*, edited by Karl P. Donfried and Johannes Beutler, 135–62. Grand Rapids: Eerdmans, 2000.

Lattimore, Richmond. *Themes in Greek and Latin Epitaphs*. Urbana: University of Illinois Press, 1942.

Laub, Franz. *Eschatologische Verkündigung und Lebensgestaltung nach Paulus: Eine Untersuchung zum Wirken des Apostels beim Aufbau der Gemeinde in Thessalonike*. Münchener Universitäts-Schriften: Katholisch-Theologische Fakultät, 1973.

Lausberg, Heinrich. *Handbook of Literary Rhetoric: A Foundation for Literary Study*. Translated by M. T. Bliss et al. Leiden: Brill, 1998.

Libanius. *The Julianic Orations*. Translated by A. F. Norman. Loeb Classical Library. Cambridge, MA: Harvard University Press, 1969.

Long, Fredrick J. *Ancient Rhetoric and Paul's Apology: The Compositional Unity of 2 Corinthians*. Cambridge: Cambridge University Press, 2004.

———. "From Epicheiremes to Exhortation: A Pauline Method for Moral Persuasion in Hellenistic Socio-Rhetorical Context." *Queen: A Journal of Rhetoric and Power: Rhetorics, Ethics and Moral Persuasion in Biblical Discourse* (2002) 1–52.

Loraux, Nicole. *The Invention of Athens: The Funeral Oration in the Classical City*. Translated by Alan Sheridan. Cambridge, MA: Harvard University Press, 1986.

Lucian. *Lucian*. Translated by A. M. Harmon and M. D. Macleod. Loeb Classical Library. Cambridge, MA: Harvard University Press, 1921–1961.

Luckensmeyer, D. *The Eschatology of First Thessalonians.* Göttingen: Vandenhoeck & Ruprecht, 2009.
Lührmann, Dieter. "The Beginnings of the Church at Thessalonica." In *Greeks, Romans, and Christians: Essays in Honor of Abraham J. Malherbe*, edited by David L. Balch et al., 237–52. Minneapolis: Fortress, 1990.
Lütgert, W. "Die Volkommenen im Philiperbrief und die Enthusiasten in Thessalonich." *Beiträge zur Förderung christlicher Theologie* 13 (1909) 547–654.
Lyons, George. "The Function of Autobiographical Remarks in the Letters of Paul: Galatians and 1 Thessalonians as Test Cases." PhD diss., Emory University, 1982.
———. *Pauline Autobiography: Toward a New Understanding.* SBLDS 73. Atlanta: Scholars, 1985.
Lysias. *Lysias.* Translated by W. R. M. Lamb. Loeb Classical Library. Cambridge, MA: Harvard University Press, 1930.
Malherbe, Abraham J. "Exhortation in First Thessalonians." *Novum Testamentum* XXV (1983) 238–56.
———. "'Gentle as a Nurse': The Cynic Background to I Thess ii." *Novum Testamentum* 12 (1970) 203–17.
———. *The Letters to the Thessalonians.* New York: Doubleday, 2000.
———. *Paul and the Popular Philosophers.* Minneapolis: Fortress, 1989.
———. *Paul and the Thessalonians.* Philadelphia: Fortress, 1987.
Marshall, Howard. *1 and 2 Thessalonians.* Grand Rapids: Eerdmans, 1983.
———. *Luke: Historian and Theologian.* 3rd ed. Downers Grove, IL: InterVarsity, 1988.
Martin, Hubert, and Jane E. Phillips. "Consolatio Ad Uxorem (Moralia 608A–612B)." *Plutarch's Ethical Writings and Early Christian Literature*, edited by Hans Dieter Betz, 394–441. Leiden: Brill, 1978.
Martin, Ralph P. *2 Corinthians.* WBC 40. Waco, TX: Word, 1986.
Marxsen, Willi. "Auslegung von 1 Thess 4:13–18." *Zeitschrift für Theologie und Kirche* 66 (1969) 22–37.
———. *Der erste Brief die Thessalonicher.* Zurich: Theologischer Verlag, 1979.
Maso, Leonardo B. Dal. *Rome of the Caesars.* Translated by Micael Hollingworth. Firenze: Bonechi, 1977.
Masson, Charles. *Les Deux Épitres de Saint Paul aux Thessaloniciens.* Neuchatel: Delachaux et Niestle, 1957.
Matera, Frank J. *II Corinthians.* Louisville: Westminster John Knox, 2003.
McGuire, R. P. "The Christian Funeral Oration." In *Funeral Orations by Saint Gregory Nazianzen and Saint Ambrose*, edited by Leo P. McCauley et al., 7–14. Translated by Leo P. McCauley et al. Washington, DC: Catholic University of America Press, 1968.
Meeks, Wayne A. "The Circle of Reference in Pauline Morality." *Greeks, Romans, and Christians: Essays in Honor of Abraham J. Malherbe*, edited by D. L. Balch et al., 305–17. Minneapolis: Fortress, 1990.
———. "Social Functions of Apocalyptic Language in Pauline Christianity." In *Apocalypticism in the Mediterranean World and the Near East*, edited by David Hellholm, 687–705. Tübingen: J. C. B. Mohr, 1989.
Menken, M. J. J. *2 Thessalonians.* New York: Routledge, 1994.
Metzger, B. *The Text of the New Testament: Its Transmission, Corruption, and Restoration.* 3rd ed. Oxford: UP, 1992.

Milligan, G. *St. Paul's Epistles to the Thessalonians: The Greek Text with Introduction and Notes.* London: Macmillan, 1908.
Mitchell, M. M. *The Heavenly Trumpet: John Chrysostom and the Art of Pauline Interpretation.* Louisville: Westminster/John Knox, 2002.
———. *Paul and the Rhetoric of Reconciliation: An Exegetical Investigation of the Language and Composition of 1 Corinthians.* Louisville: Westminster/John Knox, 1991.
Moffatt, J. *Introduction to the Literature of the New Testament.* 3rd ed. Edinburgh: T. & T. Clark, 1927.
Morris, L. *The First and Second Epistles to the Thessalonians.* Grand Rapids: Eerdmans, 1959.
Muilenburg, James. "Form Criticism and Beyond." *Journal of Biblical Literature* 88 (1969) 8.
Murphy-O'Connor, Jerome. *Paul: A Critical Life.* Oxford: Oxford University Press, 1996.
Nepper-Christensen, P. "Das verborgene Herrnwort: Eine Untersuchung über 1 Thess 4:13–18." *ST* 19 (1965) 136–65.
Nicholl, Colin R. *From Hope to Despair in Thessalonica: Situating 1 and 2 Thessalonians.* SNTSMS 126. Cambridge: Cambridge University Press, 2004.
O'Banion, John D. "Narration and Argumentation: Quintilian on *Narratio* as the Heart of Rhetorical Thinking." *Rhetorica: A Journal of the History of Rhetoric* 5 (1987) 325–51.
O'Brien, P. T. *Introductory Thanksgivings in the Letters of Paul.* Novum Testamentum Supplement Series 49. Leiden: Brill, 1977.
———. *The Letter to the Ephesians.* Grand Rapids: Eerdmans, 1999.
Ochs, Donovan J. *Consolatory Rhetoric: Grief, Symbol, and Ritual in the Greco-Roman Era.* Columbia, SC: University of South Carolina Press, 1993.
Okeke, G. E. "1 Thess 2:13–16: The Fate of the Unbelieving Jews." *New Testament Studies* 27 (1980) 127–36.
Olbricht, Thomas H. "An Aristotelian Rhetorical Analysis of 1 Thessalonians." In *Greeks, Romans, and Christians: Essays in Honor of Abraham J. Malherbe,* edited by David L. Balch et al., 216–36. Minneapolis: Fortress, 1990.
———. "Hebrews as Amplication." In *Rhetoric and the New Testament: Essays from the 1992 Heidelberg Conference,* edited by Stanley E. Porter and Thomas H. Olbricht, 375–87. Sheffield: Sheffeld Academic Press, 1993.
Palmer, D. W. "Thanksgiving, self-defense, and exhortation in 1 Thessalonians 1–3." *Colloquium* 14 (1981) 23–31.
Pearson, Birger A. "1 Thessalonians 2:13–16: A Deutero-Pauline Interpolation." *Harvard Theological Review* 64 (1971) 79–94.
Perelman, C., and L. Olbrechts-Tyteca. *The New Rhetoric: A Treatise on Argumentation.* Translated by J. Wilkinson and P. Weaver. Notre Dame; London: University of Notre Dame Press, 1969.
Pfitzner, V. C. *Paul and the Agon Motif: Traditional Athletic Imagery in the Pauline Literature.* Netherlands: Brill, 1967.
Plato. *Menexenus.* Translated by R. G. Bury. Loeb Classical Library. Cambridge, MA: Harvard University Press, 1929.
Plevnik, J. "1 Thess 5:1–11: Its Authenticity, Intention and Message." *Biblica* 60 (1979) 71–90.

Pliny. *Letters and Panegyricus* I. Translated by B. Radice. Loeb Classical Library. Cambridge, MA: Harvard University Press, 1969.

Plutarch. *Moralia II*. Translated by F. C. Babbitt. Loeb Classical Library. Cambridge, MA: Harvard University Press, 1928.

———. *Moralia VII*. Translated by P. H. de Lacy and B. Einarson. Loeb Classical Library. Cambridge, MA: Harvard University Press, 1959.

Polybius. *The Histories III*. Translated by W. R. Paton. Loeb Classical Library. Cambridge, MA: Harvard University Press, 1923.

Poulakos, T. "Historiographies of the Tradition of Rhetoric: A Brief History of Classical Funeral Orations." *Western Journal of Speech Communication* 54 (1990) 172–88.

Price, Simon. "From noble funerals to divine cult: the consecration of Roman Emperors." In *Rituals of Royalty: Power and Ceremonial in Traditional Societies*, edited by David Cannadine and Simon Price, 56–105. Cambridge: Cambridge University Press, 1987.

Quintilian. *The Institutio Oratoria of Quintilian*. Translated by H. E. Butler. 4 vols. Loeb Classical Library. Cambridge, MA: Harvard University Press, 1920–1922.

Redditt, Paul L. "The Concept of *Nomos* in Fourth Maccabees." *The Catholic Biblical Quarterly* 45 (1983) 249–70.

Rees, Roger. "Panegyric." In *A Companion to Roman Rhetoric*, edited by W. Dominik and Jon Hall, 136–48. Malden, MA: Blackwell, 2007.

Ridderbos, H. *Paul: An Outline of His Theology*. Grand Rapids: Eerdmans, 1975.

Rigaux, B. *Les Épitres aux Thessaloniciens*. Paris: Gabalda, 1956.

———. "Tradition et Rédaction dans 1 Th. V. 1–10." *New Testament Studies* 21 (1974–1975) 320–35.

Robbins, Vernon K. *The Tapestry of Early Christian Discourse: Rhetoric, Society and Ideology*. New York: Routledge, 1996.

Roetzel, Calvin J. *The Letters of Paul: Conversations in Context*. Atlanta: John Knox, 1975.

Rothschild, Clare K., and Trevor W. Thompson. "Galen: "On the Avoidance of Grief."" In *Early Christianity* 2, 110–29. Tübingen: Mohr Siebeck, 2011.

Russell, D. A., and N. G. Wilson, eds. *Menander Rhetor*. Oxford: Clarendon, 1981.

Russell, Ronald. "The Idle in 2 Thess. 3:6–12: An Eschatological or a Social Problem?" *New Testament Studies* 34 (1988) 105–13.

Salzman, Michele Renee. *The Letters of Symmachus: Book 1*. Translated by Michele Renee Salzman and Michael Roberts. Atlanta: Society of Biblical Literature, 2011.

Sanders, J. T. "The Transition from Opening Epistolary Thanksgiving to Body in the Letters of the Pauline Corpus." *Journal of Biblical Literature* 81 (1962) 348–62.

Sandys, J. E. ed. *A Companion to Latin Studies*. 3rd ed. Cambridge: Cambridge University Press, 1921.

Schmidt, P. W. *Der erste Thessalonicherbrief, neu erklärt, nebst einem Excurs über den zweiten gleichnamigen Brief*. Berlin: Reimer, 1885.

Schmithals, Walter. *Paul and the Gnostics*. Translated by John E. Steely. New York: Abingdon, 1972.

Schubert, P. *Form and Function of the Pauline Thanksgivings*. Beihefte zur Zeitschrift für die neutestamentliche Wissenschaft 20. Berlin: Töpelman, 1939.

Seneca. *Epistles 1–65*. Translated by R. M. Gummere. Loeb Classical Library. Cambridge, MA: Harvard University Press, 1917.

———. *Epistulae Morales III*. Translated by R. M. Gummere. Loeb Classical Library. Cambridge, MA: Harvard University Press, 1925.

Shin, Hyeon Woo. "The Search for Valid Criteria in Textual Criticism, Synoptic Studies, and Historical Jesus Research." PhD diss.,Vrije Universiteit Amsterdam, 2003.

Silva, Moises. *Explorations in Exegetical Method: Galatians as a Test Case*. Grand Rapids: Baker, 1996.

Smith, A. *Comfort One Another: Reconstructing the Rhetoric and Audience of 1 Thessalonians*. Literary Currents in Biblical Interpretation. Louisville: Westminster John Knox, 1995.

Smith, William., ed. *A Dictionary of Greek and Roman Antiquities*. London: John Murray, 1878.

Sourvinou-Inwood, C. *'Reading' Greek Death: To the End of the Classical Period*. Oxford: Oxford University Press, 1995.

Stowers, Stanley. *Letter-Writing in Greco-Roman Antiquity*. Philadelphia: Fortress, 1986.

Sturz, H. A. *The Byzantine Text-Type and New Testament Textual Criticism*. New York: Thomas Nelson, 1984.

Suetonius. *The Twelve Caesars*. Translated by R. Graves. Harmondsworth, Middlesex: Penguin, 1957.

Tacitus. *Agricola*. Translated by M. Hutton. Loeb Classical Library. Cambridge, MA: Harvard University Press, 1970.

Talmon, Yonina. "Millenarian Movements." *Archives européennes de sociologie* 7 (1966) 159–200.

———. "Millenarism." *IESS* 10 (1968) 349–62.

Thucydides. *History of the Peloponnesian War I–II*. Translated by C. F. Smith. Loeb Classical Library. Cambridge, MA: Harvard University Press, 1919.

Toorn, Karel van der. *Scribal Culture and the Making of the Hebrew Bible*. Cambridge, MA: Harvard University Press, 2007.

Toynbee, J. M. C. *Death and Burial in the Roman World*. Ithaca, NY: Cornell University Press, 1971.

Trebilco, Paul. *Self-Designation and Group Identity in the New Testament*. Cambridge: Cambridge University Press, 2012.

Usener, H., and L. Radermacher, eds. *Opuscula*. 6 vols. Liepzig: B. G. Teubner, 1904–1929.

Vielhauer, P. *Geschichte der urchristlichen Literatur: Einleitung in das Neue Testament, die Apokryphen und die Apostolischen Väter*. Berlin and New York: Walter de Gruyter, 1975.

———. "Introduction to Apocalypses and Related Subjects." In *New Testament Apocrypha*, edited by W. Schneemelcher, 581–607. Philadelphia: Westminster Press, 1963–1965.

Wallace, Daniel B. *Greek Grammar beyond the Basics: An Exegetical Syntax of the New Testament*. Grand Rapids: Zondervan, 1996.

Walton, Steve. "What has Aristotle to do with Paul?: Rhetorical Criticism and 1 Thessalonians." *Tyndale Bulletin* 46 (1995) 229–50.

Wanamaker, Charles A. *The Epistles to the Thessalonians*. NIGTC. Grand Rapids: Eerdmans, 1990.

———. "Epistolary vs. Rhetorical Analysis: Is a Synthesis Possible?" In *The Thessalonians Debate:Methodological Discord or Methodological Synthesis?*, edited by Karl P. Donfried and Johannes Beutler, 255–86. Grand Rapids: Eerdmans, 2000.

———. "A Socio-Rhetorical Analysis of 1 Cor. 4:14—5:13." In *The New Testament Interpreted: Essays in Honor of Bernard C. Lategan*, edited by C. Breytenbach et al., 342-43. Leiden: Brill, 2006.
Warren, J. *Facing Death: Epicurus and his Critics*. Oxford: Oxford University Press, 2004.
Watson, D. F. "Amplification Techniques in 1 John: the Interaction of Rhetorical Style and Invention." *Journal for the Study of the New Testament* 16 (1993) 101-3.
———. *Invention, Arrangement, and Style: Rhetorical Criticism of Jude and 2 Peter*. SBLDS 104. Atlanta: Scholars, 1988.
———. "Paul's Appropriation of Apocalyptic Discourse: The Rhetorical Strategy of 1 Thessalonians." In *Vision and Persuasion: Rhetorical Dimensions of Apocalyptic Discourse*, edited by Greg Carey and L. Gregory Bloomquist, 61-80. St. Louis, MO: Chalice, 1999.
Weima, J. A. D. "An Apology for the Apologetic Function of 1 Thessalonians 2:1-12." *Journal for the Study of the New Testament* 68 (1997) 73-99.
———. "'But We Became Infants Among You': The Case for nh,pioi in 1 Thess 2.7." *New Testament Studies* 46 (2000) 547-64.
———. "The Function of 1 Thessalonians 2:1-12 and the Use of Rhetorical Criticism: A Response to Otto Merk." In *The Thessalonians Debate: Methodological Discord or Methodological Synthesis?*, edited by Karl P. Donfried and Johannes Beutler, 114-31. Grand Rapids: Eerdmans, 2000.
———. "'Peace and Security' (1 Thess 5:3): Prophetic Warning or Political Propaganda?" *New Testament Studies* 58 (2012) 331-59.
———. "What Does Aristotle Have to Do with Paul?: An Evaluation of Rhetorical Criticism." *Canadian Journal of Theology* 32 (1997) 458-68.
White, Hayden. *Tropics of Discourse: Essays in Cultural Criticism*. Baltimore: Johns Hopkins University Press, 1978.
White, J. L. "Apostolic Mission and Apostolic Message: Congruence in Paul's Epistolary Rhetoric, Structure and Imagery." In *Origins and Method: Towards a New Understanding of Judaism and Christianity*, edited by Bradley H. McLean, 158-59. JSNTSup 86. Sheffield: JSOT, 1993.
———. *Light from Ancient Letters*. Philadelphia: Fortress, 1986.
White, J. R. "'Peace and Security' (1 Thessalonians 5:3): Is It Really a Roman Slogan?" *New Testament Studies* 59 (2013) 382-95.
Whiteley, D. E. H. *Thessalonians*. London: Oxford University Press, 1969.
Wikenhauser, A., and Otto Kuss. *Der Erste und Zweite Brief an die Thessalonicher*. Translated by Paul-Gerhard Müller. Regensburg: Verlag Friedrich Pustet, 2001.
Williamson, Lamar. "Led in Triumph: Paul's Use of *Thriambeuō*." *Int* 22 (1968) 317-32.
Wills, Garry. *Lincoln at Gettysburg: The Words that Remade America*. New York: Simon & Schuster, 1992.
Winter, Bruce W. "'If A Man Does Not Wish to Work . . . ': A Cultural and Historical Setting for 2 Thessalonians 3:6-16." *Tyndale Bulletin* 40 (1989) 303-15.
Wistrand, Erik. *The So-Called Laudatio Turiae: Introduction, Text, Translation, Commentary*. Berlingska Boktryckeriet, Lund: Acta Universitatis Gothoburgensis, 1976.
Witherington, Ben. *1 and 2 Thessalonians: A Socio-Rhetorical Commentary*. Grand Rapids: Eerdmans, 2006.

———. *Conflict and Community in Corinth: A Socio-Rhetorical Commentary on 1 and 2 Corinthians*. Grand Rapids: Eerdmans, 1995.

———. *New Testament History: A Narrative Account*. Grand Rapids: Baker Academic, 2001.

———. *New Testament Rhetoric: An Introductory Guide to the Art of Persuasion in and of the New Testament*. Eugene, OR: Cascade, 2009.

———. *The Paul Quest: The Renewed Search for the Jew of Tarsus*. Downers Grove, IL: InterVarsity, 1998.

———. *Paul's Letter to the Romans: A Socio-Rhetorical Commentary*. Grand Rapids: Eerdmans, 2004.

Wuellner, W. "The Argumentative Structure of 1 Thessalonians as Paradoxical Encomium." In *The Thessalonian Correspondence*, edited by Raymond F. Collins, 117–36. Bibliotheca ephemeridum theologicarum lovaniensium 87. Leuven: Leuven University Press, 1990.

———. "Where Is Rhetorical Criticism Taking Us?" *Catholic Biblical Quarterly* 49 (1987) 448–63.

Zanker, Paul. *The Power of Images in the Age of Augustus*. Ann Arbor: University of Michigan Press, 1988.

Ziolkowski, John E. *Thucydides and the Tradition of Funeral Speeches at Athens*. Salem, NH: Ayer, 1980.

Index of Ancient Documents

Old Testament

Genesis

1–3	2

Exodus

19:19	206

Deuteronomy

15:3, 12	142

2 Samuel

1:19	99
1:19–26	99
1:19ff	98
1:23	99
1:23, 26	99
1:24	99

Psalms

5:9	185n5
24:7–10	207, 208
36:23	185n5
68:17–18	203
68:17–24	203
68:18	203
118	185n5
118:5 (LXX)	185, 185n5
133	185n5

Proverbs

4:26	185n5
9:15	185n5
29:27	185n5

Isaiah

25–26	222n95
25:6–9	222n95
26:1	222n95
27:13	206
40–66	219
40:1	219
49:13	219
51:3	219
51:12	219
51:19	219
52:9	219
54:11	219
57:18	219
61:2	219
66:13	219

Jeremiah

6	234n119
6:1	234n119
6:14	234
6:17	234n119
6:24	234n119
6:26	234n119
11:20	160
12:3	160
17:10	160

Ezekiel

13:10	234

Daniel

12	29

Joel

2:1	206

Micah

3:5	234

Zephaniah

1:14-16	206

Zechariah

9:14	206, 207

Deuterocanonical Books

Apocalypse of Moses

22	206

1 Enoch

39:3	209

2 Enoch

3:1	209

4 Esdras

6.23	206

1 Maccabees

9:27	163

2 Maccabees

	21
6:29	109
7:18	109

4 Maccabees

	99, 106–9, 129, 164n97, 244
1:1-12	107, 109
1:1	107
1:2	107
1:10-11	107
1:10	107
1:13—3:18	107, 108, 109
1:15	108
2:21	108
3:19—17:6	108, 109, 130n1, 180n139
3:19	107
4	106, 165
5:1—6:30	108
5:18	107
6:10	108
6:31—7:15	108
7:1-15	108
7:16-23	108
8:1—12:19	108
9:23	108, 165
12:11-14	165
12:11	108, 139
12:14	108, 139
13:1—14:10	108
13:13-17	107
13:13-15	165
13:13	108, 139
13:15	108, 139
14:2-10	108
14:11—15:28	108
15-17	164n97
15:29—17:6	108
16:1—17:6	195
16:2	107
16:12-16	165
16:12	196
16:16	108, 139
16:22	195
17:2-6	108
17:7—18:24	107, 109
17:7—18:19	107
17:7—18:5	195
17:7	109
17:8-10	109
17:11-16	109, 165

17:15–16	196	24:37–39	235
17:16	109		
18:1–5	109, 225	**Mark**	
18:1–2	107		
18:3–4	107	13:13	134
18:20–21	107, 109	13:32	159
18:22–24	107, 109	14:58	231
18:23–24	196		

Pseudepigrapha (Old Testament)

Luke

		1:1–4	16n75
		1:79	185n5
		17:26–27	235
		23:46a	30

3 Baruch

2.1	209

John

Psalms of Solomon

		1:13	159
		1:25	159
11.1	206	10:28–29	208
		11:25–26	204

Ancient Jewish Writers

13–17	219
14:15–21	219

Josephus

16:6	29
16:16	219
16:20–22	29

Antiquities of the Jews

10.201	142

Acts 16n75

The Jewish War

		1:9	222
		7:13	222
7.72	202	7:60	166
		8:30	6
		8:39	208

Philo

11:19	163
15:16	231

The Special Laws

		16:6—18:5	16n75
2.79–80	142	17:1–10	16, 16n75, 17
		17:1–9	163n92

New Testament

17:5–10	16
17:5–7	164
17:7	168

Matthew

		17:7b	166, 167
12:29	208	17:9	166
13:19	208	17:13–14	164
16:18	231	17:18	26
24:21	163	24:2–8	133n10
24:31	207	24:10b	133n10
24:36	159		

Romans

Romans — 142, 204n43, 205n43

1:13	140n30
1:16–17	144
1:21	239
5:1	226
5:3	134
5:3b	163
8	227
8:1ff	227
8:25	134
9:2	29
9:6a	174n126
9–11	144, 174
11:15	174
11:23–26	175n126
11:25–32	174
11:25	140n30
12:12	134, 163
13:11	226
13:12–13	226
13:12a	226
13:14	226
15:10	231
15:14–33	176, 177
15:14–15a	176
15:15b–21	176
15:22–28	176
15:29–32a	176
15:32b–33	176

1 Corinthians

1 Corinthians — 18, 142, 204n43

1	2
1–4	158
1:21–25	158
4	176, 177
4:1	37
4:9	37
4:14–21	176, 177
4:16	37
7:7–8	37
8:1	231
9:1–27	37
9:25	164n97
10:1	140n30
10:23	231
11:1–2	37
12:1	140n30
13	37
13:1–13	37
14:4	231
15	204, 205, 227
15:9–10	37
15:12	204
15:12–57	227
15:20	204
15:30–34	26
15:30–32	37
15:32	226
15:50–54	29
15:51–52	204, 207
15:51–54a	34
15:53b	30
15:54b–55	34
16:22	205n46

2 Corinthians

2 Corinthians — 142, 150

1:6	134
2:1–5	29
2:14–16	202
2:14a	210
4:2	149
6:4	134, 163
6:8	149
7:2	149
7:4–7	165
8:1	140n30
8:2	163
10:1—11:15	177n133
11:16—12:10	177n133
12:2	208
12:4	208
12:11—13:10	177n133
12:14—13:13	176, 177
12:14ff	176
12:14	177
12:16–17	149

Galatians

Galatians — 19, 150, 154

1:11	140n30
2:18	231

4:12–20	176, 177	1:3	131n7, 135n13, 144, 192, 239, 246
4:16b	205n43	1:3b	1, 17
5:6	134	1:4—3:10	6, 8, 12n54, 57, 79, 108, 132, 135–73, 179–81, 183, 196, 239, 245, 246
5:25	226		
5:26	226		
6:9	226		

Ephesians 130

		1:4—2:16	151
1–3	184	1:4–10	79, 132, 140–46, 150, 151, 152, 154n72, 155, 157, 158, 162, 165, 168, 172, 173, 181, 223, 233, 245
1:20–22	203		
2:1–10	130n2		
2:11–22	130n2		
2:12b	197		
4:7–8	203	1:4–5	146
4:15	226	1:4	131n7, 132n7, 135n13, 140, 141, 142, 172, 181

Philippians

		1:5—3:10	137, 180, 245, 246
1:12	140n30	1:5—2:12	2, 149
1:27–30	164, 165	1:5–10	181
1:27ff	164n97	1:5–8	135n13
1:30	109	1:5–7	140
2:17	166	1:5–6	151, 156
2:19–24	176, 177	1:5	1, 15, 131n7, 135n12, 141, 143, 146, 155, 159, 181
2:27	29		
3:15	226		
4:3	164	1:6—3:13	131
		1:6—2:16	21

Colossians

		1:6–10	21, 132n8, 143
1:28—2:2	164	1:6–8	166
1:29—2:2	164	1:6–7	143, 144
1:29	164n97	1:6	1, 16, 21, 109, 135n12, 139, 144, 146, 163, 164, 166, 172, 173, 233
2:16—4:6	165		
4:12–13	164n97		
		1:6b	1, 16

1 Thessalonians

		1:7	184
1–3	6, 123, 130–83, 245	1:8–9	135n13
		1:8	38, 143, 243
1:1	131	1:9–10	34, 143, 144, 145, 151, 152, 156, 161, 172, 227
1:2—3:13	184		
1:2—2:16	19		
1:2–10	2, 5, 6, 19, 143, 147	1:9	37, 135n12, 140, 146, 151, 155, 238
1:2–3	6, 8, 131, 132–35, 183	1:9a	143
		1:9b	144, 215, 228, 230
1:2	133, 135n13		

1 Thessalonians
(continued)

1:10	17, 22, 37, 134, 144, 151, 192, 215, 229 239, 246
1:10a	1
1:10b	230
2–3	131
2:1—5:22	147
2:1—3:13	144
2:1—3:10	20, 233
2:1—3:3	159
2:1–18	157, 158, 219
2:1–12	1, 15, 19, 20, 37, 79, 132, 132n8, 140, 143, 146–73, 153n72, 154n72, 162, 177, 178, 181, 184, 245
2:1–8	131, 135n13
2:1–4	154, 155
2:1–2	148, 155, 156, 159, 162, 164, 181
2:1	135n12, 135n13, 141, 150, 155, 181, 191
2:2–12	40
2:2–8	157
2:2–6	150
2:2–5	173
2:2–3	21
2:2	21, 109, 135n12, 139, 141, 150, 151, 152, 163, 164, 164n97, 165, 166, 181
2:2b	1, 16, 159
2:3–7	150
2:3–4	148, 155, 156, 159, 162, 181
2:3	159
2:4	135n12, 148, 159, 160
2:4a	159
2:4b	148, 159
2:5–8	154, 155, 156, 157, 158, 162, 170, 181, 223, 245
2:5–7	159, 162, 181
2:5–7a	148
2:5	64, 135n13, 141, 148, 150, 155, 181
2:7–8	157, 181
2:7	54, 150, 168–73, 181
2:7a	155, 157
2:7b–8	155
2:7b	157
2:8	157, 159, 162, 181
2:8b	148
2:9—3:13	131
2:9–12	135n12, 155, 156, 157, 158, 162, 181, 223, 245
2:9–11	135n13
2:9	135n12, 141, 150, 181
2:9b	155
2:10	1, 17, 64, 141, 148, 150, 155, 181
2:11–12	155
2:11	54, 135n12, 141, 150, 157, 181
2:12	22, 157, 162, 186, 189, 192, 239, 246
2:13–17	164
2:13–16	6, 79, 132, 132n8, 140, 143, 151, 152, 155, 157, 158, 162, 165, 168, 172, 173–76, 181, 223, 245
2:13–14	2, 151, 156, 166n99
2:13	37, 131, 135n12, 135n13, 173
2:14–16	166, 184, 233
2:14–15	1, 21, 139, 152
2:14	16, 17, 135n12, 135n13, 144, 163, 166, 172, 173, 238
2:15–16	151, 152, 156, 161, 174

2:15	151, 163		185, 186, 188,
2:16	22, 134, 215, 229,		239, 243, 245
	230	3:11–12	186, 189
2:17—3:13	21, 176, 177, 184	3:11	185, 186
2:17—3:10	15, 19, 79, 176–	3:12–13	134
	79, 185	3:12	185, 186, 189
2:17–20	16, 132, 157	3:13	1, 17, 22, 134,
2:17–18	16		185, 186, 189,
2:17	135n13, 157, 181		191, 192, 205,
2:17a	158		227, 239, 246
2:17b	158, 176, 177, 179	4–5	22, 23, 37, 38,
2:18	109, 163, 233		131, 161, 179,
2:19–20	54, 135n13, 177		184–241, 245, 246
2:19	1, 16, 17, 22, 134,	4:1—5:28	239–41, 246
	179, 192, 205,	4:1—5:22	21, 131, 134, 143,
	227, 239, 246		144, 146, 187
2:20	16	4:1—5:15	8
3:1–10	132, 140, 245	4:1—5:11	151, 152, 154,
3:1–8	20		162, 165, 168,
3:1–5	1, 144, 164		173, 176, 178,
3:1–3	135n13		180, 181, 182,
3:1a	179		183, 184, 185,
3:1b–5	179		186, 192, 246
3:2–5	17, 177	4:1—5:10	79, 144, 158, 181
3:2–3	152, 163, 181,	4:1–12	144, 185, 187, 188
	232n116	4:1–8	1, 17, 132, 185,
3:2	21, 176		186, 187–88, 189,
3:3–5	233		192
3:3–4	16, 21, 135n12,	4:1–6	135n12
	139, 163, 166	4:1–2	188, 191
3:3	135n12, 141,	4:1	21, 135n12,
	166n99, 181		135n13
3:4	135n12, 141, 181	4:2	135n12
3:5	109, 163	4:3–8	150
3:6–9	37	4:3–4	134, 239
3:6–7	15	4:4–5b	34
3:7–10	177	4:4	135n12
3:7	21, 109, 139, 163,	4:5	135n12, 212, 215,
	179		236, 239
3:8–10	135n13	4:5b	34, 161, 188, 189,
3:8	131		192, 196, 215,
3:9–10	6, 131, 143, 179		228, 230, 239
3:9	54, 135	4:6	135n12
3:10	176, 179	4:7–8	239
3:10b–11	177	4:8–9	188
3:11–13	38, 123, 132, 134,	4:8	188
	140, 178, 182–83,	4:9–12	132, 134, 186,
			188, 189–91, 192

1 Thessalonians
(continued)

4:9–10	189
4:9	191
4:10–12	135n12
4:10–11	189
4:10	21, 188
4:11–12	1, 18, 98, 150, 188, 189, 191, 237
4:11	135n12, 191
4:12–13	34, 191
4:12	98, 189, 191, 196, 212, 215, 239
4:12a	34, 161, 189, 190, 192, 228
4:12b	190, 191
4:13—5:11	18, 20, 22, 134, 150, 185, 186, 187, 188, 191, 192, 193, 196, 223, 223n98, 227, 233, 237, 239, 246
4:13—5:10	123, 229
4:13–18	1, 17, 28, 29, 30, 132, 134, 144, 158, 186, 188, 191–222, 223, 224, 226, 229, 231, 233, 234, 240, 246, 247
4:13–18a	184
4:13–17	217, 231
4:13	26, 29, 98, 127, 135n13, 140n30, 161, 163, 166, 166n99, 188, 191, 192, 212, 215, 223, 228, 230, 236, 240 244
4:13a	233
4:13b	34, 196, 205, 233, 240, 244, 246
4:14—5:11	127, 244
4:14–16	218
4:14	34, 109, 163, 197, 205, 215, 218
4:14b	218
4:15–17	202
4:15	22, 215, 218, 223, 224
4:15a	215
4:15b	215
4:16–17	207, 217
4:16	34, 78, 197, 202, 205, 218, 223, 232n116
4:16a	221
4:16b–18	230
4:16b–17a	208, 210, 230
4:16b	205, 218, 219, 221
4:17	34, 208–13, 215, 223
4:17a	211, 215, 218, 222
4:17b–18	215–19, 240, 246
4:17b	210, 215, 217, 218, 222, 222n95, 230
4:18	21, 34, 145, 188, 210, 212, 217, 223, 230
5:1–15	222–38
5:1–11	1, 17, 132, 134, 144, 158, 188, 210, 211, 223, 224–33, 234, 235, 236, 240, 246, 247
5:1–10	228, 231
5:1–3	228, 234
5:1	223, 226
5:3–9	161, 228
5:3	202, 229, 234, 234n119, 234n120, 235
5:3a	228
5:3b–8	229
5:3b–6	229
5:3b	228
5:4–11	131
5:4–8	222n95, 226, 227, 235
5:4–8a	228
5:4–5	161, 228
5:5–7	17
5:5	1, 233, 235

5:6	223, 224, 226, 227, 228, 230, 236	2 Thessalonians	17, 154
5:6a	34, 215, 228	1:4	134, 163
5:7	228	2	237
5:8	224, 226, 227, 230, 233, 236	2:1ff	18n80
		2:1	237
5:8a	161, 228, 229, 235	2:8–9	237
5:8b–10	228	3	237
5:8b	228, 229, 232n116	3:5	185n5
5:9–11	230	3:6–15	18, 18n80, 237
5:9–10	229	3:6	17, 237
5:9	210, 228, 229, 230, 236	3:7	237
		3:11	237
5:9b	210		
5:10	34, 210, 223, 224, 230	1 Timothy	
5:11–12	150	4:7ff	164n97
5:11	21, 34, 145, 188, 210, 223, 226, 227, 229, 230, 231, 233, 236	6:11–12	164n97
		6:12	109, 164n97
5:11a	236	2 Timothy	
5:11b	231, 236	4:7–8	164n97
5:11c	231	4:7	109
5:12–22	1, 132, 187, 236		
5:12–15	236–38, 247	Philemon	
5:12–13	15, 236	21–22	176, 177
5:12	135n13	22	176–77
5:13–22	185		
5:14–15	236	Hebrews	161
5:14	1, 18, 21	1:4	161
5:14a	236, 237	2:9	161
5:14b	237	2:11	161
5:16–24	238	7	161
5:16–22	38, 238–39, 243	10	165
5:16–18	61n92, 238	10:32–33	164n97
5:16–18a	238	10:32b–33	165
5:16	238	11:33	164n97
5:18b	238	12–13	165
5:19–22	2n9	12:1	108
5:19–20	239	13	161
5:21–22	239		
5:23–28	132, 238–39	1 Peter	
5:23–24	123	2:20	134
5:23	1, 17, 34, 192, 205, 215, 227, 239, 246		
5:27	6		

Jude

3	164n97
23	208

Revelation

1:9	163
2:9	163
2:22	163
8:2–13	207
9:13–14	207
11:14–15	207
12:5	208
15:30	164n97
22:20	205n46

Early Christian Writings

St. Basil   129

Epistle to Nectarius

412B	209

Greco-Roman Literature

Alcidamas

Encomium of Poverty	145
Encomium on Death	145

Anonymous

Rhetorica ad Herennium   11

1.14	136
1.8.12	44, 141
2.20.47–49	238
3.15	72
III. 6.10	115
III. 6.11–12	115
III. 6.13	116
III. 6.13—8.15	116
III. 8, 15	116
III. 10	111

Antisthenes   49

Aphthonius the Sophist   42, 46–47, 142, 158

Progymnasmata	123
Sp. II 46ff.	43

Appian   104, 206

Roman History

III. 2.143–48	75–77
III. 143–44, 146	76
III. 144–146a	76
III. 144b, 145b, 146b	76
III. 146b	76

Aristides

Sp. II

505	40

Aristotle   9, 13, 14n67, 20, 36, 49, 129

Art of Rhetoric   11, 112–15

423	114n4

Rhetorica

1.10–15	13n56
1.2.1	11
1.3.4	155
1.3.135^{8b}.3	13n55, 13n58
1.3.135^{8b}.4	13n60
1.3.135^{9a}.9	13n55, 13n58
1.4–8	13n57
1.7.31	175
1.9	13n58
1.9.35	139
1.9.38	175
1.9.39	175, 175n128, 175n129
2.18.139^{2a}.5	13n60
3–10	36n1

INDEX OF ANCIENT DOCUMENTS   271

3:19.1	238
3.13	107
3.16.10	44, 146
135[8b]	71
I, 5.4	45
I. 3.3–4	113
I. 3.6	113
I. 5.4	113
I. 7. 35	112
I. 9. 1	111
I. 9. 33	111
I. 9.1	113
I. 9.3–25	113
I. 9.32–34	113
I. 9.35	113
I. 9.38–40	117
I. 9.38–41	114
II, 139[0b], 15	58, 142
II. 22. 6	111, 112
III, 11, 6	47–48
III, 17	45
III. 1.7	114
III. 12.5–6	114
III. 16.1–3	112, 114
III. 16.8	113

Rhetorica ad Alexandrum 11

1–2, 29–34	13n57
3, 35	13n58
4, 36	13n56

Cicero   7, 7n31, 11n47, 14n67, 20, 26, 28, 30, 38, 50, 92, 102, 103, 129, 162, 195n19, 240

Consolation 50

De Inventione 11

1.16.22	133
1.16.22–23	133
1.19.27	12
1.20	145
1.23–25	133
1.27	44
1.28	136

1.5.7	13n55, 13n58, 13n59
2.4.12–59.178	13n55
2.4.14–51.154	13n56
2.51.155–58.176	13n57
2.59.178	13n58
I. 34–6	116
II. 32–34, 59.177	116
II. 53.159–54, 165	116
II. 177	111

De Oratore

1.31.141	13n55
2.10	13n59
2.11.45–46	13n58
2.341	72
2.81.333–82.340	13n57
2.81.333–85.349	13n55
2.84–85	13n58
2.84.341	13n58
2.85.346	94, 138
3.202	45
II. 84. 341	102
II. 84.341	51, 72, 115
II. 84.344	116
II. 85.346	74, 116, 161, 179
II. 85.347–48	116
III. 55.210–12	116
xxi	116n5

On Despising Death	194
118	31

Epistulae ad Atticum

14.10.1	75

Epistulae ad Brutum

11.37	13n58

Epistulae ad Titius 28, 85

XVI.1–2	85
XVI.2	85
XVI.2–6	85
XVI.3	85

Epistulae ad Titius (continued)

XVI.4	85
XVI.5–6	85
XVI.6	85

Her

1.2	13n59
1.2.2	13n55, 13n58
3.2–5	13n57
3.6–8	13n58

Or

11.37	13n58

Orator 38–39

Philippics

2.89–91	75

Somnium Scipionis as a Consolatio 28

Sulpicius Rufus's Letter to Cicero 85–86

V.1	85
V.2–6	85
V.3	85
V.4	85, 86
V.5	86
V.6	86

Top.

24.91	13n55, 13n58
24.92–26.96	13n56
97	44

Tusculan Disputations 28, 50, 84, 86–87, 194

3:34	25
3.34	49

18.11–34	86n35
111, 118	225
Book I, 9, 24	86
Book I, 10	86
Book I, 27	86
Book I, 36–52	86
Book I, 54–55	86
Book I, 83–84	86
Book I, 92	86
Book I, 111	86
Book I, 118	87
Book II, 10–14	87
Book II, 31	87
Book II, 41	87
Book II, 42	87
Book II, 55–57	87
Book III, 7–11	87
Book III, 12	87
Book III, 13	87
Book III, 55–59	87
Book III, 76	87
Book III, 77, 79	87
Book III, 82	87
LXLIX.118	216n76

Democritus of Abedera 33, 49

Demosthenes 22, 50, 65, 66, 67, 68n103, 74n15, 94, 106, 126, 129, 141, 152, 157n80, 191, 195, 225n100, 240

On the Crown 41n20

Funeral Speech 30, 62–63, 125

1	62
1–2	62
1–2, 12, 35	212n64
1–3	62
3	62
4	62
4–26	62
4–31	62, 66n99, 130n1, 180n139

INDEX OF ANCIENT DOCUMENTS 273

5	62	LVI. 41.9b	79
7–24	212n66	LVI.34–42	200, 201
8	62	LVI.37.3–4, 40.3, 41.5	162
10	62	LVI.42.3	216–17
15–18	62, 160	LXXV. 4–5	77–80
23	62, 212n63, 212n65	LXXV.4.2—5.5	201, 216–17
27	62		
32	62	*Tiberius' funeral oration*	
32, 36	62	*for Augustus*	102
32–34	212n62	36–41	103n70, 130n1, 180n139
32–37	62, 66n99, 68, 195, 217	37.3–4	104
34	216n76	37.6	104
35	190	41.5	104
35–37	62, 109, 178, 211, 225	41.9	103n70
37	62, 63	41.9a	194

Dio

57.15.8	167n102

Dio Chrysostom 104, 129, 152, 157n80

2:17—3:10	19
29.21–22	225

Dio Cassius 104, 129, 141, 143, 152, 157n80, 240

The Consolatio ad Marciam

41.6, 9	217
41.9b	225
56.34	202

29.17–18	97
29.19–21	97
29.20	97
29.21	97
29.22	97
29.3	96
29.4–6	96
29.7–16	96

Roman History

36.4–5	160n88
41	216n76
41.3–4	31
LVI. 34	78
LVI. 34–41	77–79
LVI. 35	78
LVI. 35.3–4	78
LVI. 36–41.5	78
LVI. 36.2	78
LVI. 36.4–5	78
LVI. 37.3–4	79
LVI. 37.6	79
LVI. 39.1–4	79
LVI. 40	79
LVI. 41.5	79
LVI. 41.9a	79

The First-Fourth Discourse on Kingship 149, 171

13, 17, 20	171
40	171

The Second Discourse on Kingship

6, 67–69	171
18	164

INDEX OF ANCIENT DOCUMENTS

The Third Discourse on Kingship

14–17	171
40–41	171

The Fourth Discourse on Kingship

10, 15–16, 33	171
41–42, 74	171
44–45	171

Twenty-seventh Discourse

7–9	26n2

The Twenty-Ninth Discourse: Melancomas 95–97, 225

21	107
29.1	96
29.1–2	96
29.19–21	103n70, 194
29.2	96
29.21	109
29.3–18	96, 103n70, 130n1, 180n139
29.7–18	160n88

Oration

8.8	49
27.8–9	49

Diodorus

31.25	78

Diogenes of Sinope 49

Dionysius of Halicarnassus

44, 129, 198

Art of Rhetoric

1.2 ff.	47

Roman Antiquities

5.16	128
5.16.1—17.6	128–29
5.16–17	201
5.17.1–2	128
5.17.2–6	50
5.17.3	128
5.17.3–6	128
5.17.4–5	129
5.17.4–6	128
5.17.5–6	129
iv.40	70
V. 17.2	50
V. 17.6	51
v.17	71
VI, 2	52n72
xi, 39, 5	50

Epictetus 26

Epitaphs

Corpus Inscriptionum Latinarum (CIL) 99

2.3771	32
6.26003	32
6.26554	32, 221, 222

EG (Epigrammata Graeca)

101	192
125	209
170	209
174	209
459	192
459, 7–8	32
526, 1–3	209
595	192
646	192

IG

5, 1, 1186, 1	209
9, 2, 640, 8–9	32
12, 9, 293.3	209

INDEX OF ANCIENT DOCUMENTS 275

MAMA

| 3, 556 | 209 |

SEG

1, 464, 3	209
8, 378	209
8, 473–75	209
8, 484	209
8, 502a	209

Euripides

Orestes

| 847 | 108 |

Galen 129

On the Avoidance of Grief

91–92

1	91
2–12a	92
2–55	92
12b–14	92
29–30	92
31	92
44	92
48	92
56	92
56–84	92
62	92
65	92
80	92

Gorgias of Sicily

41n23, 45, 45n42, 126, 129, 139n27, 152, 195

Encomium of Helen 36, 41, 42n23, 52

| 14–15 | 42 |

Fragment from a Funeral Oration 63, 66n99

Olympic Speech 45

Panegyricus

| 4 | 139 |

Hermogenes 7, 42, 139

Sp. II

| 16ff. | 43 |

Hyperides 65, 66, 67, 68n103, 106, 126, 129, 143, 152, 190, 195, 225n100, 240

Epitaphs 48

Funeral Speech 125, 216n76

1–2	212n63, 212n64
2	135
3	212n66
4–5	181
8–9	212n65
28	212n62

Oration 64–65

1–5	64
2	64
4–5	64
6	64
6–9	64
6–40	64, 66n99, 130n1, 180n139
10–14, 20–23, 33, 35	160
10–14, 35	64
15–19	64
20–23, 33	64
24–34	64
31	65, 225
35–40	64
41–43	64, 66n99, 195, 217

Oration (continued)

41a	64, 68
41b	65
42	65
43	30, 65

Isocrates   66, 129, 139, 152, 225n100

Busiris

	52
4	40

Epitaphios   53

Evagoras   30, 48, 52–53

9.12–14, 17–19	52
9.12–65	160
9.12–69	52, 65n99, 130n1, 180n139
9.2	52
9.22	53
9.24	53
9.28	53
9.3	52
9.33–34	53
9.51–64	53
9.65	53
9.70–72	53
9.70–79	53, 65n99, 68
9.73	53
9.76	53
9.8–11	52
9.80–81	53, 109, 224
419.4	123

Helen   41

Panegyricus   38, 41n20, 53–55

1–14, 186	53
4	40
11	41n22
13	54
15–159	54, 65n99, 130n1, 180n139
23–25	54, 160
29, 38	54
47–50	54
52, 58	54
53	54
72, 82–84, 91	54
74	54
77, 84, 95, 186	54
87	54
95–98	54
104	54
160–89	54, 65n99
163–66. 172–73	54
182	54
186	54, 64
186–89	54
187–88	54

John of Sardis   43, 44n37

Julian   102

Epistle to Himerius

69	33, 92–93
69, 412B	209
69, 413D	225
412A	93
412A-B	93
412B	93
412B, 413D	93
412C	93
412C-413D	93
412D	93
413A	93
413C	93
413D	93
612B	93

Law of the Twelve Tables

10.4	101

INDEX OF ANCIENT DOCUMENTS 277

Libanius	104, 129, 141, 143, 152	*Encomium on the Fly*	145
		On Funerals	97–98
Oration XVIII, Funeral Oration over Julian	94–95, 102	1	97
		2–9	97
		2–24	97
18.1–6	94	9	97
18.11	94	11–24	193
18.116	95	12–14	98, 209
18.12	94	16–21	98
18.12–95	160n88	23–24	98
18.121–61	95	24	98
18.21, 28	94		
18.212–66	95	Lucretius	26
18.226	95		
18.23, 181	95	Lucretius Vespillo	
18.281	95		
18.281–95	95, 103n70	*Laudatio Turiae*	99–101, 106
18.281–96	194		
18.281–306	194	1–53	130n1, 180n139
18.282	209	3-right-hand column 1–53	103n70
18.282–83	95	7–29	100
18.296	95	11–18	100
18.296–306	95, 103n70, 217	25	100
18.298	95	25–53	100
18.3	94	30–31	100
18.304	95, 216n76, 225	30–52	100
18.308	95	54–55	100
18.39–65	95	54–59	100, 103n70
18.4	94	56–57	100
18.65	95	59	100
18.66–81	95, 104	60–66	100, 101, 103n70
18.7	94	63–64	101
18.7–280	94, 103n70, 130n1, 180n139	67–69	101, 183n146
		CIL VI 1527, 31670, 37053	99
18.95	95	Left-hand column	103n70
621	178	Left-hand column 3	100
624	182n146	Right-hand column 2–24	100
		Right-hand column 53	100
Lucian of Samosata	26		
		Lysias	74n15, 106, 126, 195
Athletics			
		Funeral Oration	125
15	108		
		71–72	178
Encomium of Muia	145	75–77	214

INDEX OF ANCIENT DOCUMENTS

Funeral Oration (continued)

77–81	216
81	108n78, 190

Lysias

1–2, 19	212n64
17–18	212n63, 212n65
20	212n66
80–81	212n62

Menander Rhetor   20, 46, 46n46, 47, 52, 125, 126, 129, 239

413.5—414.30	215
414.14–26	216
418.5—422.4	216
421.15–16	216

Division of Epideictic Speeches
          119–23, 244

368	120
369–76	120
377	120
413.14–15	120
413.15–20	120
413.24–30	120
413.5–13	120
414.17–28	121
414.5–9	120
414.7	120
418.11–15	121
418.16–25	121
418.5–10	121
419.10	196
419.1–10	121
419.10—420.5	121
419.19–20	123
419.20	121
419.20–420.5	83
420	156
420.10, 25	142n34
420.10—421.15	121–22
420.20–25	179
420.25	122
420.25—421.14	160
420.30	122
420.5	126
420.5–9	121, 123
421.1–5	122
421.10–14	122
421.15	122, 123, 126
421.16–30	122
421.20–24	122
422	122
422.1–4	182
422.2–5	122
422.3–4	238
II, 413.15	187
II, 413.25–30	187
II, 413.5–15	186
II, 414.5–22	187
II, 419.10—420.4	187
II, 421.15–25	187
II, 421.26–30	187, 224

The Imperial Oration

377,28–29	238

Nicolaus the Sophist   42, 44n37

Preliminary Exercise

47	112

Sp. III

53	42n26
491ff.	43

Oxyrhynchus Papyri

115	218

Letter from Irene

115	33

INDEX OF ANCIENT DOCUMENTS 279

Pericles	48	248b-c	61
		248d	61, 225n101
Plato	22, 26, 49, 50, 66, 67,	248e	61
	68n103, 86, 94, 106, 126, 129,	249	178
	141, 143, 152, 157n80, 195,	249a	61, 211
	225n100, 240	249c	61, 225n101

Plato — *Menexenus* 30, 59–61, 125, 126, 213, 226

235	59
235a5–6	22
235d3–7	22
236d, 246a, 247e	212n64
236d-237b	59
236d-e	59
236e	107, 123, 231
237a-b	60
237b-245b	142
237b-246b	60, 66n99, 130n1, 180n139
237b-c	60
238–39c, 242e	160
238c-239b	212n63, 212n65
238c-d	60
239–45	212n66
239a-b	60
239a-c	60
239d3	190
239d-246b	60
241a	60
241c	60
241d	60
241e	60
243d	60
243d, 247d	214
244.A, 247.D	182n146
246b	60
246b-249c	66n99
246d-249c	61, 68, 195, 217
246e	61, 225n101
247a	61, 238
247c	61, 225n101
247d	61
247d5–6	212n62
248b	61
248b-249c	224

Pliny the Younger 28, 102, 129

To Calestrius Tiro 28

XII.1–2	88
XII.3–10	88
XII.11–12	88
XII.13	88

To Caninius Rufus 28

VII.1–2	88
VII.3–9	88
VII.10–15	88, 225

To Novius Maximus 28

V.1	88
V.1–3	88
V.4–8	88

Plutarch 27, 28, 30, 50, 102, 103, 105, 129, 195n19, 240

Aristides

21.3	206

Consolatio Ad Apollonium /A Letter of Condolence to Apollonius 29, 84–85

102.A	84
102B	25–26
102.B	84
102.B—121.D	84
103.C-F	84
104.A—105.B	84
104.C	84
106.C	84

INDEX OF ANCIENT DOCUMENTS

Consolatio Ad Apollonium /A Letter of Condolence to Apollonius (continued)

106.E	84
107.A	84
107.A-B	84
107.C	84
107.D—108.F	84
108D, 109F	216n76
109.E	84
111.D—113.B	84
111.D—113.B, 114D, 120.A-121D, 117.F-118.C	194
111.D-113.B, 117.B-C	209
114.D	85
117.F—118.C	85
118.D—119.F	85
119.A	182n146
120.A—121.D	85
121.E—122	85
121.E-F	85
121F	30
122	85
611	216n76

Consolatio Ad Uxorem/ Consolation to His Wife 29, 79–84, 93, 226

608A-B	81
608B	81
608C-610F	81
608C-D	81
608D	81
608E	81
608F	81
609A-C	81
609C-E	81
609E-F	81
609E-F, 610A-D	160n88
609E-F, 610A-D, 611F	194
610A	81
610B-D	81
610D	81
610F	81
611A	82
611A-B	81
611A-C	82, 225
611A-F	81
611C-D	82
611D-612B	29, 84
611D-E	29
611F	82
612A-B	83, 225
612B	83

De Se Ipsum Citra Infidiam Laudando-On Praising Oneself Inoffensively 171

539.E	171–72
541.E-F	160
542.B-D	172
544.D-F	172–73

Lucullus

Xliii	50

Mor II

105–6	84n33

Philopoemen

21.2–3	199

Pub.

ix, 7, 102	51

Publicola

9	71

Publicolar

9.7	50

Polybius 129

The Histories

VI. 52–54	127–28, 201
VI. 52.1–11	71
VI. 52.10–11	127

VI. 53, 1	50	Pseudo-Lysias	65, 66, 68n103, 129, 143, 152, 157, 240, 244
VI. 53–54	200		
VI. 53.1	70, 71		
VI. 53.10	127		
VI. 53.1–2	127	*Funeral Oration*	30, 58–59
VI. 53.3	127		
VI. 53.3–4	71	1–2	58
VI. 53.4–5	127	2	58
VI. 53.8	127	3	58
VI. 54	224	3–9	141
VI. 54.1	127	3–19	58, 67
VI. 54.1–4	71	3–70	58, 65n99, 130n1, 180n139
VI. 54.2–5	127		
VI.53–54	50	4–6	58
		4–16	58
Polycrates	145	7–10	58
		11–16	58
Pseudo-Demetrius		17	58
	102n69	18–19	58
		20	58
Pseudo-Dionysius	105, 126, 129, 239	20–66	58, 67, 141
		21–26	58
		21–70	58
On Epideictic Speeches		23	59n87
	123–27, 244	24–26	59n87
		27–47	59
275–80	152	48–53	59
277	124	54–57	59
277–78	124	58–66	59
278	96, 124, 125	67–70	58, 67, 141
278–79	124, 142n34	69	59
278–80	124	71	59, 68
279	124	71–76	59, 68
280	83, 124, 187, 224	71–80	65n99, 195
280–83	124	75	59
281	83, 125, 126, 187, 196	77	59
		77, 79	68
282	83, 125	77–80	59, 68, 217
283	84, 125, 187, 216	79–80	59
		81	59

INDEX OF ANCIENT DOCUMENTS

Quintilian   11n47, 20, 36,
                  129, 161

Institutio Oratoria   11,
                             117–19

2.1.10	179
2.1.12	136, 168
2.11.7	136, 180
2.13.1–8	137
2.13.2	180
2.13.2–8	177
2.15	11
2.17.37	11
2.21.23	13n55, 13n58, 13n59
2.4.30	180
2.4.30–31	136
3.3.14–15	13n55, 13n59
3.4.3	13n58
3.4.7	13n60
3.4.12	13n58
3.4.13	13n58
3.4.14	13n58
3.4.16	36n2
3.7	13n58
3.7.2	72
3.7.6	41, 45, 155
3.7.6–16	141
3.7.15	44, 141, 143n38, 176, 177
3.7.16	161
3.7.28	139
3.8	13n56, 13n57
3.8.6	13n60
4.1.5	107, 132
4.1.9	133
4.1.125	137
4.2.22	132n7, 140
4.2.31	136
4.2.36	44, 135, 146
4.2.52	44, 135, 146, 179
4.2.63	44
4.2.123	179, 181
4.2.123, 125	179
4.2.123–24	137, 141, 146, 168
4.2.125	168, 180
4.2.129–31	145
6.1.1–31	77
6.1.30–31	75
7.15	78
7.6–16	160
8.3.11–12	39
8.3.53	139n27
8.4.2	156
8.4.3	175n130
8.4.3–9	156
8.4.9–14	156
8.4–9.2.4	155
8.4.26–27	156
9.2.4	156
9.3.28	174n121
12.1–4	12
II. 13.2–8	118–19
III, 7.1	71
III, 7.2	72
III. 4.5	117
III. 7.10–18	118
III. 7.12–13	118
III. 7.15	73, 74, 118
III. 7.16	73, 118, 122n8
III. 7.18, 28	118
III. 7.2	117
III. 7.24	118
III. 7.6	117, 118
III. 7.6–16	104
III. 9. 1–4	111
III.7.16	74
VIII, 3.53	45n42
VIII. 3.11–12	117
XI, 3, 153	51
XI, 3.153	72, 72n10
XL. 3.153	117, 118

Rhet. Her.

4.45	45
4.69	45

Seneca the Younger 7, 7n31, 26, 28, 30, 50, 92, 102, 103, 129, 195n19, 240

Ad Helviam matrem de consolation 50, 90n41

24	101

Ad Marciam de consolatione 28, 50, 90n41, 194

1	90
2–25	91
3:1–2	199
5.5	91
6.2	91
7.1	91
9	91
12.4	91
13.1–3, 14, 15	91
19.4–5	91
21.1	91
24.5	91
25.1	91
26	91

Ad Polybium de consolatione 50, 90n41

Apocolocyntosis

12.1	206

On Conquering the Conqueror

Ep. 30	89n37

On Consolation to the Bereaved 28, 194

Ep. XCIX	90n40
Ep. XCIX, 1–2	90n40
Ep. XCIX, 3–6	90n40
Ep. XCIX, 3–31	90n40
Ep. XCIX, 14	90n40
Ep. XCIX, 15	90n40
Ep. XCIX, 16–21	90n40
Ep. XCIX, 31	90n40
Ep. XCIX, 32	90n40

The Consolatory Letters of Seneca to Lucilius 28, 89–91

De Ira (On Anger)

2.10.7	49

On Despising Death 28

Ep. 24, 1–2	89
Ep. 24, 2	89
Ep. 24, 3–11	89
Ep. 24, 3–25	89
Ep. 24, 26	89

Epist.

CII, 15	50n64

On Grief for Lost Friends 28, 194

16	28n15, 31, 64, 217, 218
Ep. 63, 1	90
Ep. 63, 1–2	90
Ep. 63, 2–15	90
Ep. 63, 16	90, 225
Ep. 63.16	182n146

On Groundless Fears

Ep. 13, 1–3	89
Ep. 13, 4–15	89
Ep. 13, 5	89
Ep. 13, 12	89
Ep. 13, 16–17	89

Sopatros 42

Suetonius

The Deified Julius
VI 160n88

Iul.
6.1 142n33

Julius Caesar
84 75

Twelve Caesars
11 142n33

Symmachus 129

Letter 1.2: Symmachus' Father, Avianius, to Symmachus 98–99
1.2.2 98
1.2.3 99
1.2.3–7 98
1.2.4 99
1.2.5 99
1.2.6 99
1.2.7 99

Tacitus 27, 104, 129, 141, 143, 152, 157n80

Agricola 73–75, 102
1–3 73
3 74
4 74, 142
4–42 74, 103n70, 130n1, 180n139
5 74
6 74
8–17 74
16 73n14
18 74
22 74
29 74
33 74
41 75, 160n88
43 75
43–46a 75, 103n70, 194
44–45 75
45b–46a 75, 225
46 31, 64, 90, 182n146, 217, 218

Theocritus

Idyll
4.42 26, 33, 192, 194

Theodorus 48

Theon, Aelius 42, 139

The Exercises of Aelius Theon
109 111
112 112

Progymnasmata 111
5.4–11 135

Sp. II
109–10 42n24
112 42n25
118ff. 43

Theophanies 206

Theophrastus 49

Thucydides 22, 31, 48, 50, 65, 66, 67, 68n103, 74n15, 106, 121, 124, 126, 129, 152, 157, 187, 195, 225n100, 240

INDEX OF ANCIENT DOCUMENTS   285

History of the
Peloponnesian War   55–58

1.43.2–3	212n62
2.34	49
2.35	49, 212n64
2.36.2	190
2.40–41	212n63, 212n65, 212n66
2.43.1–4	107, 109
2.46.1	190
2.46.2	190n10
35.3	56
36.1	56, 153
36.2	56
36.2–4	153
36.3	56
36.3–4	214
36.4	56
37.1	214
37.1–3	56
38	56
38.1	214n72
39.1	56, 214n72
39.1—41.1–5	160
39.4	56
40.1, 2, 4	214n72
40.1–5	56
41.1–5	57
41.4	214n72
42.1–4	57
43	57
43–45	195, 217, 224
43.1	57
44	58
45	58
46.1–2	58
II, 36	232
II, 46.2	232
II, XLIII, 43	225
II, XLIII-XLV	57
II, XLVI	58
II, XXXIV-XXXV	55
II.XXXIV.1–8	220
XLIII-XLV	65n99, 68
XLIV	68
XXXVI-XLII	65n99, 130n1, 180n139

Xenocrates of Chalcidon   49

Xenophon   49

www.ingramcontent.com/pod-product-compliance
Lightning Source LLC
Chambersburg PA
CBHW071237230426
43668CB00011B/1474